ETHNICITY

SUNY Series in Ethnicity and Race in American Life
John Sibley Butler, Editor

ETHNICITY

Source of Strength?
Source of Conflict?

J. MILTON YINGER

STATE UNIVERSITY OF NEW YORK PRESS

for
George Daniel Yinger
and
Emma Bancroft Yinger
To whom no one was a stranger

Published by
State University of New York Press, Albany

© 1994 State University of New York

For information, address State University of New York
Press, State University Plaza, Albany, N.Y., 12246

Production by E. Moore
Marketing by Nancy Farrell

Library of Congress Cataloging-in-Publication Data

Yinger. J. Milton (John Milton), 1916–
    Ethnicity : source of strength? source of conflict? / J. Milton
Yinger.
        p.   cm.—(SUNY series in ethnicity and race in American
life)
    Includes bibliographical references and index.
    ISBN 0-7914-1797-2. — ISBN 0-7914-1798-0 (pbk.)
    1. Ethnicity. 2. Ethnic relations. 3. Assimilation (Sociology)
I. Title. II. Series.
GN495.6.Y56   1994
305.8—dc20   93-3455
                                                                   CIP

10 9 8 7 6 5 4 3 2 1

CONTENTS

Three interlocking problems of enormous proportions command the world's attention and are likely to be at the top of the political-moral agenda for decades to come: how to increase justice among societies, ethnic groups, races, classes, ages, sexes; how to attain peace, the elimination of the use of organized and official violence as the way to attempt to settle disputes; and how to protect the environment from overcrowding, the depletion of irreplaceable resources, and pollution.

The study of ethnicity opens a window to each of these problems. Democratic ethnic values and policies help to reduce them; coercive and separatist values and policies exacerbate them.

Although other eras doubtless faced equally daunting problems, the dangers seem greater today, for several reasons: The world's population is increasing at unprecedented speed—by nearly a billion per decade. The total of 5.5 billion in 1993 will almost certainly grow to 10 billion by the middle of the twenty-first century. In the past it was more often the wealthiest societies that were growing most rapidly; today it is the poorest.

The economically developed world, which has gained so much from its technology, is only slowly realizing the great price paid for its use. Even more slowly, it is learning the cost of dealing with technology's toxic residues—a cost that is paid by everyone, but that falls most heavily on the poor, among whom ethnic minorities are over-represented.

The enormous differences in wealth and power among societies and the ethnic groups within them were once scarcely visible to many people. They were hidden by distance, slow communication,

and social blinders. Today, a communication network sends virtually instantaneous messages around the world that document those
differences.

Struggling to find a lens that could enlarge our vision of these
problems, I sat down to write as a social theorist. But the humanist
in me kept surfacing—with unpredictable results. He, in turn, was
sometimes pushed aside by the policy analyst, asking: How can that
be done? On this topic, in this era, which may well be called the
ethnic era, these three perspectives are equally essential. They lead
us to ask: What do we know about ethnicity? What are the most
humane goals, all persons considered? How can we most nearly
achieve those goals?

I can scarcely begin to answer those questions. My hope is that
I can encourage you to find them compelling—indeed, vital—and
help you to ask them in a more creative, a more powerful way.

We need specialists in the search for insightful theories, in the
articulation of values, and in the assessment of policies. One of
these without the others, however, is an incomplete enterprise.

Kant opens his *Critique of Pure Reason* with the memorable
sentence, "Perception without conception is blind; conception
without perception is empty." Let me play with that sentence in
relation to the interdependencies among theories, values, and
policies:

> Values without knowledge are blind.
> Knowledge without values is empty.
> Both without policies are futile.

The emphasis here is analytic and descriptive—an attempt to
spell out some of the things we need to know and to understand, if
we are to respond wisely to the ethnic factor in the world today. Yet,
facts, theories, description, and analysis are of limited use if they are
separated from values (developed and expressed, one hopes, in a
democratic process of give and take) and from policies (the means
selected, in light of facts and theories, to attempt to realize those
values). It is essential that we keep these three levels of thought and
action distinct and separate in our minds while at the same time
stressing how interdependent they are.

Many of the references here are to contemporary, even current
events. A new or ongoing development—heartening, tragic, or startling—demands our attention. It is of interest and concern for itself,

for its particularity. But that is not the whole of our interest. Of each development in the world of ethnicity we can ask: What can we learn from this? What does it mean for tomorrow? Does it increase our ability to interpret the significance of ethnicity? Thus today, as I write this, our attention is rivited on Bosnia, Georgia, Somalia, Germany, Kenya, Israel, South Africa, India, Russia, the European Community, the United States. The specific events these societies face may not be the focus of attention a year or two from now. But studying them can add to our understanding of new events and help us to respond to them in a wiser, more humane way.

Having covered a wide variety of topics and theoretical perspectives, I am indebted—even more than usual—to those who have given me stimulation, encouragement, information, and correction. Some of these are identified in the footnotes and bibliography. In particular, I have benefitted from the thoughtful study and comments on the manuscript or some of the chapters by several readers. Letters, conversations, and reprints have been of great value. My sincere thanks to Thomas Pettigrew, George E. Simpson, Susan Johnson, Marc Bernstein, Frederick Starr, John Yinger, Mary Lovely, Nancy Yinger, Mark Katz, Robert Longsworth, Arthur Schlesinger, Jr., Robert Merton, Robert E. Lee, Amitai Etzioni, as well as to the anonymous reviewers of this manuscript and of earlier published papers on which I have drawn. Most of these papers were developed from manuscripts or lectures first presented at conferences or seminars. It has been my good fortune to receive sharply focused commentary on them at meetings held, appropriately for the topic, in culturally diverse settings: Uppsala, New York, Budapest, Honolulu, Oxford, Los Angeles, Tokyo, Columbus, Ljubljana, San Francisco.

The staff of the Oberlin College library has been helpful well beyond the call of duty. Phyllis Kimmel typed various versions with remarkable diligence and skill. And once again my greatest debt is to Winnie McHenry Yinger, my best friend through many years.

For any errors, awkward phrases, and vigorous assertions on controversial topics, I alone am responsible.

ACKNOWLEDGMENTS

I am grateful to the publishers for permission to use segments from papers and chapters that I wrote earlier. These paragraphs have been revised and brought up to date. My thanks for permission to use materials from:

"The Research Agenda: New Directions for Desegregation Research," in *Advancing the Art of Inquiry in School Desegregation Research*, edited by Jeffrey Prager, Douglas Longshore, and Melvin Seeman, 229–54. New York: Plenum Publishing Corporation, 1986.

"Ethnicity." *Annual Review of Sociology.* Annual Reviews 11 (1985): 151–80. Palo Alto, CA.

"Assimilation in the United States: with Particular Reference to Mexican-Americans," in *Mexican-Americans in Comparative Perspective*, edited by Walker Connor, 30–55. Washington: Urban Institute Press, 1985.

"Ethnicity and Social Change: The Interaction of Structural, Cultural, and Personality Factors." *Ethnic and Racial Studies* 6 (October 1983): 395–409. London: Routledge.

"Towards a Theory of Assimilation and Dissimilation." *Ethnic and Racial Studies* 4 (July 1981): 249–64. London: Routledge.

"Ethnicity in Complex Societies," in *The Uses of Controversy in Sociology*, edited by Lewis A. Coser and Otto N. Larsen, 197–216. New York: The Free Press, a Division of Macmillan, Inc., 1976.

Chapter 1

DRAWING THE BOUNDARIES OF ETHNICITY

This was to have been a fairly straightforward essay on ethnicity, built upon a long-standing interest. Then somebody started a revolution, tore down a wall, declared independence. People of many different inclinations leaped into the openings thus created. This is a fluid moment in human history, which, "taken at the flood" can "lead on to fortune." But it can be a time during which, opportunities neglected, we drift "in shallows and in miseries."

Humane goals, wise policies, and personal courage in the midst of ethnic conflicts mingle with revenge, personal ambition, and the fanaticism that grows out of the release of suppressed needs and desires. The conflicts command most of our attention. One is tempted to declare with Horatio, in the last scene of *Hamlet:*

> And let me speak to the yet unknowing world
> How these things came about. So shall you hear
> Of carnal, bloody, and unnatural acts,
> Of accidental judgments, casual slaughters,
> Of deaths put on by cunning and forced cause,

And, in the upshot, purposes mistook
Fall'n on the inventors' heads.

Those lines, written nearly four hundred years ago, could have been written in recent months about Bosnia, Los Angeles, Nagorno-Karabakh, Iraq, Somalia, Afghanistan, Kenya, Mozambique, Zaire, India, or Peru. This list could be greatly extended.

Other lines are being written, however, telling stories that are not so shattering. A score of African states, after reveling in their independence, have begun to discover that their homegrown tyrants have proved no better—and with the added ethnic violence, probably worse—than their foreign oppressors. Little is to be gained by backing away from the jaws of a crocodile, they are discovering, only to be torn by the claws of a tiger. The Republic of South Africa has also taken the precious early steps on a long journey toward democracy. And western European states, a generation late, are beginning to face the complex multi-ethnic situation they are carrying into their Community.

Particularly in the early chapters, I pull away from such critical and immediate events in an effort to build a solid foundation for the analytic study of ethnicity. Throughout the essay, however, the stubborn facts—often tragic, sometimes heartening—command attention.

THE DEFINITION AND MEASUREMENT OF ETHNICITY

The boundaries of things of interest to social scientists are often drawn in different ways by different observers. Theoretical perspectives, ideologies, and the data being examined all affect the process of definition. Thus "ethnic groups" range, in various usages, from small, relatively isolated, nearly primordial kin-and-culture groups within which much of life proceeds, all the way to large categories (not groups) of people defined as alike on the basis of one or two shared characteristics (e.g., Latino Americans, Asian Americans, Blacks in South Africa, the Maghrebi Muslims in France).

If groups with vastly different size, historical depth, links to other groups, and self-perceptions are all going to be called "ethnic," we must be acutely aware of the scope of the definition. Ethnic groups are a "family," a "class," or perhaps even a "phylum"—not a "species," to use the terminology of biological classification. It is of value to know that the whale, the bat, and the lion are mammals, all members of the same class to which *Homo sapiens* belongs. They share important traits; however they are also enormously different. Much would be lost if only their similarities or only their differences were studied.

And so it is with ethnic groups. It seems unlikely that the term will be pared down to some small part of the present usages. We have not yet developed a clear typology marking different points—in terms of salience, strength of individual identities, importance to societies, and the like—within the range.[1] We can perhaps suggest the outer limits by noting that current ethnic movements in developed societies are different in many ways from what can be called primary ethnic groups in developing societies.[2]

Ethnicity as a social phenomenon converges, by imperceptible steps, with related yet distinctive phenomena. Where shall we draw the line, stating that "here is ethnicity," in efforts to suggest a definition that will maximize our understanding? Both broad and narrow definitions have scientific advantages and disadvantages. One helps us to see similarities amidst differences (similarities in world views among Native Americans—three hundred or more quite diverse tribes). The other helps us to see differences amidst similarities (e.g., Oneidas and Seminoles and Sioux). In our examination of the seamless web of life, both perspectives are needed.

In a general definition, an ethnic group is a segment of a larger society whose members are thought, by themselves or others, to have a common origin and to share important segments of a common culture and who, in addition, participate in shared activities in which the common origin and culture are significant ingredients.[3] We need to distinguish a sociologically and psychologically important ethnicity from one that is only administrative or classificatory. We might call these "hard" and "soft" ethnicities. The former connects directly with many aspects of life; the latter is marginal. A hard ethnic order is thoroughly institutionalized, with clear separating boundaries and a strong ideology.[4] A soft ethnic order has blurred, permeable lines, incomplete institutionalization, and an ambivalent ideology.[5] To draw this distinction we need to expand our behavioral measures of ethnic identity; we cannot be content with naming and counting.[6]

The definition of an ethnic group I have suggested has three ingredients: (1) The group is perceived by others in the society to be different in some combination of the following traits: language, religion, race, and ancestral homeland with its related culture; (2) the members also perceive themselves as different; and (3) they participate in shared activities built around their (real or mythical) common origin and culture. Each of these is a variable, of course; hence we need to devise a scale of ethnicity. Measured by these three criteria, one can be fully ethnic or barely ethnic. Moreover, these factors vary independently of one another to some degree. If one transposes each of the three criteria into a question and answers it, for simplicity, either yes or no, there are eight possible combinations. Different forms of ethnicity have different causes and consequences. Putting them into a table, one gets a formal, and at this stage rather arid, typology of ethnic groups (see table 1.1). In particular times and places, several of the categories may be unimportant. Showing the full possible range, however, may help us to see ethnicity as a variable.

Authors concentrate on different combinations of the three variables that together mark the parameters of ethnicity. This helps to account for some of the disagreements in the literature. In my judgment, if even one of the three questions is answered yes, there is an ethnic factor operating that deserves attention, in terms of its causes and consequences. Type 4, for example, which I have called "Hidden Ethnicity," is not perceived as such either by the participants or by others. But if in fact there are activities built around a common origin and ancestral culture, perhaps hidden by a national ideology that obscures the presence of ethnic lines, the consequences may be quite significant. This is most likely to be true among members of dominant groups. One need scarcely say that

TABLE 1.1
Varieties of Ethnic Identity

	I. Are They Perceived by Others as Ethnically Distinct?			
	Yes		No	
	II. Do Individuals Perceive Themselves as Ethnically Distinct?		Do Individuals Perceive Themselves as Ethnically Distinct?	
III. Do they participate in shared activities?	Yes	No	Yes	No
Yes	1. Full	2. Unrecognized	3. Private	4. Hidden
No	5. Symbolic	6. Stereotyped	7. Imagined	8. Nonethnic

type 6, Stereotyped Ethnicity, can have important consequences, even in the absence of shared activities or perception by the individuals involved that they are ethnically distinct. Imagined Ethnicity, type 7, exists only in the beliefs of the members, but it doubtless affects their behavior and is potentially more important if the situation within which they live changes.

If the three criteria were seen as variables, rather than attributes, more subtle and refined distinctions among types and intensities of ethnicity could be drawn. We are a long way, however, from being able to measure and compare an 8–8–2 profile, let us say, with a 2–2–8 or a 5–5–5.

Examination of the relationships of ethnic groups to the societies of which they are a part reveals a different way of looking at ethnic variations. At least four major types can be found among multi-ethnic societies in the contemporary world:

A. A society can be built out of formally equal ethnic groups.
B. A society can be characterized by a major national cultural group, separated from one or more ethnic groups by a highly permeable boundary.
C. One or more ethnic groups can be strongly oriented toward an outside mother society.
D. One or more ethnic groups can be "imprisoned" as disprivileged minorities within the larger society.

These four types of societal patterns might be sketched as shown in figure 1.1.

These types are not mutually exclusive. One might think of a society built up of two or more layers each of which exhibits, to a greater or lesser degree, the characteristics of one of the societal types. It can well be argued that the United States has elements of all four types, each limiting the full applicability of the others but not excluding them entirely.

Failure to distinguish among such different societal patterns as these would deprive us of many crucial observations regarding ethnicity. It is also important to recognize that these patterns are not fixed. Societies move from one to another—or more accurately, the mix of the four types changes: boundaries become more or less permeable; equality among ethnic groups increases or decreases; orientation to outside societies grows stronger or weaker.[7]

In defining ethnicity, some contemporary writers state that everyone belongs to an ethnic group. In those rare instances where there is minimal ethnic variation, societies are described simply as

A. Society composed of several
    ethnic groups

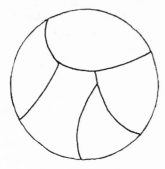

B. Society with a core cultural
    group surrounded by ethnic
    groups

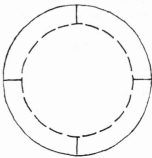

C. Society containing an ethnic
    group with outside orientation

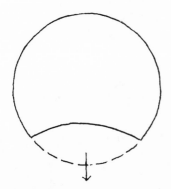

D. Society with one or more
    disadvantaged ethnic minorities

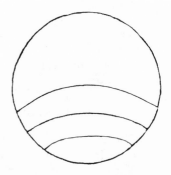

FIGURE 1.1
Varieties of Multi-ethnic Societies

ethnically homogeneous. The association of a theory of ethnicity
with the study of social conflict and discrimination—which for
long has been a major emphasis—is reduced or eliminated. In that
case, societal type B (Fig. 1.1) could not exist, since the inner core
would itself be an ethnic group.

If such shifts of definition as this can bring new insights they
can also blur important distinctions. They may come about not because of major developments in theory or a flood of new data, but
out of political or ideological interests. Arguing that a large and
dominant population in a society is or is not an ethnic group is a

political-moral position as well as an intellectual one. The choice depends on values and needs. Obviously, one does not argue against action in service of those values and needs; but it is appropriate to distinguish such action from scientific efforts to understand the sources and consequences of emphasis on ethnicity. Does one better understand England, for example, by dividing the population into an English core-group surrounded by others of Welsh, Irish, Scottish, Pakistani, Indian, Nigerian, Jamaican, and other descents, or by saying that the British population is made up of a multiplicity of ethnic groups, the largest of which is of Anglo-Saxon descent? To answer this question, I would need information on how the several groups perceive the situation and on the patterns of intra-group and intergroup behavior—that is, on the criteria of my definition of ethnicity.

In a similar way we can ask: Is there an American core group joined by a series of ethnic Americans—Mexican Americans, African Americans, Jewish Americans, Asian Americans, Native Americans, and the like? Or are we all ethnics? We all have ancestors who came from other shores—some only a few years ago, others perhaps fifteen thousand years ago.

Franklin D. Roosevelt once startled members of the Daughters of the American Revolution by opening an address to them with the greeting, "fellow immigrants." (He was never invited back.) Margaret Mead, with calculated exaggeration, said that we are all "third generation." Most Americans share the sentiments implicit in such statements. It seems much more democratic to affirm that nobody—or everybody—is a hyphenated American. It seems wise, however, not to affirm that everybody is equal if thereby we obscure the fact that some are more equal than others or make it more difficult to recognize the conflict and dissension intrinsic to many multi-ethnic systems. The idea that many large and heterogeneous societies have a core group, however diverse its origins, adds a valuable perspective to the study of social process. This is not to affirm that the core culture is intrinsically better or worse than the ethnic cultures that surround it. It is an estimatation that many people, in the United States and elsewhere, place little value on identity with their ancestral groups. They primarily are identified by others simply as Americans; they participate in few if any activities in which shared ancestry is important as symbol or substance. In addition, extensive ethnic mixture in their backgrounds makes shifts in orientation toward greater ethnic identification, unlikely.

In their recent study, Lieberson and Waters[8] note that "there are a substantial number of people who recognize that they are white, but lack any clear-cut identification with, and/or knowledge of, a specific European origin." Despite heightened awareness of ethnicity in recent years, many Americans are unaware of their ethnic origins, choose to identify with none of the ethnic groups, see themselves simply as Americans, or do not answer an ancestry question on recent polls and census surveys.[9]

A similar situation is found in France, where 80 percent or more of the population think of themselves and are thought of simply as French, despite two millennia of mixtures among a diverse group of migrants. The same can be said of China and even more strongly of Japan, where the mixed origins of the large majorities have been almost obliterated by the passage of centuries.

Invention of an ethnic label for the core group may seem to make it an ethnic group—and indeed words do both reflect and affect reality.[10] But words can also deflect us from reality. Being a WASPish fellow, I find no difficulty in being categorized as a WASP. It is purely a category, however; it has little or no social reality for me. Like tens of millions of Americans, my ancestry is so mixed that the Anglo-Saxon part of WASP has somehow to absorb a bit of Scottish, Irish, Dutch, German, and Swedish. I belong to no organizations in which WASPishness is, even informally, a criterion for membership. If everyone is ethnic, then I am a WASP, but surely a weak one, a stingless one.[11]

In renewing our attention to the important ethnic factor, we must not lose sight of earlier understandings. I would emphasize the point, made particularly by Linton, that many modern nations have as their core culture a great mélange on which most members draw and to which they have contributed. Indeed, the hybrid vigor from such mixtures has been crucial to their development.

Many will remember how Linton put it:

[I]nsidious foreign ideas have . . . wormed their way into [the American's] civilization without his realizing what was going on. Thus dawn finds the unsuspecting patriot garbed in pajamas, a garment of East Indian origin, and lying in a bed built on a pattern which originated in either Persia or Asia Minor. He is muffled to the ears in un-American materials: cotton, first domesticated in India; linen, domesticated in the Near East; wool from an animal native to Asia Minor; or silk whose uses were first discovered by the Chinese. . . .

On awakening he glances at the clock, a medieval European invention, uses one potent Latin word in abbreviated form, rises in haste, and goes to the bathroom. Here, if he stops to think about it, he must feel himself in the presence of a great American institution . . . and will know that in no other country does the average man perform his ablutions in the midst of such splendor. But the insidious foreign influence pursues him even here. Even his bathtub and toilet are but slightly modified copies of Roman originals. . . .

Breakfast over, as he scans the latest editorial pointing out the dire results to our institutions of accepting foreign ideas, he will not fail to thank a Hebrew God in an Indo-European language that he is a one hundred percent (decimal system invented by the Greeks) American (from Americus Vespucci, Italian geographer).[12]

Perhaps today we should change the well-known saying to "That's as American as apple pie, pizza, dim sum, burritos, and nouvelle cuisine." The cultural landscape would be seen as even more diverse had Linton added attention to the influence of America's indigenous population and of the many streams of immigrants and refugees. I do not need to detail here the degree to which residents of the United States are all culturally Native American, African American, Irish, Jewish, Italian, German, and so forth. It is difficult to be much of a WASP in such a setting; and it is difficult for members of some other groups, after two or three generations of ancestors in the United States, to be closely bound into a particular ethnic group, from the cultural point of view. We will examine some of the evidence for that statement under the topic of acculturation in chapter 3.

Ethnicity is a topic filled with so many assumptions, guided by such poorly defined terms, and evocative of such strong emotions that we often fail to see the culture-building process going on before our eyes. This is clearly not a one-way process; nor is there the least danger of producing dead-level homogeneity. A special issue of the *American Ethnologist* on "Intra-cultural Variation"[13] demonstrates that the fear of narrow uniformity in the absence of ethnic differences is not well founded, even in small and superficially uniform societies. With reference to the United States, the evidence does not support Novak's assertion that "the melting pot is a kind of homogenized soup."[14] Most people are aware of the great variety of persons within their own groups.[15] Failure to see it in others is a mark of our strong inclinations toward stereotypy. When thinking of persons of Irish Catholic background, should one think of Joseph McCarthy or Eugene McCarthy? Is Harry Truman or Richard Nixon the typical WASP? Is Louis Farrakhan or Martin Luther King, Jr. the standard for African Americans?

Ethnic differentiation can add strength to a society, but not because it protects us from bland homogeneity. The development of a complex core culture, drawn from many sources, may make it possible, in Cooley's words, to move from differentiation based on isolation to differentiation based on choice.

OVERLAPPING CONCEPTS: ETHNIC GROUP, NATION, RACE, MINORITY

Marking the boundaries of ethnicity is complicated by the variety of terms used to designate similar phenomena. Each of the terms I shall discuss, in terms of its relationship to ethnicity, has a vast literature and a tradition of its own. In emphasizing the degree to which they overlap with ethnicity, I have no wish to discourage their continued use. My purpose is to suggest that ethnicity is the concept best able to tie them together, to highlight their common referents, and to promote the development of a theory of multicultural societies.

Nation and Ethnic Group

The word *nation* has a variety of meanings—close to country, society, or state in some instances, and close to or synonymous with ethnic group in others. Thus the dictionary tells us that a nation is a "a country"; or, it is "the body of inhabitants of a country united under a single independent government; a state." That is probably the most commonly understood meaning in the United States (although we have some trouble with the double meaning of "state"). And the world has the United Nations, in that dictionary sense.

But the dictionary also defines nation as "a people connected by supposed ties of blood generally manifested by community of language, religion, and customs, and by a sense of common interest and interrelation." That could stand as a good definition of ethnic group, and it commonly is so used in Europe.

To complicate matters further, there are many references to "nation-state." In strictly logical terms, that is a redundancy if one uses the first definition of nation given above. And it is a contradiction if one uses the second definition, which implies a distinction between nation and state. Perhaps "nation-state" is used in an attempt to distinguish that kind of state from an American state. Or it may be an effort to emphasize a desired or exaggerated cultural unity in a given state.

I will use nation as a near-synonym of ethnic group, but will be citing others who use it differently.[16] In most instances the context will make clear the distinction. Often "nation" will refer to an ethnic group with a history of and a strong desire for sovereignty over a territory. Such groups can be called "nonstate nations,"[17] some of which are sufficiently autonomous and distinctive that they might cross the line separating ethnic group from state before these words are in print, as is the case with Lithuania, Latvia, Estonia, and Georgia in the U.S.S.R., Croatia and Slovenia in Yugoslavia, or Quebec in Canada (most of them have in fact crossed that line).

They have not thus become nation-states, however. Each is now multi-ethnic; and it seems highly unlikely that any conceivable redefinition of boundaries or any amount of migration, voluntary or forced, could produce ethnically homogeneous populations. This is one of the major, but seldom discussed, problems facing independence movements.

It is essential that participants in and opponents of ethnic movements for autonomy, as well as analysts, seek to discover how the effects of territorial separation differ from the effects of programs to achieve and protect cultural pluralism within multi-ethnic states. Here definitions are crucial. What does it mean to be a Lithuanian, a Georgian, an Israeli, a Catalan? Is the most significant boundary territorial, so that all residents are included—anyone living in Catalonia, for example, including those who speak no Catalan and who are members of other ethnic groups? Or is the crucial boundary cultural, based on descent and language?[18] The dominant ethnic group in an area seeking autonomy tends to seek both territorial and cultural separation, often overlooking or disregarding the interests or desires of smaller groups, thus cutting or deepening cleavages within the new sovereign boundaries. We need to ask: will territorial or cultural definitions be asserted, and by whom? Is the dominant ethnic group in any new state, having itself been denied cultural freedom, ready to grant it to the minority ethnic groups in its midst? Or, more precisely, under what conditions is it likely to or ready to support such a policy? How will the policies of newly dom-

TABLE 1.2
Percentage of the Total Population from the Majority Ethnic
Group in Four Former Soviet Republics

	1959	1989
Lithuania	79.3	79.6
Latvia	62.0	52.0
Estonia	74.6	61.5
Georgia	64.3	70.2

inant groups affect the treatment of their fellow ethnics who live outside the homeland?

Perhaps a simple listing of the demographic situation in four former Soviet republics, using the somewhat imprecise data of official censuses, illustrates the importance of these questions (table 1.2).

Part of the difficulty—or confusion—in the use of "nation" (and equivalent words in other European languages) is the historical shift in the process of state building. For example, Britain and France did not, at least in the earlier stages of state-building, define their people in terms of a single language and ethnicity. Although not as successful as often supposed in creating a unified patriotism out of separate nationalisms (as current ethnic movements and conflicts show), they were sufficiently coherent as societies in the nineteenth century to be able to include several ethnic and linguistic groups within the circle of citizens. As late as 1893 about one-quarter of the population of France could not speak French. There followed decades of effort, particularly in schools, to increase the knowledge and use of French and to spread the sense of a statewide citizenship.[19]

Germany and Italy, however, were more fragmented. Each used a single language as a major force in efforts, culminating politically in 1870, to build a unified society and state out of great ethnic diversity. In such efforts we see an important source of the myth of "nation-states."[20]

A substantial literature nearly equates nation and ethnic group; or, perhaps more precisely, nations are seen as a variety of ethnic group defined by a history or a mythology of statehood, or by powerful aspirations for statehood.[21]

The myths of nationhood, as Anthony Smith has shown, contain some or all of several kinds of stories: of origin; of migration and liberation; of descent; of an heroic age; of communal decline, conquest, and exile; and of rebirth, with a summons to action.[22]

Reenforced by such myths and histories, nationalism becomes the rallying cry for ethnic movements seeking higher economic and social status and independence, autonomy, or devolution.

Authors identify many different factors as the sources of movements leading to nationalistic (i.e., autonomy-seeking) ethnic groups. Underlying many of them is the "myth of common descent" (in Max Weber's words), or a "vivid sense of sameness" reenforced by, but not wholly dependent upon distinctive language, race, or religion.[23]

A second factor is the appearance of what has been called "post-industrial values." The desire to have a full share in state and international economic markets is, in some settings, qualified by or even supplanted by the desire for self-actualization, aesthetic and intellectual freedom, and a sense of belonging,[24] even if these entail high economic costs. Such "post-industrial values" join readily with some aspects of the current environmental movement in supporting a resource-modest style of life, living gently with nature, and decrying materialism.

In contrast with such ethnic movements are those that seek greater opportunities in the urban-industrial world, not drastic changes in its values. These are often led by professionals and intellectuals from oppressed groups. Among them, the pursuit of ethnicity may be a "rational choice," as Hechter argues, among the available chances.[25]

A different, but also class-based interpretation uses the language of "internal colonialism." A structure of control that links occupational and status advantages to cultural symbols leads alienated and marginalized members to ethno-national challenges to the dominating power.[26] This interpretation, however, cannot explain why it is white-collar and professional people who seek autonomy most vigorously. They experience relative deprivation more keenly as they confront barriers to full participation in the larger society. More disadvantaged members of their group, however, are also drawn, by cultural appeals and material hopes, into the campaigns for autonomy.

Altogether, I do not think it wise to see "nation" simply as a synonym for "ethnic group." Yet we must recognize the extensive overlap in their meanings and in their usage. Anthony Smith has put it well: "It seems to me that any useful definition of the nation must do justice to both ethnic and territorial conceptions."[27]

It is exactly that double meaning of nation that is reflected in the severe tensions experienced by new states and in the conflicts that disrupt the efforts to create new states. For several decades the world has experienced two powerful and contending political-cultural movements. As major empires have broken up, the many peoples in former colonies and territories have seen an opportunity to end the humiliating exclusion from power by creating their own dynamic, modern states. At the same time, however, their identification as individuals is still largely defined not by the new polity, but by language, race, locality, religion, tradition, and the associated desire to be recognized as people whose hopes and opinions matter. As Geertz emphasized near the beginning of this period, there has been severe and chronic tension between these contending motives and the associated movements. "The one aim is to be noticed: it is a search for an identity, and a demand that that identity be publicly acknowledged as having import. . . . The other aim is practical: it is a demand for progress, for a rising standard of living, more effective political order, greater social justice, and beyond that of 'playing a part in the larger arena of world politics,' of 'exercising influence among the nations' ".[28]

Those who live as ethnic groups in larger states, who have had states of their own or substantial autonomy, believe they can blend the two movements into a nation-state. But often they do not recognize how diverse would be its probable citizenry.

The boundaries of states in Africa, in most instances, were drawn by European powers at the Berlin Conference, in 1884, more to try to secure a balance of power than to correspond with any ethnic order based on cultural and lingual variation. Several civil wars have followed independence as diverse groups within these states have sought sovereignty and cultural identity.

State borders in the Middle East are equally "artificial." To an important degree they are the result of a division of influence between Britain and France after the end of the World War I and the collapse of the Ottoman Empire. Iraq's search for a Persian Gulf port, Syria's claims on Lebanon, and Israel's persistent hold over the West Bank are partly the (unintended) effects of British-French decisions.[29]

The new boundaries have meant shifts of identity. Said describes the sharp contrast with the colonial period, during which "in schools you could encounter Arabs from everywhere, Muslims and Christians, plus Armenians, Jews, Greeks, Italians, Indians and Iranians all mixed up, all under one or another colonial regime, interacting as if it were natural to do so. Today the state nationalisms have a tendency to fracture. Lebanon and Israel are perfect examples of what has happened. Apartheid of one form or another is present nearly everywhere as a group feeling if not as a practice, and it is subsidized by the state with its bureaucracies and secrete police organizations. Rulers are clans, families and closed circles of aging oligarchs, almost mythologically immune to change."[30]

After World War I, Woodrow Wilson sought to reduce the chances for conflict by increasing the cultural and linguistic homogeneity of the states of central and eastern Europe. (At the same time, treaties were drawn seeking to guarantee religious and lingual freedom where such homogeneity was clearly impossible.) Some new states were formed out of the puzzles left by the collapse of the Hapsburg and earlier, the Ottoman empires; some territorial boundaries were redrawn; and population transfers—some of them peaceful, most of them coercive—shifted hundreds of thousands of people into new and, presumably, more culturally homogeneous settings. The net effect, however, was scarcely to create or maintain any nation-states.

During and immediately after World War II, no new states were formed in Europe. Some state boundaries were changed, but more for geopolitical than ethnic reasons, hundreds of thousands of people were moved or displaced, mostly coercively; and some states were taken over militarily by the Soviet Union. Nothing approaching a nation-state has emerged from these actions.

The state-nation tension has thus become a major political fact of our time. A majority of the states in the world have been formed after the collapse of the Ottoman, Hapsburg, Russian, British, and French empires, with an assist from what remained of the Dutch, Belgian, Spanish, Portuguese, German, and Japanese empires. Over ninety of the United Nations' 165 or more member states have been created since the end of World War II.

Nor has the process ended. The crises that have destroyed the Soviet Union have not only put an end to its domination of eastern Europe, but have also revealed the grave weaknesses in its nationalities' policies. The alleged aim had been to grant maximum cultural autonomy and self-determination to the fifteen republics and the numerous other separate regions along with—and this must be emphasized—creating an overarching loyalty to the Soviet Union. There was modest progress toward both goals, continuing perhaps through World War II.[31]

Events since 1989, however, have revealed the enormous gap between policy and reality with respect to the Soviet Union's efforts to create a two-layered, non-conflicted pattern of loyalties. An editorial in *The New York Times* suggests the scope of problems:

> Minority nationalism had been growing in the Soviet Union, as elsewhere. The demands of Soviet Jews for permission to emigrate to Israel, the complaints of Ukrainian intellectuals about the slighting of the Ukrainian language and culture and the little-concealed dislike Georgians feel toward Russian domination have been frequently noted. Now the peoples of the Baltic states—involuntarily incorporated into the Soviet Union—are apparently worrying Moscow by their resistance to Russification, particularly to the influx of Russian and other Slavs who form an ever-increasing proportion of the population in the three Baltic states.

Although a few phrases in this editorial do not sound exactly *au courant*, the statement as a whole could have been written quite recently. It was written March 18, 1972. Today, more than twenty years later, and eight years after *glasnost* and *perestroika* became the watchwords of a major reform program, ethnic relations within several of the now-independent republics remain harshly conflictive. Several hundred people have been killed in the struggles for independence, in boundary disputes, and in the ethnic turmoil within the new and uniformly multi-ethnic states.

Race and Ethnicity

Do racial differences play a part in the designation of ethnic groups? Some scholars as well as many members of the general public see racial and ethnic lines as critically different from each other. This can be an indication of race prejudice; or it can be an objection to the loss of what is seen as a useful analytic distinction.[32] Others believe that we should dispense with the term *race* entirely, arguing that it has too many different meanings or is loaded with too many prejudicial connotations to be of any scientific value.

More commonly, however, race is seen as one of the defining characteristics of ethnicity. Many books and articles include both race and ethnicity in their titles or discussions in ways that indicate overlapping concepts.[33]

Use of a racial criterion in defining ethnicity varies widely in time and place. Today, the racial factor is not given major emphasis in discussions of Asian Americans or Native Americans. That has not always been the case, in the United States or elsewhere. At the beginning of the twentieth century, E. A. Ross in the United States and Gustav LeBon in France, for example, wrote of a kind of permanent biological character of the Japanese: "A Japanese may easily take a university degree or become a lawyer; the sort of varnish he thus acquires is, however, quite superficial and has no influence on his mental constitution. What no education can give him, because they are created by heredity alone, are the forms of thought, the logic, and above all the character of Western Man." Already half a century ago, after thus quoting LeBon, Ruth Benedict declared with a touch of irony: "At the present day the usual complaint is that Japan has too successfully taken over the character of the Western Powers.[34]

Nearly a century ago, W. E. B. DuBois emphasized not the biological aspect of race, but history, traditions, and joint endeavors—what one might call an ethnic group with a symbolic racial element. What is a race, he asked: "It is a vast family of human beings, generally of common blood and language, always of common history, traditions and impulses, who are both voluntarily and involuntarily striving together for the accomplishment of certain more or less vividly conceived ideals of life."[35]

To be sure, there is something to be said, under some circumstances, for distinguishing between ethnic relations and race relations. In their study of the political experiences of African Americans and European Americans, Cornacchia and Nelson found little support for what they call the "ethno-racial umbrella thesis"—that race, religion, and nationality are part of "the same theoretical and policy universe": "Nearly 125 years after the Civil War, Blacks are clearly justified in asserting that their political problems and issues are still unique and therefore warrant continued separate attention in the policy process."[36] I see little to disagree with in that last sentence; but race per se has little to do with it. Slavery has a lot to do with it; discrimination has a lot to do with it; racial beliefs and attitudes have a lot to do with it.

Ethnic groups that are seen as "races" are often those that have been brought into a society and integrated into its labor force at the bottom levels by coercion and violence. "Racial terms mirror the political power by which populations from other continents were turned into providers of coerced surplus labor. . . . These terms . . . continue to invoke supposed descent from such substandard populations so as to deny their putative descendants access to higher segments of the labor market. . . . The function of racial categories within industrial capitalism is exclusionary."[37]

Wolf's interpretation is supported by the historical record; but some qualifications are needed. The exclusionary use of the symbol of race pre-dated industrial capitalism by many centuries. And in the twentieth century non-capitalist societies have scarcely resisted the temptation to use race as one of the criteria in the occupational system and in the distribution of power and prestige. Even where economic factors played a major part in the choice of a race line, cultural and religious differences, often co-varying with racial differences, were also important. To be "heathen" and "uncivilized" was to be vulnerable to exploitation. To use cultural and religious differences as justification for economic and political coercion is no less repugnant than the use of racial differences. The greatest injustices have occurred when all of these lines of distinction have come together.

If one's aim is to focus on the unusually difficult conditions faced over many generations by a group distinguishable by race, or to highlight the intensity of use of racial symbols, it may be possible to attain a sharper focus by avoiding a more generalized ethnic vocabulary.[38] Scholars who argue that African Americans are a "unique" minority, having suffered unusually crushing experiences, seek to prevent the significance of those experiences from being lost in "sociological euphemism," as Merton[39] called the more abstract concepts several steps removed from the bite of particular events.

If one were to place American racial and ethnic groups along a scale indicating the harshness of their experience, African Americans would probably be in the most disadvantaged position, followed by Native Americans, Latinos (especially Mexicans, Puerto Ricans, and Haitians), Asian Americans (themselves highly diverse), to southern and northern Europeans. That those who have been most harshly treated are also non-white leads, perhaps too easily, to an emphasis on racial differences as the critical factor. The violent seizure of their ancestors or of their lands may be the more critical variable. The violence has powerfully influenced the prejudices of dominant groups (it is difficult not to hate those whom one has harmed) and the adaptations of the dominated, not all of which have been effective and creative.

From a similar perspective, Williams has suggested that "revised accounts of U.S. urban history imply that 'powerlessness' rather than 'race' or 'ethnicity' per se may be the primary condition needing further analysis."[40] A related theme is developed by Wilson in *The Declining Significance of Race* and in *The Truly Disadvantaged.*[41]

To these observations I would add that most of all we need to examine the interactions. Powerlessness under some circumstances is a reflection of discrimination along racial or ethnic lines. It cannot be accounted for if the history and present reality of that discrimination is overlooked.

In none of this, however, is race per se—race as a biological fact, of significance for the student of human behavior. Wherever behavior, attitude, and culture are the topics of discussion, the use of race—except as a symbolic marker for other lines of distinction—is inappropriate. This position is stated strongly by Taylor in his discussion of "ethnogenesis," defined us "the process whereby ethnic groups come into being":

> Some scholars assume a radical discontinuity between the experiences of blacks in the United States and the experiences of immigrant ethnic groups in American cities. There is a tendency to see the situation of blacks in racial rather than in ethnic terms and to emphasize the conditions of racial oppression and exploitation as exclusive sources of black sociocultural characteristics. This emphasis obscures the important role of migration, urbanization, and intergroup conflict in promoting a distinctive black ethnicity. Indeed, a review of the urban history of the black populations in northern cities suggests that the phenomenon of black ethnogenesis was inspired by essentially the same structural conditions as the development of ethnic identities and communities among white ethnic populations in American cities.[42]

In my view, race as a strictly biological concept is of no value in a theory of ethnicity. In particular we cannot accept the widespread belief that there are a few clearly distinct and nearly immutable races. Change and intermixture are continuous. Dobzhansky's list of thirty-four races is a good place to begin to think about race in its biological meaning.[43]

Beliefs about race, however, and about race as a social symbol, cannot be disregarded. In examining the racial aspect of ethnicity, the social scientist works from four premises: 1) Racial differences are minor biological variations in an essentially homogeneous species. 2) New races are continually being formed and old ones modified slowly by evolutionary processes and more rapidly by intermixtures. In many societies, persons of mixed racial ancestry— even if not so regarded—make up a significant proportion of the population. 3) Socially visible "racial" lines, based on beliefs about race and on administrative and political classifications, not on genetic differences per se, are the critical ones for social analysis.[44] These lines vary from society to society and from time to time. For example, one person with one-quarter Native American ancestry may clearly be an Indian (an enrolled and participating member of a tribe), while another with the same ancestry may be seen and responded to as white. 4) Race is important in social interaction primarily because of present and past correlation of racial differences with cultural and status differences.

For those who accept these four premises, ethnicity and race extensively overlap. In many cases, race—as well as language, religion, and ancestral homeland—helps to mark the boundaries of an ethnic group. The extent of racial homogeneity within an ethnic group can range from nearly complete to slight. Whatever the degree of homogeneity, the race factor helps to define an ethnic boundary only if it is correlated with ancestral culture or with lingual or religious differences. Such is the case, for example, among Asian Americans, Native Americans, and African Americans. In many other parts of the world the racial factor adds a symbolically important line of distinction among ethnic groups, as in the Soviet Union, Britain, Australia, Latin America, and several African states; this is increasingly true in some western European societies.

In what might be considered the "classic" case, race is fully blended into Afrikaner conceptions of ethnicity, as shown by Thompson's analysis of "The Political Mythology of Apartheid" in South Africa.[45] In the traditional Boer view, races are the basic divisions of humanity, but they are not defined simply in biological terms. Races, they believe, also differ in culture—not just as a result of different histories, but intrinsically, as part of their very nature. There has been some softening of this view in a separate-but-equal direction. The traditional Afrikaner linkage of race and culture, however, remains strong.

Minority Group and Ethnic Group

As with nation and race, the terms *ethnic group* and *minority* overlap to a large degree. In a definition by the United Nations Subcommission on Prevention and Protection of Minorities,[46] minorities are "those nondominant groups in a population which possess and wish to preserve stable ethnic, religious or linguistic traditions or characteristics markedly different from those of the rest of the population."

The anthropologists Wagley and Harris[47] use a similar definition of minority, but they make explicit what "nondominant" implies by listing five defining characteristics of minorities: They are subordinate segments of complex state societies; they have special physical or cultural traits that are held in low esteem by the dominant segments of the society; they are self-conscious units, bound together by the special traits that their members share and by the special disabilities which these bring; membership in a minority is transmitted by a rule of descent; and minority peoples, by choice or necessity, tend to marry within their group.

In a well-known definition, Louis Wirth[48] gives the experience of discrimination an even sharper focus: "We may define a minority as a group of people who, because of their physical or cultural characteristics, are singled out from the others in the society in which they live for differential and unequal treatment, and who therefore regard themselves as objects of collective discrimination. The existence of a minority in a society implies the existence of a corresponding dominant group with higher social status and greater privileges. Minority status carries with it the exclusion from full participation in the life of the society."

Much of the literature on ethnicity is focused on the study of discrimination, ranging from the absence of full cultural freedom to massive disprivilege. Or to put it another way, studies of discrimination against minorities often include—even emphasize—how one's ethnic status and what can be called the "ethnic order" influence the distribution of rewards or the experience of violence.

Although the definitions of "minority" have ethnic elements, they cannot be substituted as definitions of "ethnic group." There are ranked and unranked ethnic orders,[49] although the latter are not common. The dominant groups in a ranked system are scarcely minorities, except at times in the numerical sense. Many recent studies of ethnicity have focused much attention on cultural differences and the value of pluralism, and less attention on how ethnic differences are implicated in the distribution of power and privilege. Persons of Swedish background in the northern central United States, for example, may preserve something of an ancestral identity, but that aspect of their experience can scarcely be described in terms of of a minority or majority.

We ought also to add that a minority may mobilize or invent the rudiments of ethnicity in an effort to oppose discrimination.[50] Thus minority status can lead to ethnicity as well as the other way around.

In many instances, then, the boundaries of ethnicity and minority are coterminous. Some of the topics discussed in later chapters involve that overlap. At the same time, however, we shall need to keep clear the analytic distinction between the terms.

Other Related Terms

Nation, race, and minority are not the only terms that overlap—one might say compete with—ethnicity in contemporary discussions of the major cultural divisions within societies. Sometimes several terms that are seen as near-synonyms are used in the same sentence. As the *Economist*, in an article about the ethnic splits in the disintegrating Ethiopian empire becoming more visible, observed: "Last year the transitional government acknowledged that Ethiopia is a mixture of *peoples* by giving *tribal*-based governments seats in parliament and the cabinet, and allowing them to form parties, sometimes with their own militias. This has created a cocktail of organizations, based on *race* rather than ideology. The elections promised for 1994 will probably be fought on *ethnic* grounds."[51]

The term *tribe*, or *tribal society*, although originally a reference to one of the divisions of the Roman people, was given a wider meaning by anthropologists. Many of the following characteristics are usually associated with a tribe: it is small, usually preliterate and preindustrial, relatively isolated, endogamous (with exogamous sub-tribal divisions), united mainly by kinship and culture, but in many places also by territorial boundaries, and strongly ethnocentric ("We are the people").[52]

When referred to in this context, tribes are in no sense ethnic groups. Thousands of distinct societies in Asia, Australia, the South

Pacific, Africa, Europe, and the Western Hemisphere—before they came into contact with economically and militarily more powerful states, but perhaps more importantly, states armed with written languages—were tribes in this anthropological sense.

In the Arab world the term *tribe* is widely used, but in a more limited sense than *ethnic group.* A tribe is a combination of several extended families. They have some autonomy, particularly in areas in dispute between two states—Yemen and Saudi Arabia, for example.[53] With the formation of colonies and then states in Africa, the terms *tribe* and *ethnic group* have become more nearly synonymous, as they can both be used with reference to the earlier African empires. India has its "scheduled tribes," some 450 aboriginal groups ranging in size from a few dozen members to three million or more. To some degree isolated in forest and mountain areas and to some degree autonomous, they are nevertheless clearly part of the state of India.

The several hundred tribes in South and Central America, in Mexico, in the United States, and in Canada now have a somewhat similar relationship to the federal states to which they belong and by which they are surrounded. Earlier they were separate societies, although not without some inter-tribal political structures. The League of the Iroquois, for example, first a union of five tribes and then of six, was a kind of commonwealth led by a council of chiefs drawn from all of the tribes. Unanimity was required for League action. They first united to maintain peace among themselves and then later to fight for their shared interests against other tribes. They split apart when they could not agree on whether to support Britain or the colonists during the Revolutionary War.

After such groups became enclosed within larger state societies, subject to their polities, integrated in various ways into the larger economic system, and to some degree acculturated and amalgamated, they were still referred to, not surprisingly, as "tribes." This usage of "tribe" makes it a near-synonym for "ethnic group."[54]

I will mention only one more concept, which in some uses, overlaps with ethnicity: regionalism, or somewhat less clearly, sectionalism. Studies of regions examine the differences between areas in terms of their histories, languages, and religions, but they are also likely to focus on the natural environment and economic structures. Many regions are multi-ethnic, and the nature of their ethnic relations is an important aspect of their social structure and culture, as in the American South. Other regions are more homogeneous ethnically, but ethnically different from the society to which they belong. They can usefully be seen as ethnic groups as well as regions, as in the case of Quebec, the Basque country in Spain, or, less clearly, German Bavaria.[55]

In some cases only a detailed description of language or dialect, of history, of culture, and of self-identifications could help one decide whether a regional or an ethnic label would be the more informative.

Regional studies, or what can be called the human geography tradition, can help to remind us that the ethnic factor is not exclusively important in examination of the sub-divisions of a society. At the same time, such studies can add new dimensions to the analysis of ethnicity, enlarging the context within which ethnic relations are seen to occur.

Ethnic Group, Nation, Race, and Minority

The relationships among these four overlapping terms: *ethnic group, nation, race,* and *minority,* are suggested in figure 1.2. Segment A indicates the convergence of the four: an ethnic group that is different in race from the dominant group, that has a history or strong desire for a separate sovereign land, and that experiences discrimination.

We must recognize that this effort to bring conceptual clarity to the terms collides with their political-moral uses. They are instruments of struggle as well as communication. To conflate "race" and "ethnic group" seems to some to obscure the often overwhelming importance of racial discrimination and prejudice. To others, oppositely, it obscures what they see as the God-given immutable distinctions among the races. To conflate ethnic group and nation, in the view of some, obscures the history of and the moral right to a national sovereign area. To conflate ethnic group and minority may obscure the importance, as fact and ideology, of pluralism—a peaceful ethnic order combining relatively equal groups in one polity. It is essential that we be steadily aware of our own and others' use of these critical terms.

Of these four terms—race, nation, minority, and ethic group—the last is the most comprehensive. None of the other three is adequate to encompass the enormous range of the intergroup relations among cultural groups now so prominent within societies throughout the world.

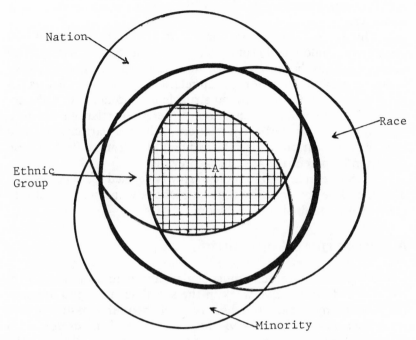

FIGURE 1.2
Relations among Ethnic Group, Nation, Race, and Minority

Some, but not all, involve race—as a symbol. Some, but not all, involve nations—groups with a history, a memory or a hope of statehood built around a sense of cultural distinctiveness. Some involve minorities—groups that face persistent discrimination (They may or may not be racially distinctive or be seen, by themselves and others, as nations).

Looking at these relationships another way, we see that an ethnic group may or may not be racially different from others in the society of which it is a part. It may or may not think of itself and be thought of by others as a nation. It may or may not be a minority. Whatever the mixture, or in the absence of these three characteristics, ethnic groups are distinguishable culturally; they are identified, by others and by themselves, as separate; and, in the fullest sense, as individuals they join in activities and share beliefs and aspirations that express their distinctiveness. Thus ethnicity is the most inclusive of these four terms. It is the most parsimonious way to focus attention on the overlapping issues to which these terms refer.

This is not to imply that a more specialized focus is unwise or impossible. Undoubtedly some intergroup relations are well studied as race relations, because in those instances, race is a major symbol of differentiation. Some intergroup relations are well studied as nations in conflict, where political struggle for autonomy or independence is the overriding issue. Some intergroup relations are well studied as minority-majority relations, where a particularly rigid form of stratification—frozen by symbols of cultural differentiation and often by potent racial beliefs—prevails.

Such research, using a more narrowly defined set of issues, can inform and be informed by the comprehensive perspective of ethnicity. Let a hundred flowers bloom.

A THEORETICAL ADDENDUM

The study of ethnicity must be tied closely to the larger field of analytic and interpretive work in the social sciences and humanities. For the most part, the discussion of theoretical issues in this essay appears—unobtrusively, I hope—as part of the examination of particular topics. A few comments, however, may illustrate the ways in which general theoretical statements can be of value to the student of ethnicity.

Granted human egocentricity, the frequency of violence, the scarcity of many goods and services, and the zero-sum quality of power and prestige, how do human societies manage to exist, often for centuries or even millennia? State boundaries change; governments are replaced; but societies stagger along, despite sharp conflict and internal divisions. At least since Aristotle, it has been asked: How to account for social order? There are four partially competing theories:

1. Social order is an expression of our inheritance. In the evolutionary process, those groups among our early ancestors that were capable of altruism and social organization were better able to survive.
2. Social order is a product of exchange and reciprocity, of perceived mutual advantages. It is through utilitarian calculations by individuals and subgroups that their interests are served—not by separation, but by live-and-let-live and by exchange.

3. It is a consequence of the power of some to command the compliance of others. Those on the bottom see little reciprocity; but the fear of loss, of pain, or heightened coercion—often a realistic fear—prevents them from opposing the order effectively.
4. Social order is the product of culture, of mutually shared values and norms—a blueprint for action that has been internalized by a set of people who have been socialized to similar standards.

Although each of these explanations of social order has its advocates. I see no reason why all four should not be recognized as important, even if to widely varying degrees in particular situations.[56]

In a minimal definition relevant to the study of ethnicity, we can define social order to mean that the structures of interaction and of the elites who manage them have a sufficiently strong mixture of power and legitimacy to prevent internal dissension or external threat from destroying the society. It does not mean lack of conflict; it does not imply that the society is fair or just by particular standards.

When one source of order is pulled from the others, whether as an explanation by a theorist or as a social reality, it becomes a recipe for disorder. Without doing justice to the subtlety of their thought, we can observe that Edmund Burke, in his *Reflections*, saw tradition and habitual allegiance ("prejudice") as the glue that held society together. For Joseph de Maistre, however, in his *Considerations on France*, it was—to put it in his harsh way—the hangman, representative of the necessary absolute power of the monarchy, on whom order depended. To market theorists, best represented perhaps not by Adam Smith but by many contemporary theorists and policy makers in the West or in the scattered pieces of the former USSR, it is exchange—the market—that is the basis of order.

It is my belief that if any one of these, as explanations or as social practice, is relied on almost exclusively, the likelihood of social conflict is greatly increased.

In various ways, we shall be asking: Granted the biological capacity for social life, how does ethnic diversity affect and reflect the balance of reciprocity, power, and culture as sources of social order in a society? As a result of ethnic divisions, are mutual advantages less likely to be perceived, or basic values and norms less likely to be shared, so that power and coercion grow in importance? Are conflict and discrimination the likely outcomes?

Or can there be continuing emphasis on ethnic diversity while maintaining or achieving pluralistic tolerance, cooperation, and equal access to power, income, and prestige?

To put the question more analytically: Under what conditions is ethnic diversity a recipe for conflict and discrimination, and when is it a recipe for cultural richness, social adaptability, and individual choice?

One of those conditions, important for the study of ethnic and many other relationships, is closely connected to the problem of order. We often find that what is a rational course of action for individuals can lead to a highly irrational result for the group to which they belong. If the village green, the commons, is opened to residents, who can freely use it to graze their flocks, each individual is best served by using it to a maximum. But if all follow that logic, the commons is over-grazed and becomes useless for everyone—the often observed "tragedy of the commons." In mathematical game theory this is studied as "the prisoner's dilemma—a trap ". . . that arises when individually rational choices aggregate with mutually undesirable results."[57]

Although current ethnic relations frequently demonstrate something very similar to the tragedy of the commons, as we shall see, it is not an inevitable process. Those who recognize interdependence and are aware of the individual vs. group dilemma, can take steps to avoid it and to strengthen a shared social order. Cues that show recognition of others' interests; sanctions; credible exchanges; monitoring by disinterested parties; a culture that emphasizes tolerance and inclusiveness—these are among the factors that can help to enlarge the human circle for whose benefit "rational choices" are made.[58]

Shifting from a macro to a more micro perspective, we need to be aware of theoretical work that examines social-psychological processes influencing attachment to our own ethnic groups and our behavior toward members of other groups. To understand intergroup relations in depth, we must add the study of these processes to the examination of economic, demographic, and other structural influences.

Principles being developed in the study of "attraction in interpersonal relations" can readily be applied to inter-ethnic contacts. One need only examine the morning news to find support for the statement that "persons will tend, where possible, to notice and distort the characteristics of others in the direction of their current motivational states."[59] Closely related are studies of "status-organizing processes." Again, our day-to-day observations, if we are alert to the processes involved, can indicate what research has documented; that "evaluations of and beliefs about the characteristics of actors become the basis of observable inequalities in face-to-face-interaction."[60]

It is often said that seeing is believing. While this is doubtless true under many conditions, it is also true that believing is seeing. Perception is affected by desire, prejudice, hatred, and personal and group needs, as well as by objective physical processes. To some degree, we make members of our own groups and members of other groups into what we need them to be. We may need others to be enemies, witches, Satan. We may need atrocity stories, over and beyond the all-too-frequent real atrocities, to reduce any ambivalence we feel about our own violence in intergroup conflict.

Most of us can look a "fact" squarely in the face and, if we already have a frame of reference that involves that fact, turn it upside down. Several decades ago, Allport and Postman described an experiment in which several people were shown a picture of a black man and a white man, the latter holding a razor in his hand. Each of the observers was then asked to tell all he could about the picture to a second person, the second to the third, the third to a fourth, and the fourth to a fifth. In over half of the cases, the razor had somehow "leaped" into the black man's hand. In several cases he was seen as threatening the white man with it.[61]

Our capacity to see or remember what we believe has not been lost in the years since Allport's and Postman's experiment. On February 6, 1991, the British Court of Appeal declined to make a judicial review of the grounds for internment and deportation of Palestinians, Lebanese, Yemenis, Iraqis, and others of Arab descent living in Britain. There had been 167 deportation orders since August 2, 1990 with no finding of law violation, only a general assertion of "national security." In denying the plaintiffs a judicial review, "Lord Justice Donaldson stated that evidence of wrongdoing was not necessary in their case because '... those who are able most effectively to undermine national security are those who least appear to constitute any risk to it.' In other words, apparent innocence is the best indicator of guilt."[62]

A strong ethnic prejudice can have an almost paralyzing effect on observation and rational judgment. In the decision of the Lord Justice are echoes of the comments of American General John De-

Witt on the forced evacuation of Americans of Japanese descent from the West Coast in 1942:

> The Japanese race is an enemy race and while many second and third generation Japanese born on United States soil, possessed of United States citizenship, have become 'Americanized,' the racial strains are undiluted. . . . That Japan is allied with Germany and Italy in this struggle is not ground for assuming that any Japanese, barred from assimilation by convention as he is, though born and raised in the United States, will not turn against this nation when the final test of loyalty comes. It therefore follows that along the vital Pacific Coast over 112,000 potential enemies of Japanese extraction are at large today. There are indications that these are organized and ready for concerted action at a favorable opportunity. *The very fact that no sabotage has taken place to date is a disturbing and confirming indication that such action will be taken.*[63]

The last sentence of General DeWitt's comment shows how *any* fact, even one that to the naive observer must seem to be an exact refutation of the conclusion, can be made to seem to support it. Again, believing is seeing.

Although we do not often hear quite such convoluted logic, the political and economic conflicts and the urban disorders of the early 1990s have exposed the less than solid grip we have on equal rights and ethnic tolerance, partly because prejudices and values of which we may not be aware intrude into our observations, distorting and limiting our understanding.

THE CHANGING ETHNIC MAP SINCE WORLD WAR II

Wars, revolutions, the rapid development of an international economy, desolate political and economic conditions in many countries, perceived opportunities abroad, and threatened population decline or shortage of workers in several developed countries are among the forces that have sent tens of millions of immigrants, guest workers, refugees, and illegal migrants across state lines. Some have moved willingly, even gladly; others reluctantly; and still others under threat of violence.

Some became ethnics in a new land, not because they moved, but because the boundaries of the country within which they lived were shifted.

Of course migration is an old, old story. Everybody in the Western Hemisphere is a migrant or a descendant of a migrant, if one thinks of a fifteen or twenty thousand year period. For a century or more, Germans have thought of themselves as one people, one volk; but they are an amalgam of many waves of migrants who have settled there over a period of several millennia. The United Kingdom unites many more groups than the English, Scots, Welsh, Irish, and the quite recent immigrants from the Caribbean, African, and Asian commonwealth countries or former colonies.[64] All of these are only the top layers of a population built up through centuries of migration and invasion.

Our reference here, however, is to shifts of populations during the last half century. The following is a partial list:

- Eighteen million or more immigrants into the United States since 1950
- Fifteen million "foreigners" into the states of western Europe— most of them "guest workers" and their descendants
- One million Columbians into Venezuela
- Nearly a million legal and illegal workers into Japan, mainly from East and Southeast Asia
- Until recently, hundreds of thousands of foreign workers into Saudi Arabia and Kuwait.

In the last quarter of a century the population of Israel has doubled, within its 1967 borders. Most of the growth is due to migration, from North Africa, Asia Minor, Eastern Europe, and—most recently—from the former Soviet Union, the source of more than 450,000 immigrants (1989–1992). The higher rate of growth among the 15 percent who are Arab Israelis, however, has meant that the percentage of Jews has fallen from 89 to 82.

Upon attaining independence, several African states put severe pressure on their citizens of Indian ancestry to leave. Of the 298,000 Asians, mainly Indians, in Uganda, Kenya, and Tanzania in 1969, only 158,000 remained in 1972.[65] The majority migrated to Britain, adding to the two million other migrants and refugees from Africa, Eastern Europe, and West Indies, and other former colonies in Asia.

Citizens of the United States tend to think of Canada as divided between a basically English society (its members sometimes seeming more English than the English) and a French society, with an interesting range of native Americans adding to the mix. In recent years, however, that picture has become less and less accurate. Annual immigration into Canada is higher than that into the United States, when stated as a percentage of the population. During the last quarter of a century, newcomers have been added to the Canadian population at an annual rate of over 150,000 (equivalent to 1½ million entering the United States). Over 40 percent, during the last decade, have come from Asia, 28 percent from Europe, and 20 percent from South and Central America, the Caribbean, and Africa.[66] Over a quarter of the population of Canada's three largest metropolitan areas (Toronto, Montreal, and Vancouver) are immigrants.

When China overran Tibet in 1950, the Tibetans became, in effect, an ethnic group in China—the border, rather than the people, having moved. In addition, 8 percent of the Chinese people are non-Han. That seems like a rather small proportion; but it amounts to 91 million people, according to the 1990 census, who belong to ethnic minorities.[67] Relatively few of them are migrants; but their share of the population is expanding rapidly.

About 18 percent of ethnic Russians (over 25 million people) live in one of the other fourteen former Soviet republics. The proportions range from 1 percent in Azerbaijan to over 37 percent in Kasakhstan. Most of the primarily Muslim republics have ethnically diverse populations, having been used as a kind of "dumping ground" for dissidents, "undesirables," or workers needed in mines and factories.[68] Twenty-one percent of the population of Ukraine is of Russian background.

Nearly as many non-Russians as Russians live outside their native lands.[69] The effect of all of these migrations, some of them before the period under review, is that none of the fifteen former Soviet republics is ethnically homogeneous. None can form a nation-state. For a time they may get a semblance of unity via their protests against Russia. "From the Lithuanians to the Tartars, Anti-Russian Tone Confronts Moscow," a *New York Times* headline declared in 1987. Their present task, however, is to create civil societies out of ethnically diverse populations.

That will be enormously difficult, not only in the former republics of the Soviet Union, but in Western Europe, which we will be discussing.[70] Migration may be less violent than in the past; it is not so often produced by the seizure of land and people. It is still often coercive and discriminatory, however, as the receiving states seek to fulfill one of their basic purposes—to secure an unskilled and semi-skilled labor force that commands, in return for their work, much less than the value of their efforts. Is it possible, if that is indeed one of the major purposes, to foresee extensive integration of the newcomers into the established civil societies? Or is it possible that such an economic purpose will become secondary to the goals of social peace and justice?

The ethnic mix in the United States is among those changing most rapidly. The country is once again the preeminent immigrant-receiving society, as measured by absolute numbers. During a forty-year interval (1924–1965) both the number and the variety of immigrants were sharply reduced. Since 1965, however, several changes in the law have increased fivefold the number of persons granted permanent visas and the chance to become citizens, annually from 155,000 to 775,000. At the same time, the narrow racial, religious, and national restrictions specifically contained in the 1924 statute or the consequence of its provisions, have been removed. In addition, a poorly measured but large number of undocumented aliens—perhaps as many as 300,000 a year during the last decade—have entered the United States. Recently, over two million of those who have been residents for several years have been granted permanent visas.

A list of the five countries sending the largest number to the United States gives a hint of the changing sources of immigrants between 1950 and 1991 (table 1.3)

TABLE 1.3
Major Sources of Immigrants to the U.S., 1950–1991

Countries of Origin	1950s	1980s	1991 (one year)
		(in thousands)	
Germany	478	*	*
Canada	378	*	*
Mexico	300	976	53
Britain	203	*	*
Italy	185	*	*
Philippines	*	477	55
China and Taiwan	*	306	31
Korea	*	303	*
Vietnam	*	266	55
Soviet Union	*	*	57

*Not in top five

Some of the items in this table reflect relatively short-run factors, but others indicate middle- or long-term developments: the disappearance of European societies from the list after the first time period shown; the prominence of Mexico (and, it can be added, of smaller Caribbean and Central American countries that send proportionately large numbers); and the growing number of migrants from Asia, from several societies not represented before 1980.

As a result of these developments, along with somewhat higher birthrates among some ethnic groups who are mainly newcomers, the ethnic mix of the United States has been changed rather dramatically. One should add, however, that the population continues to be preponderantly European descended.

Using broad, mainly pan-ethnic categories, following the census, we find the following changes in population between 1970 and 1990.

TABLE 1.4
American Racial and Ethnic Categories (Percentages)

	1970	1980	1990
White	87.4	83.1	80.3
Black	11.1	11.7	12.1
Asian and Pacific Islander	0.7	1.5	2.9
Indian, Eskimo, and Aleut	0.4	0.6	0.8
Hispanic	*	6.4	9.0
Other	0.3	3.0	*

*Not included

Because of changes in the ways the questions were asked in the census, the percentages for the different years are not strictly comparable. Self-identification was used in 1980 and 1990. More than one identity could be given, hence the numbers in the 1990 column add up to more than 100 percent. The Indian population would be greatly increased, perhaps by 500 or 600 percent, if these who claimed some Native American background were included. Nevertheless, the trends are clear. The Hispanic, Asian, and native American populations are expanding rapidly, the African-American more slowly, and the European-descended is decreasing. In the short run, at least, these trends seem likely to continue. America will enter the twenty-first century with a population of about 275–280 million people, three-quarters of mainly European descent and one quarter (c. 70,000,000) descended from a rich mixture of people drawn from all parts of the world. Because the non-European one-quarter includes 32 percent of the children under 18, it will increase quite rapidly. By the middle of the twenty-first century, if present trends continue, the United States will be a truly global society, with slightly over half of primarily European ancestry and nearly half of Latino, African, Asian, and Native American background. How the United States develops as a multi-ethnic society will be of critical importance not only for its own quality of life, but also as a model for the world.[71]

I have not included in this discussion the long list of refugees who have been a heart-rending part of the migration picture since World War II. It is difficult to draw a sharp line between refugees and migrants in more regularized programs, but the following criteria may be helpful:

TABLE 1.5
Identifying Characteristics of Migrants and Refugees

Migrants	Refugees
1. Migration propelled by hope and ambition	Migration propelled by oppression and extreme poverty
2. Migrants welcomed and absorbed	Refugees turned away or grudgingly admitted
3. Legally admitted	Enter the new land illegally
4. Permanent residence possible, even expected	Settled in temporary camps

These distinctions are overly simple. Each of these criteria is a variable, with only the end points of the range being noted in the table. Many situations, however, fall in the middle: some refugees are freely admitted and cared for; some migrants are opposed by a large part of the receiving population.

Although I do not call refugees ethnic groups, since they are identified more by their desperate plight than by their place as cultural groups within a polity, this in no way reduces their importance in the modern world. They face many of the same problems as the new ethnic groups created by migration: discrimination, the loss of human rights, the need to find a secure homeland.[72] Some, in fact, are resettled from refugee camps to new countries—a major first step toward reducing their problems. Others are admitted, as individuals or in small groups, under special refugee provisions, with the promise of long-term, even permanent residence. This is the case particularly in the United States. Between 1946 and 1989, 15 percent of foreigners gaining legal admission to the United States were refugees (2,389,000). Most of them have been granted lawful, permanent status and thus have become part of America's ethnic mix.[73]

This is not true, however, for the vast number of refugees who fled the war in Afghanistan to Pakistan, for Kurds fleeing the wrath of Saddam Hussein into Turkey or Iran, or for those trying to escape from Vietnam into Malaysia or Hong Kong or from Cambodia into Thailand. A high proportion of the eighteen million refugees in the world today are most clearly identified by the criteria listed in the Refugee column. They have been propelled by terror and hunger, turned away or admitted grudgingly, and housed in temporary shelters, most commonly in states close to their homelands. Many remain nearly stateless while the United Nations (whose High Commission for Refugees has twice, in 1954 and 1981, been awarded the Nobel Peace Prize), several states, and many private groups seek a solution to their desperate plight.

Of the several countries that have been major receiving areas, some have done so by choice, at least in part, out of both self-interest and humanitarianism. These include France, Germany, Canada, and the United States. Others are responding out of necessity, yet not without humanitarian concerns, to a task thrust upon them by their location near a major conflict—for example Somalia, Pakistan, Sudan, Jordan, Zaire. At no time since World War II have there been fewer than ten million refugees. As conflicts abate or are resolved, some have been able to return home. Yet a huge number remain, stateless persons caught in a trap the world has not learned how to avoid.

SUMMARY

This is by no means a complete picture of the changes in the map of ethnicity during the last half century. Almost every part of the globe has been involved in what is the most widespread, and probably the largest, movement of populations in human history. During this period scores of old and new states have experienced changes in their ethnic mix. When the influence of extensive internal migration is added, the significance of the ethnic factor is enlarged further.

Overarching such demographic developments is the rapid growth of the population of the world as a whole. Although the annual rate of growth has fallen from 2.1 percent to 1.7 percent in the last quarter of a century, the demographic momentum will carry the total of 5.5 billion in 1993 to the 8–12 billion range in the next half century. Most of the increase will be in the less developed countries and, within those countries, among ethnic minorities.

The United Nations graphically documents the enormous importance of changes in the rate of growth: If the replacement level (c. 2.0 children per woman) were reached immediately, the world population would peak at 8.4 billion in the year 2150. If current fertility rates were to continue, however, the world's population would reach *694 billion* in that year. 692 billion would be in today's developing countries. No one expects that to happen; but just to imagine it is to make vivid the powerful demographic momentum in the current growth rate. It is nearly twice the replacement level.[74]

Chapter 2

ASSIMILATION AND
DISSIMILATION

Despite ambiguity in usage of the term and the controversies surrounding it, *assimilation* continues to be an important concept for students of ethnicity. In these times of ethnic conflict and resurgence, assimilation has become something of a swearword. Rather than melting pots within which discriminatory differences are boiled away, modern societies are often seen as agents of "cultural genocide"—of forced Americanization, Russification, Germanification.

ASSIMILATION: REDUCING CULTURAL DIFFERENCES AND GROUP SEPARATION

No one can doubt that coercive policies against distinctive cultural groups are commonplace around the world. At the same time, paradoxically, peaceful processes that reduce the differences between members of interacting ethnic groups are also readily seen.

Both the coercive and the peaceful processes are assimilation, using the dictionary meaning of the term—to make alike, or to make similar.

As Vaclav Havel has recently written, words have histories. "The selfsame word can be true at one moment and false the next, at one moment illuminating, at another, deceptive. On one occasion it can open up glorious horizons, on another, it can lay down the tracks to an entire archipelago of concentration camps."[1] Derrida takes this point even further into the "deconstruction" of definitions and interpretations—a process that requires close examination of their premises and their often competing messages.[2]

Such statements as those of Havel and Derrida give us pause in in the effort to define *assimilation,* a word with diverse meanings. Its history cannot be disregarded. The political and valuative connotations are difficult to exclude. Although I do not share the radical relativism that can be read into these statements, I value the warning that they bring. With due caution, I shall try to develop the term in a descriptive and analytic sense. To be sure, in discussing particular situations one is likely to lament or applaud assimilation. Such evaluations, however, are not part of the definition.

Ambiguity and controversy surround the term in part because some fear that emphasis on assimilation is factually wrong, and others that it reenforces oppressive systems.[3] Still others, in contrast, fear that failure to recognize cases when some assimilation does occur under various conditions leads to poor social analysis and promotes inequities.[4] By using the concept of assimilation neutrally, I hope to reduce these various problems to a minimum.

Assimilation, then, is a process of boundary reduction that can occur when members of two or more societies, ethnic groups, or smaller social groups meet. It is a variable, not an attribute. When the process is carried to completion, "An assimilated ethnic population is defined operationally as a group of persons with similar foreign origins, knowledge of which in no way gives a better prediction or estimation of their relevant social characteristics than does knowledge of the behavior of the total population of the community or nation involved."[5]

In few instances, however, is assimilation complete. Traces of ethnic variation can persist even after several generations of social and physical mobility, extensive contact across ethnic lines, and equal opportunities. Anthropologists are beginning to give more attention to lines of division even in small and seemingly culturally homogeneous societies; ". . . Most societies give evidence, mythological or otherwise, of some stubborn survival of alien traditions."[6]

While recognizing such persistence, we must also be aware of some tendency in recent years to exaggerate the salience of ethnic identities and to overlook strong assimilative pressures. "Anthropologists who have studied truly plural societies would probably feel, for example, that attendance at Polish picnics, membership in a Polish-American voluntary association, and a reluctance to endure Polish jokes does not equate with strong ethnic identity when the individual probably speaks little if any Polish and shows scant evidence of adherence to Polish cultural traditions."[7]

Seen as a completed process assimilation is the blending into one of formerly distinguishable sociocultural groups.[8] Four principles can help us develop the term as a useful analytic tool, applicable across time and groups:

1. It is a descriptive, not an evaluative concept. Another way to say this is that the study of assimilation is simultaneously the study of dissimilation.[9] To study the conditions under which cultural lines of division within a society are weakened is at the same time to study the conditions under which they are reenforced.

   To refer to assimilation as a descriptive and analytic concept, however, is not to imply that its extent and nature are of purely empirical interest. Vital moral and policy questions are also involved. We have relatively little difficulty distinguishing among these three levels of interest when thinking about the fission and fusion of atoms. All too often, however, the empirical, moral, and policy levels are blurred when we think about the fission or fusion of groups.

2. Assimilation refers to a variable, not an attribute. Much of the disagreement surrounding the study of assimilation is due to the failure to see it as a process and to examine the effects of various degrees. One can describe 'complete assimilation' or 'complete separation', but these are rare occurrences within the context of contemporary states. When we treat it as a variable, we see that assimilation can range from the smallest beginnings of interaction and cultural exchange to the thorough fusion of the groups.

3. Assimilation is a multi-dimensional process. The various aspects of that process, which I shall be describing, are highly interactive; but they vary separately (although not entirely indepen-

dently), propelled by somewhat different sets of causes; they change at different rates and in different sequences.

4. Each process is reversible. Although there are powerful forces toward assimilation in many societies, groups can become more dissimilar under some conditions. Cultural lines of distinction that seemed to be fading are sometimes renewed; language differences can increase; and identities can shift back toward ancestral groups.[10]

Contrary to commonly stated judgments, in my view assimilation can exist alongside pluralism, except in extreme cases. Pluralism is the recognition of the legitimacy and even the value of some cultural and associational variation. As defined, assimilation and pluralism are to some degree mutually limiting, but they are not mutually contradictory. Indeed, pluralism as a value and as a policy is unlikely to appear until some assimilation occurs.

DISSIMILATION: THE CONTINUED STRENGTH AND THE RENEWAL OF ETHNICITY

We cannot develop a theory of assimilation without paying attention to its reciprocal, dissimilation—the process whereby intrasocietal differences are maintained and created around subcultural groups. Although the forces of assimilation are strong in many societies today, much more visible are the continuing strength and, in many places, the renewal of ethnic groups.

The dissolution of the Soviet Union and the sharp reduction, if not complete elimination, of Russia's commanding influence over several eastern European countries, has reduced the sense of common citizenship within each of those countries—based on their shared effort to contain the Soviet influence—and increased the sense of their separate identities. As a recent headline put it: "Ethnic rivalries are replacing cold war tensions."

For several decades, "regional conflicts"—the basis of the rivalry and often severe tension between the USSR and the USA in many parts of the world—inhibited intrastate conflicts. In many countries, either the USSR or the USA—or, in the case of Iraq, both; or as in Ethiopia, first the USA and then the USSR—cultivated and supported the dominant elites. Oligarchy was the rule; tightly controlled military power was made dominant by the aid furnished by the patron superpower. Separatist tendencies were suppressed. The sharp reduction in superpower rivalry, however, has left the dominant groups in many third-world countries with greatly reduced outside support. Suppressed ethnic groups reappear as part of the effort to fill power vacuums.[11]

Ironically, the reduction in the severity of apartheid in South Africa is beginning to have a similar effect in sub-Saharan Africa. Until recently it has been easy for repressive, one-party states—often dominated by one ethnic group—to deflect criticism and competition by pointing to the harshly oligarchic rule by the one-eighth of the population that is white in South Africa. Each change promoted by President Frederick de Klerk and pushed forward by black South Africans, however, weakens such a strategy in Kenya, Nigeria, Zambia, Zimbabwe, Zaire, Ethiopia, and elsewhere.[12]

The vulnerability of the strategy is made dramatically and harshly evident by the African writer Wole Soyinka: "The quantitative loss of humanity. The permanent brain damage of millions of famine-afflicted children. The trail of skeletons along desiccated highways. The mounds of corpses in deserted villages and in mass graves. The lassitude and hopelessness of those emaciated survivors crowded into refugee camps and forced 'resettlements' dictated by ideological formulae.

"If these images evoke the trails of slave marches, the coastal forts, dungeons and stockades, the makeshift markets filled with black human merchandise. . . . We must recognize that the African continent has again been betrayed, this time from within."[13]

Needless to say, outside cold-warriors have been as fully implicated in these tragedies as colonial invaders have been in the past.

Earlier ethnic identities can be preserved and reaffirmed even where extensive assimilation has taken place. Native Americans, for example, have experienced significant acculturation, especially since World War II. (At the same time, the larger society has continued to be influenced by Indian cultures, but the strength of the mutual acculturation reflects the great differences in size and power of the groups involved.) Various kinds of integration are evident: Scarcely a third of Native Americans live on reservations; many attend or have attended integrated schools; there has been a sharp reduction in the knowledge and use of Indian languages. And amalgamation continues more rapidly than ever, since one Indian in three now marries a non-Indian.[14]

Despite such assimilative forces, and to some degree because of them, many Indians are reaffirming their distinctiveness and promoting cultural renewal. Contact and acculturation have raised hopes, but numerous barriers still block Indians from entrance into the full range of opportunities in the larger society. In this context, many Indians have joined movements to emphasize their distinctive cultures (and to some degree, to define a pan-Indian culture that stresses the common elements among highly diverse tribes). Indian ceremonies are being revived; Indian institutes and colleges are being founded; "national" movements that go beyond pluralism to demand substantial political and economic autonomy are supported by some Native Americans.

These trends illustrate the paradox mentioned at the beginning of this chapter: powerful assimilative forces are matched by renewed attention to sociocultural differences; acculturation is not necessarily matched by integration. In examining this paradox, it is essential that we study not only the most visible movements, the politically and ideologically prominent and controversial trends—although these are likely to attract the most attention. Along with the affirmation of ethnic identity—an affirmation that usually involves the public efforts of groups—a quiet drift of separate individuals in the other direction, toward assimilation, may occur.

Under some circumstances, all four of the types of response that Louis Wirth saw as characteristic of minority groups can be found in inter-ethnic relations: In some societies today, pluralistic movements, separatist movements, and efforts among competitive ethnic groups to win domination exist alongside significant assimilative processes.[15]

How can we account for the continuing importance of ethnic attachments in spite of extensive physical and social mobility, the power of the state, communication networks dominated by mass media, the sharp reduction of language variation in many settings, and other assimilative forces? Three sets of forces are used, by various scholars, to explain this puzzling fact.

One group of writers emphasizes the continuing power of primordial attachments.[16] The concept of primordial (i.e., "its original form") has both a biological and cultural aspect. They come together in their emphasis on kinship as the foundation of ethnicity. Those who approach the study of ethnicity from a sociobiological perspective see inheritance as the very basis of their definition. Thus van den Berghe makes ". . . individual fitness (as measured by reproductive success) the ultimate currency of maximization." And he ". . . identifies nepotism based on proportion of shared genes as the basic mechanism of ethnicity."[17]

It is not clear how the sociobiological explanation of the continuing power of ethnic attachments can be applied to the large and
heterogeneous ethnic groups in modern societies—groups that have
been influenced by intermarriage, conversion, adoption, intergroup
alliances, and personal choices. "The principle of inclusive fitness
can have, at most, only a highly diluted effect in large and heterogeneous populations."[18]

'Primordial' has a cultural connotation, however, that is more
frequently emphasized. Without close attachments to a country
or in the presence of disillusionment regarding the justice or the
power of the state, or simply as a continuation of a powerfully
learned identity, one affirms that These are my people, the people of
my ancestors.[19] The one major conviction that emerged from his
study of ethnicity, Epstein wrote, "was the powerful emotional
charge that appears to surround or to underlie so much of ethnic
behaviour."[20] This is the cultural explanation.

The cultural interpretation of the persistence, or revival, of
ethnicity is most likely to be expressed by those who are close to the
communal centers of their ethnic groups. There is little doubt that
where language and religion and other major cultural elements separate a group from others in a society, ethnic identity is likely to
be maintained in all three of the senses of our definition: self-
perception, the perception of others, and associational involvement.
It is less evident that cultural factors are the basic ones in a situation where cultural differences are fading, language contrasts are
minimal, and religious sentiments and attachments are weakening.
The task, therefore, is to find reliable and valid measures of the
extent to which cultural differences persist or are reduced, and to develop a theory of the conditions under which these occur. Undoubtedly demographic factors are involved, as are spatial mobility, the
degree to which the occupational structure is open, the nature of political alignments, religious trends (ecumenicity versus denomina-
tionalizing as well as strength of attachments), and many other
factors. We are dealing with a series of interdependent variables, not
with simple cause-and-effect sequences.

We need researchable hypotheses that go beyond the simple
listing of variables. Greeley approaches such a hypothesis when he
writes "We are not ready to assume that vast cultural differences do
not persist. Our suspicion—and given the present state of the data,
it is little more than suspicion—is that the core of these differences
has to do with different expectations about close relatives; that is, in

one ethnic group the expectations of how a husband or a wife, a father or a mother, a brother or a sister, a cousin, an aunt, or an uncle should behave are likely to be quite different than in another ethnic group."[21]

The feeling that ethnicity is rooted in families or in primordial, *gemeinschaftlich* villages, is given mythic proportions in novels and stories in many lands. In an elegant study of village prose in Russia (c. 1960-1980) Parthé suggests perceptions and feelings which, with a few changes in wording, could be applied to many other societies:

> "Village prose expresses a sense of the primordial—the mystic beginnings of time in forest and field—as well as each individual's beginning in childhood. Of equal importance is its focus on the end of time in the deaths of older peasants, the abandoning of whole villages, and in the perceived threat to the distinctive rural character of Russia itself. If the past of Village Prose is full, radiant, and complex, the present is experienced as a time of loss, and the future is seen as a cultural and moral vacuum."[22]

Under some conditions, this view of the very roots of ethnic attachments is persuasive, even if not entirely adequate. One is not surprized, for example, to learn that most Kurds, their lives unfolding in Kurdish towns and villages, do not identify primarily with states to which they are attached and within which they are oppressed. Nor is it surprising that the numerous ethnic groups in the southern Sudan—different in language, religion, and race from those in the North—have fought for autonomy.[23] But how can one account for the *recovery* of an ethnic identity despite extensive acculturation? How can one account for the *choice* of an ethnic identity from among several possibilities?[24] These alternatives cannot equally be ancestral attachments. And how can one explain the appearance of *new* ethnicities, often in the form of combinations of groups that had formerly thought of themselves as quite distinct? If one thinks of himself as a Native American, rather than as a Sioux, a Navajo, an Oneida, or a Kwakiutl, it is not because of identification with one's ancestors so much as it is because of the situation created for all Indians by the dominant society.

A second line of argument seeks to answer these questions by stressing the difficulty many people feel in identifying with a large, heterogeneous, rapidly changing society. They seem surrounded by anomie, alienation,[25] and an unqualified Gesellschaft, with its emphasis on universality, rationality, and instrumental values. An ethnic attachment, it is argued, helps one to preserve some sense of community, to know who one is, to overcome the feeling of being a cipher in an anonymous world. This is the individual, or what I would call the characterological explanation.[26]

The individual explanation is plausible, particularly with reference to newcomers to a society. I find the judgments regarding the impact of anomie and alienation, however, to be too sweeping and unspecified. Almost everyone regards anomie and alienation as unhappy facts; their varieties, sources, and consequences are described in a vast literature. Much of this literature is connected with discussions of identity, for it seems reasonable to assume that alienated individuals, living in societies with high levels of anomie, find it difficult to establish or maintain an identity. At this point, the argument goes, ethnicity is affirmed or reaffirmed as a cure: One might declare: I do, in fact, know who I am—I am a Pole, a Jew, a Turk, an African American. I have meaningful attachments; my ethnic group has standards and shared values and agreed-upon norms that reduce the burden of anomie in the large society. Novak puts it particularly strongly: "The 'divisiveness' and free-floating 'rage' so prominent in America in the 1960s is one result of the shattering impact of 'forced nationalization' upon personality integration. People uncertain of their own identity are not wholly free. They are threatened not only by specific economic and social programs, but also at the very heart of their identity. The world is mediated to human persons through language and culture, that is, through ethnic belonging."[27]

It is quite easy to accept the idea that renewed ethnic attachments are a cure for overdoses of anomie and alienation. There are, however, logical and factual problems to be dealt with. If alienation and anomie are believed to be in part the *result* of loss of ethnic attachments, as is often affirmed, it isn't very helpful simply to say: Reverse the causal processes; strengthen ethnic attachments, and alienation and anomie will be reduced. This says nothing about the causes of the original situation. There is also a tendency to overlook the question of alienation from one's ethnic group and the conditions that produce it; and little is said, at least in this context, about value disagreements and structural strains—tendencies toward anomie—within ethnic groups. It is not enough, therefore, simply to affirm that neo-ethnicity or the persistence of ethnicity is to be accounted for by its value in protecting one from a pervasive anomie and alienation. We need to ask: Under what conditions is this true, and what are the side effects?

Third, it is now frequently affirmed that the persistence and renewal of ethnic attachments in spite of extensive assimilation are best accounted for by the usefulness of ethnicity in the struggle for power, status, and income.[28] Cultural symbols are highly flexible and can be used for new purposes while seeming to remain unchanged.[29] This is particularly true among those who have some latitude over which group to "join."

The pursuit of economic and political interests by means of ethnic associations is made more likely when members of the ethnic group are not fully accepted into the dominant society despite occupational, educational, or other attainments generally rewarded in that society.[30] An ethnic group movement then becomes the instrument for opposing the status inconsistency created by their rejection. It gains salience, as Bell notes, by combining interests with the affective tie to a cultural group, making the ethnic attachment an important factor in efforts to attain collective upward mobility.[31] This is most likely to occur when barriers to individual mobility are high but, paradoxically, where the culture and power contrasts are not overwhelming—that is, when a collective response has some chance of success.

Interest-based ethnic movements often occur when strong acculturative, integrative, and even amalgamative forces have raised hopes for rapid status improvement. The hopes and expectations, however, soar above the more slowly changing reality. Thus group awareness is often increased, not lowered, by the reduction of discrimination, by the movement that brought about that reduction, and by the increase in the sense of shared relative deprivation caused by the growing gap between hopes and actual conditions. Talcott Parsons, using a term from David Schneider, emphasizes the "desocialization" of ethnic groups—the reduction of their cultural content, even though they remain important as interest groups.[32] Hechter arrives at the same judgment in his study of the persistence of ethnic identities in England: "Ethnic solidarity in complex societies is best seen as a response to patterns of structural discrimination faced by certain groups in the society at large."[33] The shift of many decision-making processes from a relatively anonymous economic market to an open political arena has strongly supported the increase of communal and interest groups, "defensively to protect their places and privileges, or advantageously to gain place and privilege."[34]

In my judgment, this interest factor looms very large in the explanation of the importance of ethnicity in American society today. It may be easier in a society that tends to deny, or at least to obscure, class divisions to fight for one's economic and political interests under an ethnic label. It seems less self-serving, less "radical." It may help to aggregate greater numbers behind some policy. Hence ethnocultural rather than class myths arise.

Interest-based ethnic movements do not develop only because of inequality among groups. They also tend to appear when loyalty to the state is weak and alienation is pervasive.[35]

Although he is referring to Africa and to retribalization, Cohen's statement stands as a valuable general description of the use of ethnicity in political and economic contests. He writes that retribalization, emphasizing ethnic identity, is "a process by which a group from one ethnic category, whose members are involved in a struggle for power and privileges with the members of a group from another ethnic category, within the framework of a *formal* political system, manipulate some customs, values, myths, symbols and ceremonials from their cultural tradition in order to articulate an *informal* political organization which is used as a weapon in that struggle."[36]

Returning to the three major sources of ethnic continuity, I would add that the manipulation of cultural forces, as Cohen puts it, is possible only if some more fundamental sense of cultural connection remains, even if it is much subdued.[37]

Fallows also notes the interaction of traditional and interest sources of ethnicity, but describes a different sequence. What are seen as "primordial bonds" may be of quite recent origin. "Several million people in eastern Nigeria 'discovered,' with the help of ideologists, ethnographers and colonial administrators that they were all Ibo only during the colonial period." But the new unity became very strong; out of it came the Biafran secession movement. There were material interests; but, "The community on behalf of which these interest were asserted *had come to think of itself* as a primordial one."[38]

An interest-based ethnic movement gains salience because at least some of its members find within it a feeling of community in an anomic setting that seems threatening and chaotic. These are not, in other words, competing but complementary explanations, each influence getting strength from the others. In rapidly changing situations, however, the "interest group" interpretation of ethnic group strength is generally, in my judgment, the most powerful.

These explanations of the persistence of ethnicity are not mutually exclusive. In fact, without at least two of them ethnic identity would tend to fade quite rapidly under many conditions. The analytic distinction among the three is important, however, because their comparative weight varies from setting to setting. Scholars differ significantly in the emphasis they give to one or another of these explanations, even when describing the same situation, because the variables are not well defined and are even less well measured. Nevertheless, we need to keep them clearly in our minds as analytic variables and to search for their various combinations.

To make progress in the development of a theory that will explain most adequately the continuation and the renewal of ethnic identities in heterogeneous and mobile societies requires, in sum, attention to the interactions among three factors: the use of ethnicity in the pursuit of interests, the strength of subcultural continuity, and the effects of the experience of anomie and alienation. This is a formidable task. Until we have accomplished a large measure of it, the temptation will be strong to emphasize some part of an adequate theory, filling in the rest of the explanation with our predilections.

The Societal Consequences of Assimilation and Dissimilation

Political and moral arguments in favor of assimilation have been based on such beliefs as these: the drastic reduction of the salience of ethnic group membership supports greater equality, weakens the sources of discrimination, increases individual freedom, and helps to create a more flexible society. Political and moral arguments in favor of dissimilation—the preservation of subculture differences and even their revival—have been based on such beliefs as these: ethnic groups can be powerful centers of opposition to coercive states, can protect valuable cultural resources that are lost in a basically one-way assimilation process, and can reduce anomie and the sense of alienation by giving individuals an identity in a complex and confusing world.

Each of these statements is probably true under some sets of conditions. The task ahead for students of ethnicity is to seek to discover more precisely what those conditions are. Although we shall not attempt that here, perhaps some aspects of the task can be suggested by posing a few illustrative questions.

Does assimilation create uniformity and destroy a valued diversity; or does it, while reducing group diversity, create the opportunity for greater individual diversity (in Cooley's words, the diversity of choice rather than the diversity of isolation)? Coercive, one-way assimilation undoubtedly leads to the former; an uncoerced assimilative exchange leads to the latter.

What are the effects of organizing social conflict along ethnic rather than class lines? Or, to put the question differently: Under what conditions are societal interests optimally served by organizing competition and conflict along ethnic group lines? Assuming that social conflict is endemic, are the issues less negotiable, the parties to dispute more intractable if cultural forces and presumed ancestral attachments are involved as powerful symbols? The evidence of history and the headlines of the moment both seem to require an affirmative answer to this question. For a definitive answer with reference to specific situations, however, one would need to take account of many variables, including the degree of intra-ethnic solidarity that can be maintained (and at what costs); the attitudes—including the prejudices—of possibile allies; both the power and the values of opponents; demographic facts; and the nature of the interest being fought for.

That scarcely answers the policy question, however. Some observers will say that if "courageous" is substituted for "intractable" we will have a more accurate picture of some inter-ethnic conflicts. The alternative to an unyielding assertion of ethnicity, according to this point of view, is domination of the weak by the strong. The ethnically powerful, however, may also be unyielding when major issues are defined in the symbolic terms of ethnicity. Thus power is not more equally shared, unless weaker groups are able, by organization, to aggregate formerly dispersed resources. (I am not, by these statements, making a moral argument: Whether it is the dominant group or the weaker group who ought to succeed has to be defined by reference to specific values in specific contexts.)

Who, within an ethnic group profits, if anyone does, by the use of ethnicity to struggle for income, power, and prestige? If sheer survival is at stake, as it sometimes is, all may profit or all may lose;

but it is my judgment that in less severe circumstances, the higher strata of an ethnic group, using the powerful sense of moral identity shared with the lower strata, are more likely to gain. This is not to suggest that the higher strata consciously and cynically exploit their fellow group members, although that may at times be the case, but only that they are in a better position to capitalize on the possible gains from aggregating the forces of the ethnic group.[39]

This disparity seems greater among the members of presumed dominant ethnic groups, who also vary by class and influence, than among disprivileged groups. For decades, the "poor whites" of the American South and elsewhere were, and to some degree still are, paid off in the coin of "racial superiority." I doubt if a racial and quasi-cultural line of distinction was, or is, a good way for them to fight for their interests.

Can we have a strong emphasis on ethnicity and at the same time full civic equality, or do sharp subcultural lines reenforce group inequality in a society?[40] The conditions that made civic equality possible are rare and easily disturbed, as recent events related to the addition of millions of newcomers in the states of northwestern Europe illustrate. Of course the choice may not be between inequality and equality, but between a very difficult situation for a group, perhaps even the threat of extinction, and ethnically conscious efforts to improve the difficult situation.

How do societies vary in the impact that an emphasis on ethnicity has on the search for equal rights or other values? John Porter suggests one answer: "Ethnicity may be genuinely primordial and essential to individual survival in a former African colony made into an artificial political unit, but in a society on the threshold of post-industrialism it could, with its great emphasis on the particularistic, be considered atavistic if it were to become a salient organizing principle of social life."[41]

These questions only begin to suggest the range of issues with which a student of assimilation and dissimilation must deal.

VARIABLES THAT AFFECT THE EXTENT AND SPEED OF ASSIMILATION AND DISSIMILATION

Abundant evidence of both assimilation and dissimilation, of cultural boundary weakening and of boundary maintenance and renewal, is found on every continent in this period of history. Several historical, demographic, economic, and political factors influence those processes in ways that range from the highly assimilative to highly dissimilative. Comparative study of modern states requires attention to such variables, because ethnic differences began to present more critical issues when the relatively loose-jointed systems of control of most early empires gave way to the sterner controls and clearer boundaries of states. The great majority of states are multicultural, but not often harmoniously so. Although pluralism has been "invented," it collides to an important degree with the pressure toward statewide systems of economic, political, and educational activity. In an uncertain world, defense becomes a major preoccupation, so that the militarized state, if not the garrison state in Harold Lasswell's sense, has become almost the norm—not without some recent modifications—further defining the state as the fundamental form of social organization.

I am here neither lamenting nor applauding the emergence of the state as the dominant social structure, but only noting that comparative study of assimilation must recognize this development as a major aspect of the context within which multicultural relationships occur.[42] How are particular groups likely to be affected? Among the variables to be considered in trying to answer that question—each variable being judged in the context of other things being equal—are those noted in table 2.1.

Several comments are needed to clarify this assimilation-dissimilation table. Each of the influences listed is a variable, not an attribute, that can be seen as falling along a scale (as suggested by the nine-step format of table 2.1). They are not of equal importance. And doubtless the list is incomplete. Some of these factors refer to groups, some to individuals, and others to both. Since almost any group to whom this table might be applied is diverse, one needs to think in terms of central tendency with regard to the various influences.

Most importantly, the effect of each variable is influenced by the context. There are strong interaction effects.[43] For example, if a small group is residentially concentrated, speaks a foreign language, practices a different religion, and experiences a great deal of discrimination, its size—which under many circumstances supports assimilation—may be dissimilative in its influence or of little effect either way. Although the well-educated and highly skilled can more readily integrate, *other things being equal*, discrimination, religious or racial difference, or alienation from the

TABLE 2.1
Variables That Affect the Extent and Speed
of Assimilation of an Ethnic Group

Assimilative Influences	Of Mixed or Neutral Influence	Dissimilative Influences
1. Small group (relative to total population)	. . . . X	Large group
2. Residentially scattered (by region and community)	. . . . X	Residentially concentrated
3. Longtime residents (low proportion of newcomers)	. . . . X	Short-term residents (high proportion of newcomers)
4. Return to homeland difficult and infrequent	. . . . X	Return to homeland easy and frequent
5. Speak the majority language	. . . . X	Speak a different language
6. Share one of majority religions	. . . . X	Different religion
7. Same race as majority or dominant group	. . . . X	Different race
8. Entered voluntarily (in re the nature of the initial contact between the groups)	. . . . X	Entered by conquest or forced migration
9. Come from society culturally similar to receiving society (e.g., urban, high level of literacy)	. . . . X	Come from culturally different society
10. Repelled by political and economic developments in homeland	. . . . X	Attracted to those developments
11. Diverse in class and occupation	. . . . X	Homogeneous in class and occupation
12. High average level of education	. . . . X	Low average level of education
13. Experience little discrimination	. . . . X	Experience much discrimination

(Continued)

TABLE 2.1 (continued)
Variables That Affect the Extent and Speed
of Assimilation of an Ethnic Group

Assimilative Influences	Of Mixed or, Neutral Influence	Dissimilative Influences
14. Targets of little prejudice	.... X	Targets of much prejudice
15. Resident in an open-class society	.... X	Resident in society with little social mobility
16. Unequal sex ratio	.... X	Equal sex ratio
17. Live in an expanding economy	.... X	Live in a static or contracting economy
18. Strong outside threats to total society	.... X	Weak outside threats
19. Little shared memory of former statehood—historical and/or mythical	.... X	Vivid shared memory of former statehood
20. Full legal and political status as citizens	.... X	Limited or no status as citizens

political and economic order of the society can suppress this influence. The well-educated, in fact, can be among the leaders of an ethnic separatist movement.

Social observers sometimes disregard these interaction effects in favor of emphasis on one or another separate variable. Understanding is not thereby advanced. By analogy, one thinks of the prominent political figure (no chemist, he) who, perhaps thinking that an atom of carbon combined with two atoms of oxygen—CO_2—was not much different from an atom of carbon combined with one atom of oxygen—CO, pronounced that trees poison the air more than cars do.

Some of the variables are difficult to quantify; on others there is little evidence. Since some are of most importance in the early years of residence in a new society and others of continuing importance, change and time must be taken into account. Collectively some of their effects themselves become causes—new variables that affect the rate of assimilation. Such cybernetic processes are common in human experience, complicating our theories of cause and effect. The balance of influences at one time may lead, for example, to only a few intermarriages. Those having occurred, however, other changes may take place—shifts in residence, occupation, and attitude—that lead to higher rates of intermarriage.[44]

Without rich data and precise definitions (How to measure levels of discrimination? Against what standard do we mark a low average level of education?), applications of these assimilation variables are mainly exercises in imagination. Those exercises, however, can be valuable steps in the application of a theory of assimilation.

ASSIMILATION-DISSIMILATION AMONG MEXICAN AMERICANS

An examination, in table 2.2, of some of the variables in table 2.1 as they apply to Mexican Americans illustrate the use of this model.[45]

An argument could well be made for shifting each of my estimates, or at least for placing them on the nine-step scale in table 2.1, rather than a three-step scale. That would suggest more precision than the evidence allows. I can, however, add information with reference to several of the factors in table 2.2, pointing the way to a more confident assessment of the extent of assimilation among Mexican Americans and of probable future trends.

In these comments, let me emphasize that assimilation and dissimilation are used neutrally; they are not seen as intrinsically desirable or undesirable. I also assume that interaction between ethnic groups is two-way, although in particular situations the influence of one may be stronger than that of others. The various forms of assimilation, which we will discuss in chapters 3 and 4, may proceed at different speeds, and even in different directions. And with respect to the influence of each of these factors, one needs also to keep in mind the context of other things being equal.

The numbers that follow correspond with the factor numbers of table 2.2:

1. Of the 22 million Hispanic Americans counted in the 1990 census, over 62 percent were of Mexican background, with a number close to 14 million. With high birthrates—due in part to the lower average age—and high rates of immigration, the Mexican American population will expand quite rapidly. Mexican American birthrates are the highest among the Hispanic groups and are twice as high as those of non-Hispanics.[46]

With its long and quite open border with the United States, with a rapidly growing population of 85 million, a birthrate twice as

TABLE 2.2
Mexican Americans: Variables That Affect the Extent and
Speed of Their Assimilation

Mainly Assimilative	Of Mixed or Neutral Influence	Mainly Dissimilative
1.		A large and growing group
2.	Concentrated in the Southwest, but increasingly dispersed	
3.	Extensive immigration, but increasingly larger numbers of 2nd, 3rd, and later generations	
4.		For many, return to homeland easy and frequent
5.	Continuing high use of Spanish, but English main language by most 3rd generation	
6. Share a majority religion, including Protestantism (20%); segregation decreasing		
7.	Many of a minority race; but race line increasingly blurred and of decreasing importance	
8. Most entered voluntarily; but should not forget earlier forced entry by annexation		
9.	Mexico increasingly urban	

(Continued)

TABLE 2.2 (continued)

Mainly Assimilative	Of Mixed or Neutral Influence	Mainly Dissimilative
10. No strong pull toward political and economic developments of homeland		
11. Increasing diversity of class and occupation		
12.	Educational gap still large, but reduced by 3rd generation	
13.	Discrimination persists, but is declining	
14.	Continue to be targets of prejudice, although less commonly	
15. Resident in quite open-class society		
16.		Sex ratio near 100
17.	U.S. economy expanding only slowly	
18.		Weak outside threats to total society
19.	Little shared memory of former statehood	
20.	Full legal and political status for many, but some lack citizenship	

high, and a per capita income scarcely one-eighth as high, Mexico can be expected to continue to be the largest source of United States immigrants in the years ahead.

In the period 1981–1989, nearly one million immigrants from Mexico entered the United States—more than twice the number from the Philippines (477,000), the second largest source of immigrants. At least for the next few decades, this demographic situation is clearly dissimilative so far as Mexican Americans are concerned.

2. Seen regionally, the Mexican American population is highly concentrated in five states: California, Texas, Arizona, New Mexico, and Colorado, where over three quarters of them live. (This means, one should not forget, that nearly a quarter—3,500,000 people—live outside that region, many of them in New York, Florida, Washington, Illinois, and elsewhere.) Within the five states with the largest concentrations are several large urban communities, especially in Texas and California, where Mexican Americans are strongly represented. A third of the population of Los Angeles County is Hispanic—a majority of them Mexican American; over 20 percent in Dallas, 25 percent in Houston, and 55 percent in San Antonio are Hispanic—again, mainly Mexican American.

These numbers do not necessarily indicate, however, a strong dissimilative situation. Mexican Americans are suburbanizing quite rapidly, along with other groups, with a consequent increase in contact across ethnic lines. Their increase in political influence is based not only on separation—although that plays a part—but also on coalitions with others and on mutual accommodations. Some Mexican American leaders emphasize the protection of a distinctive Hispanic community and culture (with some non-Hispanics, oppositely, fearing the development of a "Quebec" in the United States). Others are stressing the need for more integration into the larger society—adjustments and adaptations to the requirements of life in a complex, multi-ethnic society without, however, loss of cultural identity—unless, as Vargas puts it, what we Hispanics want is to be laborers and pickers, to be on our hands and knees all our lives."[47]

Despite the high rate of immigration, the proportion of Mexican Americans who are native-born citizens is increasing. The use of English as the first language by the third generation follows the pattern of other immigrant groups.

On balance, such items as these suggest that factor two in table 2.2 is both assimilative and dissimilative; and, one must add, America is becoming somewhat more Hispanic in the process.

3. Some Mexican Americans are, of course "old American." Their ancestors entered what is now the American Southwest before there was either a Mexico as we know it today or a United States. The largest proportion, however, are more recent migrants or the descendants of more recent migrants. Half a century ago there were about 1.7 million persons of Mexican background in the United States, less than a quarter of them foreign-born.[48] Two and a half million immigrants have entered since 1940, over half of these since 1970. Without factoring in birthrates and death rates of immigrants

compared with native-born, and without estimates of the number of undocumented aliens, one cannot speak precisely. From the figures available, however, the census estimates that 70 percent of Mexican Americans are native-born Americans. Attention to the rate of immigration should not obscure the fact that most Mexican Americans are native-born.

4. The return to Mexico remains easy and, for the more recent Mexican Americans especially, quite common. Although it is difficult to gauge the effect of this factor on assimilation, I judge it to be strongly inhibitive, mainly with regard to culture. The history of seasonal and temporary migration has strengthened this pattern of return to the homeland. In a recent study of 1,000 Hispanic Americans in the Southwest, David Hayes-Bautista concluded that they were evolving into "a bilingual, bicultural culture. . . . We could come back in 100 years and the Latinos will not have assimilated in the classic sense." And Leo Estrada suggests that for a number of Hispanics, "the border has become artificial."[49]

In light of the numerous influences on assimilation, the hundred-year projection referred to above needs, perhaps, to be treated with some caution. It is based mainly on the factors that maintain Hispanic culture. Even if acculturation is minimal, however, integration in jobs, schools, residences, and marriage can create a pull in the other direction. Several of these elements are closely associated in intermarriages. Using data for Los Angeles County in 1963, Mittelbach and Moore found that 13.3 percent of first-generation Mexican-American men had married non-Hispanic wives. The rates were 23.4 percent for the second generation and 30.2 percent for the third. Intermarriage rates were particularly high, 40.4 percent, for persons in high-status jobs compared with those in middle- and low-status jobs (22.1 percent and 21.4 percent). When the two variables (generation and job status) are combined, one finds that 48.5 percent of third-generation Mexican American men with high-status jobs married non-Hispanics.[50]

Murguia notes the need for taking account not only of generation and occupation, but also of the time period and rural-urban and state differences. I will not give the details of his analysis of the effects of these variables, but will note that, using only studies since 1970, he found rates of intermarriage of 9 to 27 percent in Texas, 27 to 39 percent in New Mexico, and 51 to 55 percent in California.[51]

An increase in the intensity of ethnic attachment in recent years may have stabilized the rates of intermarriage. Pulling in the opposite direction, however, are the increases in levels of education, urbanization, and a growing proportion of third- or later-generation Mexican Americans (41 percent by 1980).

The ease of returning to the homeland and its frequency are clearly dissimilative. The importance of this factor, however, is dependent on several of the other factors we are discussing.[52]

5. The adoption of English as the first language, we have noted, is occurring among Mexican Americans at about the same rate as among other immigrant groups. It seems probable, however, that Spanish will continue to be a working language among them to a greater extent than was language preservation among earlier migrant groups that were smaller, less concentrated, more drawn by an ideology of a "new world," and less able to return to their homelands.

There are complications, however, that we need to consider in making this assessment. Naturalization requires the ability to speak and write English. Several states have declared that English is the official language—a move that may have little effect unless it reenforces the educational and job disadvantages that already increase the pressure to use English.[53]

7. Hispanics, as the U.S. Census puts it can be of any race. This is true, but even if they were racially homogeneous, that fact would be of little value in the study of the degree of assimilation. In a sense, African Americans can also be of any race: there are some almost all of whose ancestors are of European background or, less commonly, of Native American background; others are more nearly mulatto; still others are primarily of African ancestry. There is a wide range of ancestries among Native Americans, as well. And, to be entirely precise, one can say that European Americans (and, increasingly, Asian Americans) "can be of any race," in the sense that there are among them a not insignificant number who have some African, Native American, or Asian ancestors, even though they are identified, and identify themselves, simply as European in background.

Since every major census category is racial mixed, the selection of Hispanics only for the "any race" designation reflects social and political criteria, not racial ones. Referring to Mexican Americans, we can make a rough estimate that perhaps 10 percent are almost entirely European in background, 60 percent mestizo, and the remainder almost entirely Native American. (It should be added that they are also of diverse ethnic backgrounds, indicating variation within the putative racial groups.) Continuing admixtures and continuing changes of attitudes are blurring the race line further. Only residual perceptions, along with the belief that race per se is important in human interaction, make it a factor in Mexican American assimilation.

The perceptions of racial mixtures by Mexican Americans themselves are those of strength. Carlos Fuentes is speaking of American Hispanics generally, but fully including Mexican Americans, when he says: "Is anyone better prepared to deal with this central issue of dealing with the Other than we, the Spanish, the Spanish-Americans, the Hispanics of the United States? We are Indian, black, European, but above all mixed, mestizo. We are Iberian and Greek; Roman and Jewish; Arab, Gothic and Gypsy. Spain and the New World are centers where multiple cultures meet—centers of incorporation, not of exclusion. When we exclude, we betray ourselves. When we include, we find ourselves."[54]

8. Those who have become members of a society as a result of coercion are more likely, other things being equal, to retain their ethnic identity, to resist assimilation, and—under some circumstances—to struggle for independence. Thus we saw the Baltic states declaring their independence from the Soviet Union at the first opportunity. Mexican Americans, however, have selected American residence.

This statement requires two qualifications: Those living in parts of Old Mexico that were seized by the United States in 1848 (or, more diplomatically, annexed by the United States in the Treaty of Guadalupe Hidalgo), did not enter the new country freely (although some may have preferred United States rule). Many of their descendents, however, are now among the Hispanics who are most integrated into American society. The impact of the coercive history of their region is weaker than their contemporary situation. The other qualification concerns the meaning of coercion. Some Mexican Americans may believe that they did not in fact enter the United States freely. Their economic plight, resulting in part from American domination, made the shift necessary. On balance, however, I would judge that freely chosen immigration has an assimilative effect.

10. Although the return to their homeland is easy and frequent for Mexican Americans, permanent return is not common. The political and economic situation in Mexico is not a strong attractive force. As always, there are qualifications: Some who own land or have strong family connections may return. Others, whose hope for

a decent job in the United States has been frustrated or whose experience has been unsatisfying, perhaps tragic, find that Mexico looks better, by comparison, than when they left.

11. Increasing diversity of class and occupation has a variety of influences.[55] Those who have climbed the ladder a few steps may feel less well-off or experience relative deprivation. They are less likely to look down to see how far up they have come, than to look up to see how far they are below their hopes and how far behind they are compared with the highly visible standards of the majority. As a result, feelings of ethnic identity are often strengthened. Some who have climbed many steps up the ladder no longer see, hear, or identify with those on the lower rungs. They deplore affirmative action or other programs that are efforts to reduce the disadvantages of those in minority ethnic groups.[56]

12. The educational gap between Mexican Americans and the national average, although still quite large, has been slowly closing. The negative side is shown by the percentages dropping out of school before finishing high school. Between 1968 and 1988, the percentage for non-Hispanic whites fell from 15 to 13; for blacks, from 27 to 15; but for Hispanics, starting in 1972, the percentage held at about 36.[57] This figure refers to all Hispanics, among whom Mexican Americans are, on most educational measures, the least advantaged. To interpret it we must take into account the fact that "large dropout differences among whites, blacks, and Hispanics . . . diminish, vanish, or are even reversed when personal and family backgrounds are taken into account."[58]

It is helpful to compare the mean levels of educational attainment, comparing three Hispanic groups and separating the United States-born from the foreign-born or, in the case of Puerto Ricans, those born on the island.

TABLE 2.3
Mean Level of Educational Attainment, Persons over Sixteen
(in years of schooling)[59]

	Mexican Americans	Cuban Americans	Puerto Ricans
U.S.-born	10.0	12.2	12.0
Foreign-born	6.9	10.9	9.1

Gains should not be overlooked. In 1975, 86 percent of white 17 year olds had intermediate-level or higher scores in reading proficiency; by 1988 the percentage was 89. Among blacks, the gain was from 42 to 76 percent, and among Hispanics the gain was from 52 to 73 percent. Half of the disparity between Hispanics and whites (and more than two-thirds of the disparity between blacks and whites had been closed.[60]

These few data may indicate why I have placed the education factor in the middle category—of mixed influence—in table 2.2. Educational attainment is closely related to the economic situation of families. One need only note that nearly 40 percent of Mexican American children live in families below the poverty line, compared with 15 percent of non-Hispanic white children. Related to this is the fact that a large proportion of Mexican American children attend schools which, in the main, are more crowded and less well supported. And many have to deal with a language barrier. The educational influence on levels of education will change as these circumstances change.

13. I will cite only two recent studies to indicate that discrimination against Hispanics (and African Americans) persists. This is not documented simply by noting the existing large disparities in incomes and higher-level jobs, since that might indicate lesser training or experience. But suppose a large national sample of "audits"—using matched pairs of Anglos and Hispanic Americans sent out to seek employment in response to listed openings—found that "in 31 percent of the Hispanic-Anglo employment audits, the majority partner advanced farther through the hiring process," while in 11 percent the Hispanic partner advanced farther. Twenty-two percent of the Anglos received a job offer; eight percent of the Hispanics.[61]

Discrimination in housing is shown even more conclusively in an "audit" study of housing in twenty-five large metropolitan areas in the United States. The applicants again were matched as closely as possible except for ethnicity, one being non-Hispanic white, the other Hispanic. Some form of discrimination against the Hispanic applicant occurred in 50 percent of the cases involving rentals and in 56 percent in those involving purchases. (The percentages of discrimination for black applicants were 56 and 59.)[62] "Both blacks and Hispanics have a better than fifty-fifty chance of encountering some form of systematic unfavorable treatment each time they visit a landlord or real estate broker to inquire about housing."[63]

14. As measured by public opinion polls, levels of prejudice against Mexican Americans, compared with ethnic minorities generally, have clearly declined.[64] Nevertheless I have put this factor in the middle of the scale, because behavior—as shown by appeals to

anti-ethnic attitudes in political campaigns or by protests against housing integration, for example—may indicate that polls tap into the polite discourse on the topic of ethnic relationships while missing the more subtle forms of symbolism that disguise prejudice. What is sometimes called "symbolic racism" refers to beliefs that denigrated groups threaten basic cultural values, often connected with the fear that they also are a threat to job security or to the quality of education for one's children.[65] Such attitudes contain "a larger fear and a smaller contempt component" than earlier views of racial and ethnic inferiority.

15. Factor fifteen suggests that assimilation is promoted by an open-class society. Where status is not determined at birth, where opportunities for advancement are widely distributed, where the ideology applauds the chance to move from a log cabin to the White House, feelings of attachment to the larger society are likely to be strong.

I know of no societies that are fully open in this sense. Of necessity one speaks in terms of comparisons, of degrees of openness. Although I will not try to document this statement—and many will disagree—I believe that the United States is one of the most open societies in the world. That is not to say that it is very open, particularly for members of minority ethnic groups. Even they, however, are affected by the ideology and by the practices and laws that to some degree confirm it. Were America less open, dissimilative forces would be stronger.

17. This factor is labeled, "The U.S. economy is expanding only slowly." It is intended to refer not to the recession of the early 1990s, but to a longer time period, perhaps to twenty years, during which the structure of jobs (affecting the kind of labor force that is needed), the location of opportunities, the world competitiveness of American products, the skill level of the labor force, and other aspects of the economic scene have led to only modest gains. Indeed, for the bottom three-quarters of the population, there has been a steady erosion of resources. Nearly twice the proportion of Mexican American workers as of non-Hispanic workers are in low-skill jobs. Their per capita income is less than 75 percent of the non-Hispanic income, and 12 percent lower than that of other Hispanics. To an important degree these differences reflect the levels of competence in English.[66] Such disparities create a fertile ground for ethnic conflict and for dissimilation. For the present moment, I would put this factor in column three of table 2.2, rather than two; but perhaps for the twenty-year period the more neutral placement is correct.

18. Weak outside threats: When a society is being seriously threatened from the outside there is a strong tendency to close ranks, except among the most alienated and perhaps among the most universalistic in ideology. When the European colonial powers withdrew from Africa, the internal ethnic divisions within the new states became much more sharply drawn. When support for the central Soviet power declined, the newly independent or would-be independent states became much more aware of the ethnic differences within their own boundaries and of past conflicts.

Since World War II the United States has experienced, or imagined, a series of outside threats, most particularly the Soviet Union. These have included both the direct confrontations with the USSR and the regional conflicts in which the United States and the Soviet Union supported different sides, using local groups as surrogate participants in the hot battles of their cold war. With these threats drastically reduced, America's internal ethnic tensions become more salient.

Although the reduction of outside threats does not seem to be a critical factor in current ethnic relations in the United States with reference to Mexican Americans, the potential for conflict is there. Hence the factor is included among those that influence the balance of assimilation and dissimilation.

20. Ethnic groups that are blocked from citizenship or face high barriers on the road to attaining citizenship hold more tightly to their separate identities. Some European countries and Japan did not expect their "guest workers" to stay for dinner; they are now trying to decide what the legal status of the children of those "guests" should be. In the United States, those children are automatically citizens if they were born in the United States, as are the children of all legal residents. Citizenship is not automatic for immigrants, however. There is a five-year waiting period for resident aliens for citizenship. They must apply for citizenship, showing in the process their ability to read and write English.

Except for Cubans, Hispanic Americans born abroad—the largest share (4.3 million in 1990) from Mexico—are among the least likely to become citizens; their rate of naturalization is only about one-third the rate of non-Hispanic immigrants. Without citizenship they cannot vote; they have little influence over elected officials; and they are denied various social and economic benefits.

Potential Mexican American political influence is only partly realized because nearly a quarter are not citizens; of those who are citizens about half register to vote; of those who register to vote, about a quarter do not vote. (These last two constrictions of political influence are, of course, not limited to Mexican Americans, although it affects them especially strongly.)

What accounts for this limited political participation? Several influences play a part: lack of political experience in Mexico; dominance of economic considerations among migrants; little knowledge of English; lack of knowledge of the process of naturalization, registration, and voting; fear of governmental officials.

These apply most strongly to recent migrants. Integration into the American political process is becoming more common as the proportion who are native-born increases. There were 3,128 Hispanic governmental officials in the United States in 1984, 4,004 in 1990.[67] As of 1992 there are seventeen Hispanic American members of Congress, most of them of Mexican background. Such numbers reflect a rapid increase in political participation, but they also indicate continuing underrepresentation. The citizenship factor is thus of mixed influence; it is both assimilative and dissimilative. The trend depends on several of the other factors: the strength of the economy, the level of immigration, and the extent of discrimination.[68]

The reallocation of seventeen congressional seats after the 1990 census increased, for several reasons, the number of Hispanic, especially Mexican American, and of African American representatives: The Mexican American population has increased significantly since 1980. Much of the increase is in states that gained most of the seats—seven in California, four in Florida, and three in Texas. And the reallocation process, using Census computer tapes, can quickly map out districts, with information down to the block level, that can fit any desired ethnic configuration. By comparison, Judge Gerry's meandering districts were virtual rectangles.

A new district in North Carolina wanders through the Piedmont from south of Charlotte to north and east of Durham, a distance of over two hundred miles as the campaign bus rolls, according to my reckoning.[69]

This new district has been carved, or more precisely computed, ostensibly to satisfy requirements of the Voting Rights Act that districts should be designed so as to maintain equitable political rights for minorities, in this case African Americans.

Ironically, such redistricting may have increased minority representation, mostly as Democrats, while decreasing the number of Democrats in Congress.[70] It is well recognized by those designing new districts that a 65-percent minority ethnic district can be pieced together by shifting several areas that are 20- or 30-percent minority out of congressional districts where they played a balance-of-power role. A plan that makes one district safe for an ethnic group candidate can at the same time make two to four districts safe for candidates unresponsive to that group's concerns.[71]

It should be emphasized that Mexican Americans are a large population—larger than every country in Central America south of Mexico and over half of the countries of Europe—and a diverse population on almost every factor. Because reference has usually been to central tendency, that diversity may have been obscured.

From table 2.2 one can design a scale, or perhaps I should say a pseudo-scale, to indicate how tentative and preliminary it is. It would range from 20 (all factors in column one) to 60 (all factors in column three), if equal weight is assigned to each factor—clearly an over-simplification.

Using the tentative assignments I have made, Mexican Americans are very near the center of such a scale, slightly closer (with a score of 39) to the assimilative than to the dissimilative end. In the next few decades we are likely to see a slow reduction in that score; that is, an increase in assimilation as I have defined it. This will be brought about by an increase in the proportion of Mexican Americans who are native-born, by higher educational attainments and more political activity, and by the spreading effects of intermarriage, increased use of English and bi-lingualism, and doubtless other factors.

At the same time, a lively sense of distinctiveness will remain. I expect this to be pluralistic, not dissimilative in its effects. A pluralistic sense of ethnic identity can persist or develop along with an assimilationist trend. In fact, a stable pluralism requires a substantial amount of assimilation to soften the lines of separation, to reduce discrimination, and to produce toleration, respect, and accommodation among ethnic groups. However, in a society where ethnic identity is paramount for a large proportion (perhaps as a result of severe discrimination or disadvantage for some and a strong desire to protect advantages for others), mutual interests across ethnic lines, social harmony, and individual freedom to make cultural and identity choices are reduced.

Chapter 3

The Elements of Assimilation and Dissimilation: Acculturation and Integration

In common parlance, assimilation is spoken of as one-dimensional and one-directional, perhaps reflecting the most common empirical situations. To cover the full range of situations, however, I have defined assimilation in the previous chapter in a more complex way. In this chapter and the next we will examine several aspects of that complexity, seeing assimilation as a multi-dimensional and multi-directional process, the various aspects of which, although highly interactive, can vary independently at different rates and in different sequences.

The Four Elements of Assimilation

In his discussion of types of assimilation Gordon outlines seven varieties.[1] Three of these—absence of prejudice, absence of discrimination, and absence of value and power conflict—can better be seen, in my judgment, as causes and then as consequences of the extent of assimilation, rather than as types of assimilation. The other four, with some modification, can be seen as the separate but interdependent subprocesses of which assimilation is constituted. They are: integration, acculturation, identification, and amalgamation—the structural, cultural, psychological, and biological aspects of assimilation.

These four subprocesses are not usually discussed separately or distinguished in a sharply analytic way, perhaps mainly because they are empirically almost always mixed. Inter-ethnic contacts, however, vary enormously in the order in which and the extent to which these subprocesses are experienced. I shall discuss them separately, emphasizing that each is a variable, that they can change in either direction—strengthening or weakening the process of assimilation—and that they are interdependent.

In some societies all four subprocesses are reducing the sharpness of the boundaries between formerly more distinctive and separate ethnic groups. Social and physical mobility, the growth of literacy, economic changes, societal-wide governmental structures, movements seeking greater equality, and other forces tend to support assimilation.[2]

At the same time dissimilative forces, as we have noted, are also strong in many contexts; and they tend to be more visible. In the discussion of the four elements of assimilation, therefore, we will need to be alert to the strength of two contending yet interdependent influences.

Acculturation

Acculturation is the process of change toward greater cultural similarity brought about by contact between two or more groups.[3] An ethnic group is acculturated to the degree that the range of values and norms held by its members (the blueprints for action on cognitive, aesthetic, and ethical questions) fall into a pattern similar to that of the general population.

Whether cultural convergence is a result of a one-way or two-way process is not indicated in the definition of acculturation. The balance, or imbalance, requires empirical study in each instance.

To some people, to be sure, the term has strong one-way connotations. In this view, smaller groups or those lacking political or economic power lose their culture, their distinctiveness as a group, while being absorbed into the larger society built around the culture of the dominant group.

The word *transculturation* has been suggested to emphasize *mutual* change, both as fact and as value. In an effort to oppose cultural domination, however, it may obscure the wide range of actual situations, in many of which the exchange, although not one-way, documents the greater influence of some groups than of others.

It is probably true that smaller, less compact, more heterogeneous and resource-poor groups, and groups that have migrated or been brought into another society, are less likely to contribute to the cultural mix than are groups with the opposite characteristics.[4] All the groups involved in an interaction, however, are likely to be affected.[5] It is important to emphasize that, even a thoroughly dominant group is culturally influenced by its contact with other cultural groups in a society.[6]

I do not use *dominant* as a synonym for *superior.* It is an empirical estimate of the extent of influence, which I judge, with reference to the United States, to be mainly British, or perhaps northwestern Europe more generally, as molded by the new environment. The culture of the United States, however, is not simply an offshoot of British or British and northern European culture, or even British and European culture generally, to which other groups have been to a greater or lesser degree acculturated in a one-way process. The total culture contains values, objects, art, technologies, and other cultural items drawn from the spectrum of peoples who make up American society.

Whatever the balance of the exchange—a balance that varies enormously from setting to setting—the full assimilative power of acculturation has occurred when the members of formerly distinct groups can no longer be distinguished on the basis of culture. As we shall note later, acculturation can go a very long way down the road to assimilation without the group lines being erased. It is empirically mixed with varying amounts of amalgamation, identification, and integration. Although extensive acculturation can occur in advance of the other assimilative processes, as Gordon argues, that is not the only time sequence. In a society where one group possesses overwhelmingly stronger power, other groups may be brought into the economy (integrated to a degree), before anything more than minimal acculturation has taken place. Under the same circumstances, sexual exploitation may make amalgamation an early process. And in a few cases, members of a group unable to defend its way of life may identify with the dominant society before they are acculturated to its ways. Thus the timing of acculturation in the sequence of intergroup processes is a question to be kept open for examination in each situation.

Anthropologists and historians have long emphasized the extent to which the cultures of almost all complex societies—the United States in particular—are the result of the convergence of many cultural streams. That process continues. Even casual observation in regions outside as well as inside their major concentrations reveal the cultural impact, for example, of Jews, African Americans, Native Americans, Hispanic Americans, and Italian Americans on the total cultural repertoire of the country.

America is by no means unique, however. We may miss the often slow process of acculturation in some settings because our attention is drawn to current conflicts. In India today, for example, the turmoil involving Muslims and Hindus is too easily and erroneously seen as a sign of a cultural polarity. As Sen has observed: "The point is not simply that so many major contributions to Indian culture have come from Islamic writers, musicians, and painters, but also that their works are thoroughly integrated with those of Hindus. Indeed, even Hindu religious beliefs and practices have been substantially influenced by contact with Islamic ideas and values."[7]

The speed and ease with which different parts of a culture are transferred to members of another cultural group vary widely. Appropriate behavior in a new culture may be learned quite easily, even though it is difficult to experience the associated emotions.[8] Items of material culture may be quite readily shared; but basic values, although not independent of material culture, are adopted much more slowly. Value shifts are likely to occur only if individuals can find a secure and rewarding place in the group proffering the new values—an outcome that either his own or the receiving group may facilitate or block.

Clarity in the discussion of acculturation is reduced by failure to distinguish between individual and group referents. It is one thing to say that some individual members of group A have absorbed various values, beliefs, and behaviors characteristic of group B, perhaps thinking of themselves as somewhat deviant as a result. It is something else to say that group A has absorbed those values, beliefs, and behaviors as part of its own normative system, using them as new cultural items, which are taught to the young through the normal process of socialization. Throughout history, for example, some individual American Indians have been acculturated to the predominant national culture. That is quite different from the adoption of the horse, the rifle, and other cultural items by whole tribes and the absorption of these new items into their own established culture complex. If we call both of these processes acculturation, it is important to distinguish them conceptually, because their causes and effects are quite different.

Additive versus Substitutive Acculturation

Both theoretical and policy issues are involved in another question regarding acculturation. Does it mean the mutual or one-way *giving up* of some elements of one culture, with replacements from another; or can it mean, as well, the *addition* of values, norms, and styles, creating for those involved a more complex cultural repertoire from which to draw? In the latter case, acculturation does not mean a loss or impoverishment. It can be seen as enrichment, unless one sees a given cultural complex as integral and complete.

Under some conditions, additive acculturation is quite unlikely—for example, in contact between two highly antagonistic or culturally disparate groups. Put another way, cultural groups separated by many traits that could be exchanged only by substitution will have low and conflicting rates of cultural assimilation. For example, those Native American tribes whose economies were built around the bison could not simply add settled agriculture; nor could the white settlers accept the Indian economy.

Under other conditions, however, such as high social and physical mobility, with strongly interdependent groups coming into extensive contact, acculturation is likely to be additive as well as substitutive. One does not need to give up accustomed foods,[9] or music, or language, but adds those from other cultures. Wynton Marsalis, the black trumpeter, need not give up his fondness and skill at jazz to play classical European music, even on a Baroque instrument. Even religious acculturation can mean, in some traditions, not only conversion from one faith to another, but also the adding of new religious elements. (Religious purists, to be sure, are likely to claim that such addition is, *ipso facto*, substitution. What one person calls ecumenism—a friendly blending, another calls syncretism—the harmful absorption of elements from a contrasting religious tradition.)

Additive acculturation is close in meaning to the concept of 'biculturism' or, seen as a process, to 'dual socialization'. Under some conditions, often those that require adaptation to a dominant culture by members of a disadvantaged ethnic minority, many individuals will learn and act according to both the "mainline" culture and the ethnic subculture. This implies a dual identity, not just the addition of some cultural elements—language, for example—from another group. Particular situations strongly influence which identity will be activated.[10]

Additive acculturation does not imply a dual identity. It refers to the enlargement of one's cultural repertoire by acquiring skills, values, tastes from another ethnic group or society. The line separating biculturism and additive acculturation, however, is not sharp.[11]

Triandis has also developed a related concept, additive multiculturism, and strongly advocates it as "an essential step toward a pluralistic society." The great civilizations of the past have been characterized by heterogeneity. "Thus, rather than banish heterogeneity we must discover ways to harness it. We must discover ways to make optimal use of it."[12] Additive multiculturism does not refer primarily to individuals' acquisition of tastes, skills, values from another culture, blending them with their own. Rather, it emphasizes "interdependence, appreciation, and the skills to interact intimately with persons from other cultures" as essential in heterogeneous societies.[13]

Additive acculturation takes this one step further. Not only is there tolerance and mutual appreciation, but also the absorption by individuals or groups of other tastes, skills, and values into their own cultural repertoires. The two concepts, to be sure, are complementary, not contradictory.

An additive approach to acculturation, if it is accepted as part of the process, helps to account for the continuing strength of ethnic traditions in many places despite extensive integration and substitutive acculturation. Some American Indians, African Americans, Mexican Americans, and others have been strongly "Anglicized," while continuing to hold fast to many aspects of a distinctive subculture. The possibility of additive acculturation raises several questions that a theory of assimilation must examine: What conditions make it most, and least likely? What aspects of culture are most likely to be additive, which ones only substitutive? What are the consequences, for individuals and for groups, of these two forms of acculturation?[14]

If mutual acculturation often seems very slow even after decades of contact, one should not be surprised. The barriers to cultural learning—prejudice, resource competition, in-group pressure—and the opportunities for "cultural misunderstandings," to use the title of a book by Raymonde Carroll, are impressive.[15] Some African American students do poorly in school because of a shared belief that academic success is a sellout to the white world.[16] "Acting white" means, among other things, pursuing academic success, using standard English, listening to "white" music, being on time.

Dominant groups are often poorly informed about the extent to which they have absorbed cultural elements from others. For example, European Americans are only slowly beginning to realize how much they have been acculturated to the ways of Native Americans. Most of this borrowing has been additive. It has not simply changed the cultural options; it has increased them. The English language is filled with Indian words and names. The literary tradition of Longfellow (*The Song of Hiawatha*) and Cooper (*Leatherstocking Tales*) has not quite been obliterated by "Cowboy-and Indian" movies; and that tradition is now being reenforced by wider circulation of the work of Native American writers and award-winning movies that more accurately portray life from an Indian perspective (*Dances with Wolves*).[17]

Not only the United States but most of the world has been acculturated to foods first domesticated by Native Americans: "Irish" (sic) potatoes, corns, beans, squash, sweet potatoes. Contemporary pharmacology, not to mention various illegal activities, uses a number of drugs first used by Native Americans, among them: curare in anesthetics, cinchona bark (quinine), ephedra (ephedrine), and coca (novacaine, cocaine).

Indian arts and crafts (pottery, rugs, silver work) are part of the American mix. Indian music has been affected by Euro-American music, but it has also had its own impact. Elements long found in Indian music, such as unusual intervals, arbitrary scales, conflicting rhythms, and polychoral effects, have been studied and used by composers who visited reservations, especially in the early twentieth century. Anton Dvorak did not become less of a European musician for having studied and adapted melodies and rhythms characteristic of the music of both Native Americans and African Americans. During the year (1893–94) that he spent in the United States, he traveled widely, attending festivals, talking with native musicians, and visiting reservations. His symphony "From the New World" was composed and had its premier in New York during that year. In the symphony we hear, in some segments, the pentatonic scale characteristic of American Indian music and the syncopation frequently heard in African American music. These were not simply direct borrowing from native materials. They were Dvorak's rendering of the "color," the feelings aroused in him as new sounds and sights suffused his experience.[18]

Of course stronger currents of acculturation have flowed the other way. One needs spend only a little time on an Indian reservation or in an urban neighborhood whose residents are mainly Native American to realize how extensively they have been acculturated, in both the additive and the substitutive senses.

Some forms of ethnic contact reduce the likelihood of additive or even substitutive acculturation. Alongside them and to some degree replacing them is a process that one might call "subtractive acculturation." When the dominant group brings pressure toward one-sided change, and when opportunities to attain full participation and respect in the larger society seem to minority ethnic groups to be sharply limited, the acculturation process can be stopped, even reversed. There may be a reciprocal turning back toward origins, real or imputed. Whereas dominant group pluralism leads to mutual modifications of cultural contrasts, small step by small step, ethnocentrism leads to rigidity. "Tolerance may provide a congenial climate for cultural convergence, while the drastic application of assimilation may provoke a group into an isolationist stance."[19]

We must distinguish, then, among (1) cultural values that are mutually contradictory (only substitutive acculturation is possible); (2) cultural values that are neutral vis-a-vis each other; (3) and cultural values that can be additive.

Values are not frozen in one or another of these categories. Some may move from the first to the second; for example religious values may shift from interreligious conflict to tolerance. Values may shift from the first or second category to the third; for instance musical or dietary tastes may expand, with training and experience. However, the shift may be in the opposite direction, from the third or second category to the first: tolerance may be lost in conflict situations; sharp distinctions between cultural values may be emphasized. In the United States today there is evidence of all three of these acculturative processes. The third shift in particular requires comment.

An Inclusive American Culture versus Exclusive Cultures

One can detect in the United States today some shrinking of the common ground of culture. Subterranean streams of acculturation continue to flow, I believe, but they are hidden by what Richard Bernstein calls "a new tribalism,"—a heightened sense of ethnic and racial separateness, a "cult of otherness," a tower of Babel. Especially in the arts, "the common ground is shrinking fast."[20]

"In academic circles these days," from the perspective of some minority ethnic groups, "the very idea of a common culture is under assault, seen merely as a tool used by what is called the white, male, heterosexual establishment to exercise its 'hegemony'."[21] In contrast are those who seek to protect "the canon"—that core of ideas and books that many regard as the foundation of modern society, the essential mental equipment for the educated person.

On many campuses, faculty and students (with both groups represented on both sides of the controversy) are asking: Should there be a list of courses and books required of all students? Who should select the list? Should it contain titles from a wide variety of perspectives, male and female authors, representation from a variety of ethnic and racial groups, and studies of the history and cultures of many civilizations?

In autumn 1990, a symposium held in the Library of Congress celebrated the publication, by the *Encyclopaedia Britannica*, of the sixty *Great Books of the Western World*, updated to include a few twentieth century authors. Alterman reports that the list of authors included four women and no persons of color. The consultants who made the choices included one woman, one Canadian of African descent, and no African Americans.[22]

Continuing intellectual and moral controversies surround such "great book" lists. Since the issues involved in those controversies are vital in ways that go well beyond educational policies, every student of ethnicity must examine them carefully. To do so we can counterpose the *Great Books of the Western World* with *A Curriculum of Inclusion*, prepared for the New York State Department of Education.[23] Noting the large and growing diversity of students in New York schools, the task force chosen to prepare the curriculum (most of its members were from ethnic minorities) proposed a large increase in attention to the customs, backgrounds, and contributions of African, Hispanic, Asian, and Native Americans.

These proposals, when pressed with ideological fervor, bring the risk that the additions will be made at the expense of American and European history and literature. Rather than promoting the more diverse yet shared and common heritage needed by students from ethnic minorities as well as by students from the majority, the "curriculum of inclusion" can become a curriculum of separation. The challenge is to avoid a zero-sum contest by designing a program that enlarges everyone's vision. This requires that multicultural additions to a curriculum be part of expanded study of human rights, of the nature of societies and of democratic processes.[24]

In a letter published in *Newsday* (June 29, 1990), twenty-eight historians organized by Diane Ravitch and Arthur Schlesinger, Jr., strongly opposed the curricular recommendations. "The Western tradition is the source of ideas of individual freedom and political democracy to which most of the world now aspires. The West has committed its share of crimes against humanity, but the Western democratic philosophy also contains in its essence the means of exposing crimes and producing reforms. This philosophy has included and empowered people of all nations and races. Little can be more dangerous to the psyches of young blacks, Hispanics, Asians and Indians than for the State of New York to tell them that the Western democratic tradition is not for them."[25]

Before white Americans make a judgment on such letters, perhaps they need to walk a mile in the shoes, moccasins, sneakers, or sandals of persons from minority ethnic groups. Some of them see tasks, such as the creation of programs that instill group pride and self-respect, that come prior to the study of "Western democratic philosophy." Glorious traditions aside, they see existing school programs as agents of powerful ethnic groups, designed to create willing workers or docile citizens.[26]

Ethnic Americans have been awakened to the devaluation of their own cultures, the neglect of their own histories. They want full recognition—and indictment—of the European and the European American record of slavery, the destruction of native peoples, and colonization.[27]

In his thoughtful dissent from the majority view of the New York State Social Studies Syllabus Review Committee, Arthur Schlesinger, Jr., writes: "The underlying philosophy of the report [urging the use of public education to celebrate and promote separate ethnic heritages], as I read it, is that ethnicity is the defining experience for most Americans, that ethnic ties are permanent and indelible, that the division into ethnic groups establishes the basic structure of American society and that a main objective of public education should be the protection, strengthening, celebration and perpetuation of ethnic origins and identities. . . . The ethnic interpretation, moreover, reverses the historic theory of America—

which has been, not the preservation and sanctification of old cultures and identities, but the creation of a new national culture and a new national identity."[28]

"Nothing changes more regularly and reliably than the canon," Schlesinger observes. And the writers included are in many instances among the sharpest critics of American injustices and inadequacies. He skillfully argues that nothing is to be gained by substituting "under-dog history," designed as a weapon or as therapy, for the "top-dog history," used to justify the status of the ruling class. "Low self-esteem is too deep a malady to be cured by hearing nice things about one's own ethnic past. . . . The cult of ethnicity exaggerates differences, intensifies resentments and antagonisms, drives even deeper the awful wedges between races and nationalities."[29]

These statements seem to me to be true, yet seriously incomplete. Schlesinger said once or twice but, granted his fervor in criticizing ethnic history and separatism, might well have said in every chapter: European Americans invented the cult of ethnicity and many still belong to it. With Tocqueville we need continually to emphasize that civic participation, which springs from hope and a sense of justice, is the clue to commitment to democracy. An invented or distorted history, to be sure, is poor therapy. What is needed is rigorous history in a context of equal opportunity and non-discrimination.

Many among the successful and the comfortable no longer see the regnant institutions in the United States as credible, legitimate, trustworthy. How much more difficult it is to maintain a strong sense of identification, to resist the appeals of a "cult of ethnicity," among those who face continuing discrimination, growing inequality, greed in high places, and self-selected leaders. Little can be accomplished simply by stating that ethnic histories are inadequate, that separation is destructive. Change will come when the problems that make such histories and activities appealing are put high on the public agenda.

Even among those who see much to admire in Schlesinger's interpretation of "the historic theory of America" (a group that would include, I believe, many minority ethnic persons as well as those from the majority), there is still room for disagreement over timing, strategy, and policy regarding the most effective way to resume "the creation of a new national culture and a new national identity," to repeat his phrase. It is easy to understand the criticism of the sometimes harsh separatism and exaggerated or invented histories that are part of the anti-acculturative protests among some American ethnic groups. Members of dominant groups would be wiser, however, to examine the sources of those protests in the persistent discrimination against minority ethnic groups—and, having examined those sources, seek diligently to remove them.

At the same time, if separatism is to be reduced, the definition of American culture will need to be broadened to take fuller account of its diverse sources and of its continuing development under the vastly changed conditions of advanced or post-industrialization. Only then will the voices of Americans of European background on the topic of cultural unity and diversity be heard, by the most alienated and disillusioned Americans, as something more than self-serving ethnocentrism.

What I would emphasize more than Schlesinger does is the belief among protesting minorities that the present "common American culture" is already separatist because of its Eurocentric emphasis. That belief is continually being reenforced when a harshly divisive candidate gets over half of the white vote in a governor's race, when a successful presidential candidate accepts, without protest, a political ad that reenforces negative racial stereotypes, or when job and housing discrimination against Hispanics and African Americans are powerfully documented.[30] What group is most strongly represented, one might ask, among those who are thus acting out—even while arguing for a unified society—the belief that "ethnicity is the defining experience for most Americans"? Ethnic minorities are responding to the "real" American culture, while we want them to respond to the "ideal" American culture, to use a distinction made by Ralph Linton decades ago. That contrast can be prevented only when the gap between the two—the real and the ideal—has been significantly reduced.

The debate over a canon neglects an important point: How can America develop lifetime readers? Some books are better than others; and the sixty-book canon may contain many excellent ones. When should they be read? Often, I believe, they are most significant after reading something that speaks directly to one's immediate experience, something that draws one into the world of books.

The dispute arises not only around different choices of what should be read and when it should be read, but also for what purposes. For all sides "the purpose of reading is none of the varied and delicious satisfactions [that reading can bring]; it's medicinal. The chief end of reading is to produce a desirable kind of person and a desirable kind of society. A respectful, high-minded citizen of a unified society for the conservatives, an up-to-date and flexible sort for the liberals, a subgroup-identified, robustly confident one for the radicals. . . . Read the conservatives' list and produce a nation of sexists and racists—or a nation of philosopher kings. Read the liberals' list and produce a nation of spineless relativists—or a nation of open-minded world citizens. Read the radicals' list and produce a nation of psychobabblers and ancestor-worshippers—or a nation of stalwart proud-to-be-me pluralists. . . . Books cannot mold a common national purpose when, in fact, people are honestly divided about what kind of country they want—and are divided, moreover, for very good and practical reasons.[31]

Probably most societies have their equivalents of Sixty Great Books. Few of them, however, are very open to "additive acculturation." The kind of vigorous controversy that we see in the United States, however slow it may be in enlarging the canon can scarcely be imagined in some societies. Those best trained in the dominant cultural forms—and perhaps best served by them—cannot hear minority protests.

V.S. Naipaul describes a meeting he had about a decade ago with a young poet in Java. The poet had had a modern education, with some influence from various cultural traditions; but he was quite unable to explain to his elegant, cultivated mother why he wanted to be a poet. Was she not proud that he wanted to be a poet, Naipaul asked him? She would have no sense of what it meant, was the poet's reply. The poet's mentor at the local university noted that he might try to explain it as poetry in the classical tradition, but his mother would find that absurd and reject it as an impossibility," because for the poet's mother the epics of her country—and to her they would have been like sacred texts—already existed, had already been written. They had only to be learned or consulted. . . . That particular book, it might be said, was closed: it was part of the perfection of her culture. To be told by her son . . . that he was hoping to be a poet would be like a devout mother in another culture asking her writer-son what he intended to write next, and getting the reply, 'I am thinking of adding a book to the Bible.' "[32]

To use this as a parable for the American situation, we can note that not many new books are being added to that mainly secular, academic bible, the "canon." A lively debate continues, however; a few changes are being made; and that first step in the process of mutual acculturation—awareness of differing positions and possibilities—has been taken.

Perhaps we can learn from this that when a strong, integrative movement slows down or stalls after a quarter of a century, as it has in the United States, when it reaches a plateau or falls back to some degree an accompanying acculturation process also stalls. People are more likely to sort themselves into familiar groupings, seeking to reduce the stress that accompanies social change.

An oppressed group may be acculturated to the "ideal" culture of the dominant group while suffering under the "operative" or "real" culture. If the oppressed resent and protest against their treatment, they may be regarded as uncivilized and uncultured, while they regard themselves as having been too trusting, too well acculturated to the ideal culture patterns.

Such a situation is poignantly described by Rita Maran in her discussion of torture. As French military officers tortured Abdelaziz Boupacha in Algiers, 1960, he cried out, "Un peu d'humanité!" They replied: "Pas d'humanité pour les Arabes!" Yet Boupacha went on to declare: "Long live France and justice."[33]

Although he uses different terms, Triandis, in his research among black and white Americans, draws a similar distinction between normative beliefs and behavior. He studies the sources of deviation from widely accepted "subjective cultures"—that is, standards accepted by both black and white respondents—on the part of unemployed, black, male ghetto dwellers. They may be acculturated to the same norms and values, but those from ghettos "Look at the world around them in a manner very different from the way other samples of blacks look at the world."[34] They see the environment as chaotic; they do not trust other people, the dominant institutions, or other blacks who have "made it." Triandis calls this "ecosystem distrust." He sees it as the natural outcome of extreme poverty, discrimination, rejection, and the unpredictability of life. Such distrust can develop in one environment and persist in another, reducing the likelihood that the distrustful will take advantage of opportunities that do exist.

Thus the behavioral outcomes of acculturation to widely shared "ideal" cultural values depend in part on the situation. Deviation is not proof of contrasting values, of sharp ethnic differences. It documents the impact of experience and opportunity.

An additional refinement is needed in a full analysis of the process of acculturation. It is not simply the transfer of some elements of culture from group A to group B or group B to group A, reciprocally. It includes, at least as background forces, the shared modifications and additions to culture that result from a whole set of circumstances acting on both A and B. These circumstances include demographic, environmental, technical, and international influences that suggest or even demand cultural changes of all the affected groups.

For example, if a society is weakening the ozone layer or increasing the proportion of carbon dioxide in the atmosphere, with attendant risks of more exposure to ultra-violet radiation or higher average temperatures, new values and norms more sensitive to the environmental damage may emerge in all the affected groups. They are being *mutually acculturated to new standards.* Of course this might not happen, or it might not happen rapidly or extensively enough. The resulting damage can increase ethnic conflict if there are different assessments of the sources of the problem or of the distribution of costs and burdens.

INTEGRATION

I shall use the term *integration* to refer to the process of structural assimilation of persons from two of more formerly separate sub-societies into a set of shared interactions. These interactions occur in situations that vary from the relatively impersonal contacts within economic and political institutions to the personal contacts within neighborhoods, friendship circles, and marriages.[35] As with the other assimilative processes, integration can occur at various points in the sequence of change. The beginning of structural integration can come first, as when workers from isolated regions or from other societies are incorporated into the work force of an industrial society. This almost certainly leads to at least some acculturation, identification and amalgamation; but these do not necessarily precipitate still further integration. Dominant groups may be unwilling to let structural integration go beyond the unequal status contacts produced by the work situation, even though the other assimilative processes continue. And those ethnic communities able to furnish quite complete institutional services tend to retain their members.[36] Under other circumstances, integration proceeds *pari passu* with the other processes, with change in one supporting change in the others and stability in one tending to produce stability in the others.

As with acculturation and, as we shall observe later, amalgamation, it is important to distinguish between individual and group aspects of integration. Individual integration exists to the degree that persons from groups A and B belong to the same social groups, including private associations, and interact within those groups on the basis of equality. Group integration, which we shall call "pluralism," exists to the degree that A and B as groups are accorded the same rights and public privileges, the same access to political and economic advantages, and share the same responsibilities as citizens and members of the total society, while at the same time they are accepted as legitimate subdivisions of the society, with partially distinctive cultures and identities. Full integration into the economy, for example, implies similarity between groups in their occupational distribution and incomes. (There is, of course, another tradition in the use of the term *pluralism* that emphasized the cleavages and inequalities often found in multi-ethnic societies.)[37] Group integration as a process of assimilation stops short of extensive interaction within personal networks; it implies the continuing existence of separate groups. Yet it can exist despite extensive acculturation and amalgamation. In fact, strongly acculturated persons of mixed ancestry are often leaders in movements to define the boundaries and win the rights implied by pluralistic structural integration.

Switzerland is perhaps the clearest illustration of integration in this sense, with its three longstanding groups of German, French, and Italian origin. One can also add the small Romansch-speaking group. Pluralistic integration, however, does not include the nearly one million "guest workers" and their families, from diverse origins, who have been brought into the lower ranks of the occupational system. This is only a moderate degree of integration; few have moved up the economic ladder, and that climb is matched by only small steps toward political and educational integration for the newcomers. Their stay in Switzerland is limited to a clearly specified time. Barriers to citizenship are high.

Belgium's situation is quite similar. Dutch-speaking Flanders, French-speaking Wallonia, and bilingual Brussels, the capital, make up a federal republic of nearly equal parts, as regards rights and public privileges. The earlier dominance of Wallonia has been reduced by the transfer of such services as education to the separate federal units. As in Switzerland, although not quite so constrained, the guest workers and their families are only minimally integrated, in either the individual or the group sense.

Human Rights As an Indicator of Integration. There are many variables that might be used to assess the extent of integration of ethnic groups within a society—for example, demographic, economic, political, educational, and religious factors. With such an abundance, one looks for an index, a variable that is simpler or relatively more easily measured but which is highly correlated with others that are also important. The distribution of human rights can be used as such an index. If one can determine the similarity or difference among ethnic groups with respect to human rights, one can speak with some confidence about the degree of integration.

To be sure, the extent to which human rights are protected or denied is not itself readily measured. If we have the concept before us, however, it can serve as a valuable guide to the integration process.

"Human rights are entitlements granted to people as individuals or members of groups because they are human beings."[38] They can be classified as (1) *civil* (rights to life, security, physical movement, legal equality, due process, freedom from cruel and unusual punishment; (2) *political* (freedom of speech and assemblage, unrestricted right to vote and to seek political office; (3) *cultural* (rights to educational opportunity, religious freedom, family life, cultural diversity; or (4) *economic* (rights to the essential means of subsistence—adequate food, shelter, health care, minimum level of income).[39]

To put this in the language of the first two articles of the Universal Declaration of Human Rights, adopted by the United Nations in 1948,

> All human beings are born free and equal in dignity and rights. They are endowed with reason and conscience and should act towards one another in a spirit of brotherhood. . . . Everyone is entitled to all the rights and freedoms set forth in this Declaration, without distinctions of any kind, such as race, colour, sex, language, religious, political or other opinion, national or social origin, property, birth or other status.[40]

In its review of the "Second Decade to Combat Racism and Racial Discrimination," the United Nations Centre for Human Rights noted that "it is recognized by the overwhelming majority of States that individuals are entitled to equality of treatment before the law, and most states have passed legislation to that effect."[41] The various states used quite similar language: "All the nations in the State have equal rights" (Austria); "All are equal before the law" (Brazil), "All nationalities in the People's Republic of China are equal" (China); "The people of Iran belonging to whatever ethnic or tribal group shall enjoy equal rights" (Iran).

The only major difference among the several score of such declarations by the United Nations is that some refer to the rights of nations or ethnic groups, while others refer to individuals. Both kinds of rights may be inferred, but the emphasis on one or the other can have political and legal significance. The United States has not prepared such a statement for the United Nations, relying instead on its own constitution, a document susceptible to various interpretations on human rights. Persons opposed to affirmative action, for example, find no support for group rights. Those who support affirmative action believe that individual rights cannot be protected if some groups are particularly vulnerable to discrimination and severely limited opportunities.

The most critical question regarding state declarations of human rights is whether they express only pious affirmation or are protected in laws, courts, administrative actions and, above all, in the attitudes and behavior of the individual citizens and private groups.

During the last generation, even as the world was rapidly becoming more integrated economically and politically interdependent, many new or renewed states have been formed. They have developed primarily out of the former colonies or regions of collapsing empires. Because they start with little or no experience in democracy, autocratic control—now home-grown—has often been the rule. Some have chosen democracy, however, perhaps after a period of authoritarian control. Human rights have been acclaimed, but the governing records of new states and newly elected leaders have yet to be assessed.

The distinction between declarations of human rights (which are essential for countries seeking support and aid from developed states) and consistent actions to protect those rights will be of great importance to students of ethnicity as they follow the human rights records of the newly independent states of the former Soviet Union. While still part of that union, the Ukrainian constitution declared: "Citizens of other Union Republics enjoy equal rights with citizens of the Ukrainian SSR. . . . Citizens of the Ukrainian SSR of differing races and nationalities have equal rights."[42] We are likely to see the effects of what I would call romantic nationalism in a contest with the development of the civil, pluralistic state implied in the constitutional statement. Of course, Ukraine is not alone. The same contest is likely to be sharp in Georgia, Lithuania, Azerbaijan, and perhaps especially in Russia. Indeed, I can think of no state where this political and moral contest will not be high on the public agenda for years to come.

The Influence of Political Structure on Ethnic Integration. The degree and kinds of integration of ethnic groups within a society are strongly influenced by the extent of power concentration in a centralized government. The possibilities can be seen as falling along a scale, from most to least concentrated (table 3.1):

TABLE 3.1
Extent of Power in Centralized Governments

Centralized or Unitary States	*Federated States*	*Confederations of States*	*Commonwealths, Associations of States*
Most power resides in the central government	Power is shared between provinces and the central government	Separate states hold most power but yield some to their mutually created governmental structures	Mainly a symbolic union, with some joint action and reciprocities

States are not easily placed along this scale, since change is almost continuous and even written constitutions are unreliable guides to the actual governmental processes. The United States, for example, is a federation. Specific powers are assigned by the tenth Amendment to the Constitution to the central government; all other powers not so designated "are reserved to the states respectively or to the people." The practice moves back and forth, but the long-run trend has been to increase the power of the central government.

At this writing, what the successor to the Soviet Union will be called and what its membership and its boundaries will be is not certain; nor is it clear what powers the newly independent republics will grant to their joint union, if such a union evolves. It seems likely that they will be called something close to the Commonwealth of Independent States (perhaps even the Commonwealth of European and Asian States, as Andre Sakharov suggested a few years ago). The degree of centralization, however, may prove to be a matter of day-by-day improvisation and negotiation, with movement to the left, as in Table 3.1 (*left* has no political connotation in this context), a likely trend as shared problems and opportunities become more visible and independence less glamorous.

Ethnic nationalisms are powerful forces among the newly independent former Soviet states. If they continue to be dominant, only a minimum of an "association of states" seems possible.

The "European-Asian Commonwealth" will have before it the experience of the European Community, which even now debates the kinds of powers to be granted their joint endeavors. Will a common currency, a single military force, a market with no barriers to trade be added to the free movement of people, the extensive reduction of trade barriers, and the beginnings of a common parliament—decisions that have already been made? Will the European Community, in other words, continue to move from a commonwealth toward a confederation? Will it become a gigantic Switzerland? It will be able to do so only if ethnic differences, both within the states and between them, are fully recognized but at the same time are not the source of ethnic nationalisms.

Some kind of balance between pluralism and integration may be more readily attained in France, where most of the immigrants speak French, and in England, where most speak English, than in Germany, where Turkish immigrants, and even some of the ethnic German migrants, know little German.

Unfettered additional migration across the boundaries of the states within the European Community may further increase the importance of policies regarding ethnic groups. Other issues—agricultural and monetary policies, whether to admit new members to the Community, the degree to which governmental powers are centralized in the inter-state commissions and councils—all will influence and be influenced by the emerging ethnic order.[43]

Attitudes and policies toward ethnic groups vary with the degree of centralization of governmental power, but not in a direct way. One might start out by noting that unitary states either have few ethnic divisions or are sympathetic to their identification. Commonwealths, on the other hand, almost always combine states

of different ethnic mixes—lingually, religiously, and historically—
hence recognition of ethnic diversity is built into their very
structure.

These two broad generalizations need to be qualified. Japan, for
example, is near the "unitary state" end of the scale; it has been
pridefully homogeneous ethnically, despite Korean, Ainu, and other
residents and citizens; citizenship has been denied to most non-
Japanese. Now, however, Japan finds itself on a road that Western
Europe entered upon some forty years ago (and the Americas, five
hundred years ago). Population growth below replacement level
combined with an enormous need for workers to staff a rapidly
growing economy have led to a sharp increase in legal and illegal
migration. Not only Koreans, but Filipinos, Malaysians, Thais, Iranians—several hundred thousand, altogether—have entered Japan
for work. One is beginning to see headlines that have been commonplace in the United States and Europe for several decades: "12,000
illegal workers deported in early 1991."[44]

In this context, Japan begins to ask questions about its homogeneity. Racist "slips of the tongue" by prominent officials enter the
public debate. A few are beginning to declare that "the pervasive
Japanese belief in ethnic homogeneity is a dangerous myth which
must be dispelled if we are ever to be fully integrated into a family
of nations."[45]

The European Community, in contrast with Japan, is near
the commonwealth end of the scale. From the beginning the members have been fully aware of the cultural differences among the
states and the long-standing ethnic divisions within them. These
have proved not to be a major barrier to closer association among
the states. What remains as problematic, however, is the presence
of millions of persons from ethnic backgrounds not formerly
represented in large numbers. Who are these relative newcomers?
To what degree are they being integrated into western European
societies?

LEVELS OF ETHNIC INTEGRATION IN WESTERN EUROPE

Although most European countries are a blend of diverse people when seen over several centuries, many of them have come to
think of themselves as fairly homogeneous. That is not true of Switzerland, the Netherlands, Belgium, or Spain, where regional-

linguistic lines are quite clearly drawn. Even within each of them, however, the sense of a shared European culture, participation in a shared state polity, and similar economic patterns create links across the ethnic lines. That is, their levels of group integration are quite high. Perhaps the United Kingdom should be placed on that list. I believe, however, that it stands between those with clear ethnic divisions and the somewhat more integrated (in fact and in ideology) states, such as France, Germany, and Italy.[46]

Whatever the levels of integration, pluralistic or individual, half a century ago, the pattern has been strongly challenged by three waves of migration since World War II. Put in terms appropriate to our definition of integration, knowledge of a person's ethnicity now gives evidence of his or her probable occupational and political positions and rights as well as some knowledge of language use and religion.

The three waves of migrants, overlapping in time but typically in this order, are: immigrants from former colonies; the guest workers; and refugees from the dramatically changing countries of Eastern Europe and the Soviet Union.

Of the nearly 13 million foreign residents in the states of the European Community in the late 1980s (not counting those who have entered illegally), 38 percent were from the Community, 61 percent from outside, from Turkey, Yugoslavia, Algeria, and from several other countries in Asia, Africa, Europe, and Latin America. Seventy-eight percent of the total are found in three of the largest countries in the community: Germany (these data refer to West Germany alone), France, and the United Kingdom. Another 18 percent reside in Belgium, the Netherlands, Italy, and Spain. The numbers have increased significantly in the early 1990s, especially in Germany.

Taking off from small beginnings in about 1950, the surge of newcomers had become a sizable presence by 1970. The prevailing policy was to treat the migrants as guest workers, a rotating labor force that would keep its primary attachment to the countries of origin. Such a policy did little to motivate employers of the host country government to grant civil rights, to find adequate housing, or to plan for the education of the migrants' children. The arrangements and their consequences were similar to those in the Untied States, from World War II until 1964, in the bracero program. Mexican workers were brought in for a few months, under an agreement between the Mexican and United States governments, mainly to do

TABLE 3.2

Foreigners in European Community Countries, c. 1987–1990

	Population 1990 (000,000)	Foreign Residents (000)	Percent Foreign	From European Community	Percent from EC	From Outside EC (000)	Percent from Outside EC
Belgium	9.9	859	8.6	537	11	322	4
Denmark	5.1	137	2.7	27	1	109	1
France	56.4	3,680	6.5	1,578	32	2,102	27
Germany, West	63.2	4,489	7.1	1,276	26	3,213	41
Greece	10.1	217	0.2	108	2	109	1
Ireland	3.5	84	2.4	66	1	17	0
Italy	57.7	407	0.7	90	2	317	4
Luxembourg	0.4	96	24.0	89	2	7	0
Netherlands	14.9	592	4.0	157	3	435	6
Portugal	10.4	94	0.9	25	0	69	1
Spain	39.4	335	0.9	194	4	141	2
United Kingdom	57.4	1,785	3.1	766	16	1,019	13
Totals	*328.4*	*12,775*	*3.9*	*4,913*	*100*	*7,860*	*100*

* Adapted from *European Communities Encyclopedia and Directory, 1992* and from Martin, Hönekopp, and Ullmann, 1990.

the hard "stoop labor" of agriculture. For most of them, living conditions were primitive. There were few educational opportunities for their children.

In Western Europe a kind of "myth of return" developed, despite the growing reality that many were staying in the new country, that families were being formed, that the economies were becoming increasingly dependent on the migrants, and that undocumented workers were growing in number. All of the interested parties had at least some motivation to cling to the myth of return: It helped the migrants deal with hardship and discrimination; it helped the host countries rationalize their own practices and to push out of their minds the problems that were developing; it helped the sending countries, who were also benefiting financially, to continue to claim some control over and concern for their citizens. (In the mid-1970s they were receiving 6.6 billion dollars annually.)[47]

By the early 1970s, however, reality—or additional aspects of reality—came into view. Most of the host countries perceived themselves to be homogeneous culturally. In no case was this literally true, especially if viewed historically; but seen against the immediate situation it seemed true enough. The oil crisis of 1973 and the more general slowing of economic growth added to the feeling that immigration should be curtailed. It was, in fact, brought nearly to a halt, but efforts to encourage migrants to return to their countries of origin had little effect. Millions remain, with their children and now some grandchildren.

Indigenous Ethnic Groups in Western Europe. Most attention in recent years has been focused on the three waves of immigrants into Western Europe since World War II—the migrants from former colonies, guest workers, and the migrants from Eastern Europe and the former Soviet republics. These groups have significantly changed the ethnic makeup of most western European countries. Several of those countries also contain what I will call indigenous ethnic groups. These groups of long standing in their present locations, often with histories of independent statehood or substantial autonomy are now subordinate parts of a larger state.

Illustrative of indigenous ethnic groups are the Scots, Welsh, and Northern Irish in Britain, the Basques in Spain and France, the Catalonians in Spain, and the Alsatians in France (although, with their Franco-Germanic history, they fall less clearly in this group).

When world attention is focused on one of these groups, it is less likely to be seen in the context of a process of integration than in one of disintegration. Ethnic movements demanding devolution, autonomy, or full independence are often in the headlines. The Basques' situation can illustrate some of the factors involved.

The 1978 Spanish Constitution, with its reference to self-government and autonomy, was sufficiently vague that the Basques could find it too constrictive and the government could see their efforts as attempts to win independence.

Why push for autonomy? Although I use the Basques as my point of reference, the factors involved are quite similar in the political movements of other indigenous ethnic groups:

The increase, almost everywhere in the economic and political power of central governments, can lead, among the members of an indigenous ethnic group, to the belief—and often the reality—that the "periphery" suffers from economic and political disadvantages due to the central dominance.

Oppositely, some members of the ethnic group may work for independence or greater autonomy as a way of gaining economic advantages. Critics of Basque separatism say that "money is what lies behind the recent expressions of nationalistic fervor."[48]

Those who look back to what they believe were better times fear the current situation threatens their culture and their language. Yet the umbrella raised by the European Community may offer some protection from state domination to the smaller, indigenous ethnic groups.

Ethnic conflicts elsewhere in the world can give added impetus to an independence movement. Although they do not fit the model of indigenous ethnic groups very closely (having been independent states a few decades ago), the struggle in Latvia, Estonia, and Lithuania for independence from the Soviet Union "heightened nationalist yearnings of Basques," as a New York Times headline put it.[49]

Each of these factors plays a part in recent Basque separatism. They had been granted a large amount of autonomy under the Spanish monarchy. The Franco regime, however, was much more restrictive with respect to schools, publications, and Basque language use. The Basques had sided with the defeated republic.

The struggle at first focused on the loss of local rights, the concentration of power in the state, the increase in immigrants into Euskadi (the Basque country)—outsiders whom they did not want to assimilate—and threats to their language. Among some, it became a struggle for a pure "Basqueness," even including at first a belief in racial distinctiveness.[50]

For several years beginning in the late 1960s, the conflict became violent, and was violently repressed by the federal government. Several hundred were killed. In recent years, Basque nationalism has become less focused on primordial culture and language, more on what they see as political and economic domination. Some have used the language of internal colonialism: we are a dominated region. Thinking regionally, the Basques have not so sharply excluded immigrants.[51]

Factors Influencing Ethnic Integration in Western Europe

In their extensive survey of "minorities at risk," Gurr and Scarritt (1989) found that among 126 countries with populations over one million, ninety nine contained such minorities. Every continent was represented. In almost every setting, the granting or denial of human rights is undergoing dramatic shifts in this last decade of the twentieth century, as are other questions related to the extent of integration. This is one of the dimensions of the changes taking place in Western Europe as twelve (or more) countries seek to establish a European community, while at the same time dealing, within their own legal value systems, with the fact that fifteen million or more persons of foreign origin are resident there, many having established families since World war II. Some have entered illegally; but more have been invited, even sought after, to take the less skilled jobs.

Four factors account for most of this rapid demographic development: The native populations in these countries have been growing slowly or not at all. Their economies were expanding rapidly, especially between 1950 and the early 1970s, creating the need for both skilled and unskilled workers. Native residents moved quickly into higher skilled, higher paying jobs, leaving an occupational vacuum which if not filled would serious hamper economic growth. And workers from countries all over the world, their societies devastated by war or revolution, their populations expanding rapidly, and their economies poorly developed, eagerly moved to the countries of Western Europe.

Additional factors must be taken into account, however, to explain the nature of the migrant workers' experiences. To some degree, employers sought to reduce their labor costs by a policy of bringing in workers for fairly short periods, thus hampering their ability to organize or to gain seniority. Yet they also needed a stable and experienced work force. By the mid-1970s, when the guest worker programs were substantially ended, several million "migrants" had lived in Western Europe for a number of years. In Germany, for example, by 1978 more than a quarter of them had been in residence for ten years or more. Nearly 80 percent had lived in Germany for more than four years.[52]

Labor unions, one might suppose, sought to keep the migrants in the poorly paid jobs to protect their interests in a "split labor market."[53] That is only part of the truth, however, for at the same time they did not want to give employers a chance to undermine the solidarity of workers. In Germany the unions trained immigrant officials, provided language courses, and secured contracts specifying "equal treatment in the labor market and in the area of work-related rights."[54] These were steps toward economic integration of the migrant worker, although they were insufficient to take them out of their disadvantaged status.

Barriers to integration are built in part by what Hechter has called "a cultural division of labor."[55] A defensive ethnic response to economic hardship and discrimination can take the form of ethnic communities (not necessarily defined by separate residential areas) or by a cultural revivalist movement. This has been the case, for example, among some of the Turks in Germany. Turkey itself had striven for seventy years to build a secular society. "The growing reaffirmation of cultural traditions and primordial loyalties in Turkish immigrant enclaves represents a radical departure from official state policies, [but] . . . in Europe, the migrants can freely carry their commitment to Islam to its most conservative extremes."[56] Ironically, some of the resulting movements are proscribed in Turkey.

In the context of such factors as the three mentioned here (profit maximization on the part of employers, protection of favored jobs by workers, and cultural preservation by many of the migrants) Western Europe is pursuing a mixture of policies and is experiencing a mixture of "foreign worker" responses.[57] The possibilities can be shown as follows:

Assimilation	Democratic Pluralism	Ethnic Enclaves	Return to Homeland

One can find evidence of all four of these possibilities in Western Europe, whether as a result of policies or of individual actions.

Tens of thousands of guest workers did return home after a period—usually only a few years—of higher earnings than they could have received in their homelands, but also after experiencing discrimination and cultural conflict. The number who returned has been much smaller, however, than the host countries expected and sought to attain; and it has been tiny for the children of migrants.

On the other end of the scale, we find clear evidences of assimilation. It is mainly one-way, with the migrants becoming in some measure acculturated to the ways of the dominant society and integrated at a modest level, into the economy, the educational system, and the polity. This is not equally true, of course, of all the diverse migrant groups in a country. With regard to Britain, for example, Robinson concludes on the basis of evidence from the 1981 census, the biennial Labor Force Surveys, and other sources" that Britain's major black groups are seeing an important improvement in their aggregate social class profiles. That is, they are becoming more similar to the profile of the society as a whole. This improvement is dramatic in the case of Indians and West Indian women, but is less so for Pakistanis and West Indian men."[58]

The extent and nature of the education of migrants, and even more the education of their children, are critical in the process of integration. It is estimated that by the year 2000 one-third of the young people in West Europe will be the children of guest workers, immigrants, or illegal migrants.[59] Will it be assumed—is it now being assumed—that their training should mainly prepare them to continue in the jobs held by their parents? Or will the wider range of options available to the native population be opened to them?

Answers to these questions will depend partly on the values and policies of the receiving societies, partly on the cultures and practices of the migrant families. Children of Yugoslavian parents, for example, are more readily integrated into German schools than are children of Turkish parents. The cultural contrast is less, the Yugoslavian children are more likely to know some German, and their parents are more involved in their education than is typical for the Turks.[60]

Whatever the policies adopted and whatever the aims and responses of immigrant families, educational systems in Western Europe are likely to experience drastic shifts as they seek to train an increasingly diverse group of students. The opportunities and the problems they face, it seems fair to say, will become more like those in the United States.

The nature of assimilation, whether one-way or two-way, is strongly influenced by the nature of previous contact between a society and its immigrants. Although both France and Germany have large Muslim populations, the Maghrebi in France (the North African Arabs from Algeria, Morocco, and Tunisia) have a closer historical and cultural tie to their new homeland than do Muslim Turks in Germany. In France, most of the children of immigrants become citizens. France has had naturalized army veterans from North Africa for at least two generations.[61] The intermarriage rate of Maghrebi, mainly men to French women, is about 7 percent, which is twice the Turkish-German rate.[62]

The acculturation is not all one-way, especially in France, where more than 40,000 persons have converted to Islam, a rate many times higher than in Germany. Many, but not all, of these conversions are among the intermarried.[63]

The major ethnic tension in Western Europe during the next several decades, however, is not likely to be that between assimilation and return to the homeland, the end points on the scale of possibilities. The tension is much more likely to be between forces supporting democratic pluralism and those supporting ethnic enclaves wherein the "newcomers" live in a society but are not of that society.

Democratic pluralism implies not only tolerance but some mutual acculturation, not only acceptance of newcomers but a substantial amount of integration into the economic, political, and educational systems. Referring to the Muslims in France and Germany, Safran observes, "One might reasonably expect a gradual westernization of selected religious and social attitudes and practices: a greater role for women; a partial displacement of Islamic fatalism by the protestant work ethic required for upward mobility; the printing of the Koran and other Islamic books in French and German; and perhaps, ultimately, the use of the languages of the host country in Muslim prayer."[64]

This trend will stop short of full assimilation, however, for many reasons: The nation-state is no longer seen as possible, or even desirable to many western Europeans, despite its glorification by visible political minorities (and its much stronger ideological pull in other parts of the world). There are limits to the degree that Islam can adapt to a secularized and urbanized world. Multilateral agreements with the sending countries, containing standards for equitable treatment of their former nationals, give them an identity and to some degree a protected place. And, despite official, if somewhat limited opposition in the countries of Western Europe, discrimination and prejudice persist, enhancing the sense of ethnic identity among the targets of such actions and attitudes and increasing their support for stronger Muslim communities and institutions.

At the same time, pluralism is a cause and a result of some acculturation and integration among the dominant groups of the host society. We are likely to see, Safran suggests, more multicultural training for French and German students, the appointment of Islamic clergy as military chaplains, the adjustment of Sunday closing laws to provide alternative days of rest for devout Muslims, state support of programs on Muslim culture and religion on television and radio, and less ethnocentric approaches to history.[65]

If the conditions supportive of democratic pluralism prove to be weak, however, even while the western European states become more diverse ethnically, existing enclaves will become stronger, reciprocal prejudices will increase, and some of the conflict-laden predictions of the more reactionary individuals and groups in those two states will come true. "Reactionary" is not automatically a swear word. It means here simply desiring to go back to an earlier imagined or real situation. A moral judgment has to be added, presumably on the basis of expected consequences of given actions, to support a negative assessment of "reactionary." My own judgment is that the oppression of new or culturally and racially different groups cannot lead a country back to a culturally homogeneous and conflict-free existence. The ways in which we need to be more alike and the ways in which we permit one another to be more diverse need to be continually reviewed. The balance between democratic pluralism and persistent ethnic enclaves—both are likely to be found—depends on many factors:

The perceived sharpness of ethnic difference and ethnic conflict.

The strength of the belief that ethnic enclaves are a good way to defend interests—one's own or one's group interests.

The sense of relative deprivation—aspiration levels having been raised higher and more rapidly than attainments, or even the perceived possibilities of attainments in light of highly visible prejudice and discrimination.

Political, religious, and economic developments abroad, including those in one's ancestral homeland, such as a religio-nationalism.

The strength and health of the larger society or, in the case we are examining, of the European Community.

These and doubtless other factors are highly interdependent. Their collective impact will strongly influence the possibility of and the nature of the development of the European Community into a peaceful confederation or federation in the decades to come.

The Evolving German Ethnic Situation

Although the situation in each of the countries in the European Community is to some degree unique, they share some common interests and concerns in connection with the increased diversity of the populations. We shall use the German situation as a kind of case study.

During several visits to West Germany, in 1969–1976, I found that scholars and officials were beginning to ask themselves such questions as: How long will our "guests" remain? How can we encourage them to return to their homelands? Are we being fair to them? What obligations do we have to their children, born in Germany, often speaking German, who never had any other homeland? Do we need to reassess the meaning of citizenship? What are their human rights?

These questions remain, but new ones are being added: What are likely to be the political and economic effects of the migration of roughly one million eastern Germans to the West (1989–1991)? Should we continue to admit freely all those of German ancestral ethnicity (many from the USSR), some of whom speak little or no German (No, is being heard more often.) How does the task of integrating East and West Germany influence our options on non-German migrants and our policies toward non-German residents? Are we, almost in spite of ourselves, becoming an immigrant society? Have we always been one? In what ways does the imminent strengthening and possible enlargement of the European Community affect our options and the wisdom of our policies?

This last question is being asked throughout the Community. How far east will the European Community extend? To the western frontier of the old Soviet Union, or less far, or farther? Many of Germany's leaders want to push ahead with European unity, to deepen the community; but they want also to widen it, to reach out to the East and to the members of the European Free Trade Association

(Austria, Finland, Norway, Sweden, and Switzerland). "But many people at the highest levels of the EC consider deepening and widening to be not complementary but contradictory goals."[66] Those who hold this view see a serious dilemma: If a primary goal is to move from a European Community to a "united states of Europe," east central Europe will come in late or never. If east central Europe joins the Community soon, a united states of Europe will develop late or never.[67]

Of the basic human rights, the migrants into Germany who are not of German ethnic background are least likely to be given civil rights, particularly citizenship and legal equality. Barbara John, a member of the German Government's Special Commission on Integration has observed that of the five million foreigners, more than three million are Turkish guest workers and their descendants, some of them third-generation residents of Germany—but still foreign. "Each year, about 20,000 of them are nationalized, but 79,000 babies are born. So you have a permanent and growing group of excluded people. . . . We're an ostensibly non-immigration country with proportionally the world's largest immigration. . . . We also have the world's most outdated definition of nationality."[68]

Several million persons of German background who had been settled in Czechoslovakia, Poland, the Soviet Union, or other Eastern European states by Nazi Germany, or had moved east earlier, were forced out after 1945. They were readily repatriated in Germany and automatically granted citizenship. Some did not speak German. Other migrants, however—the Turks, Yugoslavians, Poles, Czechoslovakians—have a precarious legal status. To become citizens they must prove eight years of residence; there are many reasons for deportation; they face discrimination in housing and wages.[69]

Perhaps we should add, to give a complete picture, that what Dahrendorf calls "secondary political rights" are more widely available.[70] Freedom to join organizations, the creation of ethnic groups, and participation in worker councils, union elections, and church activities have seldom been proscribed. In fact, when pressure to stop further worker migration mounted, so did pressure to liberalize the treatment of those who remained. It had become clear that many migrant workers and their families were likely to remain, so the question of how to integrate them into society became critical. Employment restrictions have been eased. The International Labor Organization has emphasized the need for "migrant equality" in connection with employment, social security, labor union membership, and cultural rights. Germany, for example, "tied the worker importation ban to a more liberal integration policy—workers would still be encouraged to leave, but those who remained could obtain permanent resident status, unite their families in Germany and remain eligible for most social services.[71]

The unification of Germany has great implications, not only for Germany, but also for the European Community, for Eastern Europe, and—in the area of our interest—for ethnic relationships. This is to say, it has great implications for all of us, for the whole planet.

The first steps in the merger were taken rapidly; but the nature and speed of full integration are not easy to predict. "For 40 years, Germans on both sides of the Wall believed the people across the divide were essentially the same. Both spoke the same language, read the same literature and thought the same way, according to the common wisdom; easterners and westerners might have had different political systems, but they really did understand each other."[72]

Now, many Germans seem to believe that judgment was wrong. The enormous difference in standard of living was well recognized. The different experiences, the different laws and customs over a period of several decades could not be overlooked. The great emotional divide between Ossies and Wessies, however, the "wall in the head," came as a shock. Stereotypes developed, or were reinforced. In the former East Germany, despite remarkable changes, a sense of hopelessness is widespread. Crime, suicides, and violence against foreigners have increased.[73] Since the integration that has occurred has mostly been in one direction, with people in East Germany having to change in the direction of West German economics, politics, and customs, they face a kind of identity crisis. In its more severe forms it is a *wenderkrankheit*—a turnabout illness.[74]

Although it would probably be to stretch the term too far, there is something to be said for thinking of East Germans as a situationally created minority ethnic group. Two-thirds of its population had lived only in a divided Germany until 1990. Their historical memories, their self definitions, and to some degree their culture divided them from the West. To eliminate this division as rapidly as possible, the Bonn government put $85 billion into the reconstruction of former East Germany in 1991, and perhaps as much in 1992.[75] This expenditure has begun to integrate the infrastructure of Germany as well as integrating individuals in or from the eastern region. This has not, however, been without social costs. "Already one hears of second generation Turkish-German citizens losing their jobs to east Germans. It is here, on the streets, that the political culture of the Federal Republic will be put to the test."[76] Attacks on "foreigners," some of them longtime residents, continue, based on the belief that they are taking jobs, apartments, and government assistance that belong to "natives." Eighty such attacks occurred during the first nine months of 1991, compared with twenty during all of 1990.[77] One must add that there are strenuous protests against such attacks on the part of German citizens and the government.

An additional ethnic problem increases the tensions caused by the need, simultaneously, to unify the country and integrate the five million non-Germans who have migrated to Germany or been born there since 1950. Increasing population pressure from Eastern Europe has brought a haunting specter of "a post-communist *Völkerwanderung*. This is a formidable challenge for the whole European Community, but for Germany above all."[78] In principle, the German government is committed to allow visa-free access to Hungarians, Czechs, and Slovaks. The policy is less clear about Poles and about Jews and others from the former Soviet Republics. "The press conjures up an alarming picture of millions of people inside the Soviet Union flooding towards the eastern frontier: those huddled masses yearning to share in the prosperity that many West Germans are reluctant to share even with other Germans."[79]

In America we are familiar with the ethnic-political situation where a large and economically deprived population in a country resides just across a river from an economic giant. Desperate workers are pushed across the river by their lack of opportunities at home and pulled across by the need for workers on the other side. Seeing migration as their only hope, they journey toward the river, sleeping in cheap hotels, guided by people who promise them secretive entry into the promised land. Over the Rio Grande from Mexico to the United States? Yes. But I was thinking here of the journey over the Oder and Neisse Rivers from Poland to Germany. Or one can change the picture a bit to describe the trek, perhaps from Bulgaria, Rumania, or Hungary, over the mountains from Czechoslovakia to Germany.[80]

As in the United States there are sharp differences of opinion in Western European countries about what the best response is, to the wave of migrants. There is debate first over whether they are political refugees, fleeing from civil war or harsh political turmoil, or economic refugees seeking a better life. International understandings give countries less latitude in dealing with political refugees. However that debate may be resolved, perhaps the more persistent questions in Germany will be: What does our economy require? Will the needs be met by the integration of East and West Germany? We have only begun to integrate the five million persons of Turkish, Yugoslavian, and other backgrounds. How shall we now deal with still a third wave, from Eastern Europe?

A few in Germany are contending that the country needs more immigrants, as workers and consumers. More are saying, We need to find a democratic way to stem the flood, to build a legal wall. More precisely, one ought to say To prevent the flood, if one is thinking of non-German migrants from Eastern Europe. In the first nine months of 1991, 140,000 refugees asked for asylum in Germany—about half of the refugees from Eastern Europe—but eight percent of applicants, those seen as fleeing political violence or oppression, were granted asylum.[81]

One aspect of such a prevention program is the treaty of friendship and non-aggression signed by Germany and Poland in 1991. This treaty required that the two countries come to terms with some harsh historical realities and memories: the brutal six-year occupation of Poland by the Nazis, the transfer of a large tract of land from Germany to Poland after World War II, the expulsion of many Germans from Poland and the denial of human rights, until the dramatic change in the Polish government in 1989, to those who remained. If the 1991 treaty and the political realities in the two countries during the coming years prevent such past conflicts from having continuing political significance, the potential flood of migrants may be reduced and the integration of persons of Polish background now in Germany will be strengthened.

Important as Polish-German relations are, other problems now seem larger. For several years Germany has been carrying on a strong, even harsh, debate with itself over its general immigration and refugee policies. By the mid-1980s, after admitting hundreds of thousands of refugees, at first mainly from Eastern Europe but increasingly from third-world countries, Germany began to take in the welcome mat put out after World War II. In mid-1992, Chancellor Helmut Kohl and his coalition proposed a constitutional amendment designed to curb the flow of refugees. The first response of the political opposition was to call it a shameful concession to rioters who were attacking immigrants, burning cars and houses; but in December they joined the government in support of the amendment. Labor contract workers will be limited to 100,000 per year. Ethnic Germans will be admitted in numbers not to exceed by more than 10 percent the 220,000 who were allowed to remain in 1991 and 1992. Even that number was, by 1993, beginning to seem large, seen in context with the five million who may be eligible in eastern Europe and the former Soviet Union. At the same time, several neonazi groups have been banned; special police units have greatly increased the efforts to stop anti-foreign rioting; several rallies—some with 250,000 or more participants—have protested the violence; and President Richard von Weizaecher has called for a broader definition of "citizen" to include six million Turkish and other foreign residents.[82] Germany is deeply divided on that issue.

There is more agreement in Germany, and to some degree elsewhere, for major economic support to the countries of Eastern Europe, to encourage their people not to wander. This seems politically more acceptable and has already begun. Whether the aid, not from Germany alone but also from other members of the European Community, from Japan, and from the United States, will be anywhere nearly adequate to rebuild the broken economies one cannot guess. The probable outcome, if extensive help is not given, however—continuing enormous efforts to escape to the West—may make a massive aid program seem to be the wisest course in the prosperous countries. In its absence we are likely to see not only a wave of migrants, but also authoritarian states. The area could become not a democratic, liberal Central Europe, but "an area of weak, undemocratic states, riven by social and national conflicts. This would obviously be bad for all of Europe, but it would be especially bad for Germany, since the resulting chaos would be just fifty kilometers east of the capital, Berlin. The pressure of immigrants would grow not decline, and they would be knocking first at Germany's doors."[83] In response to such possibilities, the German parliament has voted to deny entrance, beginning July 1, 1993, to all refugees seeking assylum from any country believed by Germany to be free of persecution.

The outcome of these various actions will be strongly influenced by developments outside as well as inside of Germany: Russian and eastern European economic and political trends, the effects of the European Community on the flow of population, the nature of the settlement of the war among the South Slavs. With regard to the last of these, one should note Germany's recognition of the independence of Solvenia and Croatia—earlier than most western European countries and the United States thought wise, although they followed suit in mid-January 1992. Germany hoped that such recognition would stem the flow of political refugees and improve their economic situations. The opposite happened. An ethnic war started that has sent more than half a million refugees into Western Europe, half of them into Germany.

The Break-Up of Yugoslavia. Seeing no chance to hold Yugoslavia together, Serbia launched a military campaign to seize areas in other regions where numerous Serbs lived. Several conditions converged to bring about a violent struggle. Over seventy years as a single state had created numerous economic links and a mix of populations in all of the republics, but these forces were insufficient to overcome the conflict-producing forces: historical grievances and myths; differences in religion and language; economic hardship; ethnic zealotry and conflict reverberating around the world; ambitious and authoritarian leaders; and a fluid, not to say chaotic, political situation. Add to these the fact that Serbia is the largest of the former Yugoslavian republics (one-third of the population) and has command over most of the arsenal.

In the early stages of the civil war thousands of Serbs were killed or driven from their homes even as they seized control over the Krajina—a third of the Croatian territory. The Croats also encountered severe losses. The Krajina is still occupied by the Serbs, although a United Nations peace-keeping force has reduced the fighting there. In 1992 the main battle shifted to Bosnia and Herzegovina, a mainly Muslim area but inhabited also by Serbs and Croats in several scattered enclaves. By mid-1993, over twenty thousand Bosnians had been killed as the Serbs, and in lesser measures the Croats, sought to "cleanse" those parts of the Republic they sought to control by killing, driving out, or imprisoning those who lacked the proper ethnic credentials. Several cease-fires have lasted ony a few hours or days. They have been insufficient to stop the pillaging, the killing, and the barbarous treatment of prisoners.

Slobodan Milosevic won a contested election to the presidency of what remained of Yugoslavia in December 1992. This consolidated his already strong support among the Serbs of Bosnia and of Kosovo (who dominate the far more numerous Albanians there), and the Krajina area of Croatia. Some of them seem even more unyielding than he in their demands for a "greater Serbia."

The continuing efforts of the United Nations to find a political solution (perhaps keeping sovereignty in the Bosnian republic but creating autonomous Serb and Croat areas) will require each group to yield something now being demanded at the point of a gun. Whatever the political-military outcome of the struggle, it is unlikely that any of the republics of the former Yugoslavia will be ethnically homogeneous. Living with diversity is an essential skill in the modern world.[84]

In the effort to understand the tragedies that have swept across Yugoslavia, ought our attention be focused on Balkan history? Are the belligerents driven by the memory of ancient conflicts, never solved, only held in check by empires and Tito's political skill? It is a valuable insight to say, with George Santayana, that those who cannot remember the past are condemned to repeat it. I believe it is also true, however, that those who remember the past only to sanctify it, to give it a mythical grandeur and terror, thus to make it an instrument of current ambitions, are destined once again to suffer its tragedies. They are likely to forget that others also remember—and sanctify—their own versions of the past. This collective ignorance and these colliding memories are destined to distort the present and to obscure its pitfalls, opportunities, and new necessities.[85]

"Nationalists everywhere turn the historical record into a narrative of self-justification. In the Balkans, the contestants have a particular interest in turning their history into fate, so that the past can then serve to explain away their hatreds." However, Ignatieff goes on to say, "there is no reason why outside observers should do the same.[86]

The violence destroying Yugoslavia is ". . . not driven by irreducible historical or ethnic differences," although those differences furnish the rhetorical weapons. The conflict ". . . was ignited by nationalist ideologues who turned the narcissism of minor differences [Freud's phrase for the making of enemies out of those who are close] into the monstrous fable that the people of the other side were genocidal killers, while they themselves were blameless victims."[87]

We must indeed study the past, but to that we must add the study of the sociology and psychology of violence and of the current appeal of harsh and separatist nationalism. "What is truly difficult to understand about the Balkan tragedy is how such nationalist lies ever managed to take root in the soil of a shared village existence. . . . These people were neighbors, friends, spouses, not inhabitants of different ethnic planets."[88]

They are also people seeking a sense of stability in a chaotic situation. Power and ideological vacuums have been left by declining political structures and fading beliefs in a setting of uncertain boundaries, discrimination, and unequal access to force. All over the world identities have shifted down to smaller groups that seem to bring a sense of familiarity and control in a strange new world. But hopes and visions collide. Under these conditions ethnicity is less a source of strength than a source of conflict.

The tragic civil war in the former land of the South Slavs can serve as a parable for many other lands. If I seem to write harshly of Serbia here, it is not because I believe it to have tendencies toward violence over and beyond those of other societies within and outside of Yugoslavia. Sadly, few societies have escaped such destructive attacks as we have been witnessing in Yugoslavia. This is not to excuse it or to dismiss it. I seek only to wring from it some greater understanding of the part played by ethnic divisions in human violence. One could substitute another time and another place or think of different antagonists to develop the parable.

The swift recognition of the independence of Croatia and Slovenia by Europe and the United States, leaving Serbia the overwhelmingly dominant force in the reduced Yugoslavia, was made without first demanding that full civil rights be guaranteed for all. This critical message was lacking for Serbia as well. Such demands were incorporated into the treaties ending World War I, only to be frequently violated, except by Czechoslovakia. In the early 1990s, however, Europe and American were in a much stronger position to enforce such civil rights provisions, primarily by withholding recognition and financial help, than they were in 1918. Instead, like much of the world, they seem to be enamored of the vision of nation-states, of which almost none exists. Most states, indeed, are becoming more multi-national.

Ethnic groups, like religious groups, will be free to enjoy and enrich their various heritages only when they are freed from the power demands and the dogmas of statehood. This applies to the dominant groups within states as well as to the smaller ones. The overwhelming need is for civil societies, granting full rights to all. Only such societies will be—as some are now—in a strong position to create a world order within which cultural differences are not the source and the symbol of irreconcilable conflicts.

How can there be a "greater Serbia" when for hundreds of thousands, particularly of young men, to be a Serb has meant, for many months, to act in a thoroughly uncivil way toward nearly helpless populations of different ethnic backgrounds? Are they to be confident of their greatness because of the new areas they dominate at the cost of an enormous number of casualties inflicted on others and suffered themselves? Will that be the source of pride, rather than the music they could have composed, the games played, the children nurtured, the inter-ethnic marriages saved, the churches made beautiful, the environment protected, the richness of other cultures studied and perhaps enjoyed? Such qualities and achievements will be nourished when Serbia rediscovers its ability to live peacefully and justly within a multi-cultural world.

Ethnic Intolerance in Western Europe

Laws to protect the human rights of all residents and social programs to guarantee at least minimum economic, medical, and educational support are universal throughout the states of the European Community. At the same time, protests against the "newcomers"—a larger and larger share of whom were born in Western Europe—have been widespread, these range from political movements to mob violence. It is difficult to estimate the degree to which these protests are supported—as it is difficult in the United States—but electoral results and public debates can give us clues, which are at the same time clues to the extent of integration.

In 1988, the National Front party of Jean-Marie LePen won 14.3 percent of the votes for Parliament, with strong support particularly in southern France. His support in public opinion polls in 1991 was 15 to 17 percent. The National Front won 14 percent in regional elections in March 1992. This can best be understood against the historical background. For millennia, France has been built from a variety of nationalities and races. Although the degree to which this diversity has been melded into a unified whole has been exaggerated in the French tradition,[89] there has been a significant amount of integration and acculturation. In the last few decades France has continued the historic pattern by absorbing many waves of migrants—Poles, White Russians, Hungarians, Cambodians, West Indians—and they have been widely accepted as French if they adopted the French language and, to a substantial degree, its culture. By 1931 there were three million naturalized foreigners and immigrants in France.[90]

Since the French-Algerian War, however, with its great wave of refugees accompanied by the large demand for workers created by major economic expansion, newcomers have come in at a rate greater than the fact-and-ideology of French assimilation could handle. Looking ahead, the French (and of course the other states, as well) realize that with the consolidation of the European Community, Greeks, Italians, Germans, and all the others in the community will be free to settle and work wherever they wish within the twelve states, with other states perhaps to be added.

Who, then, is French in France? Such a question is threatening to some. Over 30 percent share LePen's exclusionary views.[91] A vocal minority excludes North African Arabs, the largest group of recent migrants, and the growing number of sub-Saharan Africans as not truly French. Anti-semitism, which lies close to the surface in France, is given a boost. And the minority ethnic groups themselves, the victims of stereotypes and discrimination, react with anger and with reemphasis on their own culture.

In 1990, four days after a renovated and refurbished section of Lyon was dedicated, primarily as a residence for North Africans, rioting broke out between young Arabs and police. The new housing development was an expression of the fact that most French leaders, outside the far-right National Front, were seeking "to redouble their effort to prevent the nation's four million immigrants, half of them Arab, from living on the social and economic margins. . . . there is widespread agreement that more should be done to integrate alienated youths into society."[92] The youths, however, seemed to be saying This is a mere gesture. What we need are jobs, respect for our culture, full human rights.

This is the context within which LePen defied a police ban to hold a demonstration in Paris to blame French immigration policy for "injustice, insecurity, corruption and decadence. . . . The French want to be at home in France."[93] More startling have been the remarks of Jacques Chirac, a former prime minister and the head of the Guallist Rally for the Republic. His conservative party and coalition easily defeated the socialist coalition in the 1993 election for Parliament. At the same time LePen's vote fell significantly, partly because Chirac had been bringing some of the same message. He spoke of a French worker who lived next door to an immigrant family "with a father, three or four wives, some 20 children, that receives 50,000 francs [$8,300] per month in social welfare, obviously without working. Add to that the noise and smell and the French worker goes crazy."[94]

The quotation from Chirac reminded me of a similar statement by the mayor of a suburb of Paris a year earlier: "Let's take the immigrant from Mali. He has four wives. This wife has eight children, this one has seven children, this one has two. His fourth wife has none. That makes 17 children whose schooling our town has to pay for. . . . We all believe in integrating French society, but how can you do that when you have 20 foreign children in a class and just 2 French children?"[95]

Not many words would need to be changed to turn these comments on France into an American story. Direct and indirect reference to the costs of welfare, the deterioration of education, and increasing violence—attributed primarily to the members of new or poorly integrated ethnic groups—have been persistent themes in American politics and public discourse up to the present.

Jörg Haider's Austrian Freedom Party did not get enough votes in the first round of the presidential elections, April 1992, to be eligible for the final round. It did, nevertheless, win 16.3 percent of the vote with its anti-foreigner, antisemitic, and thinly disguised Nazi attitudes.

I am not primarily interested here in identifying the heroes and the villains of this drama. There are significant problems to be addressed. The focus of attention should be on the development of strategies to reduce those problems. Those strategies must be concerned, however—and here I do have my own heroes and villains— with the welfare of all, not just some favored individuals and groups. They must avoid one-sided interpretations of the roots of the problems. In particular, political movements that seek to persuade the most disadvantaged individuals among the most advantaged groups that their difficulties are caused by the even more disadvantaged ethnic minorities are not strategies for solutions. They are themselves a serious problem.

I will not undertake further descriptions of ethnic antagonisms in the countries of Western Europe. Each case is unique, yet strangely similar to the others. Let a few comments and headlines hint at the similarities: "Call for government counter-attack on 'racist elements.' " (The London Times, Dec. 1, 1976); "Britain needs an affirmative action plan, and soon: its police and black underclass are on a collision course." (Washington Post National Weekly, April 20, 1987); "Tories in uproar over black candidate." (The New York Times, Dec. 6, 1990); "Black Britons describe a motherland that has long held them inferior." (The New York Times, March 31, 1991).

Racial discrimination and conflict became public issues and their study an important task earlier in Britain than on the continent, reflecting in part the earlier flow of immigrants from Jamaica and the newly independent India and Pakistan.[96] In the 1960s and 1970s, Enoch Powell took a political stance in Britain similar to that of LePen in France in the 1980s and 1990s. Strongly opposed by most British voters and leaders, Powell gained his limited support by the persistence of the violent conflict in Northern Ireland and by the frustrations felt by those Britons least protected, culturally and economically, from the changes occurring in a society that was rapidly becoming more diverse.

There had been immigrant workers in Germany well before the surge of the 1950s and 1960s. In 1908, 800,000 were in residence, 1.5 percent of the population.[97] And there was a vastly coercive use of foreign labor during the Nazi era, although there was little thought that more than a few of them would become German residents. Thus the post-World War II situation is quite different in the magnitude of the immigrant group and in the nature of public policy. By the mid-1970s, the aims have been to reduce conflict and discrimination and to increase human rights. German nationalism, however, and economic pressure on the less skilled German workers, in a context of new waves of immigration, are reflected in anti-foreigner protests. They may be more strongly represented in the headlines than in public support, but they have created a great deal of anxiety.

Few of the societies of Western Europe are free of ethnic intolerance, as indicated by such items as these: "Swedes discover their dark side: racism." (*The New York Times*, Feb. 24, 1980, E-5); "Swiss doing soul searching as nation marks 700 years." (*The New York Times*, Aug. 11, 1990, p. 1). Most of the million foreign residents in Switzerland are from Italy, Spain, and Portugal, "but nonwhite citizens from Sri Lanka and Turkey are clearly less welcome." In the most recent general election, the most anti-foreigner party in Switzerland (Partie des Automobilistes—Party of Cab Drivers) increased its representation in Parliament from two to eight seats. Support for Jörg Haider, leader of the Freedom Party in Austria, increased in October, 1990, from 9.7 percent to 16.0 percent, placing 30 deputies in Parliament.[98]

On balance, such miscellaneous items do not add up to a signal that ethnic intolerance is a major political fact in Western Europe. One is tempted to say that despite persistent tension between several of the governments and their indigenous national ethnic groups, despite an even larger and more diverse wave of migrants from former colonies, despite another wave of guest workers who are now permanent residents, despite another wave from Eastern Europe—neither its current nor its probable future size yet measured—potential xenophobic movements have been constrained.

Major tests, however, are yet to come. Discrimination is widespread and often harsh. Changes required by the expanding role of the European Community can exacerbate the intrastate conflicts between nationalistic and pluralistic political movements. As in the United States, there is not much room for error. To succumb to the temptation to yield a bit to the cultural chauvinists, to win a political contest, is to seriously endanger the development of civil societies that are at the same time democratic and multi-ethnic.

The Changing Record of Human Rights and Ethnic Integration in Sub-Saharan Africa

The new states of Sub-Saharan Africa are probably even more diverse ethnically than the former Republics of the Soviet Union. Between 1957 and 1990, all won their independence; but they came to statehood with little experience in democracy. Ethnic hostilities that had been partially contained by the overarching authority of the colonial powers were released almost everywhere, often justified by the claim that multi-party politics would only intensify ethnic conflicts.

Within the Organization for African Unity (OAU), agreement among the ruling groups to accept the boundaries set by the colonial powers has kept inter-state conflicts at a minimum. Many ethnic groups within each of the states, however, have felt—often with good reason—that they were even more cruelly repressed by their ethnic overlords than by the imperial powers. Or, independence left ambiguous the balance of power among several groups, with colliding visions of how the new states should be organized. The results: several bitter and prolonged civil wars and authoritarianism turned into oppression, with human rights only for the dominant ethnic groups.[99]

A few comments on several of these conflicts will indicate the range of ethnic situations in sub-Saharan Africa.

On March 21, 1990, Namibia became an independent state, after a prolonged civil war and several years of intensive effort through the United Nations to obtain a settlement. Thus the colonial period has ended; and only South Africa remains under white rule. Sub-Saharan Africa has entered a new period. What can we expect now? The cold war, which intensified several of the civil wars, is over; the colonial powers are gone; nations in many other parts of the world are protesting monolithic party systems and authoritarian rule; the painful knowledge grows that despotism and civil war have wasted vast resources; and the ethnic hostility has left not victory for anyone but only a trail of bitterness. "African despots don't have Pretoria to kick around anymore," may be to put the matter too strongly, but as long as apartheid was at full strength "there was always one injustice that black African rulers could point to that was more repugnant than those they inflicted on their own people."[100]

Can we then expect expanded human rights and pluralistic societies? A flood of changes or proposed changes make it seem possible that in the 1990s Africa will move from a transitional, even chaotic period of post-colonialism to a period of incipient democracy. "In Africa, 16 of the 50 states are democratic or are moving in that direction, with others under intense pressure to follow suit."[101] What events document or challenge that assessment? Here is a sample. Although these events will soon be outdated they can indicate both the small beginnings of political change and the enormity of the obstacles in the way of protecting and extending those gains.

In October 1991, Frederick Chiluba, a trade union leader, defeated Kenneth Kaunda—Zambia's president since 1964—in a multi-party election. "The Stream of democracy, dammed up for 27 years, is finally free to run its course as a mighty African river," Chiluba declared at his inauguration.[102] Kaunda turned over his power peacefully and remains on good terms with Chiluba.

One of the deadliest civil wars, in Angola, resulted in a half a million deaths, an economy in ruins, and deepened ethnic hostilities. It was made more severe by the participation of the Soviet Union (via Cuba) and the United States (via South Africa). The end of the cold war made negotiations possible. In October 1991, Jonas Savimbi, a leader of the largest tribe (35 percent of the population), and supported since 1975 by the United States, returned to Launda to campaign for his rebel movement in the first multi-party election. Having been defeated in that election, however, Savimbi has been unwilling to accept its result, his intransigence perhaps encouraged by America's failure until May, 1993 to recognize the new government and by the fact that his armed rebellion dominates a substantial area of the country. Acting President Jose Eduardo dos Santos barely failed to win a majority (49.6%), but in the face of the fierce rebellion has been unable or unwilling to call the required runoff election. As of mid-1993 more than 20,000 have been killed in the renewal of the civil war.

It has proved unwise, after a prolonged and bitter ethnic war, that, in a first election, a winner-take-all rather than a negotiated multi-party government should be put in place.

Mobuto Sese Seko, the longtime leader of Zaire, agreed in 1990 to multi-party elections. He was not quick to call them; but under mounting pressure he agreed to a coalition government. In October 1990, Etienne Tshisekedi, leader of the opposition was made prime minister; defense, however, remains in the hands of Mobuto supporters. Although outright civil war has been avoided, mob violence is common, with ethnic divisions often involved (Ngbandi *vs.* Katangan *vs.* Kasai). Mobuto has sought to prevent the prime minister from governing; and by his control over a Special Presidential Division has substantially succeeded. In the view of a western diplomat in Kinshasa (quoted by the *Washington Post National Weekly* (March 1–7, 1993): "There's been no effective government here since the first of December."

Mobuto is now widely believed to have looted the national treasury of Zaire of many millions of dollars, not to mention the United States Treasury, from which he has received a great deal of support.[103] Despite an economy in ruins and a divided army, however, he remains in power, as of May 1993. The small steps toward a more open society have not led to greater ethnic equality.

For several years after attaining independence, Kenya was relatively open politically and economically successful. The current president, Daniel arap Moi, who once was one of the dissidents who made it so, now declares his monolithic party essential and the opposition illegal.[104] In recent months, however, he has faced growing opposition. A crowd of 100,000—the first legal anti-government demonstration in two decades—cheered as a former vice president, Jaramogi Oginga Odinga, condemned the "incompetent, corrupt and unimaginative government" of President Moi and called for his ouster.[105] Recent ethnic conflicts, however, with hundreds of deaths, have again documented the fragility of the movement against authoritarian rule in states where ethnic identities are primary. In an election that required only a plurality, Moi won the first multi-party election in January 1993; but the legislature has a large number of representatives from minority parties.

After one of the worst post-colonial civil wars, Nigeria has worked, with modest success, to soften ethnic animosities and

Islamic-Christian tensions by an ethnic-tribal system of governance alongside the state system.[106] A declining economy, however, and the continuing dominance of the military under President Ibrahim Babangida make problematic the effects of the June, 1993 election, which he has annulled.

Ghana, with seventy-five ethnic groups, has bound them relatively peacefully together in a way similar to Nigeria by using the power of village chiefs and tribal laws in local matters combined with the apparatus of a modern state.

The newly established government of Namibia, in pursuit of national reconciliation, includes some white members. Whites make up about 7 percent of the 1,500,000 population. The constitution is democratic.

In two countries where ethnic violence has been particularly severe, at least small changes have been made. In Burundi the Tutsi tribe is outnumbered by the Hutu by eight to one. Nevertheless the Tutsi rule, in the past by brutal repression. Since 1987, when Pierre Buyoga came to power in a bloodless coup, there have been efforts to end the hostility; opportunities for Hutu have been increased.[107] Violence beyond the control of the central government, however, has continued.

In Rwanda it is the Hutu who rule; the Tutsi, who are outnumbered about six to one, have been rebels since 1959. In 1990, President Juvénal Habyarimana, who had ruled in a one-party state since 1973, called for a multi-party system.[108]

Zimbabwe, like Namibia, has a small but economically influential white population. About half of the 250,000 whites left after full independence in 1980, leaving them with a little over 1 percent of the ten million total. The settlement that ended the seven-year war called for racial reconciliation and promised that there would be no reprisals. This has not been entirely the case, either with respect to the whites or the smaller African ethnic groups,[109] but economic integration has been the rule. White farmers, who owned 42 percent of the land in 1980 still hold one-third. Some of those who left the country, most for South Africa, have returned. Prime Minister Robert Mugabe's ZANU-PF party (mainly from the Shona tribe) is represented in the Parliament in numbers matching its proportion in the population (c. 75 percent), with Joshua Nkomo's PF-ZAPU (mainly Ndebele) in opposition. Although the government is dominated by Mugabe, public opposition is beginning to surface. That opposition may be a major factor in planned redistribution of up to half of the land of white farmers. The large farms will be divided among landless black peasants or those who have small plots in a move to reduce the large disparity between black and white farmers.

In assessing the significance for ethnic integration of such items as these, it is necessary to remember that only one-third of the sub-Saharan states have taken steps that promise some pluralism in economic and political activities. The steps taken so far are small. The military, usually led by ethnically oriented authoritarians, is broadening the base of power only grudgingly or not at all. The pre-colonial political structures and traditions, having been virtually destroyed by a century of European domination, individual aggrandizement, and ethnic group control, quickly became the rule. Rapid population growth and economic corruption have stalled economic development.

And yet, in the face of all that, glimmers of hope, hints of protest against cruel and authoritarian rulers, and small signs of change have begun to appear.

What seems lacking is a vision of a civil society, where all are citizens first, whatever their ethnicity. If that idea is difficult to maintain even in prosperous societies with a democratic tradition— as it surely is—how much more difficult it is in the new states.

It is necessary also to emphasize that the Republic of South Africa, the economic giant in the area, is a critical influence on development in most of these states, particularly those on or near her borders and economically interdependent with her. As we noted in chapter 2, South Africa is in the midst of dramatic changes, although it remains to be seen whether they are as powerful as they are dramatic.

These changes did not leap onto the scene in 1990. Individual churchmen, writers, and intellectuals had been opposing apartheid for many years. "In the late 1970s, a number of white South African lawyers thought it was an opportune time to establish legal organizations dedicated to fighting for human rights.[110] From a single office staffed by four people, the Legal Resources Centre has grown to six offices, which "handle thousands of cases each year and provide training and assistance to a network of advice centers throughout the country."[111] At about the same time, the Centre for Applied Legal Studies began its work in defense of the rights of labor and other human rights.

More recently the South African Government, under the leadership of President F. W. de Klerk—and under persistent protests from the disfranchised black population and international economic pressure—has repealed the pass laws, which have been basic in the apartheid system; public facilities have been desegregated; and parliamentary groups for Asians and Coloured South Africans, even if they have no governing power, have widened the debate on public issues. South Africa's version of *glasnost* extends to the African National Congress. Today it "holds open news conferences, issues statements daily that criticize Government behavior and promulgates documents laying out its views on issues like nationalization and land reform."[112]

Almost daily we read such stories as these: "Pretoria is ready to negotiate plan for interim rule"; "Apartheid is beginning to dissolve at local level"; "Mandela urges his Congress to recruit more nonblacks." Negotiations to create a government representative of the whole population are underway, a date—April 27, 1994—if not a clear plan having been agreed upon for the first universal election.

Of course that is only part of the story. We also read: "Afrikaners are staking out an enclave for whites only"; "Despite peace agreement, South African killings persist"; "Even in 'New South Africa,' apartheid's legacy lives on"; "Segregation's legal foundations are going; the economic chasm remains"; "A strident, well-armed minority of South African whites is preparing to foil further dismantling of apartheid."[113] All of these are headlines or story lines from the 1990s.

In sub-Saharan Africa, ethnic divisions are less sharp and ethnic conflicts less violent than they have been through the last thirty years. The changes are hopeful, if small. A long journey begins with but a single step.

A COMMENTARY ON SCHOOL INTEGRATION (AND DIS-INTEGRATION) IN THE UNITED STATES[114]

Ethnic integration can be viewed from many perspectives. With a wide-angle lens we try to see a society, or even inter-society relations. We get a sharper picture, however, by focusing on the ethnic factor in a particular institution. To illustrate these contrasting methods, we shift now from a general survey of the barriers and openings for integration in Western Europe and sub-Saharan Africa to a more focused examination of one aspect of integration (education) in one country (the United States). Our interest, however, continues to be not only in the specific evidence in a particular situation, but also in the more general principles that can be of value in understanding other situations—in France, Germany, and Britain, for example, where school integration or segregation have become major public issues.

The opportunities and the controversies resulting from efforts to promote school integration (or, as a first step, desegregation) are based in part on issues of social class and neighborhood. They express more strongly, however, questions related to ethnicity and race.[115] Analysis of this complex topic must be based on both micro and macro perspectives, terms whose limits are not self-evident. What is macro in one context—e.g., the school system of a community when one is focusing on individual students—is micro in another context—e.g., the study of the impact of federal policy or of demographic trends on particular school systems. The task, whatever the appropriate boundary in a given study, is to see their interdependence. The influence of neither can be identified without reference to the other, for we are dealing with "simultaneous equations," each containing unknowns. The equations can be solved only together. They are part of a single field.[116] The field can be visualized simply, as in figure 3.1.

The likelihood of a given action, as suggested in Fig. 3.1, depends not alone on the strength of individual inclinations nor only on situational opportunities and costs. It develops from a conjunction of a certain set of inclinations, positive and/or negative, and a set of opportunities and costs. Integration will not proceed if individuals ready for it, in terms of most of their attitudes and skills, interact in a school setting that is poorly designed to promote it. Oppositely, if school districts are desegregated but little attention is paid to the individual attitudes and skills or to the interpersonal encounters within the desegregated setting, the outcomes are likely to be disappointing. Neither theory nor policy can avoid the truth of the adage: No chain is stronger than its weakest link.

The need to study individual tendencies and situational influences as interacting parts of a single field is emphasized in the extensive literature that examines the relationship of attitudes to behavior.[117] It is well established that attitudes toward school and housing desegregation have become much more tolerant in the United States in the last quarter century;[118] but it is equally well established that resistance to desegregation has sometimes been strong. Does this simply reflect the fact that those who have remained intolerant are resisting? Or is there a difference between

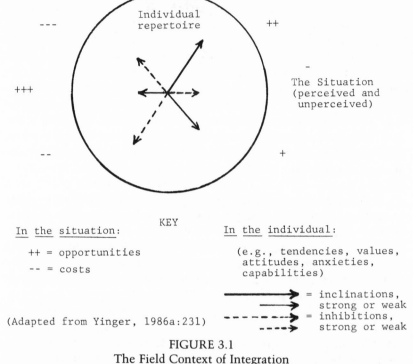

KEY

In the situation:

  ++ = opportunities

  -- = costs

(Adapted from Yinger, 1986a:231)

In the individual:

  (e.g., tendencies, values,
  attitudes, anxieties,
  capabilities)

  ⟶ = inclinations,
  ⟶   strong or weak

  - - - -⟶ = inhibitions,
  - - -⟶   strong or weak

FIGURE 3.1
The Field Context of Integration

generalized attitudes and those that are activated in particular contexts? Indeed, it is sometimes true that behavior changes first, sometimes under compulsion, followed by attitude change that helps to reestablish some consistency?[119]

The Roots of Segregation

To understand school integration we must understand school segregation—the forces that created it and the forces that sustain it. These range from the institutional structures of power to demographic trends, to the legal and customary processes of school decision making, to parental ambitions and attitudes, and to the tendencies of students and teachers. Such factors as these are highly interactive; they can be understood only as part of a field of forces.

Various factors in the system of segregation have been emphasized by different authors. Ogbu has made a distinction between immigrant and subordinate groups, based on his argument that schools and families have collaborated to socialize black children to the expectation of failure or little social mobility. In doing so they simply reflect and seek to adapt to an occupational system that needs a corps of unskilled—and nearly powerless—workers. Historical, demographic, and attitudinal influences have left the door open for immigrant groups, but not, Ogbu believes, for the subordinate groups. He rests the distinction mainly on the degree of volunteerism in the move of various groups to America, with Native Americans, African Americans, and—less clearly—Mexican Americans being most strongly coerced. Europeans and Asian Americans have come more voluntarily.[120] This is a useful distinction if not drawn too sharply.

The distinction Suttles makes between insiders and outsiders in our national myths is similar to the immigrant-subordinate contrast drawn by Ogbu. Some new groups are incorporated into insider status by the historical reconstruction of the national myth.[121]

Gutman has developed a similar theme, although he speaks of more impersonal forces. Relatively recent patterns of migration reflecting economic changes, not the drag of history, have been in effect a new Enclosure Movement. "Peasants" have been driven off the land at a time when the lower rungs of the skill ladder in the urban occupational system have been cut away. "Neither the economy nor those who dominate the political decision-making process have as a priority the creation of useful work for those driven in such numbers from the land."[122]

These are valuable concepts if we take them not as statements of hard reality but as analytic contrasts. If we treat "immigrant" and "subordinant" or "insider" and "outsider" as points on a scale, we are led to ask: What conditions affect placement on the scale? What conditions cause or permit changes? How does placement in one or another of these categories influence preparation for and attitudes toward integration? How does the great diversity *within* subordinant or outsider groups—in class, occupation, family experience, and individual tendency—qualify the impact of the labor market and the prevailing national myths?

The temptation is strong to explain segregation, with its accompanying disadvantages, either as a result of the structure of power or of the prejudices and other attitudes of individuals. Even together these are inadequate. To some degree segregation is the unintended and unwanted consequence of action that may temporarily seem to serve an individual purpose but that, in the long run, injures individual purposes and collective interests—the long-observed "tragedy of the Commons" or, in more current terms, the problem of the critical mass, or what we can call "the Schelling effect": "In some schools, the white pupils are being withdrawn because there are too few white pupils; as they leave, white pupils become fewer so that even those who didn't mind yesterday's ratio will leave at today's ratio, leaving behind still fewer, who may leave tomorrow."[123]

To explain this result by reference to individual motives is often wrong. It is the interplay of attitudes and the ways they are activated by the initial distribution that is crucial. Each parent, pressing hard for the best school for his or her own child, may take action that alongside the actions of other parents can have the opposite result from the one sought.

In *Fatal Remedies*, Sieber discusses a dishearteningly long list of such unanticipated negative consequences. We know little about how to anticipate the unanticipated. It is easy to agree with Sieber's recommendation that "the same measures be taken to assess the negative outcomes of social interventions as are increasingly taken to assess the second- or third-order consequences of new technologies."[124] But anticipation is not enough. Thinking for the moment on the policy level, we need to learn how to prevent these self-defeating actions. It is a good start to remember, with Cooley, that much of the harm in the world is done with the elbows, not the fists (he was not anticipating current basketball styles), that we bump and injure without intending to. Knowledge alone will not be persuasive; it must be accompanied by ability and willingness to take a long view, which in turn requires confidence in the system.

Little is known of the possibilities of what might be called "stopper variables"—new factors that are introduced into a system to prevent tipping from continuing to its "logical" conclusion of resegregation or desegregation without integration. These stoppers might include different patterns of reward that change parental and student priorities—superior curricula, payments to stay in school, credits toward expenses, for example. The tipping process is "inevitable" only if no new elements are added to the system within which it has begun.

Stoppers that prevent or inhibit segregative actions are needed as well as those that facilitate integrative actions. Thus, policies that indicate that there are no longer all-white communities to which prejudiced persons can escape—based for example, on scattered subsidized housing or on more open housing policies—could help to block the tipping process.[125]

Effects of School Segregation and Integration

Of the numerous effects or possible effects of integration, four have been given most attention: Effects on the self-esteem of students from minority groups, on achievement, on the extent and friendliness of new contacts, and on the racial and ethnic make-up of the communities involved. I will comment briefly on each one.

Sources and Effects of Levels of Self-Esteem. Although early studies of the self-esteem of African American children were focused more on prejudice and discrimination than on the degree of segregation, they seemed to confirm what was held to be a fairly self-evident fact: the burdens of minority status and its personal consequences lowered self-esteem. Methodological weaknesses, however, raised doubts. The samples used were small and nonrandom; seldom was there a white comparison group; the children were required to select from few options; and self-esteem was not clearly distinguished from group-esteem.

By the late 1960s, self-esteem was being measured by survey methods based on probability samples of both blacks and whites. Respondents came from a broader age range. And self-esteem, not group-esteem, was clearly the focus. The results of numerous studies sharply challenged and to a large degree contradicted the earlier studies. Black self-esteem is not lower and is sometimes higher than white self esteem. When the question of segregation is introduced as a variable, it has usually proved to increase, not decrease, black self-esteem.[126]

What is the significance of this body of literature for the study of integration in schools? Although recent survey methods have many advantages, the verbal behavior they measure may not correspond with other behaviors that express levels of self-esteem. Many events, typified by the direct training of the Rev. Jesse Jackson, have been teaching black children to say: "I am *somebody.*" One needs to ask: Does day-by-day experience reenforce that declaration?

Rosenberg has emphasized that to understand the roots of self-esteem we must see the world from the child's point of view, although he rejects any tendency to define this as the only point of view of significance for behavior.[127] Looking out at the world from the child's perspective, we must ask, Rosenberg notes: How much does a child care about a given appraisal? How much confidence does he place in it? In segregated settings, he believes, reflected appraisals and social comparisons are more positive than in integrated settings. Attribution of blame to oneself is deflected by "system blame," made easier by knowledge of discrimination. At least, one can infer this tendency from studies that show that African Americans score higher on measures of perception of the external locus of control. That inference may not be correct, however. Taylor and Walsh found system-blame to be correlated with low self-esteem, not a way of avoiding it.[128] And Hughes and Demo found that black Americans with a strong sense of personal efficacy—that is, a low sense of external control—are significantly higher in self-esteem. Personal efficacy is enhanced by education, the quality of family and friendship relations, interracial contacts, religious involvement, and other variables. This is shown by their regression analysis of the data from the 1979–1980 National Survey of Black Americans.[129]

In assessing the effects of segregation and of integration on ethnic minority children, we need to note that segregation doesn't mean lack of contact. It may be associated with menial, degrading contact. Symbolic contact through the mass media may be extensive. Adults significant in the child's life often have contact with the dominant group that affects the signals they send. We need ways to measure the extent to which verbal self-esteem corresponds with deeper feelings and with behavior.

Although integration can have negative effects on ethnic minority children, it also has positive effects: higher academic achievement; the opening of more post-school opportunities; more stable families; less crime.[130] If lower self-esteem, as presently measured, is a negative outcome of integration, we need to ask whether there are ways to reduce this deflationary effect. Perhaps it is produced, not by desegregation per se, but by some of the processes—labeling, tracking, internal resegregation, and the like—that are sometimes the accompaniments of desegregation. Knowledge that self-esteem can be lowered under some conditions is a new variable that can lead to counseling, discussion, and other activities that can prevent it from happening.

A similar experience affects some white students who attend academically selective colleges. Ninety per cent of them are likely to have been in the top 10 or 20 percent of their high-school classes; but two-thirds of them are in the bottom two-thirds of their college classes. This "desegregation" is a shocking experience for some and a blow to their self-esteem. Yet most of them stay; they find new grounds for self-esteem, they borrow from the prestige of the college, they employ a larger comparison group, and most of them believe they have made the right choice. If this analogy is of any value it may lead us to be alert to the long-run as well as the short-run effects of integration on self-esteem.

There is a fascinating parallel between the shifts in self-esteem studies and two other significant areas of research in ethnic and racial relations: slavery and language use. I shall only hint at that parallel here. Discrimination and inequality, said Clark and Clark and many other researchers in the 1940s and 1950s, had a crushing impact on self-esteem. Slavery, said Elkins and in a somewhat different way Stampp, had a devastating effect on personality development, leading to a childlike "Sambo." Isolation and deprivation, said Bernstein, created restrictive language codes.[131] All of these scholars described in sympathetic—but also mournful—tones the destructive power of segregation and discrimination.

All three positions have now been challenged, the parallel changes suggesting a new moral and political climate as well as continuing research. Interpretations are now more "upbeat," emphasizing the creativity and powers of resistance among the disadvantaged. Taking a child's-eye view, Rosenberg and a host of other researchers now say, we see that a segregated environment contains numerous resources and processes that enhance self-esteem. Slavery created a harsh and demanding context within which self-enhancing community and subcultural supports were created by the slaves, say Genovese, Fogel, and Engerman, and especially Gutman. Labov and many other contemporary linguists declare that Bernstein missed the "expressive richness and syntactic complexity of the nonstandard dialects," as Jules-Rosette and Mehan put it.[132]

How can we account for these shifts in emphasis on the effects of segregation and discrimination? Are they the result of new and better evidence; of new paradigms that produce different questions and perceptions; of shifting ideologies that demand that we express not only opposition to discrimination and sympathy for the unjustly treated, but also appreciation of their creative powers?

In my judgment we know more now than we did twenty-five years ago with respect to those questions. The speed with which the received wisdom shifted, however, gives me pause and causes me to wonder what tomorrow's scholars will think of today's knowledge. It is imperative that we be aware of these rapid changes—in some cases nearly reversals—in our explanations. That awareness may lead us, in terms of the immediate topic, to more powerful explanations of self-esteem and of the effects of integration on it. We may find that the swing of the pendulum was caused not simply by better research designs and evidence. New problems are being addressed, new questions asked. When changes of interpretation occur we are less likely, looking at them in this way, to say that "discrediting this tradition is, we believe, necessary.[133] The task is to build on the tradition. We can also share Adam's concern that the newer studies of self-esteem may deflect attention from study of the negative impact of discrimination. (He does not assume that such deflection is inevitable or that the evidence and argument of those studies should simply be set aside.) "Self-esteem has become a psychological abstraction," Adam writes, "which allows the effects of a racial social structure simply to fade away . . . the fundamental problem raised by the early writers, of the production and reproduction of social order, has been side-stepped and ultimately obscured by the redefinition of the self-esteem concept over time."[134]

Those who have found evidences of positive self-esteem even in the face of discrimination are unlikely to agree with Adam's statement. To find that individuals have ways of coping with prejudice and discrimination is scarcely to deny their negative impact. Both observations are essential. The value of the enormous body of research on self-concept and self-esteem for expanding our knowledge of the effects of school integration will be sharply reduced unless we can avoid these swings of the pendulum. Pettigrew has wisely suggested a framework within which the diverse, but not necessarily contradictory, findings can be drawn together:

(1) Oppression and subjugation do in fact have 'negative' personal consequences for minority individuals that are mediated by behavioral responses shaped through coping with oppression.
(2) There are also some 'positive' personal consequences for minority individuals as well as negative personal consequences for majority individuals. . . .
(3) Many of the 'negative' consequences for minority group members are reflected in personality traits that in a range of situations can act to maintain, rather than challenge, the repressive social system.
(4) Not all minority group members will be so affected nor are most traits of most minority members so shaped, since a sharp dis-

tinction between the 'real,' personal self and the racial self is generally possible.

(5) Thus proud, strong minorities are possible despite 'marks of oppression.' And this strength becomes increasingly evident as the minority itself effectively challenges the repressive societal system.[135]

Desegregation and Academic Achievement. Findings regarding the effects of the desegregation of schools on academic achievement vary widely. Although to Weinberg the preponderance of the evidence indicates beneficial results, Bradley and Bradley see little gain.[136] Does this difference in the findings reflect better or poorer methods of research, does it indicate study of different sets of facts and different conditions or, most likely, does it show both of these things? Reference to the numerous influences on academic achievement will help to bring us an answer.

This topic has been the focus of extensive research; but here I will simply list some of the variables that have been studied, limiting comment to a few of them. The list is quite long and could be made longer, for we are dealing with a complex situation. By facing the complexity we may reduce the tendency to retreat into oversimplification. (Many of these variables affect not only academic achievement but the probability that a school will remain multi-ethnic.)

1. The effects of various ratios of different ethnic groups, races, and classes. On one hand, the "solo" literature indicates that a group with small representation is likely to be isolated and stereotyped. We do not know the ratios or absolute numbers required before these effects are reduced, although 20 or 30 percent is sometimes suggested.[137] This proportion, however, begins to lead to the opposite problem—reactions stemming from the feeling that the "other" group is too large. Recent public opinion polls indicate that three-quarters of white parents say they would not object to having their children attend schools in which half of the pupils were black; but there is some evidence that withdrawals increase when the ratio reaches 30 percent. This may be because schools with such ratios suffer various disadvantages—poor financial support, location, a class mix deemed undesirable by the parents—and not because of the ethnic ratio itself. Or it may be that the one-quarter of parents who say they would object to sending their children to schools

in which half of the pupils were black begin to withdraw them when the ratio reaches 30 percent, creating a higher ratio for those remaining, and thus stimulating additional withdrawals—the Schelling effect.

2. Influence of age at which children enter desegregated schools.
3. Strength of an academic emphasis in the national school culture. If it is weak, students are more likely to sort themselves into partially conflicting "subcultures," with boundaries that correspond quite closely with racial and ethnic boundaries.[138]
4. Preschool preparation. The evidence is not yet decisive; but it now seems likely, contrary to earlier judgments, that children who enter school with some preschool educational experiences are indeed off to a "head start." Insofar as such experiences are less available to students from minority ethnic backgrounds, their academic achievement will be comparatively weaker.
5. School control methods: discipline vs. a progressive approach. Either a clear pattern of authority and discipline or a more relaxed and open style can work among students trained to one or other of these expectations. A mixture, however, may weaken both. One wonders how much this might be modified if a teacher laid his or her cards on the table, talked about the dilemma, and self-consciously sought to create a blend. There is evidence that firm discipline accompanied by respect, love, and parental involvement significantly increases the level of academic achievement.[139]
6. Sorting processes, by tracking, counseling, labeling. There is now substantial evidence not only of official and planned tracking of pupils but also of unplanned and unintended steering and labeling. This tends to reinforce differences in academic achievement and to increase segregation.[140]
7. Degree of teacher and staff integration and special training in problems likely to be faced in integrated schools. Such training, which is not widely used, interacts with the values and attitudes that teachers and administrators bring into the school situation.[141] It is often emphasized that teachers are role models. They may not be in desegregated schools—indeed, they may seem to be opponents—if they are not encouraged and helped to see the nature of the new teaching situation.
8. Goals of those who are dominant in society and the post-school opportunities they furnish, or deny, members of various ethnic groups.

9. Presence or absence of generational continuity in attitudes and values. With calculated exaggeration, Margaret Mead once remarked that for the first time in history, people no longer have (cultural) ancestors, just as they have no descendants. There is wide variation in the degree to which this is true—variation that is reflected in differences of academic achievement.

10. Cultural "fairness" in the curriculum and throughout the school. This is the school version of the *Great Books of the Western World* vs. *A Curriculum of Inclusion* controversy we discussed in the section on acculturation. Few would disagree that cultural fairness is not adequately served by holding an ethnic fair or celebrating X Week. But there is much less agreement on what it does entail in nonacademic as well as academic programs and what it does, if anything, to reduce the sharpness of the pluralism-universalism dilemma. Under what conditions do programs based on the value of cultural fairness accentuate boundaries and reinforce sorting processes that work in the opposite direction from those intended?[142]

This partial list of the variables that affect academic achievement in desegregated schools perhaps suggests the complexity of the research task. If we also recognize the various meanings attached to the term "academic achievement," the reasons for controversy are even more apparent. At least three questions need to be asked as one tries to assess the extent and the effects of school integration:

1. Does "academic achievement" mean attained level or extent of improvement over the entering level? Both measures are important; but in my judgment the extent of improvement (or loss) is the more significant.

2. Does it mean acquisition of certain skills or, in addition to that, a set of values favorable to intellectual growth generally? In a society in which rapid changes of occupational and other patterns demand flexibility, the learning of specific skills must be complemented by attitudes favorable to continuing education and retraining. Studies of integration have taught us little about its effects on such attitudes. Our measures of attainment are designed almost entirely to show levels of information and skill. The acquisition of attitudes and values favorable to continuing development can be parts of the culture of a school. Is that culture promoted by desegregation? Does desegregation bring some

students into schools, from which they formerly were excluded, within which that culture is strong?

3. Is the sheer fact of remaining in school and getting a diploma or degree the main achievement, or is level of competence the chief measure? Considering how poorly academic record predicts later success, except in a few occupations, and yet how much can be predicted by knowledge that a person has a diploma or degree, without knowledge of class rank, we need much more study of the effect of completing a course of study in segregated compared with desegregated schools. Persons who answer these questions differently are going to make different appraisals of the effects of integration on academic achievement.

Desegregation and Contact. Another topic of great interest and importance is the effect of desegregation on interracial and interethnic contact, and then the effect of various levels of contact on academic achievement, job placement, and other actions and tendencies—of teachers as well as students.[143] Many of the variables affecting academic achievement noted above also affect the extent and varieties of contact. Ratios, age, and sorting processes ought particularly to be mentioned in this regard.

In studying contact, we need to be aware of the barriers and gateways brought into the school as well as the opportunities for contact furnished or blocked by the school. As Blalock emphasized, we are greatly in need of analysis of the intrinsic costs and rewards of contact (those applying to persons experiencing the contact) and of the extrinsic costs and rewards (coming from persons not directly in the contact situation) under various sets of conditions. It should not require emphasis, but seems often to be forgotten, that if contact seems to some participants mainly to entail costs, with little perceived opportunity for gains—judged against their past experience and the interpretations of their groups—contacts will be resisted or used as an opportunity to try to improve their competitive situation.

The range of contacts is scarcely measured by sociometric tests that, for example, identify only dyadic ties with three best friends in a fixed-choice procedure. "Weak ties" are also important, not only in themselves but also because they link persons who move in different circles, thus furnishing direct and indirect group contacts.[144]

Neglect of study of weak ties should not be overcome by failing to study strong ties. Granovetter suggests that emphasis on the latter is associated with an assimilationist model. He observes that African Americans with strong ties to whites may so weaken their ties to other blacks that networks are not enlarged. I wonder if weak ties are not of significance precisely because there are some strong ties, and that without the latter weak ties are experienced as tokens. Whether or not this is true, much more extensive research is needed on the full range of contacts and the conditions under which they occur. Granovetter notes that, although weak ties "provide access to information and resources beyond those available" to one's closest associates, those with whom one has strong ties are more strongly motivated to help and are more readily available.[145] What needs study, I believe, are the results of various combinations of weak and strong ties. Under what conditions is a strong ethnic organization in a high school, for example, a separating barrier that prevents weak ties with others? And under what conditions is such an organization a source of self-confidence and of leadership able to promote the cultivation of weak ties?

Without imaginative teaching methods, classroom contact among persons of widely different levels of preparation can reenforce stereotypes. Large amounts of cooperative team learning and small amounts of tracking (e.g., no student put into a "homogeneous" classroom for more than one subject) can help to prevent that reenforcement. Unhappily, school policies more often reflect the opposite choice.[146] Various sorting procedures can effectively segregate ethnic groups within the walls of a "desegregated" school.

Outside the classroom, extra-curricular activities, playgrounds, and summer programs affect or have the possibilities of affecting interracial and interethnic contact. In the early 1960s, studies by Clark and Coleman were valuable maps of the internal "thematic" structure in schools. Students differ significantly in the strength of their attachments to "academic," "fun," or "delinquent" subcultures. We need now to know more about the way in which these thematic subcultures interact with or cut across ethnic subcultures, not only because they influence the amount and kinds of contact, but also because they affect levels of achievement. Where ethnic subcultures are kept within bounds by offsetting interests and contacts, Suttles observes, students do not 'burn their bridges' to school before they attempt to enter the job market."[147]

Community Effects of School Desegregation. A great deal of public attention and social research has been focused on the effect of school desegregation, particularly if brought about by court order, on the communities involved. Housing, job, and politics, as well as education, are strongly affected. The adversarial nature of research on this issue persists not only because of different premises and values, but also because the research task is extremely complicated. Different segments of a population were already moving, and at different speeds and at different rates of acceleration or deceleration, before school desegregation had begun. This situation can have effects that "masquerade as effects of desegregation," leading some to emphasize "white flight" from integrated schools, rather than earlier changes and trends, as the source of segregation.

We are confronted with the puzzling fact that public attitudes have become steadily more liberal regarding integrated housing and schools at the same time resistance to particular plans and policies has often been severe. The tendencies engaged when one is asked how he or she would respond to a given level of integration are often different from those activated when a specific plan is being discussed or carried out.

One can desegregate schools either by changing the racial and ethnic household mix in communities or by changing the mix of children in schools, or by a combination of the two. The two processes, in fact, are inevitably linked. Less attention has been paid to the prior integration of communities, however, except perhaps by urban economists. Far more than white flight is producing quasi-segregated communities along with the suburbanization of most of the white middle class. Clotfelter has observed that "relatively innocent market forces, including rising incomes and changes in production and transportation technology; public policies providing subsidies to transportation and middle-income housing; and outright discrimination against blacks, causing them to be concentrated in central cities and underrepresented in suburbs relative to their economic status" are three major factors.[148] These and other influences operate in an environment where the Schelling tipping process can readily be set in motion, because there are some with strong opposition to integration and others who are opposed if the minority exceeds some critical proportion—30 percent being a figure often given. The result can be more extreme segregation than almost anyone wants.

Of course households have always sorted themselves by income. Government-induced suburbanization, however, has facilitated the growth of separate—and ethnically segregated—school districts. There are actions that can be taken, and some have been taken, to counter the process of metropolitan segregation. Insofar as they are successful, school desegregation will be one of the results.

Open-housing laws by themselves are useful but incomplete, because they run into house buyers' prejudices (and the "Schelling effect"), sellers' prejudices (not unaccompanied by their economic interests), sales conditions with monopolistic elements, and wide income differences between whites, Hispanics, and blacks—conditions that furnish incentives to brokers to discriminate. "Only a theory that involves discrimination can explain why blacks are concentrated in a central ghetto, why blacks pay more for comparable housing than whites in the same submarkets, why prices of equivalent housing are higher in the ghetto than in the white interior, and why blacks consume less housing and are much less likely to be home owners than whites with the same characteristics."[149]

New and imaginative action is required to break up this pattern. In addition to strengthening open housing laws, desegregation bonuses could be awarded to communities and individuals. The profit from segregation could be reduced by an increased flow of information in the housing market. Present multiple listing services are incomplete, often excluding minority brokers or limiting their access.[150]

Changes in these structural factors will retard the resegregation of communities and thus of schools. Those changes are likely to be slow in coming, however, so that the problem needs to be approached from the other end as well—direct efforts to desegregate schools. Under many circumstances this helps to desegregate communities, setting a beneficient cycle in motion.[151]

Although disagreements are numerous in the vast literature on this topic,[152] at a minimum one can say that school desegregation brought about by individual household mobility, e.g., the suburbanization of black families,[153] or occurring in relatively small school districts or in school districts where minority enrollment is not more than one-third of the total, is likely to contribute to rather than reverse community desegregation. This may occur only after a year or two of influence in the opposite direction.[154]

On the other hand, where changes are piecemeal, where school desegregation occurs only on the borders of ghetto areas, and where administrative policy is vacillating, school desegregation is likely to be associated with resegregation of the communities involved. This is not to say that school desegregation caused resegregation in the form of white flight. It may simply be that the items mentioned are correlated with the diminishing appeal of the largest central cities, that diminishing appeal being the cause of suburbanization for any family with such an option, as Orfield put it.[155]

The possibility of a new kind of white flight has developed in the U.S. since 1989. Eight states now allow students to enroll in any school district, subject to a few restrictions. Some people thought that black and other minority students would be most likely to use this choice. The evidence now shows, however, that white students select the option more frequently. Their families are better able, on the average, to afford the costs of transportation and are often motivated to avoid an integrated school without having to move. It is ironic that opponents of busing now find themselves its willing users.[156]

Thus school districts can be caught between a federal requirement that they achieve racial integration and a state-mandated student choice policy that can have dis-integrative effects.

I have come to the conclusion that to continue to try to determine the proportion of the resegregation of city schools and of the cities themselves due to white flight from desegregation, particularly when produced by busing, is a nearly useless exercise. (I cannot resist adding, however, that in my judgment, major long-run structural changes in our metropolitan areas and the economy are the root causes. Where those causes are operating most strongly, in Detroit, for example, school desegregation can have a multiplier effect on the suburbanization of whites.) However that may be, we do know that resegregation has occurred in many cities. If school desegregation is desirable, even mandatory, as I believe it is, then we need to ask: How can the causes of that resegregation be dealt with? The problem must be approached from both ends: desegregating communities in order to desegregate schools, and desegregating schools in order to desegregate communities. That is a controversial statement. Some will say there is no legal or judicial mandate to desegregate communities. That is the position taken by the Supreme Court in *Milliken v. Bradley* (1974). If schools can be desegregated only by maintaining or bringing about integrated communities, however, and if school integration is mandated, then the 1974 Supreme Court decision in the Detroit case cannot stand. That is the position taken by Justice Douglas in joining the minority of four on the Court: "When we rule against the metropolitan area remedy we take a step that will likely put the problems of Blacks and our society back to the period that antedated the 'separate but equal' regime of *Plessy v. Ferguson.*"[157] Recent developments have, in the main, supported that view.

We need to know much more about the legal, attitudinal, and structural (often impersonal) forces standing in the way of metropolitan area remedies, starting both from the school and the community end. In my view, no research related to the study of school desegregation can be of greater importance.

CONCLUSION

Our questions, research strategies, and judgments would be influenced, I think for the better, if we recognized explicitly that we are dealing with a two- or three-generational problem. I take this to be a sound empirical judgment, albeit not easily documented, and in no sense the expression of a desire or a counsel to go slow. Insofar as it is true, assessment of the impact of desegregation should refer to trend lines, not to goals obtained in a year or two. Research can be based on the study of settings where change is rapid and extensive compared with settings where it is slow, accompanied by study of the degree to which these various settings are becoming more common.

We need to be as alert as possible to unintended effects, not only the one most commonly studied—resegregation—but those that may occur in particular communities, schools, and individuals. Does desegregation increase parental involvement? Does it stimulate greater awareness of the growing language issue in the United States? Does it have spillover effects on other aspects of community life—e.g., home prices, school taxes? Does it lead, among some, to a loss of the sense of "my school," with accompanying alienation, when one's ethnic group can no longer be seen as the only or main group? And how do these unintended effects feed back into the desegregation process, strengthening or deflecting it?

Research on the effects of media attention and interpretation, both before and after school desegregation, is in short supply. It is a truism that conflict gets the best press. Reports of events then feed back into the ongoing reality of events, partly shaping them.

To a degree, changes that the desegregation of schools brings about involve, not only gains for all but some transfer of advantages—zero-sum gains. There is little doubt that many of the opponents of desegregation believe that what others might gain, they and those with whom they identify are likely to lose. In examining the issues of equality vs. dominance, we need to study this possibility, indeed the probability in my judgment, that educational and occupational opportunities are to some degree zero-sum. "Society as a whole" is likely to benefit, but some individuals pay a price. And—to show the toughness of the stratification system—it is mainly the least well-off of the dominant group who pay the price and the best-off of the subordinate groups who profit from the changes. Until we learn how to spread the cost of dominance reduction to include the best-off of the dominant group and spread the gains to include the least well-off of the least advantaged groups, we will have satisfied only poorly the requirements of justice, as I understand them. The research question, purified from these politico-moral judgments, is: Which forms of school integration are or could be progressive (in an income tax sense), which ones proportional, which ones regressive?[158]

There is now substantial evidence that academic competence and even intelligence, as measured by standard tests, are strongly influenced by activities—or the lack of activities—during the summer months.[159] Since differences in academic competence are among the factors influencing attitudes toward and the success of desegregation, the differences among children in the nature of their summer experiences, and especially the kinds of summer experiences that link strongly to the programs of the academic year, are of critical importance. Without such linkage, without follow-through, the effects of summer enrichment are likely to face quite rapidly. In *Middle Start,* my colleagues and I found that there were three ingredients to a successful summer program: A decisive new, stretching, and stereotype-breaking experience; a sponsor to show that new possibilities were available and to explain each step, because each step was into "foreign" territory; and a circle of "supporting others," complementing the instrumental guidance of the sponsor with emotional support.[160] Whether or not these ingredients are essential in all instances, we can be sure, I think, that wide differences in the way summers are spent compound other difficulties faced in the process of desegregation.

Finally, we need to keep continuously in mind the several levels, from the most macro to the most micro, and their interdependence if we are to advance our understanding of the complicated process of school integration. It might be useful to note these levels.

We are dealing with a very complicated part of nature. The several levels of analysis and the illustrative variables listed here surely

TABLE 3.2
Levels of Analysis of School Integration

Level of Analysis	Variables to Consider
Society as a whole	Demography
	Major technical and economic changes
	Housing policies
Relationships among school districts	All of the above, plus laws bearing on desegregation
	Court decisions
	Media attention
Relationships within school districts	All of the above, plus School board policies with regard, e.g., to school locations, busing, teacher selection and training
	Ratios of different groups
	Sorting processes
Relationships within a school	All of the above, plus
	Methods of discipline
	Peer groups, youth cultures
	Language variation
	Processes affecting weak ties
	Teaching methods
	Effects on self-esteem
Relationships within a classroom or other specific activity	All of the above, plus
	Age of the students
	Socio-economic status range
	Criteria for participating in the activity
The individual	All of the above, plus
	Racial or ethnic group
	SES
	Attitudes concerning desegregation
	Levels of competence
	Ambition, distinguishing plans (aspirations) from motivation (expenditure of effort)

give us pause. Nothing is to be gained, however, from the belief that by studying one or two levels and a few variables we can enlarge our understanding of the sources and effects of school integration or the costs of its absence.

Chapter 4

THE ELEMENTS OF ASSIMILATION AND DISSIMILATION: IDENTIFICATION AND AMALGAMATION

Having discussed the cultural and structural elements of assimilation, we turn in this chapter to the psychological and biological aspects. Although one or another of the elements may be critical with reference to particular topics and questions, they can be fully understood only when all of them and their interactions are taken into account.

IDENTIFICATION

"We don't even know who we are anymore. They tell me I am a 'Russian' now. What does that mean? Does it mean that my parents, who live in Uzbekistan, are foreigners? Will I need a visa to visit them. ... I am all for the changes in this country, but I am completely confused. What does it mean—'Russian'?"[1]

Who indeed is he? And who are they? Who am I? Who are you? In many times and places these become crucial questions. Answers formerly taken for granted no longer suffice. The sense of urgency that drives the search for new answers often leads, in this period of history, toward ethnicity. Even where extensive integration and acculturation have softened the ethnic attachment, an affective tie may remain strong or be reenforced because it helps to clarify who we are in a time of puzzling uncertainties.

The psychological process of *identification* refers to a set of related aspects of assimilation. Individuals from separate groups may come to think of themselves as belonging to the same society—a new society, blended from their societies of origin.[2] Shifts in identification, however, may be more one-sided, with members of group A identifying with society B, or members of group B identifying with society A. All three of these identificational processes may go on at the same time, and the nature of their mixture tells us a great deal about the situation in which they occur. Some Americans of Indian ancestry identify themselves simply as Americans, along with a large number of European Americans, as we noted earlier, and some Hispanic, African, and Asian Americans. Throughout American history, a few white persons have identified themselves as Indians, have lived in tribal villages, married Indian wives, and sometimes have become chiefs.[3]

In the United States the term *Hispanic* is often used in official documents and public discourse to identify a highly diverse population. For many of them, however, that is not the preferred label. In a recent study of nearly 3,000 persons who are "Hispanics" in the census, a majority identified themselves by their place of origin and others simply as Americans.

In this sample, less than one-fifth selected a pan-ethnic label. Yet ethnic identities can shift upward to a new pan-ethnic cluster, or downward to a segment of a society that had been constructed and defined by an outside power.

Some people have a kind of negative identity, defining themselves more by who they are not, rather than by who they are.

Ethnic identities are strongly influenced by the other assimilative processes—by the levels of integration, acculturation, and amalgamation. We need to keep these interdependent processes analytically separate, however, because they vary in distinctive ways, being affected by different sets of causes. Identification is some-

TABLE 4.1
Preferred Identification among "Hispanic" Americans[4]

	Prefer to Be Identified by Place of Origin	Prefer Pan-Ethnic names, (Hispanic, Latino, etc.)	Prefer American
Mexicans			
Born in Mexico	86%	14%	—
Born in U.S.	62%	28%	10%
Puerto Ricans			
Born on the island	85%	13%	3%
Born on the mainland	57%	19%	21%
Cubans			
Born in Cuba	83%	12%	5%
Born in U.S.	41%	20%	39%

times the major causal influence in the ethnic order; at other times it is more nearly dependent on the levels of integration, acculturation, and amalgamation.

In 1980, the United States census sought information, not just of the ancestry of parent and grandparents, but of the respondents' ancestry more generally. Persons of mixed ethnic origin could give more than one ancestry. Thirty-seven percent did so; 60 to 80 percent of the various European groups cited multiple ancestries. Nearly 50 million named English and an equal number named German among their ancestral lines; 40 million named Irish, 27 million French, 12 million Italian. The interesting new response was that 12 million gave American as their ancestry.[5] This is a conservative estimate since the census listed "American" only if no other response was given. It was the choice of last resort. Mexican Americans were recorded as Mexicans. Those who gave "black" as their response to a racial question but did not answer "black" to the ancestry question were excluded from the American ethnic category. Such classification decisions reflected an effort to get as full a record as possible of the ancestral backgrounds of the population; but they had the effect of obscuring the appearance of a new category, particularly among persons of more than three generations of ancestral background in the United States.

Instructions to the interviewers taking the 1980 census make clear the primary aim: "Some persons may not identify with the foreign birthplace of their ancestors or with their nationality group and may report the category 'American.' If you have explained that we are referring to the nationality group of the person or his or her ancestors before arriving in the United States, and the person still says that he or she is 'American,' then print 'American.' "[6]

Lieberson and Waters refer to those who think of themselves simply as Americans as "unhyphenated whites." Most are of European background, but they are saying: I am not British-American or Italian-American, just American. We need to note, however, that "white" in the label is not entirely precise. Through the last twenty generations there has been a significant amount of racial mixing in America. A person with one great-grandparent who was Native American who identifies himself as white and is also thus identified by others (although he may well remember with pride that one-eighth of his ancestry is Indian) may find "American" the appropriate label. Many persons with one or more African ancestors but with a predominance of European ancestors have "passed" into the white population. And what is the identification of a person such as General Benjamin O. Davis, of European and African descent, when he states that he does not like the term *African American;* he finds it misleading and thinks it segregating? "Everybody I know is mixed up. . . . I prefer to be an American."[7] Perhaps we need simply to note the presence of many "unhyphenated Americans."

Census classifications only get us started in thinking about ethnic identity. We need to examine several questions:

Who am I? How is the question asked; what options for answers are open; who asked the question; is the answer given in words or in actions?

Who are we? Do you include me in your ethnic circle, and I you? Do we agree on the boundary that separates us from them? The meaning of a person's identity is strongly affected if, when he says, "I am a Frenchman," someone else says, "you are not; you are a dirty Arab." In asking who we are, we are also asking who you are and who they are.

Thus, along with various processes of self identification are the assignments of others to insider or outsider groups. Psychological assimilation of others has occurred to the degree that "they" are believed to be part of us. It is often true that self-identification and identification by others are not correspondent. Prejudices on the part of the dominant ethnic groups may prevent the granting of full membership in a society to members of ethnic minorities, even

though the latter think of themselves only in terms of the larger society. Oppositely, however, group solidarity among members of a
group may block identification even with an open society.

There may be subconscious as well as conscious levels of ethnic
identity, both of self and others. And there may be a lack of correspondence between the levels, as revealed by changing circumstances. Some African Americans who have visited Africa have
discovered that they are more American than they had realized, as a
result both of their own feelings in the new situation and of the way
they are identified by the Africans with whom they interact.[8] Some
persons in Britain have discovered that the identification of all
members of the Commonwealth as co-citizens collides, under conditions of social stress, with subconscious identification of some as
outsiders. This ambivalence is reflected in legal changes. In 1947
the British Nationalities Act granted, or reaffirmed, British citizenship for migrants from former colonies, many of Asian or African
background. In the early 1960s, however, their rights as citizens began to be curtailed by a series of laws. As a consequence, feelings of
ethnic nationalism have increased: If we are not Xs (full citizens)
some are declaring, then we shall by Ys (identifying ourselves first
as Sikhs or Pakistanis, or Jamaicans).[9]

Each person has several identities. Even ethnic identities are
not fixed and unambiguous. Which of various possibilities is dominant at a particular time depends in part on other people, on individual choice, and on the circumstances of the moment. Alex Haley
investigated his "roots" in Africa, but also, on third or fourth
thought, in Ireland as well.

If you had asked a person from the mountains of northern
Georgia in 1942 during the "Great Patriotic War," Who are you? he
might have answered, "I am Soviet." Twenty-five years later, at the
height of Russian dominance over the USSR, he might have said, "I
am Georgian." Today, during the struggle in Georgia to define the
meaning of its independence, he is most likely to say, "I am
Ossetian."

Four samples of black women in different areas of South Africa
were asked to select their *first* identity from among three choices:
Ethnic (Zulu, Xhosa, etc.), Black, or South African. The answers varied widely.

Who they are—or how they label themselves—varied with the
context. Soweto and Pretoria, both in the Transvaal, are heteroge-

TABLE 4.2
Variation in Choices of First Identity[10]

Choices	Durban	Reef/Pretoria	Soweto	Eastern Cape
Ethnic	55.0%	29.9%	20.4%	19.2%
Black	33.9%	40.9%	33.6%	43.3%
South African	11.0%	29.3%	46.0%	37.5%

neous ethnically; they contain many migrants. Durban, in Natal, is 90 percent Zulu; the eastern Cape is mainly Xhosa.

Verbal ethnic identities at least, and perhaps behavioral identities as well, vary through time. In 1971–1972 the United States census sought to find the consistency of response to an ethnic question by asking the same people in two successive years what their ethnicity was. Consistency was very high for Puerto Ricans (96.5%), Blacks (94.2%), and Mexicans (88.3%). It was much lower for Irish (57.1%), English, Welsh, Scots (55.1%), and "don't knows" (34.9%).[11] The last group clearly did not know. Some of the "inconsistency" may be accounted for by the possibility that different adults in the same household were asked in different years; but presumably that factor affected all the groups. The main source of the difference in consistency was probably the higher proportion of persons with mixed ancestry among the inconsistent. They had a choice.

The Salience of Ethnic Identities

We do not know very much about an individual's ethnic identity nor about the ethnic order of a society if we know only labels and classifications. How important is the identity in the life of individuals and in the interactions of a society? Identifying the home of one's ancestors is a very weak measure. We need information about consistency of identification, as we have seen, about behavior, and about the effects of various contexts on the salience of ethnicity.

Identities can be inherited, chosen, assigned, or merely inferred from some bit of evidence. If one strengthens the definition of identification to make it more than simply a label or category, one can, with Royce, think of it as *validated* place in an ethnic group. It is not merely ascription. Some ethnic identities have to be achieved; and they have to be maintained by behavior, by ethnic "signaling." "Adequate performance in an identity is much more rigorously judged within a group than it is by outsiders. For the latter, a few tokens of the identity are usually sufficient. . . ."[12] The Census Bureau is content with "I am X; my ancestors were X's." To insiders, lack of knowledge or inability to signal properly can mean that identity can be challenged. "In this sense, cultural illiteracy is as crippling as illiteracy in a language."[13]

The physical and symbolic qualities that connote "home" can send such signals. What is kept? What heirlooms? Are objects that are ethnically identified treasured; or are they discarded and removed?[14]

In later chapters we will discuss situations where the ethnic language and religion differ from the predominant ones. They are among the most powerful signals of one's ethnic identity.

Ethnic signaling can be influenced by the situation. For example, there may be consistent differences in the perception and choice of appropriate foods when one is eating with business associates, as contrasted with eating with one's parents.[15]

Artists are important sources of the symbols that signal one's identity. African American artists, from the poets, dramatists, and novelists of the Harlem Renaissance in the 1920s to the musicians, rappers, and filmmakers of the 1980s and 1990s have been important in defining what it means to be black.

One has to earn or achieve an ethnic identity under some conditions. Under other conditions it is thrust upon one. Individual choices are constrained. Deviants from the proclaimed norms are "Uncle Toms"; differences among the members are downplayed or repressed. The emphasis of those who assert the ethnic orthodoxy is backward looking, to reclaim a "revered and forgotten tradition." In some Mexican American or Native American groups, for example, "to be successful economically, or to participate socially with dominant status white, is by definition to be a 'falso' or a deserter. . . . Members from early on may be prevented from taking on other linguistic or social usages by group sanctioning."[16]

Pressures to belong start very early in some ethnic situations "and cannot be separated from the development of a sense of self." Family experiences are often critical in self-definition, but so also are peer groups, particularly where families are broken or seem to offer inadequate guidelines in a hostile or chaotic world. "Compared with the experiences of the waves of European immigrants, there seems today to be more difficulty in educating children of Mexican-American, Puerto Rican, Black, or American Indian background. It is evident to me at least that for these children to be amenable to learning majority norms, the influence of their minority peer groups against such norms must be overcome. Threats of expulsion from the ethnic peer group are a strong force against the formal educative processes in the schools."[17]

Critics of De Vos' statement are likely to say: What is so good about majority norms? Perhaps any disagreement can be reduced, however, if we take him to mean by majority norms the widely shared goal of education for all, not the all too imperfect practices so widely found. We need also to emphasize the diversity within the groups he mentions. It is the severely disadvantaged among them who are most likely to develop a self-protecting response—sometimes a counterculture—to serve as a shield against persistent discrimination.

"There are those for whom schooling has been a torment from the beginning. Poorly prepared lingually or by the range of their experiences for the process of formal learning, their first regular contacts with the world beyond the family are marked by failure, and they fall continuously farther behind. In a loud voice the schools say: You are no good. Some students come to believe that, and they join with others hearing the same message to design an inverted culture where they *are* good, where they have a chance to be somebody. Insofar as possible, those who don't share that culture are assigned to a category of persons who don't count. The fact that values are reversed, however, in the effort to repress lingering hopes and ambitions, is an indication of persistent ambivalence."[18]

A "mentor program" in a drug-infested, violence-ridden area in Washington, D.C. seeks "to capture the boys before the streets do," to prevent a countercultural ethnic identity from dominating their lives. "Think of a little boy who is growing up in that environment. He is like a canoe floating in an ocean without a compass. . . . If your kid has to walk through a den of dope pushers and addicts every day just to get to school, that's an incredible thing."[19] "I wanted these young boys to realize there were black males who are caring and who work hard. If you listen to the guys on the corner you'd think working hard was passé. I wanted the boys to see something other than the drug dealer."[20]

The shared and inverted values and the ambivalence associated with them that develop in such anomic settings suggest that more commonly, or certainly more visibly, coerced ethnic identity is produced largely by outsiders. Opportunities denied, stereotypes, and legal and political definitions restrict one's ethnic options.

They can be part of a self-fulfilling prophecy in which those kept outside a dominant ethnic circle (or who are treat *unfraternally*, to use a term we will develop later) assert their distinctiveness. In the United States, participation in a Chicano movement or a sense of strong identification with *La Raza*, for example, expresses a situation where slowly expanding opportunities fail to keep pace with rapidly increasing levels of aspiration.[21]

Are Ethnic Identities Additive or Substitutive?

In the discussion of acculturation, we noted that one can think of it as substitutive or additive. The same issue needs to be raised in connection with identities. Are they zero-sum, so that if one goes up, another must go down? Or are they additive, allowing a person to take on new identities without setting aside or downgrading others? If I become aware that I am a WAIF (one of the White American International Folk), am I thereby less an American, less human, less an individual? Or have I simply added to my identity repertoire, as one would add a new piece of music or engage in "role accumulation"?[22]

It is perhaps most likely that some identities are mutually exclusive or competitive; an increase in the salience of one entails a decrease in the salience of the other. Other combinations, however, may be compatible, allowing one to build up more complex structures of identity. If this is the most useful way to explore the issue of additive vs. substitutive identities, the critical question becomes: With what other identities are ethnic identities compatible or incompatible, and at what levels of salience?

Nisbet believes that increasing emphasis on ethnicity (along with an increase in fundamentalism and the rise of the "cultural Left") is in part the result of the repudiation of the political state. "Throughout recorded history there is a high correlation between alienation of individual loyalties from dominant political institutions and the rise of new forms of community—ethnic, religious, and others—which are at once renunciations of and challenges to these political institutions."[23] In many instances, of course, one would need to speak not of new but of persistent or renewed forms of community.

Are we to believe, then, following Nisbet, that a resurgent white ethnic identity in the United States, of Georgian in an independent Georgia, of German in an increasingly multi-ethnic Germany indicate repudiation of the political state? It is more likely that minority ethnic groups, feeling unrepresented, perhaps even persecuted, will become more strongly ethnic as their sense of alienation grows. The dominant ethnic groups, well represented in the political structures, feel more strongly identified with the state, even chauvinistic about it, as their ethnicity becomes more intense.

Although some identities clash—if one grows in strength the others become less salient—others are nested into a compatible structure of identities. The smaller, more intimate identities are surrounded by larger and more impersonal ones. Think of the family, the community, the ethnic group, and the society as concentric circles of identity. At any given time, any one can be the most salient, preferences varying, alternating sometimes on a calendrical rhythm (at culturally regulated intervals) and sometimes on a critical rhythm (the timing being determined by an event, perhaps a crisis, the occurrence of which cannot be determined).

Shelby Steele describes two such circles: "in the writing [of *The Content of Character*], I have had both to remember and forget that I am black. The forgetting was to see the human universals within the memory of the racial specifics. One of the least noted facts in this era when racial, ethnic, and gender differences are often embraced as sacred is that being black in no way spares one from being human. Whatever I do or think as a black can never be more than a variant of what all people do and think."[24]

For some people, perhaps for all of us at one time or another, the feeling of attachment to one of the identities becomes so intense that the other identities are lost. In this period of history, ethnic and religious identities, often in combination, are most likely to be thus embraced. These are zealous times, if we mean by zealotry the nearly exclusive attachment to one identity. The result: civil conflicts and civil wars in unprecedented numbers. At a time when inter-state wars are few, scores of intra-state wars, many of them overwhelmingly violent, are breaking states apart. Most of these internal conflicts that typify the late twentieth century involve an ethnic element. They indicate the prevalence in many settings of what I call identity compaction: Nothing matters to me except that I am X; I will do anything, I should do anything, to attain its goals. Such zealotry sometimes collapses into fanaticism, which I define as a condition in which the goals no longer matter; the means have taken over. A fanatic is one who, having lost his way, redoubles his efforts.

Some individuals, of course, identify themselves with two cultural groups, while feeling marginal to both. We cannot here explore the extensive literature dealing with marginality[25] more than to say that the ambivalence it expresses is connected with the experience of dual acculturation, integration, and often amalgamation as well. One is caught between two worlds and is unable, both because of outside forces and because of forces within oneself, to move fully into either one.

Some persons, to be sure, are able to overcome the anxiety-laden aspects of this duality and to use it for highly creative purposes. DuBois wrote impressively of his "double consciousness."[26] One might call it a kind of stereoscopic vision, while most of us see out of only one ethnic eye. Similarly with Senghor, the poet and political leader who "cannot write many pages without evoking the word *métis*. He means primarily cultural intermixture, as in his own career he crossed passionate Negritude with passionate Frenchness,"[27] an expression of Senghor's belief that Senegal must stand for tolerance, a belief now challenged by a militant Islam and ethnic nationalism.

Shifts in Ethnic Identity. In many settings most individuals carry an ethnic identity with them from birth to death. Due to the powerful early experiences of socialization, one's ethnicity is built into self-definitions. The original ethnic group, wanting to maintain or enhance its strength, brings pressure on its members not to be deserters nor to forget their roots. Outsiders, trying to protect their own ethnic boundaries, create barriers to shifting. A person may be thoroughly acculturated and integrated, speak without a "foreign" accent, have no identifiable physical differences from a dominant group, and yet be sought out and "exposed" if he seeks another ethnic identity. Some, of course, are more readily identified by culture or appearance and are thus more easily prevented from passing.

Despite such barriers to identity shifts, under some conditions shifts of ethnic identity are quite common. In the United States the local, tribal, or regional lines among immigrants are replaced to some degree by enlarged pan-ethnic clusters. Immigrants from Italy might identify themselves as Sicilians, perhaps from a particular region of Sicily. Their descendents become Italians, the shift in identity being toward a "high" Italian culture not previously their own.[28] Then perhaps they become unhyphenated Americans with an Italian flavor. Mexicans, Puerto Ricans, Cubans, Costa Ricans, and many more, become Hispanic Americans, although less in their own identifications than in public records and in identification by others.

Shifts in identification are not, however, only a one-way process toward larger and more inclusive groups. That has been the dominant trend in the historical development of states. It also prevails under colonial conditions if groups that think of themselves as different are defined by a common term and treated similarly by the ruling power. As Horowitz notes, identity expands with an expanding context. By the same token, however, it contracts when the significant territorial boundaries contract. Tribal identities in Africa, for example, gained additional salience when states shaped by European powers attained independence. Horowitz put it well:

> The moving force of assimilation and differentiation is the sense of similarity and difference from others sharing the same space. As the importance of a given political unit increases, so does the importance of the highest available level of identification immediately *beneath* the level of that unit, for that is the level at which judgments of likeness are made and contrasts take hold.[29]

Muslims within pre-independence India felt a common bond. When the Muslim League won a separate Islamic state, however, in the form of a multi-ethnic Pakistan, a new basis of identity—set over against the state—was created in East Bengal. Twenty-five years later, after years of ethnic conflict, the new state of Bangladesh was formed, with its own ethnic divisions.

Under many conditions, identity shifts tend to be from lower to higher status groups. Where social mobility is hindered by prejudice and discrimination, however, many members of lower status groups will reaffirm their shared identity and seek to facilitate group mobility.

Changes in the rules and classifications of governments and other institutions can cause changes in ethnic identities. "It is almost certain that the rules will deviate from the reality in the direction of meeting the needs of the dominant population and/or the organizations themselves."[30]

Continuing Ethnic Identity among the Highly Assimilated. There is a great deal of evidence that Americans of European background are highly assimilated. This is particularly true of those of mixed ancestry and of those whose ancestors came to America four or more generations ago. Evidence includes the high rate of ethnic intermarriage (to be discussed later), similar occupational, educational, and income profiles, self-designation simply as American in the census by many, as we have noted, and the almost universal use of English as the first language.

Nevertheless, a majority still identify themselves ethnically, as one of their several identities. This connection can be very loose, a "dime store ethnicity," as Stein and Hill have called it[31]; "symbolic," with more expressive than instrumental functions[32]; "situational," the identity of choice under some conditions; or a more continuous, "authentic" identity despite substantial acculturation and integration.

Why this persistence of an ethnic identity even under conditions containing strong assimilative pressures? The answer, to some interpreters, is quite self-evident: Ethnicity expresses a basic human attachment, a primordial bond to one's ancestors and one's cultural roots. I do not want to dismiss this argument quickly. The emotional intensity of contemporary ethnic-nationalisms document the way ethnic identities can persist, perhaps beneath the surface of awareness, and then surge with energy in a changing situation.

Even if there is a persistent primordial element, however, we have to ask why it lies nearly dormant for a time, only to be revived in other circumstances. In the American case, I think these are among the reasons:

The experience of anomie (living in a society of highly diverse and, to some degree, clashing values and norms) and feelings of alienation from that society because of its value complexity (some part of which seems repugnant or crass to almost everyone) sends us in search of a more coherent moral order. One aspect of that search is the rise, in many parts of the world, of fundamentalist religious movements. They seek to capture and to hold separate a kind of holy space protected from the "sinful space" of a changing world. Although some of these movements have a universalist emphasis, many draw the boundary between us and them along national and ethnic lines.[33]

There is an effort among some members of the more prosperous ethnic groups (particularly the less prosperous individuals among them) to differentiate themselves from ethnic minorities whose identity is likely to be unambiguous and in a sense more authentic because of the discriminations they experience. "Ethnicity does not stand on its own but stands because it is draped over the skeletal structure of inequality."[34]

In her study of suburban whites near San Francisco and Philadelphia, Waters shows how their basically symbolic ethnic identities are nearly costless for them. They are voluntary; they do not, for the most part, limit the choices of marriage partners, friends, residences, or jobs. Nor do they make it more likely that one will experience discrimination, although the same cannot be said for the non-voluntary ethnic identities of some of their grandparents.

Is symbolic ethnicity "a lovely way to show that all cultures can coexist and that pluralist values of diversity and tolerance are alive and well in the United States?"[35] Yes and maybe no, Waters writes. In addition to the positive, amusing, and creative aspects of the celebration of ethnic identity, ". . . there is a subtle way in which this ethnicity has consequences for American race relations."[36] When Michael Novak wrote[37] that the "new ethnicity" was the best hope for confronting racial hatred, he "could not have been more wrong."[38] The "new white ethnics" were among the strongest opponents of many aspects of the civil rights movement. Because their ethnic identities were voluntarily chosen, were nearly costless by the 1960s, and provided enjoyment, they could not well understand the costs, "the everyday influence and importance of skin color and racial minority status for members of minority groups in the United States."[39] Since "everybody has the same opportunities" it doesn't matter what their background is, as one of Waters' respondents put it. If the members of some groups are not doing well, it is not the result of discrimination, but of individual inadequacies or cultural weaknesses. Affirming their ethnic identity, then, is, among other things, a way for those of European background to distance themselves from the plight of those whose ethnicity is not simply symbolic but a harsh daily reality.

The affirmation of a rather soft ethnic identity can also be understood as a way of dealing with the often observed tension in America between the values of individualism and community. This duality is similar to the observations made by Tocqueville 160 years ago, and those of many others since, of the strain in American life arising from efforts to expand both liberty and equality. Similar observations have been made about other societies. At least since Goethe there have been discussions of "the two Germanys"—a methodical, controlled, obedient quality and a romantic, emotional, extravagant quality. Erik Erikson has remarked that a culture "is much more richly defined by such point-counterpoint tensions than by a list of mutually consistent values."[40]

The tension between individuality and community is dealt with by a soft, symbolic ethnicity. "Being ethnic makes them feel unique and special and not just 'vanilla,' as one respondent put it. They are not like everybody else. At the same time, being ethnic gives them a sense of belonging to a collectivity. It is the best of all worlds: they can claim to be unique and special while simultaneously finding the community and conformity with others that will not interfere with a person's individuality."[41]

Efforts to reconcile two contrasting desires, as in symbolic ethnicity, are not uncommon in human experience. Lionel Trilling once remarked that many of us admire both nonconformity and community, so we decide that "we are all nonconformists together." This is reminiscent of Sapir's comment that fashion is the result of the effort to satisfy two opposite desires: one wishes to stand out, to be unique and independent; yet one wishes to belong, to share the security of group identity. The variations in fashion which carry the impression of individual choice, but are kept within the bounds of group definitions, allow one to pursue these contradictory desires with a feeling of "adventurous safety."[42]

In their widely read *Habits of the Heart*, Robert Bellah and his colleagues stress their belief that the emphasis on independence has overwhelmed the experience of community.[43] They see ethnic "communities of memory" as ways of redressing the balance. Even if some lessening of the individualism-community dilemma can be achieved, however, it may be at the cost of reduction of tolerance across communal lines and of injury to the universalistic values and social structures that are increasingly essential in an interdependent world. Ethnicity is strong medicine. A little can improve the quality of life; large doses can kill us.[44]

AMALGAMATION

In a strictly biological sense, two or more groups are amalgamated when the genetic makeup of their members has been drawn from the same gene pool. Seen as a variable, groups are amalgamated *to the degree that* the genetic makeup of their members is drawn from the same gene pool. A more limited definition, however, is appropriate to our interests: Groups are amalgamated when no *socially visible* genetic differences separate their members.[45]

In chapter 1 I expressed the view that the most significant racial lines were those that were socially visible, not those that were genetic. In a similar sense amalgamation ought not to be seen in strictly genetic terms. Many similarities and differences in genetic makeup are disregarded in drawing racial lines. In a society, the process of racial designation starts with a biological substratum; but in the end it is socially constructed. Who is and who is not white varies from time to time and place to place. Who is and who is not black also varies. What can be called "perceptual amalgamation" occurs when a visible physical difference that formerly was thought to indicate a racial difference, and often an ethnic difference, is no longer thought to do so.

The blurring of genetic distinctions has been taking place in many parts of the world for thousands of years, opening up for societies a variety of ways in which they can draw lines distinguishing "genetically different" groups and individuals. These ways change with shifts in the degree and kinds of sensitivity to differences in ancestry, class, and culture. Before 1850, Williamson notes, free mulattos in the United States constituted a kind of third class. Relationships with whites "had a distinct West Indian flavor." In South Carolina and Louisiana there was some intermarriage. As tensions over slavery mounted, however, whites rejected this ambiguous way of drawing the line between African and European, a rejection that holds quite firm in most parts of the country even today.

To cite an extreme example: As late as 1983 the courts upheld a Mississippi law that classified a person with one thirty-second or more of African heritage—that is, with one great, great, great African grandparent—as a Negro. It is not clear how such a statute could have been applied. After millennia of contact among Europeans, Near Easterners, and Africans along with centuries of black-white contact in America, millions of "white" Americans would be classified as African Americans by this criterion.

In any event, with the repeal of the law, and a Supreme Court decision shortly thereafter declaring such laws unconstitutional, virtually all persons with a few African ancestors—perhaps one in eight (one great-grandparent)—are now "amalgamated" without any change in the biological mixture.

Estimates of the number of European Americans who are European-African Americans are necessarily rough. Stuckert has estimated that over 20 percent of the "white" population of the United States has some degree of African ancestry.[46] Since most of these ancestors are quite distant, their contributions to the gene pool are small: 1 to 2 percent in the case of whites; 20 to 30 percent in the case of blacks.

Current rates of intermarriage of "Europeans" with Native Americans, Hispanics, and migrants from Asia (rates that average, as we shall see, between one-quarter and one-third), indicate that the American multi-racial population is continuing to expand. A large proportion of migrants from the West Indies are of mixed ancestry. The distribution of Indians, Mestizos, and Europeans in Mexico is not well established (30%, 60%, and 10%?) and is even less clearly understood for Mexican Americans; but few would doubt that 50 percent or more of the latter have both European and Indian ancestors.

Thirty-five years ago, Edward Dozier, a Native American anthropologist, said to me that his studies had convinced him there were more persons with some Indian ancestry living as whites than there were as identified Indians. Asian and Hispanic ancestry among the socially white will grow quite rapidly, from an unknown base, if present rates of intermarriage continue. Only a small number "passing" in each generation has an expanding influence on each succeeding generation.

These crude estimates suggest that the amalgamation aspect of the assimilation process deserves careful attention. This is not because amalgamation by itself is particularly important. It is not in my judgment. It is, however, an important index of the degree of social separation among ethnic groups. Current rates of intermarriage among several groups in the United States are quite high; and the impact is cumulative. If one assumes that the offspring of the intermarried do not simply marry among themselves, but marry proportionately persons from their two parental lines; and if we assume also a relatively small difference in the birth rates of the intramarried and intermarried; then, even with no increase in rates of intermarriage, over three-fourths of the offspring in the smaller group (e.g., Mexican American) would be of mixed ancestry by the third generation.

In the period of two or more centuries during which western European states, the United States, and Russia dominated many "colonies" (to use that term to refer to a variety of power arrangements), the millennia-long process of ethnic and racial mixing was given a new push. Substantial numbers of Eurasians and others of mixed inheritance were added to the populations of India, Indonesia

(Dutch East Indies), the Philippines, Indochina, Hong Kong, Singapore, Sri Lanka (Ceylon), Hawaii, the areas dominated by Russia both before and after 1917, Guyana, South Africa, and many other parts of the world.[47]

"In the United States miscegenation of Negroes with Indians and whites occurred from the very beginning. . . . Equality of social status between Indians and Negroes favored intermingling. The whites had little interest in hindering it. . . . Whole tribes of Indians become untraceably lost in the Negro population of the South."[48] Perhaps a quarter of African Americans have some Native American ancestors.

Because Americans may tend to think in terms of broad racial categories we may overlook the continuing process of amalgamation, associated with the increasing rate of intermarriage. In recent years, the number of babies born to interracial couples has increased rapidly in the United States, from one percent of all births in 1968 (32,500) to 3.4 percent in 1989 (117,000).

Between 1968 and 1989 the total number of births increased by 15 percent. Children born to black-white couples increased over 500 percent (from 8,700 to 45,000). In 1968, children born to Native American couples outnumbered those born to Native American-white couples by two to one (13,800 to 6,800). By 1989, the proportions were nearly reversed, with 59 percent being born to Native American-white couples (21,000 to 15,000). The larger total may be due partly to an increase in the number who identify themselves as Native American.

A similar trend characterized Japanese Americans. The percentage of children born to Japanese American-white couples increased from 40 percent to 58 percent between 1968 and 1989. This shift is partly due to the fact that most Japanese Americans are now second or later generation. Their immigration rate is low. The trend among all "Asian and Pacific Islanders," to use the census term, is in the opposite direction, reflecting the large proportion of recent immigrants, among whom intermarriage rates are low. In 1978, Asian-white couples had 59 percent of the children, Asian American (both partners of Asian background) 41 percent. By 1989 the percentages were reversed.[49]

The United States is not unique in its rates of amalgamation. Eleven percent of the population of South Africa is Euro-African (coloured), not to mention those of mixed ancestry who are socially part of the European-descended or the African-descended group.

Although most households in the republics of the former Soviet Union are ethnically homogeneous, ethnically mixed households, used here as an index of amalgamation, ranged in 1970 from six to twenty-five percent.[50]

War and military occupation have further blurred ethnic and racial lines since World War II. Although the data are inevitably imprecise, American servicemen, white and black, are the fathers of perhaps 200,000 children in Japan, Korea, the Philippines, and Germany.

There are several possible outcomes of the continuing process of miscegenation. It can be the source of a new ethnic group that demands and is able to win a status separate from or superior to the "lower" of its ancestral groups, as illustrated by the Anglo-Indians during the time when India was a colony, the coloured in South Africa, or the Eurasians in Indonesia who, before independence from the Netherlands, won a substantial place in colonial administration.

More often, the mixed inheritance proves to be a barrier to other assimilative processes, often for generations. This is due both to the way they are viewed by the dominant ethnic groups (as in Japan, Germany, and Korea, where the children of American servicemen who have remained with their mothers have faced a great deal of discrimination) and to their own response to marginality, which has often been to assert strongly a single identity.[51]

Mixed inheritance can, however, be a factor in an assimilation process, not a barrier to it, in those situations where acculturation and integration are continuing. It seems probable that amalgamation need not be biologically complete (that is, no difference in ancestry between persons in formerly distinctive groups) before socially visible genetic differences fade. What is likely to happen is that as the other assimilative processes continue, the inherited lines that divide "us" from "them" will shift.[52] In the United States, for example, more and more persons of European background will see those who have a few Native American, Asian, or Hispanic ancestors as "amalgamated." This process will be slowest for those of predominantly African background. On an ideological level, Blacks have been less likely during the last twenty-five years than formerly to pay attention to differences in racial mixture among themselves ("black is beautiful"). Behavior of African Americans and of whites, however, sends a different message. Using data from a National Survey of Black Americans, 1979–1980, Keith and Herring found that variation in skin tone, other things being equal, affected educational attainment, occupation, and income. The disadvantage of darker African Americans, on the basis of this evidence, is an indication of persisting discrimination.[53] Some whites, however, have developed a more differentiated picture of black Americans, on the basis of variation in education, occupation, and other social characteristics.

In common usage, amalgamation refers only to racial blending. This is due not so much to the assumed larger genetic differences involved, but to the fact that early racial contacts were correlated with large differences in culture—in religion, language, and custom. Amalgamation must be studied as part of the assimilation process, in fact, because this historical background has made visible genetic differences almost everywhere an important factor in the nature of contact between groups.

I will not examine here the myths and conflicts surrounding the term *race*. Most of the criteria by which the human species is genetically differentiated today can be detected and measured only by use of sophisticated instruments and analysis. These have lead Dobzhansky to list thirty-four races, some of them the result of recent blends.[54] Perhaps it is sufficient here to say that the United States population, using it as an example, contains very large—and internally diverse—numbers from three categories or clusters of races. Based on their ancestral backgrounds, I will call them simply African, Asian, and European. Such crude categories are least satisfactory for the "Asians," since the ancestors of over two-thirds of them migrated to the Western Hemisphere ten- to twenty-thousand years ago. To describe our population in this simple-minded way, I hope, will remind us how arbitrary our conceptions of amalgamation can be. All of these groups are genetically blended to an important degree, and the blending continues, within and between them.

Amalgamation and the Other Assimilative Processes

It is generally recognized that groups that are biologically distinct from each other (have few common ancestors) and are distinguishable by appearance or genealogy as separate in inheritance, are less likely, other things being equal, to experience psychological, cultural, or structural assimilation. By the same token, where *amalgamation* has taken place or is taking place, other processes of assimilation are often made more likely. This statement of the influence of amalgamation must, however, be qualified, particularly if groups of unequal status are involved. The mixed population resulting from amalgamation can be assigned by the dominant group to lower status, given a separate and intermediate status, or absorbed into the higher status group, with widely varying effects on other processes of assimilation. Intermarriage can mean the transfer of a group's most acculturated members to the larger society, thus lowering the average level of acculturation among those who remain in the group.

Under some circumstances, individual choice plays an important part in determining the effect of amalgamation. In the United States, some persons with three Indian (Native American) grandparents and one white grandparent regard themselves and are regarded by others as white. Other persons with one Indian grandparent are Indian. The influence of biological assimilation, it is clear, can be understood only when it is examined in context with particular levels of identification, acculturation, and integration.[55]

It is important sociologically to distinguish between the individual and group levels of amalgamation. It is one thing to say that approximately 80 percent of Americans of primarily African descent have some European ancestors. It is something else to say that perhaps 20 to 30 percent of their "gene pool" is European. Partial amalgamation is creating a new "brown" race (Afro-European, with a small mixture of Native American ancestry). It is not, at this stage of American history, producing an amalgam.

Strictly speaking, all human beings, with a few pure white—albino—exceptions, are brown. The density of the melanin, carotene, and other pigments that, along with the environments, determine skin color, however, varies widely, producing color differences that range from the pale shade of the Laplanders to the dark brown of the residents of the rain forest of Central Africa. Also, within each group there is extensive variation.[56]

It is often emphasized that amalgamation occurs late in a succession of assimilative processes.[57] This is doubtless true of amalgamation resulting from intermarriage, which is likely to occur only after extensive acculturation and integration. Where two groups are very unequal in power and status, however, or when migration from a dominant colonial power includes mostly males, sexual exploitation can occur in the early period of contact. A semilegal concubine system may develop.[58] Amalgamation may thereafter decline, even though acculturation continues. At a still later stage, if prejudice and inequality decline, intermarriage may become more common.

Although amalgamation is usually regarded as a one-way process, like the other aspects of assimilation it can be reversed. The proportion of a given group's biological inheritance that comes from other groups will decline if there is a differential birthrate between the full-blood and the mixed-blood segments. It is also reduced by "passing"—the shifting of persons of mixed ancestry from one group to another, in terms of their own sense of identity and their identification by others. Passing may be secretive or it may be openly encouraged, as when a dominant group absorbs those of mixed heritage. Of course the passing that reduces the degree of amalgamation in one group increases it in the receiving group: as we have noted, the "white" population of the United States has absorbed several million persons with some degree of African and Native American ancestry (the latter made up partly of those of Mexican background), thus experiencing an unknown but significant degree of biological assimilation. A similar process has occurred, of course, and is occurring at varying levels of intensity in many other societies, from South Africa to Brazil, India, southern and western Europe, and elsewhere.

INTERMARRIAGE

Although I have referred to intermarriage several times in this discussion of amalgamation, the two terms are not synonymous. There can be intermarriage without amalgamation (childless couples). There can be amalgamation without intermarriage (extramarital children), which in some contexts is the commoner pattern. Nevertheless, at the present time, the extent of intermarriage is probably the best index available of the levels of amalgamation in various inter-ethnic settings. For that reason I discuss it here, rather than in the section on integration, where it might as reasonably have been placed. It is often used, in fact, as the best measure of the extent of integration between two groups.

The definition of intermarriage is not self-evident.[59] Studies that use national or other survey data are almost always limited by the one-variable categories available, so that European Americans who marry Mexican Americans or African Americans are intermarried, however much the partners may be similar in other ways. They may be alike in level of education, social class, religion, native language, and favored leisure activities, yet be seen as intermarried if they differ ethnically or racially. There is a substantial literature examining religious intermarriage, which often has an ethnic element; but seldom are the ways in which the partners are alike given full attention. This indicates, of course, the way in which ethnicity or race or religion are seen to be the critical indicators of difference or similarity.

If only one item is used to determine who is and who is not intermarried we have a simple yes-or-no measure. If several items are used, indicating in how many significant ways a couple differ or are alike, intermarriage is seen as a variable. A couple can be more or less intermarried. Those from different ethnic backgrounds but similar in education, native language, and religion are less intermarried than those who are different not only in ethnicity but also in one or more of the other attributes.

At first it strains our imaginations to transform a long-held dichotomy into a variable. In fact, I will not do it in citing various studies of ethnic intermarriages that use a single variable. It may be useful, however, to keep the idea of a scale in mind, recognizing that without it the causes and effects of ethnic intermarriage will be only imperfectly understood.[60] We need a "thick" description, and in its absence will have to interpret cautiously the significance of intermarriage.

Intermarriage can be defined as marriage across a socially significant line of distinction. Not all will agree, however, that a given line ought thus to be regarded. In Honolulu, I once asked a friend of Japanese and one of Chinese background whether marriage between a Japanese American and a Chinese American was an intermarriage. Both said "of course." When I asked if marriages between Americans of English and German background were intermarriages, both said "of course not." On the whole, studies of intermarriages deal with the generally acknowledged "of course" variety; but we need to be aware of possible disagreements and of the unexamined assumptions on which the designation rests.

Attitudes of the majority, it should be noted, are not an entirely reliable indicator of the probable rate of intermarriage in a society, since only a small percentage of the majority intermarrying can mean a large percentage of a minority. In Britain, about 80 percent are opposed to interracial marriages, yet approximately 20 per-

TABLE 4.3
Rates of Individual Marriage Exogamy by Ethnicity and Sex
Labour Force Survey, United Kingdom[61]

| | Exogamy with Whites | | Exogamy with the Other Specified Groups | |
| | Percent | | Percent | |
	Men	Women	Men	Women
West Indian	22	10	8	2
African	27	11	19	17
Indian	8	4	3	2
Pakistani	7	2	3	7
Bangladeshi	11	—	3	—

cent of Britain's black and Asian marriages are to a white partner. Another 12 percent are inter-ethnic among those who have migrated fairly recently to the United Kingdom.

Factors That Influence Rates of Inter-ethnic Marriage

Families are widely regarded as the major force sustaining ethnic groups. To put this in the opposite way: marriage across ethnic lines is seen as a major indicator of assimilation. This can mean three different things: the assimilation of a smaller or less powerful group into another, a dominant group; the co-assimilation of both into a new group, a new ethnicity or pan-ethnic cluster; or the beginnings of a new society formed out of the blending, the amalgamation, of several ethnic groups into one people.

The last of these processes has probably happened often in human history, in centuries-long consolidations of small groups into larger ones. Tendencies in that direction are apparent in many multi-ethnic societies today. They are not very powerful, however, nor easily visible, because the time span is long and because such societies are steadily changing as a result of the addition of people from other societies.

The first two processes, however, are quite common today, especially in urban societies. They are seldom carried to completion, at least in a time frame of two or three generations. Nevertheless they can strongly affect the ethnic order of a society. Rates of inter-marriage reflect the extent of acculturation, integration, and identity shifts of individuals; but in turn, they affect those processes and add to them the influence of amalgamation.

There is an enormous literature dealing with intermarriage in the United States. I will use it to help answer a more general question: What demographic, attitudinal, historical, legal, and cultural factors affect the rates of inter-ethnic marriage? Each of the factors listed here should be preceded by the phrase "other things being equal," and their interdependence should be recognized.

- To the degree that integration and acculturation have increased in a society, some of the barriers to intermarriage are reduced and, as a result of more inter-ethnic contact, opportunities to meet are increased.
- Individuals from large groups, or those who make up a large proportion of a population, have low rates of ethnic intermarriage.
- In the urban world we seldom "marry the girl next door"; but propinquity plays a part. The more homogeneous a neighborhood or community the lower the rate of intermarriage.
- Some ethnic boundaries coincide with lingual, religious, or class boundaries. When that is true, intermarriage is less likely.
- Individual attitudes, values, prejudices related to other ethnic groups affect the intermarriage rate, often in a way that corresponds rather closely to a scale of "social distance."
- Laws, widely shared customs, and religious proscriptions are often involved in drawing the boundaries separating the ethnically preferred partners from the tolerated and the proscribed. In some settings such legal and religious norms are nearly definitive. In contemporary America, however, all legal barriers to ethnic or racial intermarriage have been removed, customary norms have been softened, and strong religious opposition has been reduced in most instances.
- Persons of mixed ethnic ancestry, indicating earlier intermarriages, are more likely to intermarry than those of single ethnic ancestry. This is closely correlated with the number of generations they have been resident in a society.
- Marital selections are arranged in some societies, made with strong family influence in some, and based on individual choice and romantic love in others. Of course all three influences may be involved in many instances. Where individual choice is strongest, the likelihood of intermarriage is increased.

Although these eight factors have been derived from studies of ethnic intermarriage in the United States, some of which I shall be discussing, it seems probable that they have wider applicability.[62]

Several technical adjustments are needed to interpret inter-marriage rates based on survey or census data: Data on heterogamy are sometimes given as the number of intermarriages and some-times as the number of individuals who are intermarried. Since the proportions derived from the same numbers differ, if one is a calcu-lation of the group rate and another of the individual rate, quite dif-ferent interpretations can follow. It takes two to make an *intra-marriage*, but only one from a particular group to make it, for that group, an *intermarriage*. If 40 percent of the marriages of urban Na-tive Americans are to persons of other ethnic groups, then 25 per-cent of individual Native Americans are intermarried. The sixty homogamous marriages would include 120 Native Americans; the forty heterogamous ones would include forty, or one-quarter of the total number of Native Americans involved.[63]

Rates of ethnic intermarriage are also affected by population ratios. If marriage partners were a matter of sheer chance, so far as ethnicity is concerned, then Italian-American women would wed Italian-American men about five percent of the time, since men with at least some Italian ancestry make up 5.2 percent of the rel-evant population. In fact, the Italian-American women married men of their own ethnicity 39.5 percent of the time; they outmar-ried 60.5 percent of the time.[64] If this seems to be a high proportion of out-marriages, one should compare it with the fact that women of Italian background were nineteen times more likely to marry men of Italian background than were other women. Since we do not have adequate data on the eight factors that influence rates of inter-marriage that we discussed earlier, we cannot assume that the eth-nic factor accounts for all of the difference. It does furnish a way, however, to compare groups on the extent to which they exceed the proportion of in-group marriages that one would expect on the basis of random choice—that is, with no ethnic factor influencing the results.

From the same data set, Lieberson and Waters note that 48.6 percent of German American women in-married, compared with 39.5 percent of the Italian-American women. However, since men of at least some German background made up 24.5 percent of all hus-bands, chance might have accounted for half of the German in-marriages, but less than one-eighth of the Italian in-marriages. What appears to be a higher rate of exogamy among Italian-Americans is, when seen this way, a much lower rate.

Among African American women, 98.7 percent in-married. By chance one would expect 7.4 percent, the proportion of African

American men in this sample. Thus less than 8 percent of the in-marriages would have occurred if only chance were operating.[65] These are 1980 data, however, and the rate of interracial marriage among African American men is higher than the rate for women. In total, black-white marriages numbered 65,000 in 1970, but 246,000 in 1992—nearly four times as many. There were also 32,000 black-other races, 883,000 white-other races, and 1.2 million Hispanic-other ethnic group marriages.[66] Such an increase indicates the steady if not dramatic shift in many of the factors that influence rates of racial intermarriage. Yet this rapid increase from a low base leaves black-white marriages much less common than other racial mixtures.

Altogether, mixed-race couples in the United States have in-creased by more than 300 percent since 1970, while the total popu-lation has increased less than 25 percent.

Another constraint on intermarriage, this one purely numeri-cal, exists when one group makes up more than half of a population. In the United States, for example, about 65 percent are Protestants. If everyone of the 35 percent who are not Protestants intermarried with them, 30 percent of the Protestants would be left to marry among themselves. To put this same fact another way, if 30 percent of Catholics marry Protestants, that is only 12 percent of Protes-tants, since they are about 2½ times as numerous.[67]

Measures of intermarriage sometimes refer to the group mem-berships of the partners at birth and sometimes to their adult iden-tities, which may not be the same. Persons of mixed ethnic ancestry may shift to that of the spouse, or to look at the religious aspects of ethnicity, for which the data are best, one or the other partner may convert. Data from the 1980 General Social Survey of the National Opinion Research Center indicate that 59 percent of Catholic men and 68 percent of Catholic women were married to persons who had been raised as Catholics. At the time of the survey, however, 80 per-cent of the Catholic men and 83 percent of the women were married to Catholic spouses, indicating that just about half of the non-Catholic spouses had converted. Among Protestants, 84 percent of the men and 80 percent of the women were married to persons who had been raised as Protestants; but 92 percent of their wives and 88 percent of their husbands were Protestants at the time of the survey, indicating that about half of the non-Protestants had also converted.

Thus rates of intermarriage are inadequate guides to the extent of shifts in ethnic or religious identity. Not only does one need to ask whether one or the other partner converts to the religion of the spouse, but also to ask in what faith the children are raised, and what are the trends. A recent survey of the Jewish population in the United States by the Council of Jewish Federations noted that between 1970 and 1990 the Jewish population had increased by 2 percent while the total population had increased by 22 percent. Religious intermarriage accounts for part of the difference. The rate has increased steadily from 9 percent among Jews married before 1965, to 52 percent among those married since 1985.

The rates of conversion of the non-Jewish partner to Judaism are lower than those formerly reported: 18 percent among those married before 1965; 9 percent among those married since 1985.

Among the children of Jewish-gentile marriages, 28 percent have been raised as Jews, 31 percent in no religion, and 41 percent in another faith.[68]

These trends raise a dilemma for American Jews. The high rates of intermarriage can be seen as a threat to the survival of a group with virtually no population growth. Yet America is treasured for its openness and its "unprecedented acceptance" of Jews. As a result of the higher rates of immigration of Jews in the early 1990s, the dilemma may be less sharp for a time. This effect will be small, however, so long as current attitudes and demographic trends continue.

In the United States, during the last few decades, laws forbidding racial intermarriages have been repealed, religious proscriptions have been modified or removed, and individual attitudes have become somewhat more accepting, although not without some fluctuation. According to Gallup polls, in 1968 76 percent of those interviewed opposed interracial marriages. This had fallen to 50 percent by 1983, with 43 percent approving and 7 percent giving no answer. Sixty-three percent of persons 18–19 years of age approved. Data from the 1990 General Social Survey allow some ethnic comparisons. Respondents were asked how they felt about a close relative marrying a person from various groups, a somewhat different way of asking the question. The percentages for the national sample are given in table 4.4.

As shown by the data in table 4.4, 16.3 percent would object or strongly object to a close relative marrying a Jew; 57.5 percent a Black; 42.4 percent, an Asian American; and 40.5 percent, a Hispanic American. When the data indicating how each group felt about intermarriage are compared with the general sample, we find

TABLE 4.4
Acceptance of Intermarriage[69] (percentages)

	Jews	Blacks	Asian Americans	Hispanic Americans
Strongly favor	7.2	7.0	2.9	4.4
Favor	12.3	4.5	6.6	6.9
Neither favor nor oppose	63.1	29.9	49.4	46.4
Oppose	11.3	25.1	27.4	25.2
Strongly oppose	5.0	32.4	15.0	15.3
Do not know	1.2	1.1	1.8	1.4

that the percentages are quite similar except for African Americans, whose opposition was stronger than that of the total sample. The percentages of each group that would be opposed to a relative marrying a person outside the group were: 16.8 percent among Jews, 65.3 percent among African Americans, 41.7 percent among Asian Americans, and 41.2 percent among Hispanic Americans.[70] These percentages are inversely correlated, as we might expect, with the actual rates of ethnic intermarriage of these groups.

Minority ethnic groups that face discrimination and segregation are caught in a dilemma in dealing with the question of intermarriage. They oppose discrimination and exclusion, but they may also oppose intermarriage. As the barriers they deplore go down, intermarriage goes up.

African Americans have, through the years, responded to this dilemma in a variety of ways: Frederick Douglass, more than a century ago, was proud to be black, but he also emphasized a universalistic view of the future that tied that pride to the right to be on equal and intimate terms with non-blacks. For W. E. B. DuBois, black pride said no to intermarriage but insisted on protecting the abstract right to intermarry. More recently, those who have emphasized black power say more directly: black people marry other black people.[71] And today, as we have noted, about 35 percent say they would have no objection to a close relative out-marrying.

Summary

A majority of marriages in the United States are ethnically homogamous. One must quickly add, however, that trends in several of the factors that affect the rates of intermarriage (I have noted eight above) are making intermarriage more likely.

Among European Americans, marriages across ethnic lines are almost without restrictions. This does not mean that they occur in random fashion, so far as ethnicity is concerned, because group size, residence, time in America, and other factors continue to play a part. Forty percent of Italian-American women marry men of Italian background. But 60 percent do not; and many of the spouses are of mixed ethnic background.

Thirty to 40 percent of Native Americans marry persons of other ancestry. Hispanic American intermarriages rates are from 15 to 50 percent, depending on the Hispanic group involved, the area of residence, and the generation of residence in the United States. Intermarriage rates among Asian Americans fall within the same range, with the same factors influencing the trends. African American intermarriage rates are low—from 2 to 6 percent—but they are highest among the youngest cohorts.

The United States is rather rapidly expanding its Native-European American, Asian-European American, and Hispanic-European American populations. It has long since created a mainly African-European American population. America may not be a "melting-pot," except for its population from Europe; but it is much more than a tossed salad.

There are numerous and somewhat contradictory outcomes of the current trends. Intermarriage rates do not need to be high to affect other assimilative processes. When many who are themselves intra-married have relatives and friends who are intermarried, contacts and attitudes begin to change. Even the perception of what constitutes an intermarriage changes; the lines within the large pan-ethnic clusters begin to disappear.

The rather high rates of intermarriage of Asian Americans, Native Americans and Mexican Americans (who in a majority of cases also have Indian ancestors) indicate clearly that some generalized "racial difference" factor is of little help in accounting for the extent and direction of intermarriage. Historical, cultural, demographic, and status factors are the critical ones. Some of them are becoming more favorable to intermarriage, with the result that some racial lines are continuing to become less clear. Amalgamation continues.

This does not mean that ethnic identities will disappear. They have a continuing lively place in American political, economic, and educational matters. Identities are reenforced by the struggles to maintain advantages or to oppose discrimination. Some who are able to choose and others who have no choice will embrace their ethnic identities as "havens in a heartless world" and guides in times of anomie. Those of mixed ancestry do not necessarily assimilate into a dominant group. They may be blocked out; they may try to protect what they see as a precious cultural treasure; they may become leaders of a persecuted group. Their numbers may be replenished by immigrants.

For many others, however, ethnic identities are becoming situational, symbolic, even recreational.

Granted its "head start" in ethnic relations, its democratic polity, and its enormous resources, what the United States does or does not do to create a tolerant, non-discriminatory, multi-ethnic society, where ancestral identities do not dominate more inclusive human identities nor dictate individual choices, can be of enormous importance to a world in which similar ethnic complexities have become almost universal.

Chapter 5

Ethnicity, Stratification, and Discrimination: A Field Theoretical Approach

In most multi-ethnic societies the several groups in the ethnic order vary in wealth, power, and status. Ethnicity is a major factor in the stratification system. In many instances, the political and social struggles of those most seriously disadvantaged to improve their situation are major forces of social change. At the same time, an established ethnic stratification system is very difficult to tear down. How did it get built? Why is it so tough? Are there offsetting forces?

The Sources of Discrimination

Perhaps we can begin to answer these questions by describing a kind of historical parable. Two groups collide as a result of one group migrating into the territory of the other. Each group believes itself superior to the other; but the greater economic and military power of the invader gives one kind of reality to their "superiority," as when Europeans overwhelmed the Native Americans. There were great economic and military advantages to be derived from this domination—the first cause of Indian subjugation. To force them into and keep them in minority status was profitable. This seems quite crass and unjust from the contemporary perspective, as it probably did to many European settlers. Most made it seem less unjust, however, not by eliminating the discrimination, but by developing a comforting rationalization: The Indian is "a lying, thieving, murdering savage." Not everybody believed this, but it became such a well-established part of the culture that many persons who had never seen an Indian "knew" what all of them were like. Ethnic stereotypes thus help to reenforce the system of ethnic discrimination based, in the first instance, on economic and military interests.

To these two sources we can add a third. Some individuals in a society carry heavy loads of hostility. Perhaps because life has been cruel to them, their most serious needs for security and affection unsatisfied and their expectations frustrated by neglect or capricious treatment from parents and others, they have come to believe that the world is a jungle. They have a powerful urge to strike out at a world which has treated them so badly, as they see it. But they also need security. Therefore they do not attack those who are powerful or those who are close to them. If society furnishes them an ethnic group that is relatively powerless, however, one that is characterized—so the stereotype teaches them—by evil and inferior ways, and that is sufficiently different and distant that they feel no attachment to its members, then they can vent their hostility on this group, feeling all the while that they have struck a blow for freedom and justice.

Insofar as the hostility results from neglect and cruelty of one's own group, it may be displaced onto members of an ethnic minority because it is relatively powerless and alien. However, guilt as well as hostility may be shifted—that is, projected. Many European settlers may have felt guilty for things they had done: Hundreds of thousands of Indians were killed by those who were in the process of taking over their land. Granted the gains thus attained, however, and the comforting stereotypes, this guilt seldom came fully into view. It was projected: It is not I, it is he who is guilty. This is a very effective disguise. It follows the principle of the "big lie": no one

would think of believing a story like that unless it were the truth—
yet it nearly reverses the truth. One would almost think that it had
been the Indian who had invaded Europe, driven back the inhabitants, cut their population to one-third of its original size, unilater-
ally changed treaties, and brought the dubious glories of firewater
and firearms.

Thus we have economic conflict, cultural training, and some
intricate personality mechanisms reenforcing each other, helping to
maintain stratified ethnic orders.

With three such roots—I shall call them structure, culture,
and character—ethnic discrimination is not easily reduced. And
that is not the end of the story. As it persists, discrimination is built
into the normal operating procedures of institutions. In some settings, it no longer requires much personal animus, cultural support,
or perception by the dominant group that they gain by it. What today is often called "institutional racism" is, in the first instance, an
effect of the three basic causes. For that reason, I find attempts to
explain ethnic discrimination primarily as a "result" of institutional racism of little value. Nevertheless, in analyzing the cybernetic systems so common in the social world, we cannot neglect
it as part of the tough system. Established procedures, patterns of
seniority, and social networks perpetuate discrimination without
members of the advantaged groups thinking much about it. It is
partly "indirect," an effect that has outlived the original sources. It
is to some degree ". . . independent of the dominant group's present
'tastes,' attitudes, or awareness."[1]

Still another influence adds toughness to systems of discrimination: the very victims of such systems, in their efforts to mitigate
their condition, in some of their responses designed to deflect the
blows of an oppressive society, can reenforce that very system. If an
oppressed ethnic group fights back (and they are seldom passive targets), it may increase the hostility and the belief in the justice of
their own ways among members of the dominant group.

In addition, there are powerful pressures which, in some measure, make the oppressed into the kinds of persons the stereotypes
say they are. Many Indians did become cruel, lacking in ambition,
untrustworthy. If, on the basis of the belief that they are inferior, one
gives to a group poor schools, poor jobs, few opportunities for self-
respect, and little chance for advancement, one soon proves the belief to be partly true, for one has created the conditions for its

reenforcement. The ethnic stratification system is bound into a vicious circle.

I want to state this very carefully. There are now those who emphasize, without reference to the total system, the responsibility of an oppressed ethnic group to solve its own problems. They point to the gains, however modest, in reducing the root causes, and then say Let those who have suffered past discrimination cure themselves of its ill effects.

This is one part of the response of many leaders of minority ethnic groups; but it is put alongside sharp criticism of persistent discrimination. Among African Americans, for example, it is an important theme in the work of W. E. B. DuBois, Martin Luther King, and Jesse Jackson. Some other African American leaders, however, give the self-help theme major—sometimes almost exclusive—emphasis. That was the case with Booker T. Washington and, on the current scene, with Shelby Steele, Thomas Sowell, Glenn Loury, and Supreme Court Justice Clarence Thomas.

More commonly, however, it is a member of a dominant ethnic group who relies most fully on a self-help approach to the reduction of discrimination. Peter Hamill, for example, has expressed this view in "Breaking the Silence: a Letter to a Black Friend." He is not a social scientist but a prominent publicist, whose pop sociology is probably not far from that of many white Americans. After citing what he saw as major reductions in discrimination, he wrote to his black friend, "Instead, you have retreated defensively into the cliches of glib racialism. Your argument is simple: the black Underclass is the fault of the white man. Not some white men. *All* white men. You cite various examples of a surging white racism: the antibusing violence in liberal Boston, the Bernhard Goetz and Howard Beach cases in liberal New York, a resurgent Klan in some places, continued reports of whites using force to keep blacks from moving into their neighborhoods, white cops too quick to arrest, abuse, or shoot down black suspects, persistent examples of racial steering in middle-class housing, the Al Campanis controversy. Certainly racism continues to be real in the United States; only a fool would deny it."

After such a statement, one might expect a fairly complex analysis of causes and a multifaceted policy. What we get is an exclusive focus on point 6 in figure 1, cut off from the system of which it is a part: "So I've come to believe," Hamill writes, "that if there is a solution to the self-perpetuating Underclass, it must come from blacks, specifically from the black middle class. Blacks might have no other choice."[2]

We have no other choice than to be wiser than Hamill.

THE CYCLE OF CAUSES OF ETHNIC DISCRIMINATION

To emphasize self-help as the "solution" to ethnic discrimination is to tell a seriously incomplete story. What in the first instance was an effect is made into a basic cause, history and biography having been forgotten. To start with the responses of a disadvantaged ethnic group (often seen stereotypically) in an effort to understand discrimination is the essence of folly. To start there in forming policies designed to reduce discrimination is futile.

Once the three root causes have been identified and reduced, however, attention to these effects-turned-causes is essential, as part of the larger view. In figure 5.1, I attempt to describe the interactions within this system of ethnic discrimination, treating it first as a closed system, unaffected by any outside forces, to emphasize how tough a social structure it can be.

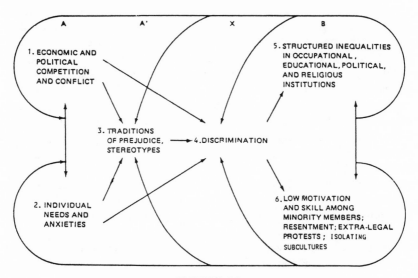

FIGURE 5.1
The Field Context of Ethnic Discrimination
(Adapted from Simpson and Yinger, 1972: 157.)

Seen as closed system, the message of figure 5.1 is: This is the process by which a dominant ethnic group is led into a pattern of discrimination to its own advantage and is able to maintain that pattern despite many forces seeking to change it.[3] A time sequence is implied, moving from left to right and then back to the left through a series of feedback reenforcements; but this time sequence is not intrinsic to the argument. However started, as suggested in figure 5.1, discrimination can develop into a very tough system in which even the victims play a supporting part.

The different points in figure 5.1 require brief explication, even though it is the general thesis presented there—that ethnic discrimination is perpetuated by an interacting system of forces—with which we are mainly concerned. I take it as a given that economic and political resources are scarce (by definition) and that their allocation will involve some forms of competition and conflict in most situations. Class, region, age, and sex often furnish the critical dividing lines along which competition and conflict form: and so also do ethnic groups. History and the contemporary world are filled with illustrations of a process whereby one ethnic group is able to designate others as outsiders or inferiors not deserving of political and economic equality. If one thinks of this part of the system of discrimination as the starting point, not yet reenforced by other parts of the system, one stresses the military, economic, and political forces that are more available to some than to others.[4]

There is a clear analytic distinction between economic and political discrimination, and at times a group may find itself possessed of one power more than the other, as in Malaysia. More commonly, however, the two are empirically connected, with political power being used to bolster economic advantage or vice versa.[5]

Tendencies toward discrimination and prejudice do not vary simply with different locations in the social structure, with different opportunities for economic and political advantage. As indicated by point 2 in figure 5.1, they vary also with levels of anxiety and individual needs. Ancient wisdom has been supported by contemporary research that shows how hostility is often displaced and guilt frequently projected onto 'outsiders.' *The Authoritarian Personality*[6] and the vast related literature stressing the personality sources of discrimination seem to me to exaggerate the importance of those sources, particularly if they are examined in isolation from the system of which they are a part. Nevertheless, there is substantial evidence that high levels of hostility and anxiety, the need to reduce the confusing complexity of the social world, the burden of self-doubt, and other psychological forces play a part in inter-ethnic discrimination.[7]

In some situations, personality factors are of major significance; in others they are minimal. In well-established "stable" discriminatory systems, reenforcement from personality needs tends to be slight. In systems where economic, political, and cultural factors are unstable, with divergent forces at work, personality factors have greater impact.

In my judgment, economic and political factors are primary in the origins of a system of discrimination. It is unlikely that authoritarianism or other personal tendencies would express themselves in the form of ethnic or racial discrimination in the absence of the belief by many that discrimination serves an economic or political advantage—thus giving it a kind of "rational" justification. Granted economic and political conflict, however, personality factors add power to the system of discrimination. Once tied into the system, they give it greater strength, because they are more impervious to changing social conditions; they rest on more irrational and unconscious grounds. Discrimination based on economic and political factors is more sensitive to changing conditions and shifting interests.

We need say little about point 3 in figure 5.1. Persistent discrimination against minority ethnic groups becomes "justified" by a tradition of prejudice. Stereotypes "explain" why certain groups are in disadvantaged positions. Even those persons who in no way stand to gain economically or politically absorb the culture of prejudice and thus help to perpetuate discriminatory ethnic patterns for others.[8]

Parts of the culture of ethnicity are the sets of contrasting images of one's own and of other ethnic groups. The reciprocal of stereotypes applied to others is the ethnocentrism that many, probably most, ethnic groups apply to themselves. Ethnocentrism is the belief in the unique value and rightness of one's own group and its way of living.[9] It may seem, under some circumstances, to serve a protective, morale-building purpose. Under different conditions, however, ethnocentrism (We are the best; We are number one) can add inflexibility and blindness that prevent actions needed for the group's own welfare as well as for peaceful intergroup relations.[10]

Since many groups value tolerance and hospitality, along with their ethnocentric views, dividing lines between some groups and some individuals may be much more permeable than a strict theory of universal ethnocentrism implies.[11] In any given ethnic-conflict situation, the depth and the breadth of in-group and out-group stereotyping require careful analysis. In chapter 3 we discussed the violence dividing the former republics of Yugoslavia, violence that has cost tens of thousands of causalties, particularly among the Bosnians, but also among the Croatians and Serbs. Four or more states now stand—or perhaps I should say lie—where Yugoslavia stood. The several centuries of historical entanglement and several decades of common citizenship have scarcely softened their mutually antagonistic ethnocentrisms and stereotypes. These beliefs came easily to the surface when stressful times (the near-collapse of worldwide communism, severely restricted immigration to Western Europe, economic weakness) increased the strength among each group of self-interest policies. This is true especially of the largest and strongest of the former republics. An almost fanatical emphasis on the differences among them has served to justify a reign of terror.

Discrimination flows from these mutually reenforcing structural, personality, and cultural sources, even in relatively peaceful times. As it persists, it gets built into institutional patterns that embody the vested interests of the dominant ethnic groups.[12] Occupations, education, politics, and religion reflect and reenforce the status structure, as suggested by point 5 of figure 5.1. What is often called "institutional racism" becomes the most visible expression of the system of discrimination, of its persistence and its self-fulfilling qualities, as ethnic groups caught in poor jobs, with poor educational opportunities and little political power experience a vicious circle of forces that keep them trapped.

Stable, institutionalized discrimination is not the only consequence of the persistent disadvantages experienced by ethnic minorities. Those caught in the vicious circle are less likely to acquire necessary skills; they may become acquiescent or poorly motivated; feelings of efficacy—the sense that they can control their own lives—may be low; they may form isolating subcultures that reenforce the system of discrimination; they may develop a strong resentment, expressed in illegal protests that seem to the dominant ethnic groups to justify their own actions (point 6, figure 5.1). In this sense the victims of discrimination help to perpetuate it.[13]

As I have described it, the system of ethnic discrimination is extraordinarily resilient and tough. Efforts to change one part of the system may be frustrated by adaptations in other parts that restore the earlier arrangements. Racially segregated and discriminatory schooling in the United States in some cities has been modified by judicial and legal acts only to be reestablished by demographic trends, by the expansion of private schools, by the system of housing allocation, and by continuing and sometimes accelerating suburbanization of the white population. Opportunities for ethnic minorities may be increased but only partially exploited, due to lack of resources, preparation, or motivation.[14] The sense that one is a member of a group mainly under external rather than internal control,[15] the perception if not the full reality of lack of choice,[16] or a pervading feeling of alienation[17] may prevent action needed to take advantage of the new opportunities. Violent protest against ethnic discrimination may change the majority somewhat;[18] but at the same time it may lower the trust within the minority community that is essential to consolidate the gains.[19]

THE CYCLE OF CAUSES SUPPORTING TOLERANCE AND EQUALITY

It is time, however, to emphasize that seldom is the system of discrimination as tightly closed as the explication of figure 5.1 would make it appear to be. In most societies one can also describe a system of non-discrimination, an interacting group of forces that support some social mobility and equality. Those forces may be less visible, less "newsworthy," and, to be sure, less powerful. To neglect them, however, is to weaken one's analysis of ethnic relationships. In some settings there is a culture of pluralism, ranging from a minimum of live-and-let-live among ethnic groups to a more expansive sense of a shared larger society. Interdependence and common interests, as well as cultural differences, may be recognized. And ethnic minorities may possess resources which, when mobilized, enable them to challenge their status assignment. Thus we need to study, in any society, the balance of strength between two open systems that are part of the larger field of forces determining ethnic relationships.

In figure 5.2 is outlined what I shall call a system of equality, a beneficent cycle. Although it is drawn as a closed system, I emphasize that it is in fact open to many situational influences.[20] The pattern is parallel to that of figure 5.1. Structural, personality, and

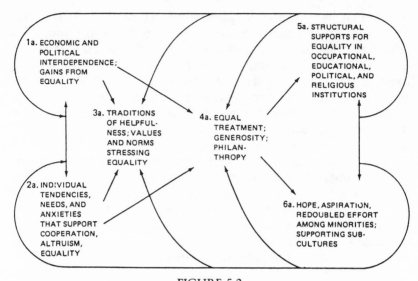

FIGURE 5.2
The Field Context of Forces Supporting Equality among Ethnic Groups
Adapted from J. Milton Yinger, 1983: 402

cultural factors are shown leading to equality of treatment. That
outcome is consolidated both in dominant institutional forms and
in the motives, values, and community structures of ethnic minorities. Although research dealing with this positive system is less
common than research dealing with the negative system of discrimination, some recent work has begun at least to examine its constit-
uent parts. In this interdependent world, poorly trained and
motivated workers, poverty-stricken customers, and alienated citizens are recognized by dominant groups, in some contexts, as costly
burdens rather than exploitable resources.

In this system, gains from equality, as suggested by point 1a,
not gains from exploitation, are emphasized. On the individual level
(point 2a) humankind is seen not simply as "the imperial animal"
dominated by aggressive impulses, but as a creature selected in part
by a capacity for altruism and cooperation.[21] Religious and political
ideologies (point 3a) consolidate these tendencies into norms and
values that stress helpfulness and cooperation.[22]

These structural, individual, and cultural forces lead almost
everywhere, according to this thesis, to some degree of equal treatment, generosity, or philanthropy (4a). Although these may be

shown most often within fairly narrow "fraternal" circles, under favorable conditions they cross over ethnic and societal lines. They are expressed not only in individual actions, but are also embodied in institutional form (5a), giving them greater continuity and influence. In India, particularly since Gandhi and the post-independence constitution, ethnic groups are legally equal. (The traditional hierarchies of the varna and caste systems have not, of course, been eliminated, but the Dalits—the Scheduled Castes—and other disprivileged groups have increased opportunities for status improvement.) Despite the persistent ethnic violence, India has maintained a democratic polity. And the United States, during about the same period, has had a veritable constitutional and legal revolution that has weakened the institutional supports for ethnic discrimination while strengthening the institutional supports for equality. These changes are in place and affect our daily lives, despite the vivid demonstrations that discriminatory forces remain strong.

Point 6a suggests that, seen from the perspective of this "equality system," individual members of minority ethnic groups are not simply helpless victims, governed by feelings of powerlessness and hopelessness.[23] The dominant institutions and policies as well as the perceptions of ethnic minorities support aspirations to change. Minor improvement in opportunities may stimulate major improvement in effort.[24] Even the crushing conditions of slavery in the United States did not prevent active—even if often disguised—resistance and creative adaptations on the part of the oppressed.[25] The caste system in India has often unrecognized fluidity to it that has permitted occupational and status change. Sanskritization, westernization, changes in religious identity, and other processes are factors in that fluidity.[26] In *India: A Million Mutinies Now*, Naipaul sees the constant turmoil not as disintegration but as a sign that the dispossessed of India are struggling out of their old inertia, rejecting rejection.[27]

In the contemporary scene, dominant groups may be ready to permit, even to encourage, the training and ambition of individual minority-group members, even when they are far less supportive of significant change in the social structure. Or, without intending to stimulate minority activity, majority ethnic groups may create the perception of greater choice. Such personal influences can combine with impersonal demographic trends to strengthen processes of change. Danigelis[28] suggests such a combination at work in connection with political activity among African Americans:

Coalescing factors
(e.g., urbanization)   ↘

                Norms of   High political
                political → activity level
                activism   among blacks

Hope of surmounting ↗
barriers

The equality system suggests a beneficent cycle, not a vicious cycle. A series of interacting forces keeps alive the possibility, and to some degree the reality, of change toward greater equality. To realize the potential of this system often requires that individual resources be aggregated by a group. Many of the religious and political movements among ethnic minorities are efforts to attain such aggregation. The right to vote is of little value if, as often happens, it is disregarded by many minority group members. When opportunity and a growing sense of efficacy combine, however, minorities can have significant impact in competitive political systems.

Cultural and historical factors strongly affect the accumulation of economic resources. Small amounts may be efficiently aggregated into a fund of value for economic growth within a minority community, as by a rotating credit association[29] Or they may be inefficiently aggregated at great overhead cost by a pseudo-financial institution such as numbers gambling.[30] But even "playing the numbers" is a sign of some economic potential that, under conditions of greater hope, could be used for economic growth and development.

Is There Evidence of a "System of Equality" in South Africa?

A severe test of the search for a system of equality, paralleling and to some degree offsetting the system of discrimination, is to look in South Africa. There, against a background of decades of repression, discrimination, and cruelty experienced particularly by the black population, but also by the mixed race and Asian (mainly Indian) population, some slight movement toward pluralism and democracy began, to pick an arbitrary date, in the early 1980s.[31] Doubtless reluctantly for most, but nevertheless clearly, whites began to accept the fact that their lives and those of the non-whites were bound closely together. This movement has been able to draw on, and then contribute to, the widely scattered humanitarian and egalitarian forces noted in figure 5.2.

Blacks make up nearly three-quarters of the forty million population of South Africa; persons of mixed race and Asians are, together, almost another eighth. If the one-seventh who are white hope for a skilled and well-motivated labor force, cooperation from an increasingly strong black labor movement, a political movement capable of negotiation, not just confrontation, and the other qualities of a modern democratic society, they will have to support—and many are supporting—the dismantling of apartheid. If they want their white athletes to compete in the Olympics they cannot deny opportunities to their black athletes. It took twenty-one years for the white controllers of this decision to realize their interdependence. Since they have, the International Olympic Committee lifted the ban, thus permitting South Africa to participate in the 1992 summer games.

Referring to figure 5.2, then, I suggest that even in societies with harshly repressive ethnic orders, interdependence and common interests furnish some support for a "system of equality," as in point 1a. In this system, gains from equality, not gains from exploitation, are emphasized. As Afrikaner Frederik van Zyl Slabbert remarked, after a conference between seventeen members of the African National Congress and sixty-one South African whites, "We found that we have a great deal in common, and although there are some differences, we found that there is a great deal of flexibility and negotiability on those points."[32]

Closely related to the recognition of interdependence are changes in attitudes that have increasingly, during the last decade, made modifications of apartheid politically possible. A 1985 poll of white South Africans found 32 percent unhappy with apartheid. In 1986 it was 45 percent.[33] A government-sponsored sample survey, taken through a period of several years by the Human Sciences Research Council, found that more than two-thirds of the white respondents favored equal rights for all racial groups. "White opinion has been moving much more rapidly toward multiracialism than toward a last stand for apartheid."[34] These data illustrate that, as suggested in point 2a in figure 5.2, individual attitudes—and we can add needs and anxieties—are not all supportive of racial separation and white dominance among white South Africans.

Even in the midst of an authoritarian apartheid system (as experienced by seven-eighths of the population), there were cultural elements (point 3a) defending racial equality and multiracialism. These could be hampered but not repressed. As sharply contrasting as they are with the dominant picture many people in the West have of South Africa, as well as contrasting with the dominant reality, these too are part of the reality of South Africa. They are part of the potential for a more liberal multi-ethnic society—a potential that has grown during the last few years. I will simply mention three elements within the dominant system that have, at the least, kept alive a more egalitarian prospect:

Perhaps best known are the novelists who, while portraying the cruelty of the apartheid system have at the same time helped us picture more humane possibilities. (The same can be said, of course, for some of the writers in the Soviet Union, the United States, and elsewhere.) In South Africa a literature of dissent goes back several generations; and since World War II we have heard the voices of Alan Paton (*Cry the Beloved Country; Too Late the Phalarope*), Nadine Gordimer (*The Conservationist; Burger's Daughter; July's People*), and J. M. Goetze, a coloured writer (*The Life and Times of Michael K.; Waiting for the Barbarians*), to name some of the most prominent.

Although South African universities have been severely constrained by the apartheid system—formally by the 1959 Extension of University Education Act, designed to keep black students from attending "white" universities—they have found ways to resist segregation. By law, to attend a white university a non-white student required government permission. This was to be granted only if the institution designated for his racial group did not offer work in his discipline. "But in the last few years the loophole has widened to the point of becoming a gap, practically a tunnel, and a process that elsewhere might be called integration is occurring at an accelerating pace. The number of non-white students at theoretically white universities now exceeds 4,000, twice what it was five years ago."[35] These universities have judged themselves to some degree by international norms as "open" institutions. This is shown not only by their readiness to admit students from "forbidden" groups, but also by the several institutes for the study of ethnic and racial relations.

The 4,000 black students in white universities in 1981 were only a fragment of the number of black South Africans who would be getting university training a few years later. By 1989, 65,000 were enrolled in universities and another 10,000 in advanced technical colleges. "Add the other racial groups and 40 percent of all South African university enrollment is non-white. . . . A quarter of all pupils in private schools around the country are black, though state schools are still segregated."[36]

This expansion has not been without tension. Although there has been little conflict between coloured and black students, some Indian South Africans have resisted the admission of Blacks into a university designated by the apartheid regime as one for Indians.[37] And to keep the full reality before us, we must note the continuing impoverishment of the "native" universities.

Some signs of the "culture of equality" are also found in the churches. They are commonly seen as bastions for support and legitimation of apartheid.[38] This has been true particularly of the white branches of the Dutch Reformed churches, to which a majority of the white populations and of government officials and legislators belong.

Beliefs among the Boers about their place as chosen people with a God-given destiny to dominate South Africa go back to the early nineteenth century. This belief system began, or was reenforced, by the 1838 battle with the Zulus, from which came the myth of a covenant made with God by Andrias Pretorius and his band of Voortrekkers that they would maintain their particular view of a Christian society if He would bring them the victory.[39] The myth has been maintained by the persistent struggles between the Dutch- and English-descended South Africans.

Segregation of black from white churches in South Africa became the standard in the nineteenth century and has, for the most part, continued. The walls of separation, however, have been lowered. Individual ministers and theologians have renounced apartheid and joined black churches.[40] After several decades of isolation from the World Council of Churches, which has condemned apartheid, the Dutch Reformed Church—the major Afrikaner church—"which justified race laws for 40 years, has joined other Christians in declaring apartheid a sin and admitting its responsibility for the suffering of millions of blacks."[41] Although the impact of this action on local churches and on the politics of lay members remains to be seen—and is likely to be small—we nevertheless see that the religious culture contains resources for those who oppose apartheid.

Those resources are most strongly used by the predominantly black churches, where "liberation theology"—binding religious thought and action closely to questions of justice and equality—has become prominent. Opposition to apartheid, however, is increasingly found in the predominantly white churches as well.[42]

In my judgment, churches of dominant groups seldom take the lead in major social changes. Having been moved to make small adaptations, however, by economic, political, and demographic changes and by protests from their midst, they become part of a bundle of forces, each affecting the others. Religious universalism gets renewed attention.[43] Churches affect the speed with which changes occur and the methods used. In South Africa today, religion and the churches, having long strengthened apartheid, are now beginning to support the "culture of equality."

Figure 5.2 (points 1, 2, and 3) suggests that interdependence, supportive attitudes, and elements of pluralistic, even universalistic cultural values are resources on which some egalitarian and democratic activities can draw, even in a society that is harshly divided ethnically. These resources, in turn, reenforce institutional supports (point 5a) and the resolve of disadvantaged ethnic minorities to change the ethnic order (point 6a).

In the comments on cultural values supporting a more egalitarian society, I have mentioned churches and universities. These can also be seen structurally, as institutional locales for the pursuit of those values. Just as "racism" can be institutionalized, so can pluralism and egalitarianism. That is, they can be built into established social structures, with professional and lay personnel and "routine" procedures that support them.

Most recently, in South Africa, such institutional support has been expanding in legal and political matters. The onerous "pass laws"—the pillar of apartheid, as they have been called—have been repealed.[44] So also have laws reserving land and neighborhoods for whites only.[45] New laws regarding the racial-ethnic order scarcely guarantee rapid changes in behavior. Yet they come into play at a time when much freer discussion of ethnic relations is possible, partly due to the quasi-legislative role now played by Asian and coloured South Africans,[46] and when progressive representation in the all-white parliament has increased significantly. Add these developments to the increasing support for egalitarian policies in the educational, religious, and sports establishments, and one seems justified in noting that support for a more open, democratic society in South Africa, however modest, is now firmly a part of the establishment.

Perhaps the strongest clue to institutional change, although still primarily symbolic, was the referendum (March 18, 1992) on a question proposed by President de Klerk (to the white-only electorate!): "Do you support the reform process which the State President began on Feb. 2, 1990, and which is aimed at a new constitution through negotiation?" 68.6 percent said yes, with many declaring that date to be the beginning of a new South Africa. A few months later President de Klerk offered a multi-race election, on April 27, 1994. The outcome would almost certainly be to give South African its first black president.[47]

Turning to point 6a, to complete this illustration of Figure 5.2, we should note that the aspirations and activities of coloured South Africans, those of Indian background, and particularly of the far more numerous black South Africans, are increasingly important during this period of change and turmoil. A protest movement has been building for over a quarter of a century, powered from within by the growing importance of ethnic minorities in the labor force— and their growing resentment of the severe restraints of apartheid— and encouragement from outside South Africa by the breakup of colonialism throughout Africa. "It is our contention," van den Berghe wrote at the beginning of this period, "that any attempt to implement the *ends* of apartheid, given a modern, technological, industrial, urban society must use the *means* of Fascism. The control of an increasingly educated and politically conscious non-European population of twelve million [now over thirty million] (which are either actively or passively opposed to apartheid) is a different matter from the control of a few hundred thousand Africans divided into ethnic groups on the fringes of 19th century White settlement."[48]

The repressive measures of apartheid document this assessment (although I agree with Adam and Giliomee that use of the term *fascism* obscures important differences from Germany or Italy.)[49] The African National Congress, founded on the active non-violence tradition that Gandhi had established in South Africa, and still influenced by that approach to social change, has through the years developed a more confrontational style.[50] In recent months, divisions within its ranks have complicated but have not stopped efforts to negotiate with the government of President de Klerk to obtain the complete dismantling of apartheid.

Divisions among black ethnic groups have also weakened their campaign for political and economic equity. There are not only differences in strategy, as between Chief Buthelezi's "work within the system" approach and Nelson Mandela's "confrontation, but if possible without violence" approach, but also harsh conflict among the ethnic groups themselves, as between the Xhosa and Zulu, often with violent outcomes.

Despite these conflicts, there are also abundant "hope, aspiration, redoubled effort, and supporting subcultures," to use the description of ethnic-minority activity in point 6a of figure 5.2. There is substantial agreement among black South Africans on the strategy of active nonviolence and strong pressure on the government toward the goal of a democratic multiracial society of fully equal citizens—the "unbroken thread" of Frederikse's title. Polls show strong majority support for Nelson Mandela and Bishop Desmond Tutu, major proponents of this strategy and goal. They stand between those who support Chief Buthelezi's preference for relatively autonomous "homelands" and, on the other side, the black South Africans who see violence as the only way and a totally black government as the goal.

In late 1992, rival black African groups—the African National Congress, led by Nelson Mandela, and the Inkatha Freedom Party, led by Mangosuthu Buthelezi, agreed to meet in an effort to stop the violence between the often harshly contending groups. Their conflicts have claimed thousands of lives in the last decade. At the same time, Mandela offered white South Africans an assured place of power, indicating that he did not envisage simply a shift from white domination to black domination.[51]

Several black unions, with over half a million members, have formed the Congress of South African Trade Unions, supporting a non-racial approach to political change. A multiracial United Democratic Front, now expanded into the Mass Democratic Movement, with most of its members from urban areas, has strong trade union participation.

To understand these developments, one needs to study the whole system outlined in figure 5.2. For example, point 1a, "economic and political interdependence; gains from equality," is closely linked to 6a. "Taking off the ideological brakes [regarding who could hold what job] meant scrapping job reservation and allowing blacks to meet the industrial sector's desperate need for skilled manpower. It meant blacks had to be trained for these skilled jobs, which in turn meant upgrading their education and admitting them to previously whites-only technical institutes and universities. A skilled work force, moreover, must be allowed to unionize in order to regularize labour relations and prevent it from becoming anarchic."[52]

In South Africa there is a powerful "system of discrimination." For many years we have seen it as an almost impenetrable, closed system, capable of defending itself against all but an overwhelming violent attack. Perhaps now we are permitted to see the elements of a "system of equality," never absent from the scene but only recently of sufficient influence to be able to challenge apartheid in significant ways. On a long and difficult road, whose twists and turns we cannot now foresee, South Africa is moving toward a multi-ethnic polity.

By using South Africa as an illustration of the concept of a "system of equality," I have no desire to minimize the entrenched power of apartheid nor to forget the distance to go before something close to a democratic society can be achieved. I want simply to show that even in a harshly conflictful ethnic order there may be other forces pulling in the opposite direction. A few recent headlines and lead sentences may pull us back to the harsher side of reality: "Afrikaners are staking out an enclave for whites only." "Black radicals target whites." "De Klerk concedes military had a role in township strife" (during which twenty-eight were killed while participating in an anti-apartheid demonstration). "Even in 'new South Africa,' apartheid's legacy lives on." "Segregation's legal foundations are going; the economic chasm remains"—a statement that could apply almost as well to the United States twenty-five years ago and not entirely falsely today.[53]

As I have once again reexamined (that is not a redundancy) the South African scene, now under the leadership of Frederik de Klerk, I have been struck by a most unusual parallel with the U.S.S.R. The "hard line Afrikaners," one might say, are "the communists of South Africa," or, the hard-line communist opponents of change in Russia and some of the other now-independent republics are "the Afrikaners of the defunct U.S.S.R." In similar ways they are trying to preserve their positions in the old order, bolstered in their efforts by some public support, but more strongly by their firm—not to say rigid—ideology and their entrenched positions in the Party and the government bureaucracies and in most of the institutions on the current scene.

They are being challenged, however, by many forces: political and economic changes around the world; increased opposition from the disadvantaged and repressed in their own societies; doubts and schisms among the old rulers; new rulers thrust up by these developments; increased human resources for focusing opposition; and a powerful combination of old and new methods of communication that deny the old rulers their former near-monopoly over what is known to the majority. Perhaps most important, it has become apparent in both societies that the seeds of dissent and protest had been planted many years ago.

The public performance of social subordination is in contrast with the disguised and hidden activities ". . . that takes place offstage, out of earshot, and so away from the surveillance of the powerful." Thus ". . . the powerless create for themselves social space, alternative ideologies, dissident subcultures, and forms of disguised, low profile, and undisclosed resistance. . . ."[54]

Early sprouts of such dissent were cut down, but the roots were not destroyed.[55] When the environments, both internal and worldwide, became somewhat more favorable, liberalizing movements developed rapidly. All of these, and doubtless other forces, have opened new possibilities and have led to new strategies of change.

Perhaps by studying two vastly different societies which, despite their differences, are experiencing similar stresses and responding to some degree in similar ways, we can find clues of more general applicability to the task of moving from there (inegalitarian and authoritarian regimes riven by ethnic conflict) to here (pluralistic and democratic regimes) in the contemporary world. One searches almost in vain to find a society for which such clues would not be of inestimable value.

THE FIELD CONTEXT OF SOCIAL CHANGE IN INTER-ETHNIC RELATIONS

We need now to return to a more analytic discussion of how interaction between the system of discrimination and the system of equality affects the process of social change. The two closed systems I have described are, of course, imaginary. They are in reality open not only to the influence of each other, but together they also interact in a larger field of forces. Technical, economic, demographic, ecological, and international changes all influence the unfolding of the patterns of inter-ethnic relations. Figure 5.3 is an attempt to suggest this larger field. In my judgment, effective mobilization of ethnic groups to work for greater equality is strongly dependent on our understanding the interdependencies and interactions within this field. Strategies for change that focus on only one or a few of the factors are unlikely to be effective. In a given setting, at a particular time, one or another may deserve the greatest

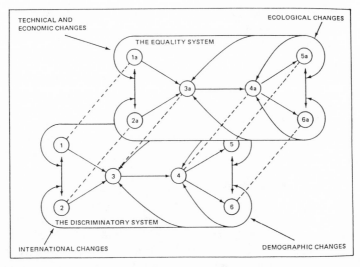

FIGURE 5.3
The Field Context of Two Open Systems, One Supporting
Discrimination, the Other Equality
Adapted from Yinger, 1983: 405

effort, but it can be successful only as the several interdependent factors are taken into account.

It is almost useless, for example, to try to reduce the ethnocentrism and prejudices of individual members of dominant ethnic groups (figure 5.2, point 2) if institutional discrimination and minority group demoralization (points 5 and 6) are strong. Or, the most powerful attack on the system of discrimination will be insufficient in a context in which we disregard major ecological and demographic problems.

In many parts of the world today, minority ethnic groups (that is, groups, regardless of their proportionate size, that are disadvantaged in power and status) are striving to improve their situations, to attain equality. What are their chances of success? Under what conditions are the processes of social change likely to be in the direction of greater ethnic equality? There is something paradoxical about any discussion of the mobilization of ethnic minorities to improve their status. Presumably, as minorities, their power is limited. Are we asking whether or not they can pick themselves up by their own bootstraps? Are there ways in which they can break free from the conditions that constrain them in lower statuses? Our discussion of this question is futile unless one or both of the following statements are true:

1. Minority ethnic groups, despite their relative lack of power, possess *potential* strengths that can be mobilized to their own advantage. Even the most disadvantaged groups have potential strengths.[56] To explore this issue, scholars and policymakers must ask what those strengths might be, why they have not been utilized, and the conditions under which they can be changed from potential to actual strengths.
2. A minority ethnic group seeking to mobilize its resources must recognize that dominant groups also can mobilize.[57] The advantages of dominant ethnic groups, however, and the discriminatory system in which they are embedded are not consistent: individual ambivalences, cultural contradictions, and structural diversities represent potential strengths for movements seeking to change unequal ethnic arrangements. To explore this issue, we must seek to discover these hidden and contradictory aspects of the dominant system of discrimination and ask what conditions make it possible to use them to increase equality, perhaps by the formation of coalitions or by focusing on the non-discriminatory qualities of the dominant system. The tendency to regard existing systems as monolithic, utterly lacking in capabilities for change, can blind one to possibilities hidden in their contradictions and interdependencies.

I shall assume that both of these statements are true. I believe them to be true in virtually all societies. One further assumption seems justified: effective action requires a correct appraisal of the situation into which ethnic relations are bound and of the conditions under which social change occurs. It is not only that good practice makes good theory, as many contemporary "critical" scholars affirm, but good theory makes good practice. This dictum is applicable, I believe, to the process of change in any society. Policies based on ideologies that draw overly simple pictures of a society are less likely to be able to use the resources for change.

The members of minority ethnic groups are likely to be mobilized only for symbolic movements of societal transformation if their aspirations and hopes are raised without an increase in opportunities and a reduction in institutional discrimination. It is somewhat more difficult to make an opposite point: Structural and cultural changes (an increase in the strength of the structural and cultural supports for equality vis-à-vis the supports for discrimination) can finally be effective only if there are matching personality changes. Because of some reduction in discrimination and some increase in opportunities, it is now possible for a person like the Rev. Jesse Jackson to emphasize "self-development"—personality changes that keep pace with structural changes. "The thrust of my argument," he wrote, "is that black Americans must begin to accept a larger share of responsibility for their lives. For too many years we have been crying that racism and oppression have to be fought on every front. But to fight any battle takes soldiers who are strong, healthy, spirited, committed, well-trained and confident. . . . Many leaders who are black, and many white liberals will object to my discussing these things in public. But the decadence in black communities—killings, destruction of our own businesses, violence in the school—is already in the headlines; the only question is what we should do about it. Others will object that to demand that we must meet the challenge of self-government is to put too much pressure on the victims of ancient wrongs. Yet in spite of these objections, in spite of yesterday's agony, liberation struggles are built on sweat and pain rather than tears and complaints."[58]

Such a message is one ingredient necessary for ethnic mobilization for change. Not only its content, but its "social movement" quality affects the response. Mobilization of resources is not simply drawing from some social bank account. It must engage shared dreams and frustrations, giving them the energy of collective purpose.[59] Insofar as Jackson's movement is successful it will strengthen the process of structural change that, to a degree, made it possible. In the absence of continuing expansion of opportunities, however, the message would soon be perceived, as Jackson recognizes, as meaningless, if not indeed a hoax. It is a strong minority group, one that is experiencing a growing self-confidence and some increase in opportunities, that will produce and listen to such a message.

The point that Jackson made some fifteen years ago—as many other black leaders did earlier—has been repeatedly emphasized in recent years, but without connecting it, as he does, to strong opposition to persistent discrimination. By itself, such "bootstrap" strategy propounded by a few of those who have won out over the odds (with talent, hard work, good fortune, and sometimes a keen eye for the main chance) is of little value for the great majority of those of average talent and average luck still facing severe discrimination.

Effective mobilization in any setting requires an accurate appraisal of the balance between each item in the system of discrimination with its matching item in the system of equality. We might imagine scales ranging from -1.0 (maximum discrimination) to +1.0 (maximum equality), with the zero point indicating an equal degree of influence. We do not have the information, of course, to use such scales; but I would guess that in most societies all of the comparisons between the two systems are negative—that is, below zero. The discrimination system seems tougher than the equality system. This does not mean, however, that resources for equality are lacking. Such resources are there to draw upon and are being drawn upon.

Referring to the United States, I believe the evidence shows that in the last forty years the balance has shifted upward in each segment of the diagram, even if the balance is still negative.[60] For example, the following comparisons seem appropriate with reference to Figure 5.3:

1 and 1a   Economic and political interdependence is now more clearly recognized.

2 and 2a   Individual prejudice has declined.

3 and 3a   Cultural supports and justifications for discrimination are weaker.

5 and 5a   Important changes have occurred in several major institutions. Although every fact that we can cite has its negative aspects, we need to note some of these changes. Minority-ethnic representation in local, state, and federal political offices has increased dramatically. There were three black congressmen forty years ago, twenty-four in 1990, and thirty-nine in 1992. (Fifty would be the proportionate number.) The armed forces have been desegregated, if not fully integrated. The minority-ethnic middle classes have expanded, partly under legal pressure, which itself indicates institutional change.

6 and 6a   Individual members of ethnic minorities have grown in self-confidence, skill, and morale. Their collective efforts are more powerful, with better aggregation of political and economic resources. (At the same time, a large and perhaps growing number of individuals remain alienated and resentful.)

Because I am arguing that the whole system, not just one part of it, must be shifted, the fact that several related changes have occurred is significant.

Yet there are serious lags that keep feeding discriminatory influences back into the system, weakening the impact of the changes toward equality. In the United States, what is often referred to as institutional racism (I prefer the term *institutionalized discrimination*)—established patterns of discrimination that rest less on individual prejudice or perceived self-interest than on customary ways of doing things, on the effects of past discrimination, and on inertia—continues to operate powerfully in the full range of institutional life. It too has declined, as I have suggested, but less than other parts of the system of discrimination, because its sources are less easily detected.

The strategies of ethnic groups seeking to increase their power and income often contain an implicit if not explicit theory of resource mobilization—that is, a theory of the best ways to draw in and activate members, to aggregate their resources into an effective size and strength, and to secure outside help. The resources are not simply those possessed by individual members, which may be relevant to their individual status improvement, such as skill, money, courage, and readiness to sacrifice. Interpersonal resources are also vital: community cohesion and trust, cooperative relationships among the variety of groups in a movement, and effective contact with the media and with the dominant authorities in a society.[61] This is true because we are dealing with "the problem of how a distinct subgroup in society, with little power and without direct resources for gaining more power, can nevertheless come to gain those resources." Coleman is using the term *power*, "not in the sense of power over another group but a position in society having as much power over one's own life and over community and national actions as other citizens"[62]—a definition harmonious with the idea of a pluralistic ethnic order.

"Feelings of solidarity with the group seeking change are essential in order to deal, among other things, with the "free rider" problem. This refers to the fact that changes that are won often benefit those who did not work for them as well as those who did. If many try to be free riders, of course, there will not be any ride; hence the need to emphasize shared interests and a nearly exclusive identity—we versus they."[63]

Identity is enforced positively by emphasizing that we are bound together by kinship, friendship, and common values. It is enforced negatively by emphasizing the barriers to our mobility that we believe are imposed by the dominant group or an opposing ethnic group. "There is a delicate problem of balance in this aspect of resource mobilization: How to increase cohesion without at the same time increasing the cohesion of a majority opposed to the goals being sought . . . and, as a corollary, how to emphasize an exclusive identity without losing ties to those in the majority who can be valuable allies, bringing resources of their own to the efforts to reduce discrimination."[64]

Resource mobilization is a means, not an end. Analysts as well as moralists need to ask not only how it can be obtained, but also toward what various ends it is directed. Is ethnic conflict necessarily a zero-sum game? Or is it the case that ethnic groups, living in a small and interdependent world, cannot achieve their goals simply by attaining independence or by replacing a dominant group only to become dominant themselves?

Almost continuously during the last several years, accounts of ethnic conflicts in many parts of the world have brought forcefully to our attention the dilemmas of ethnic mobilization. Some of the conflicts involve a minority ethnic group versus the center, or the dominant group. Others involve two or more groups, each struggling for dominance over a shared territory: Azerbaijanis vs. Armenians; Serbs vs. Bosnian Muslims; Israelis vs. Palestinians; African Americans vs. Jewish Americans; Soviet Georgians vs. Ossetians; Molaccas vs. Indonesians; Karens vs. Mynamar (Burma); Tamils vs. Sri Lanka. In no case, nor in the several others that could be listed, does one get the sense of a cultural resource indicating that the adversaries have learned how to balance the need for solidarity and a strong group identity with a matching need among those with whom they contend. Such a resource might prevent the sense of an exclusive solidarity among opposing groups from creating an impenetrable line of separation.

To be sure, the world has invented mediation, arbitration, and courts of justice. There are several peace institutes and centers for the study of conflict resolution. International negotiating teams have recently been more frequently in evidence. The United Nations has been strengthened by the thawing of the cold war. Many countries have civil rights laws. "Residents of West Europe now can turn to outside institutions to protect human rights. Since the 1975 Helsinki Accords, minority rights everywhere in Europe have been codified, and violations can be referred to the European Conference on Security and Cooperation."[65] In addition to such mediating institutions, there is a large and, in my view, valuable literature on conflict resolution.[66]

All of these give one hope. But the words are not often acted upon, nor the institutions widely used, or even known. Learning how to soften the sharpness of the ethnic dilemma remains one of the most critical questions facing the world today.

The Larger Context of the Discrimination-Equality Systems

Around the boundaries of Figure 5.3 I have noted four influences not directly tied to the systems of discrimination and equality, which nevertheless can strongly affect them, positively and negatively.

Ecology. Ecological thinking requires thinking across boundaries of time and space. It is the study of *Eixos*—the habitation, "with its sacred hearth, bonding the earth to all aspects of society."[67] We are common inhabitants of this miraculous planet, capable of supporting enormous diversity, yet increasingly fragile. Many of the celebrated accomplishments of *Homo sapiens*—for example, the extraction and processing of the earth's materials—have been strictly man-centered, with little regard for long-run effects on our air, water, soil, and on the other species with whom we are interdependent. If I may tamper with Shakespeare: Our degradation droppeth as the acid rain from heaven.

When Brazil began extensive lumbering from its rain forests, this was not in any direct sense an expression of ethnic conflict, but the Indians native to the forest are gravely affected, as are all of us in time. In the United States, as in many parts of the world, the poor—among whom ethnic minorities are overly represented—live and work in the most polluted parts of the environment, thus bearing the heavier load of illness and premature death.[68]

The world, particularly the industrialized part, has obtained the resources needed to maintain and expand its economies by adding to renewable resources (virtually the only ones available for millennia), the extraction and consumption of exhaustible resources.[69] In time—fifty years? a century? a millennium?—when we have consumed those that are not replaceable, while polluting the environment with their residue, we shall have to adapt fully to a renewable economy. The timetable is being shortened by the unprecedented growth in the world's population and by the rising expectations and demands of those just entering the industrial age.

Economic and political interdependence, rather than conflict, are more readily recognized under conditions of expansion of resources for all. Dominant ethnic groups and states more willingly accept changes when they are moving upward, even if more slowly than ethnic minorities. Even a "small" recession exacerbates ethnic tension. The world faces a cruel dilemma if the expansion of resources now begins to seem not simply finite, but quite limited. An ecologically sensitive program to protect the environment and steps toward a resource-modest style of life may reduce the chances for improvement in the lives of disadvantaged ethnic groups. This dilemma calls powerfully to our attention that the systems of discrimination and equality that we have been describing are open not only to the influence of each other, but are part of a larger field, including ecological forces, that strongly affects their interaction.

Demographic Factors. The size, location, and composition of populations are influenced by the ethnic order, but their trajectories also have their own internal propulsion. These can have a strong impact on the systems of discrimination and equality. In many societies (e.g., the United States, many European countries, Canada) disadvantaged ethnic groups are growing more rapidly than the advantaged. The first effects may be to weaken their chances for improvement of status. The larger families may be less able, on the average, to support the health and education of their children. Dominant groups may feel more threatened. Population policies, even if they are made without reference to the comparative advantages of ethnic groups, affect the distribution of advantages. In time, however, particularly in democratic societies, the groups growing in size can have a larger impact.

The comparative sizes of relatively equal ethnic groups can also be a major factor in their developing relations, as in Malaysia, where the combined population of persons of Chinese and Indian background has fallen below that of the Malays.

The location as well as the size of ethnic populations is important. In South Africa, the black population is not only becoming a larger part of the total, but it is rapidly urbanizing. The changing location affects their attitudes—and those of whites—and their opportunities. In the United States, where the black population is now largely urban, new political opportunities have been opened. Although still only 2 percent of elected officials are African Americans, the number has increased rapidly, from 1,472 in 1970, to 4,912 in 1980, to 7,226 in 1989.[70] As noted earlier, in 1946 there were three black members of the House of Representatives; thirty-nine were elected in 1992. Of the twenty-four elected in 1990, fifteen were from districts where African Americans were the majority, seven from districts where the Hispanic and black voters together made up a majority, and two from majority white districts. Currently, one African American governor, several mayors, and one senator have been elected by a majority white electorate.

American Civil Rights Law requires that district lines be drawn in such a way that they neither dilute minority voting strength unduly (dividing a community that is large enough to elect a representative among two or more districts, in none of which it can elect one) nor concentrate it unduly (creating a 90 percent African American district, for example, when a 60–30 division might well lead to the election of an African American in one district and give them substantial influence in another.) I will not explore the strategic issue involve here. Political scientists, however—ethnic and otherwise—will want to examine the comparative value of representation by a member of one's own group versus strong minority representation in the choice of two or more non-ethnics who are responsive to (court the support of) one's ethnic group. To put this in the form of an over-simplified question: Ought Hispanics interested in maximizing their political influence in California or Texas seek a district that is 60 percent Hispanic, to make reasonably certain that they will be directly represented; or would they be wiser to support a plan that gives them a 20 percent representation in three districts in which the 80 percent non-Hispanics are divided 40–40 between two parties? The latter situation does not foreclose the possibility of electing one or more from one's own group, but makes it unlikely. At the same time, it increases the "balance of power" possibilities. The different strategies may produce different kinds of representatives and have various other effects on the issues that get acted upon and on the nature of the political debate. Perhaps a mixture of the two strategies, varying among districts, will give a minority ethnic group its strongest representation.

On the national level, had African American voters divided their support equally between the Republican and the Democratic candidates in 1960 and 1976 (rather than about 12–88), neither President Kennedy nor President Carter would have been elected. Such results have complicated and ambiguous implications for minority political strategy. Should African Americans, for example, have a party of their own, thus to be able to speak clearly about the issues that concern them most? Or should they support both majority parties about equally, hoping to influence whichever one is in office?

I raise these questions only to indicate some of the ways in which the size, location, and composition of populations have significant implications for ethnic relations.

Technology and the Economy. Changes in the economic and technological environment are a third "outside" influence on the ethnic order. Developments in the structure of occupational systems have increased the economic advantages of the more educated and skilled parts of industrialized countries. In the United States, many members of the more severely disadvantaged ethnic minorities are unemployed, require welfare support, and are seriously demoralized, not simply because of institutionalized discrimination or the prejudices of the majority, but also because of these shifts in the occupational structure. For example, Lori Kletzer has studied a sample of workers who had held jobs for at least three years and then lost them, between 1979 and 1986, not due to temporary layoffs but due to plant closings and structural changes in an industry that eliminated their jobs. "Black workers bore a relatively heavier burden of widespread job displacement during the 1980s because of the industries and occupations in which they were concentrated; they were also less likely to be reemployed and were out of work longer."[71]

International Changes. The relationships between ethnic groups within a society are affected not only by the local and national scenes, but also by international forces. In the 1990s we are more keenly aware that many of the violent conflicts within societies have been exacerbated by the after-effects of the cold war. Seeking greater power or more resources or constraints on each other, the Soviet Union and the United States used different ethnic groups as surrogate fighters in their cold war.

As tensions eased between the Soviet Union and the United States, new opportunities and new problems appeared in the societies where they had backed antagonistic ethnic groups. In Namibia, the end of the cold war has led to the withdrawal of foreign troops and a sharp reduction in inter-ethnic violence. In 1990 an independent government was put in place, with major help from the United Nations, marking the end of European colonialism in Africa after more than a century. A democratic constitution has been adopted. Although some of the nearly 200,000 white Namibians (about 11 percent of the population) have left, most seem ready to accept the new government. They continue to occupy major economic positions and some in the government. By the end of the century we will be able to gauge the dimensions of this success story in ethnic relations.

Ethiopia, since 1991, is no longer dominated at the center by a minority group supported by the USSR; but the breakup of central control has increased the centrifugal forces tending to pull it apart. Three thousand years old, yet newly defined by outside powers after World War II, it is torn by bitter ethnic conflicts. Tens of thousands have starved while rival armies have cut off food and medicine for weeks at a time. It remains to be seen whether three or more countries will emerge from the vacuum at the center. "U.S. plans to be 'midwife' to a new rule in Ethiopia," says a recent headline; but those plans face the fact that "In Ethiopia, as in so much of the third world, the ties of dependency that attached poor countries to either Washington or Moscow were easier to establish than they are now to untie."[72]

Eritrea, the northern region of Ethiopia, has won a precarious independence after a disastrous thirty years of civil war. A referendum scheduled for 1993 will indicate whether the several ethnic groups in Eritrea can create a stable, independent, and pluralistic state.

Thus the effects of international changes impinging on ethnically divided societies range from promising to highly problematic. In an optimistic mood, one can say that in the last few years there have been some tentative signs of pluralism and multi-party politics spreading quite widely across Africa. These reflect in part the changing international environment, including the sharp reduction of tension between the United States and the Soviet Union and the small steps in South Africa toward democracy. (Authoritarian rule in black African states can no longer be so easily justified by pointing to South Africa's apartheid regime.)

The most advantaged members of ethnic minorities are less strongly affected by the ecological, demographic, structural, and international changes we have illustrated. The trends, in fact, may blur the lines drawn by ethnicity on one hand and by class on the other, tending to create a split within a minority that hinders the aggregation of its resources and sharpens the dilemma—individual vs. group struggle—so common in minority movements.[73]

Until these impersonal structural forces are precisely identified, their effects recognized, and suitable action is taken to offset their impact, social change toward greater equality can be effectively blocked, despite a favorable legal and political situation, increasing goodwill among the majority ethnic groups and higher levels of self-confidence and skill among the minorities.[74] Each situation has its own set of possibilities and limitations. But in the final analysis, social change toward greater ethnic equality requires modification of the whole system.

Chapter 6

LIBERTY-EQUALITY-
FRATERNITY—AND ETHNICITY

To understand ethnicity—and, understanding, to seek to shape it into an enriching part of human experience—we shall have to look at it through a wide-angle lens, with respect both to theory and to policy. An excessive sharp focus on ethnicity per se will blur the contexts within which it is embedded.

In this chapter, using that perspective, I shall be exploring a thesis: We cannot understand the course of events in connection with ethnicity without studying the basic values of a society. It is not only power, demography, and economic self-interest that govern ethnic relations, important as they are. Culture, which makes up a large part of the context within which ethnic dramas are played, is also important.

In using a cultural approach one does not imply that culture is simply an independent cause. It is part of a cybernetic system, an effect as well as a cause as it interacts with material forces and with particular individuals and groups, with their diverse biographies and histories.

As a kind of literary device, I shall develop this theme around a study of liberty—equality—fraternity, separately and in interaction. Of course this device will give us only a partial picture of the cultural aspects of ethnic relations; but I believe it can be a particularly valuable part.

Although I shall be citing many facts, this is not primarily an empirical study. Instead I shall examine ethnicity as a generic aspect of most societies, seeking thereby to strengthen our sociological understanding. As we seek to increase the power of our theories of ethnicity we must tie them to more general theories—of social change, of socialization, of conflict. Vladimir Horowitz once remarked, as he pointed to the notes on a score, "The music is behind those dots. One must search for it." When he played, he did not simply reproduce the score, he recreated it. And so it is with our topic: The truth is behind those facts. One must search for it. One must let her or his imagination flow. Facts are not a score simply to be reproduced. They are a challenge to our theoretical powers.

Perhaps only in France is that famous trilogy—liberty, equality, fraternity—combined into a kind of official motto. As three distinctive values, however, they are widely acclaimed. Their interdependence or, oppositely, their mutual contradictions are analyzed in an enormous body of literature. We can see the sources of many of the disagreements among students of ethnicity by commenting on some of that literature. Policy deadlocks or controversies regarding ethnicity are often tied to different rankings of the three values or different judgments about their compatibility. Are these values competitive, perhaps even mutually contradictory? Or is progress toward one a sine qua non of progress toward the others? Or do they move independently, their interactions depending upon the context? How does extensive emphasis on ethnic identities and distinctiveness interact with the liberty-equality-fraternity value cluster?

I am using liberty-equality-fraternity as shorthand for a democratic culture—that is, the culture of societies wherein the majority selects the leaders; where all have ready access to those selected; where all minorities have full rights to seek to make themselves into the majority by peaceful means; and where tolerance of difference is widely practiced.

These criteria imply peaceful transfer of power, the presence of many countervailing powers—non-governmental as well as governmental—and fully open access to such basic resources as education, health, and self-respect.

I will resist the temptation to go back to Aristotle, or even to Tocqueville (at least at this point) to show the historical depth of interest in the study of these values. A brief reference to sociological interest in those values, however, seems appropriate.

A century ago Sumner succinctly expressed a view that is widely held today: "Liberty, inequality, survival of the fittest . . . carries society forward and favours all its best members."[1] Cooley's view was quite different. In his description of primary groups, he described the development of what he called "primary ideals"—loyalty, lawfulness, and freedom. In such "we" groups, the golden rule is a natural expression of their unity. He then examined "the extension of primary ideals"—the effort by the world religions and by democracy to extend the reach of those ideals. They often fail, he observed, partly due to individual inadequacy; but viewed sociologically "the failure is seen to be the difficulty of organization. . . . The creation of a moral order on an ever-growing scale is the great historical task of mankind, and the magnitude of it explains all shortcomings."[2]

Weber raises the issue in a somewhat different form; but his powerful discussion of "Class, Status, Power" can readily be transposed into a discussion of equality, fraternity, and liberty.[3]

When Myrdal wrote about "an American dilemma," he was discussing the complexity, the contradictions of the value system, not only on the societal level but also within individuals; "even a poor and uneducated white person . . . who is violently prejudiced against the Negro and intent upon depriving him of his civic rights and human independence, has also a whole compartment in his valuation spheres housing the entire American creed of liberty, equality, justice, and fair opportunity for everybody. He is actually also a good Christian and honestly devoted to the ideals of human brotherhood and the Golden Rule."[4]

Echoes of Myrdal can be heard in the work of several recent writers who have pointed to what they see as distortions in the portrayals of working class and lower-middle class white ethnics by many liberal observers. What might be called the Archie Bunker stereotype is challenged by more sympathetic accounts both of the problems they face in contemporary America and the (sometimes hidden) democratic values to which they adhere.[5]

Empirical studies of American values, while using a variety of terms, have consistently found liberty and equality, or equivalent terms, high on the list, with fraternity less clearly seen. Humani-

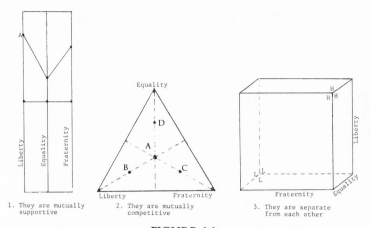

FIGURE 6.1
Three Possible Relationships among Liberty, Equality, and Fraternity

tarianism, equality, freedom, and democracy are on Williams' list of fifteen primary values; but so also is racism.[6] Rokeach's list of eighteen "terminal" values includes freedom, equality, true friendship, and a world at peace.[7]

It is, of course, essential in the sociological study of values to distinguish between values as ideology and values as one of the elements influencing behavior. When values conflict, when interests intrude, when ignorance prevails, when group pressure is strong, values are likely to be a poor index of behavior.

THE RELATIONSHIPS AMONG LIBERTY, EQUALITY, AND FRATERNITY

It is possible to imagine several different relationships among liberty, equality, and fraternity: 1) They are mutually supportive: What encourages or increases one also expands the others. 2) They are mutually competitive or contradictory; they stand in a zero-sum relationship: What encourages or increases one leads to the decline of the others. 3) They are independent of each other: All possible combinations can occur, because each is influenced by a distinctive set of causes.

The three relationships can be sketched as shown in figure 6.1.

The three charts represent no actual situation. Aspects of all three may operate in some societies under various sets of circumstances, allowing persons with widely varying views to find support for their interpretations of the relationships among liberty, equality, and fraternity.

In chart 1, I suggest that a society cannot increase liberty—move upward on the scale—without simultaneously increasing equality and fraternity. From this perspective, if white South Africans want to be free of fear and free of the restrictions imposed by many other societies, they must become more egalitarian and fraternal across racial lines. Liberty, equality, and fraternity are lashed together like mountain climbers. Movement upward for one requires upward movement of the others also. To continue this metaphor: there is a little slack in the cords that unite them (without such slack, it is difficult to move at all). A great deal of slack, however (line A in figure 6.1), creates a situation where a precipitous fall of one or two of the climbers brings down all three.

In chart 2, point A is equidistant from the maximums of each of the values (represented by the corners). It is the point of least total distance from the three value corners taken together. Any movement toward one of the corners (points B, C, or D) will increase the distance from the other corners. A strong push for liberty, if this model is correct, means a retreat from goals of equality and fraternity. For fifty years or more the USSR made strides toward equality, both of opportunity and of income, but at the expense of liberty and, at best, modest gains in fraternal feelings across the land.[8] Since 1985 there has been a strong push for liberty, affecting speech, religion, politics, and occupations. Our emphasis on equality, many Soviet reformers were saying in the last several years, has made us "equal in poverty" while creating a system that has sharply curtailed our liberties. As ideological fervor faded, the "free-rider problem" became more severe; i.e., why should I work hard when no one else does and when I receive my equal share of the pittance in any event? That attitude, say the reformers, can be changed only be rewarding effort, by recognizing differences in achievement—by increasing inequality while expanding liberties.[9]

The great majority in Russia and the other republics that made up the USSR, however, have not at this writing benefited from the liberties in the more open society, even as they learn that the egalitarian ethic they were taught had by no means been equally applied. Their suspicions that party officials, black marketeers, mobsters, and others were very well off are now openly confirmed.

With the modest security of egalitarianism lost, envy at any sign of economic success, more than enterprise, has been the result. Ethnic prejudices and conflicts have been reinforced. Azerbaijanis and Armenians attack each other; the Russian suspicions of Georgians as bourgeois exploiters increase; antisemitism is reinforced. In the short run, at least, the increase in freedom and the explicit support for a more inegalitarian reward system has had very unfraternal consequences.

Such tensions among liberty, equality, and fraternity are the stuff of headlines in many parts of the world, certainly including the United States. In France, at the height of a flood of immigrants in the early 1970s—a flood accompanied by exploitation, discrimination, and violence—Jean-Paul Sartre wrote: "We will not accept the rebirth of this sick ideology [a new racism; police and gang brutality] which we knew all too well during the time of the Algerian war. Or else, let us take away the word 'equality' from the three words we are told form the French motto. (It is true that we could also take away the other two [Sartre added], but that is another story)."[10]

To the extent that chart 2 correctly suggests the empirical situation, a democracy does not seek to maximize any one of the three values. It seeks to optimize them, that is, to achieve the most total value of the three taken together.

In chart 3 liberty, equality, and fraternity are depicted as relatively independent values, not specifically interdependent, as in chart 1, or inevitably competitive, as in chart 2. The social space represented by the cube can hold every combination, whether of high salience or low, of the three variables. Width represents fraternity; depth, equality; and height, liberty. The corner marked by three "l s" is the low point on each of the scales; the corner with three "H s" is the high point where liberty, equality, and fraternity are all at a maximum. This model leaves open the possibility that many different combinations of the three values can be found, depending upon a variety of conditions.

Liberty

Freedom is nothing. The really arduous task is to know what to do with it.

— Andre Gide

Inevitably each of the three terms has been defined in a variety of ways. Liberty is most commonly thought of as freedom from the tyranny of leaders and from constraints by the majority where those restraints are unnecessary for the larger public good. It is the right to participate in decision-making in matters regarding one's own self. Liberty is the availability of a choice among good alternatives. It is "freedom from arbitrary, despotic, or authoritarian rule or control" (*Oxford English Dictionary*). In a more sociological sense, "liberty means that the capacity to resist oppression is widely distributed."[11] In the often-cited words of John Stuart Mill: "The sole end for which mankind are warranted, individually or collectively in interfering with the liberty of action of any of their number, is self-protection. . . . the only purpose for which power can be rightfully exercised over any member of a civilized community, against his will, is to prevent harm to others. His own good, either physical or moral is not sufficient warrant."[12] (It is a bit surprising to find a predecessor in Hobbes, who declared that a free man is one who is not hindered to do what he has a will to do.)

Mill emphasized freedom *from*, what Isaiah Berlin has called "negative liberty," believing that unless men are left to follow their own paths, civilization cannot advance. Truth will fail for lack of a free market in ideas. Constrained by tradition, people will find little room for spontaneity, originality, or moral courage.

Mill is not entirely clear on the extent to which he saw such liberty as based upon a framework of law and individual responsibility. Many critics, however, have emphasized "those wise restraints that make men free"—a slogan that sends shudders through staunch individualists. Tawney affirmed that the liberty of the strong must be restrained lest the liberty of the weak be destroyed.—"Freedom for the pike is death for the minnow."

A century before Mill, Rousseau, in helping to pave the way for the liberté asserted by the French Revolution, saw such liberty not as unrestrained individual freedom. "but the possession by all, and not merely by some, of the fully qualified members of a society a share in the public power which is entitled to interfere with every aspect of a citizen's life."[13] As Berlin has observed, nineteenth-century liberals saw clearly that such "liberty" could destroy their "negative liberty." "They pointed out that the sovereignty of the people could easily destroy that of individuals."[14] This is a highly contemporary controversy, to which we will return.

In the early history of the struggle for liberty, it meant "protection against the tyranny of political rulers." At a larger stage, constitutional checks that guaranteed such protection were sought. Then the idea emerged that governors should be delegates of all, that their terms of office should be temporary, and that their positions be revocable. Later it came to be seen that the will of the people might also become the "tyranny of the majority."[15] Mill's insight concerning the need for protection against prevailing opinion and feeling, as well as against the power of rulers, is frequently confirmed. To illustrate this, one need only examine the crush of popular sentiment in the United States during the recent war and the fragile victory over Iraq.

Thus liberty can mean collective freedom from the unconstrained domination by King Louis XVI or King George III. Or it can mean, in the American idiom: Don't fence me in; I'll do it my way; I'm king of the wild frontier. Concerned with this ambiguity, if not contradiction in the meaning of liberty, Mill wondered how societies can adjust to both independence and interdependence. In a similar way, Durkheim was concerned over "the malady of infinite aspiration," of insatiable desires. Liberty, as he saw it, was the fruit of regulation, not just the chance to do what one pleases. To be free is to be master of oneself, to act rationally, and to do one's duty.

The belief in the value of "free enterprise," so strongly emphasized in the United States during the last several years, exalts the name of the Adam Smith of *The Wealth of Nations* (each person working diligently in his own behalf benefits the society as a whole) while neglecting the Adam Smith of *A Theory of Moral Sentiments* (sympathy and altruism are natural and essential aspects of human societies).

Some recent students of American individualism, a concept often associated with liberty, see a strong tendency toward lawlessness in the emphasis on individualism. They stress the lack of a sense of civic responsibility, the neglect of the obligations associated with liberty by Adam Smith, Durkheim, and by political and religious traditions, which at an earlier time both promoted and contained it.[16]

In Eastern Europe today, the "romance of the market" so attractive to some of the reformers expresses the same tensions. Gavril Popov, former mayor of Moscow, while working for a free market notes the contradictions that can develop between such reform and democratization—a society with widely shared opportunities and participation.[17]

Equality

Equality is similarity in the distribution of scarce goods and services. It is "the condition of having equal dignity, rank or privileges with others" (*Oxford English Dictionary*). Except in some communes, equality is seldom taken to mean identity of income and privilege. There is, however, a continuing debate between those who emphasize equality of opportunity and those who emphasize equality of result. R. H. Tawney in *Equality* developed the classic argument for greater attention to results, without which, in his view, neither liberty for all nor equality is possible. Tawney believed that in America the concept of equality has come to mean, for most people, an equal chance for those of rare ability to get ahead; "The consolation which it offers for social evils consists in the statement that exceptional individuals can succeed in evading them." This is wrong, he believed, because it suggests "that opportunities to rise, which can, of their nature, be seized only by the few, are a substitute for a general diffusion of the means of civilization, which are needed by all."[18]

The ways in which people are seen as equal or unequal—differences that make a difference—vary from society to society and through time. Among the most common criteria are income, wealth, diverse skills and personal characteristics, manners, dialects, ethnic and racial identities, and titles or other honorific marks. Historically in the United States, individualism, most clearly connected with liberty, also had an egalitarian side. Not only are all men "created equal," but they are also "endowed by their creator with certain inalienable rights"—life, liberty, and the pursuit of happiness. That resonant 1776 declaration was reaffirmed by President Lincoln "four score and seven years" later, when he proclaimed the United States as "a new nation, conceived in liberty and dedicated to the proposition that all men are created equal."

By the late nineteenth century, however, the triumph of industrial capitalism, Harold Laski argued, "made liberty a function of one's place in the market's hierarchy of power."[19] The connection with that aspect of individualism that was tied to equality was broken. Yet he added that "no one has yet been able to make a successful frontal attack on the idea of equality."[20]

One might argue that Laski cannot have it both ways. The two quotations are separated by 300 pages; perhaps he had changed his mind by the time he got to the second statement. I think not. Viewing the American scene from the English Left, he saw a continuing, if weakened, influence of the idea of equality. Many, probably most, Americans were familiar not only with the phrases from the Declaration of Independence and Lincoln quoted above, but also with the words of a first-century Jewish radical: "It is easier for a camel to go through the eye of a needle than for a rich man to enter into the Kingdom of God."

The degree of equality or inequality is a major influence on ethnic relationships. In many countries there are ethnic groups substantially worse off than the dominant groups. (I need mention only the United States, South Africa, Israel, and most of the countries of Western Europe.) In other countries, competitive ethnic groups compare themselves not only with each other, but also with living standards abroad that are vastly higher than their own—differences that today are widely known (for example, Russia, many of the countries of Eastern Europe, Sri Lanka, and Malaysia).

Insofar as ethnic tension and conflict are a product of such inequality, many societies face an extraordinarily difficult challenge. Even if average incomes go up, the relative differences, which are the critical ones in social interaction, can sustain the fear of loss among those on top and the sense of injustice among those on bottom.

We also have to ask ourselves, however, whether in the foreseeable future average incomes may not decline worldwide. Sixty years ago, Lord Keynes speculated that the day might come—perhaps in the next century—when everybody would be rich, a condition within which, he believed, humankind will "once more value ends above means and prefer the good to the useful."[21] Those who take such an optimistic view are not concerned with relative deprivation, nor with the exhaustion of irreplaceable resources. And they believe that advances in technology will allow the earth to support its probable ten billion human inhabitants by the year 2050 while safely dealing with the trash and pollutants they create. Although I have no firm evidence, I believe such views are dominant today, at least in wealthy societies.

Beginning about twenty years ago, however, a movement concerned with environmental and demographic problems developed a different view. Referring to the wealthy societies, those who hold this view declare: "We are waging economic war against our own grandchildren by consuming a vast proportion of the world's irreplaceable resources and leaving them, in place of those resources, a legacy of garbage, junk, chemical pollutants, and radioactive waste, some of it with a half-life of 32,000 years, that we have only barely begun to learn how to contain."[22] When we think of the economically poor societies, and the disadvantaged ethnic groups within them, we are reminded by their rapid growth that it took until 1800 for the human population to reach one billion. Now, at an accelerating rate, the world will add the sixth billion in ten or eleven years.

As Lasch has recently written, we can no longer hope to solve the problem of poverty by making everyone rich. "Earth's ecology will no longer sustain an indefinite expansion of productive forces."[23] Read that alongside such facts as this: For the world as a whole to use as much energy per capita as is now used by the wealthiest one billion would require a five fold increase in energy production. Now double the present world population—a near certainty within fifty years—to see what the energy situation could be like half a century from now.

If this view of the near future is correct—a view that stresses the ecological costs, the resource loss, the population growth—dominant ethnic groups may find themselves forced to a lower resource-using, lower consumption style of life. The scramble among the rich may become fierce (perhaps I should say even more fierce.) The plight of the poor will become more desperate. Unless income is distributed more equitably and resources used more carefully, ethnic conflict is likely to be intensified.

But perhaps Lord Keynes is our prophet. In that case, we shall have to worry only about the effects of relative deprivation.[24]

Fraternity

These comments on liberty and equality would lose much of their relevance for the study of ethnicity if the two values seen separately and in interaction were not connected with *fraternity*. Who is to have liberty? To whom am I equal? Against whom or what must I struggle for liberty and equality? Who will be my brother and my sister in that struggle?

Fraternity, the dictionary tells us, is pertaining to brothers, to brotherliness. (Today we must mean fraternity-sorority or humanity, although I use fraternity, often quoting others, in the generic sense.) It means relative similarity in the distribution of social honor, so that each is close to, the brother or sister of, the other. Or each is a potential brother or sister if they happen to meet. Or, to put it perhaps even more strongly, each is a potential brother- or sister-in-law.

In contrast with the enormous amount of commentary on liberty and equality, fraternity is seldom analyzed. The critical question, especially as it relates to ethnicity, is the diameter of the circle that encloses the metaphorical family. We are all children of God, say the world religions in their sacred texts and sermonic flourishes, if not consistently in their institutions and activities. For some, however, "brother" extends only to the five or six members of their "gang." More commonly, it reaches only those with whom one shares an ethnic identity, a political ideology, a religion; and even those boundaries often prove to be too expansive.

Sébastien Chamfort, the aphorist, having witnessed many innocents killed, wrote this parody of a motto for fraternity in the French Revolution: "Be my brother or I'll kill you." Half a century later, on an optimistic note, Victor Hugo wrote "A day will come when you, France; you, Russia; you, Italy, you, England; you, Germany—all of you nations of the [European] continent will, without losing, your distinctive qualities, be blended into a . . . European fraternity."[25] Will 1993 and the years that follow prove him right?

The same contrast as that between Chamfort and Hugo can be found in America's attitudes toward brotherhood. McWilliams has shown how difficult it was, even for the Puritans, to hold to an inclusive fraternal view.[26] Although the universalist theme was not lost, fellow believers were not immune from exclusion. Pushing out at least to the country's boundaries, Americans sing: "God shed his grace on thee; and crown thy good with brotherhood, from sea to shining sea." More often, however, they sing of bombs bursting in air—a less fraternal image.

Thus ambiguity surrounds the meaning of fraternity, as of liberty and equality. It speaks of unity, and of separation. It implies comradeship, but also conflict. Edwin Markham expressed his view while capturing this ambiguity:[27]

> He drew a circle that shut me out—
> Heretic, rebel, a thing to flout.
> But love and I had the wit to win.
> We drew a circle that took him in.

How wide must the circle be before we speak of fraternity? And how shall we gauge the diameter? Ideological measures are easy to find—both restrictive and expansive; but behavioral measures are rare. Dostoyevsky suggested one which, by its application, led him to a pessimistic view: "Until you have become really, in actual fact, a brother of everyone, brotherhood will not come to pass. No sort of scientific teaching, no kind of common interest, will ever teach men to share property and privilege with equal consideration for all. Everyone will think his share too small and they will be always envying, complaining and attacking one another."[28]

"To share property and privilege with equal consideration for all"—Dostoyevsky has given us a good definition of fraternity. It suggests a severe test. Judging by behavior, conceptions of "all" seldom extend past one's own society, and within that, one's ethnic group or even local community. Robert Reich has recently documented the extent to which the wealthiest fifth of American families have separated themselves into quite homogeneous residential clusters, aided by federal tax policies and expenditures.[29] "The fortunate fifth," he suggests, "are quietly seceding from the rest of the nation" into relatively ethnically homogeneous neighborhoods. Their contributions to charity are scarcely half, in percentage terms, of those of the poorest Americans. And they give mostly "to the places and institutions that entertain, inspire, cure or educate wealthy Americans. . . . If inhabitants of another area are poorer, let them look to one another. Why should *we* pay for *their* schools?"[30] If the available tax base in American cities is shrinking, while the need for public support is growing,[31] that need not trouble the comfortable. They can move farther out, support federal policies that reduce federal grants to cities, and turn over the deteriorating inner cores, demographically and politically, to the ethnic minorities who remain.[32]

This is not a complete picture of course. Every sentence in the several previous paragraphs needs to be qualified. But those qualifications, in my judgment, will not strongly challenge the evidence that fraternity, at this point in American history, is being enclosed within narrow bounds.

Many different circles are also being drawn in Eastern Europe. Marx's idea of fraternity and that of communism generally was not universalistic. The aim was to attain a unity of working classes across international boundaries in a common struggle against the ruling classes. But even the fraternity of comrades exalted in communist societies is now being challenged in Eastern Europe by a revival, in some societies, of chauvinism, of ethnic nationalism. While one of the major efforts in Eastern Europe is to move toward democracy and pluralism, another is to redraw the old national lines. Dahrendorf sees in this development the threat of fascism. By that he means a "combination of a nostalgic idea of community which draws harsh boundaries between those who belong and those who do not with a new political monopoly of a man or a movement."[33] Exaggerated emphasis on ethnic self-determination can lead to a politics of chauvinistic mobilization, not one of freedom of choice.

Although these two faces of politics are found in many parts of the world (they are not lacking in the United States) they are most clearly seen in a disintegrating Yugoslavia and in Eastern Europe, as the Commonwealth of Independent States and the former satellites of the USSR search for new structures to replace a disintegrating communism. In Russia two types of anti-Communism contend not only with remnants of the old regime but with each other. One "is liberal, pluralistic, and European; the other . . . is xenophobic, authoritarian, turned toward the past and toward restoring the life of the past."[34] Russia and Russian culture have been nearly destroyed, in the view of the latter group, not simply by communism, but by a decadent Western civilization, of which communism was one of the offspring.

The fraternal line, for those who hold such views, is an ethnic line. A nation-state, not a cosmopolitan, pluralistic state, is their goal.

Though the two faces of anti-communism can be seen most vividly in Russia and some of the other republics from the Soviet Union, they are visible throughout the region. In Poland "there are certain people who hold aliens and foreigners—Russians, Germans, Jews, cosmopolites, Freemasons—accountable for bringing communism."[35] Contrasted with those who see the future of Poland as part of Europe, they see it in ethnic terms. In Bulgaria, some seek to deny Muslims the right to use their own names. In the Transylvanian region of Romania some are attempting to prevent those of Hungarian background from attaining full rights as citizens, an expression of an ethnic conflict that goes back at least to the dual monarchy of the Austro-Hungarian Empire, 1848ff, during which Romanians were the ones living under severe cultural restraints. And the fragile fraternal ties in Yugoslavia have been cut, even in multi-ethnic, thoroughly European Sarajevo.[36]

Such constrictions of the circles of fraternity may seem far removed from the American experience. If we study them more carefully, however, we may find them highly relevant. Consider the work of Andrei Sinyavsky as he discusses the dissident movement in the last years of the Soviet Union. It is a struggle, he writes, not for material privileges nor even for democracy. "It fights for the individual. After a hiatus of fifty years, the Soviet man suddenly discovered that he was a person, not an impersonal sociopolitical category. . . . Dissidence reintroduced into Soviet civilization the notion of the individual."[37] Joseph Frank wonders if this might not cast a new light on the American scene: "In these days, when American universities are filled with people insisting that 'persons' can only be defined (or should be defined) in terms of 'race, class, and gender,' Sinyavsky's pages might help them to see what occurs when impersonal sociopolitical categories take precedence over individuals and are used as unquestioned guides to social action."[38]

In a paradoxical way, emphasis on the individual can help to enlarge the circles of fraternity.

Lest this be read to apply only to minority ethnic groups or women, one must emphasize that prejudice and discrimination by those in dominant groups have most clearly drawn the lines that mark "impersonal sociopolitical categories." Those lines will be erased or weakened when, as a first step, prejudice and discrimination have been significantly reduced. Then more members of disadvantaged ethnic groups will be able to say: I am treated as an individual. I can now give less attention to my "category," more to my individuality.

AFFIRMATIVE ACTION: DOES IT INCREASE LIBERTY?

To give greater immediacy to the rather abstract definitions and illustrative comments on liberty, equality, and fraternity, I have selected three topics for more detailed analysis. Each is particularly relevant for one of the trilogy of democratic values, but all apply as well to the interdependencies among those values. My aim, again, is to show that studies of ethnicity require attention to a wide range of theories which, when combined, give us a richer understanding of the several levels of influence on human behavior.

Many inter-ethnic controversies and intellectual disagreements are severe because the cultures of each of the groups as well as their shared culture furnish strong support for competing values. The disagreements and conflicts over the preferred kinds and degrees of liberty, equality, and fraternity are seen not only between ethnic groups, but also within groups and within many individuals.

Affirmative action illustrates in a powerful way just such clashes of values. Opposition to affirmative action, to be sure, rests in part on self-interest. While documenting that connection in their study of national survey data, however, Kluegel and Smith also found that negative racial feelings, perception that affirmative action has egalitarian effects, and beliefs that opportunities are already equal had stronger influences.[39]

We need to add that self-interest and racial hostility are insufficient by themselves to explain opposition to affirmative action. Some persons with no evident self-interest and with tolerant ethnic and racial views are also opposed. They see affirmative action as a constraint on individualism, a restriction on the rights of employers to select the most efficient work force or colleges to select the best qualified students, and an unjust imposition of burdens on some who have not themselves discriminated. In the terms of this chapter, they value what Isaiah Berlin calls "negative liberty" over programs designed to increase equality. They oppose group oriented efforts to increase opportunities as collectivist threats to the liberties of an individualistic society.[40]

The disagreement over values seems to me to be deeper than the disagreement over facts, and indeed to be a substantial cause of the latter. We readily understand why persons who believe they or those with whom they identify will be helped or harmed by affirmative action support or oppose it. But such direct interests are often not involved, or they are reenforced by reference to basic values. It would be desirable if our various judgments of fairness were made by application of John Rawls' criterion (that is fair which is agreed upon by well-informed persons of good faith who don't know to which group they will belong), but our judgments are more primordial—buried deep within our biographies and group histories.

Proponents of affirmative action believe that the protection and growth of liberty require substantially more equality than now exists in most societies. They share the view of R. H. Tawney that when the capacities of some are stifled by the social environment, equality of opportunity is a myth. "As though opportunity for talent to rise could be equalized in a society where the circumstances surrounding it from birth are themselves unequal."[41] A false dichotomy is often drawn between equality of opportunity and equality of results. They are closely bound together. It means little to admit persons to the contest who formerly were excluded or were made to play under restrictive rules, if they have no shoes, or no coaching, or no experience, or no breakfast.

Sources of support for or opposition to affirmative action programs and the consequences of such programs vary from society to society; and they vary through time, as circumstances change. In Malaysia, "The groups that receive the benefits of affirmative action policies are the ones who have the political power to legislate them."[42] There it is the Malays who are economically disadvantaged but politically advantaged. Similar situations developed in Kenya, Uganda, and Indonesia—post-colonial societies—where the strongest ethnic groups, suddenly in power, have seized advantages, legislatively and coercively. Indigenous minority ethnic groups, but more particularly immigrant minorities (Indians and Chinese), have faced economic and political barriers including, in some cases, violence and expulsion.

These situations have some similarity with the United States. Until the late 1930s, those with power maintained private and quasi-public "affirmative action" programs (racially exclusive labor unions, a gender- and ethnically-labelled occupational structure, racial barriers to political participation). These strongly reenforced the advantages of those who made the rules. Such advantages, as we shall see, have not been eliminated.

The explicit affirmative action program in Malaysia has worked in the sense that it has improved the economic situation of Malays and, less certainly, the country as a whole. The least advantaged members of all the ethnic groups, however, have received few if any benefits; and ethnic tensions remain, particularly between the Malays and those of Chinese background. For a quarter of a century, however, violent confrontation has been avoided.

Affirmative action in India emerged out of a very different kind of situation. It has not been a case of the politically powerful seizing or protecting advantages. The democratic ideology that propelled the independence movement included a kind of civil rights program for the so-called "outcastes"—the scheduled castes, the Harijans (children of God in Gandhi's term), the Dalits, as they now call themselves. They are the recipients of specifically labeled educational grants; approximately one-seventh of government jobs and of seats in parliament and the state legislatures are assigned to Harijans, reflecting their proportion of the population. This unabashed quota system has been the source of some controversy; violence against Harijans continues. Nevertheless, affirmative action has meant significant educational, economic, and political gains for some members of this and other highly disadvantaged groups.[43]

The United States has a mixture of affirmative action for the powerful and affirmative action for the disadvantaged. Although they are not typically labeled as such, there are dozens of ad hoc "affirmative action" programs that for the most part benefit members of the dominant ethnic groups. These programs and actions are sometimes private, sometimes public. They are not typically designed, of course, to assist a particular ethnic or racial group, although the benefits are unequally distributed among such groups. "Rules get stretched to meet extraordinary social needs when a Lockheed must be bailed out or the S&L debts redeemed. "Favoritism" toward one company or social sector is justified by social need. Welfare for the rich makes people very lax about the rules."[44]

Discrimination plays a part in maintaining advantages for some ethnic groups over others. In 1991 the Urban Institute reported a study of the results of job applications. Matched pairs of white and black young men (476 pairs in all) were sent on interviews for the same job, from a list drawn at random from classified advertisements of entry-level jobs in the Washington *Post* and Chicago *Tribune*. The white candidates (or auditors, as they are called in this kind of study) moved further along in the job process 20 percent of the time, the black candidates 7 percent of the time. Fifteen percent of the white young men, 5 percent of the black young men were offered jobs—significantly different rates.[45] Since the auditors were competing against real applicants, there was no expectation that one of the auditors would, in most cases, receive a job offer.)

In 1990, the Urban Institute used the auditing method to assess the level of discrimination against Hispanic jobseekers. In 31 percent of the audits of matched Hispanic-Anglo pairs in San Diego and Chicago, the majority applicants advanced further through the hiring process than the Hispanic applicants. In 11 percent of the cases the Hispanic applicant advanced further. The 20 percent difference is even larger than the Black-White difference found in the later study. Job offers were made to 22 percent of the Anglos, 8 percent of the Hispanics.[46]

A similar study with a larger and more representative sample, this one dealing with housing, has recently been completed. Nearly 3,800 audits, using matched pairs of black or Hispanic and non-Hispanic white prospective home buyers or renters, were carried out in twenty-five major metropolitan areas. Five of these areas were selected because of their large Hispanic and black populations (to make certain they were in the pool); the other twenty were selected randomly. Each audit was based on a sample of housing advertisements in the major Sunday newspaper.

I will give only the summary figures, based on a multinomial logit analysis: 58.9 percent of potential black home buyers and 56.0 percent of black renters faced discrimination; 56 percent of Hispanic home buyers and 50.1 percent of Hispanic renters faced discrimination. "Both blacks and Hispanics have a better than fifty-fifty chance of encountering some form of systematic unfavorable treatment each time they visit a landlord or real estate broker to inquire about housing."[47]

Studies of job and housing discrimination based on publicly advertised openings leave unanswered the extent of discrimination in situations where the jobs or residences are obtained by private contacts of various sorts; but informal evidence suggests that discrimination is more prevalent in such circumstances.

These studies of job and housing discrimination furnish clear evidence of affirmative action—in these cases largely by private agents, but with lack of attention, at the least, on the part of public officials—favoring the dominant majority.

Objections to affirmative action programs designed to help the disadvantaged are partly based on the concern that qualified Xs will be subordinated to less qualified Ys. There are several questions related to this concern: Does it rest on false perceptions? What qualifications are taken into account and how are they measured? Does discrimination play a part in causing any differences among ethnic groups in the levels of qualification?

Dovidio and Gaertner wondered whether it might not be a threatened reversal of statuses, rather than or in addition to the belief that the less qualified would be promoted, that causes opposition to affirmative action programs.[48] To test the hypothesis that perceptions of status played a part, they introduced to alternate partners in an experimental task, black or white males who had been designated as either subordinate or superiors in the project. They were also described, allegedly on the basis of previous tests, as being higher or lower in competence, in cognitive ability, than the subjects. Perceptions—or more accurately preconceptions—led to different evaluations of the white and black members of the experimental groups. The higher-ability blacks were evaluated as less competent, but the experimentally designated higher-ability whites were recognized as superior. In "helping behavior," which was part of the experiment, black subordinates were favored relative to black supervisors, regardless of ability; but the high-ability whites elicited more help than the low-ability whites.

The recent study of job discrimination indicated again that ethnic perceptions affect economic opportunities. Stereotypes continue to influence the choice of workers, as illustrated by the comments of a store manager: "It's unfortunate, but in my business I think overall [black men] tend to be known to be dishonest. . . . They're known to be lazy. . . . Go look in the jails."[49]

Although in the United States there has been a forty-year decline in such stereotyped beliefs,[50] they are still widespread. In his 1990 analysis of General Social Survey data, Smith found that a majority of whites still believe that Hispanics and Blacks prefer welfare to hard work, and are lazier, more violence-prone, less intelligent, and less patriotic than are whites. He also found that these images significantly predict attitudes toward such programs as affirmative action. These "images," as Smith calls them, "brand minorities as undeserving of help."[51]

It seems wise to listen to Dovidio and Gaertner: "Although affirmative action programs may initially generate negative reactions, they may be important steps in breaking down the barriers created by stereotypic thinking."[52]

Some Questions Related to Affirmative Action

How reliable and valid are the measures used to determine qualifications of candidates for professional training or for jobs? In April 1991, a white student at the Georgetown University Law School wrote in the student-run *Law Weekly* that a sample (obtained surreptitiously) of recent LSAT scores averaged 36, out of a possible 48, among black applicants and 43 among the white applicants. There was a similar difference in undergraduate grade-point averages (3.2 to 3.7). Are these adequate measures of talent? If so, talent for what? A Georgetown professor wrote that "preferential treatment in law schools is old hat. The preferred group, however, has been the children of affluent whites."[53]

Perhaps neither the student nor the professor made the right point. It is of little value if schools replace one mistaken admissions procedure with another. And it is of little value to point out that pre-matriculation test scores are lower for some, if post-graduation careers take those with the lower scores into communities and jobs for which they are especially qualified and where they are strongly needed.

Is there an alternative to affirmative action programs that has increased or might be expected to increase minority ethnic representation significantly throughout the educational and occupational systems? That was one of the tests of the "Brennan group" of the Supreme Court in the Bakke case. The deans of the four publically supported law schools in California pointed out, in their brief filed with the Supreme Court in that case, that without "special admissions" programs the great underrepresentation of minority persons in law (and we can add, in professions generally) will continue. In 1970, 1.08 percent of lawyers were black. The ratio of Mexican-Americans was even lower.[54] As Erwin Griswold notes: "Law and medicine are inevitably involved in politics in the broad sense, and minority groups will be under-represented in the political process if their members cannot gain admission to the professions."[55]

What has happened as a result of affirmative action? By 1981, 4.4 percent of accredited law school students were black, 2.4 percent were Hispanic, quadrupling their representation in a decade.[56] Black enrollments in schools of medicine went up between 1968–1969 and 1979–1980 from 2.2 percent to 5.7 percent, and those of Hispanics from 0.2 percent to 3.9 percent.[57]

Does this mean that less qualified persons have been admitted in preference to some who are more qualified? "A study of 1,088 students in 14 classes at the University of California School of Medicine in San Francisco concluded that there is virtually no relationship between those scores [applicant test scores] and medical school grades. Standardized tests have often eliminated those persons who are most humane and empathetic."[58]

Some students have been judged by their placement among others of their own ethnic group—sometimes called a race-norming procedure. A National Research Council study has concluded that such a procedure more accurately predicts the job performance of black and Hispanic applicants than does the use of a single list.[59]

George Will, a journalist of generally conservative inclinations, commented on the decision of Congressman William Gray—a powerful member of the House of Representatives—to resign from the House to become head of the United Negro College Fund. The forty-one colleges, Will noted, may educate in the next decade close to one million students. "The students range from needy inner-city and rural blacks, *who for cultural reasons do not test well but who are college material,* to upper-middle class blacks (the Huxtable children) seeking an intensely black experience."[60] Will may one day conclude that the same logic ("who for cultural reasons do not test well") applies to the admission of some ethnic minority students to predominantly white colleges. From both the individual's and society's standpoint, it is the extent of the gain, not the score at the start, that is critical for wise policy.

Race-norming, like affirmative action generally, is highly controversial. It may be wise to compare it, not with some faultless process, but with the real-life procedures with which it competes. In citing data about the increase in the number of black police officers and firefighters. Thomas Edsall notes "the use in some cases of hiring procedures that do not strictly follow civil service selection of those who do the best on test batteries. [This is] arguably in less variance with merit selection than patronage, old-boy networks and nepotism historically characteristic of city, union, and private sector job allocation."[61]

According to census data, affirmative action programs have significantly increased the number and proportion of black police officers and firefighters in the United States. Between 1960 and 1989, the percentage of black police officers increased from 3.7 to 13.1; and the percentage of black firefighters from 1.9 to 12.0.[62] With unemployment rates up, however, and real wages dropping steadily over a fifteen-year period, those figures are seen as threats, not accomplishments, by those to whom they represent lost opportunities. One of the respondents in a recent Washington *Post*/ABC poll, a Chicago firefighter, declared: "The guys they are stepping on are middle-class white Americans, and we are leaving in droves to vote for the Republican Party."[63] Such sentiments are indicated by the 80 to 17 percent opposition to racial preferences in jobs, the 76 to 22 percent opposition to preferences in college admissions. In fact, racial preferences are rarely used. The increases in minority representation come mainly from the reduction of discrimination.

At the same time, there is widespread recognition of discrimination against non-whites. Fifty-eight percent believe that equally qualified blacks are less likely to be promoted; 13 percent say they have a better chance.[64]

It has recently been argued that affirmative action is not only unfair—it is reverse discrimination—but that its side effects hurt those for whom its benefits are intended far more than they can gain from its presumed benefits. This is the view taken by Shelby Steele in his widely publicized *The Content of Our Character.* "One of the most troubling effects of racial preference for blacks," he writes, "is a kind of demoralization . . . an enlargement of self doubt. Under affirmative action the quality that earns us preferential treatment is an implied inferiority."[65]

Julian Bond, with tongue just barely in cheek, plays on this theme. President Bush and Congress, he writes, have overlooked an important reason for passing a civil rights bill: "to help white men overcome their feelings of inferiority. . . . Many whites and some blacks now argue that preferential racial treatment creates deep-seated feelings of deficiency and mediocrity in its beneficiaries. . . . Think of it. For decades, white men have know they've received favored, front-of-the-line positions in jobs, education and the benefits of a race-conscious society. . . . The knowledge that maids, porters, garbage collectors, unemployed teenagers and cotton pickers were suspicious of their credentials took a heavy psychic toll on white American males." The civil rights movement, Bond suggests, helped to reduce that sense of inferiority; but because of recent court decisions that weakened civil rights for ethnic minorities, those feelings of inadequacy have returned. "If President Bush has any compassion, he will move swiftly to remove the awful stigma of race. These victims have suffered long enough. Free white men!"[66]

How adequate are the selection criteria? Affirmative action programs can lead to the reassessment not only of the modes of measurement, but of the criteria being measured, because such programs help also to reveal the culture of a society and its power structure. One way to explore this question would be to ask: Are there particular contributions that underrepresented groups can make that are not now included in the selection criteria? This is an extremely complicated set of questions, with ethical and policy issues pressing into every empirical examination of them. Twenty-five years ago, before the term *affirmative action* had become current, but long after the issues to which it is connected had become important, Arthur Hertzberg wrote about one of the most significant, indeed poignant, illustrations of affirmative action: "The real question is what love and justice mean, concretely: how many Jewish school principals are commanded by the joint Negro-Jewish commitment to morality, and Jewish memories of persecution to go sell shoes, so less well-trained Negroes can hold their jobs?"[67] Perhaps we need to note that whether a person or group is "less well-trained" depends in part upon what one wants accomplished. Is a black teacher less well-trained to motivate black children to stay in school, to be sensitive to the aspirations and perspectives of the black population, to introduce perspectives on American culture and history that express more fully the roles of black people—perspectives essential for all who live in America?

Lest this seems to make standards of excellence completely relative, let me add, "Even granted that they are less well-trained now, is there any other way to achieve parity than to offer special opportunities for experience to overcome past disprivilege?"[68]

The Short View and the Long View on Affirmative Action

There are several varieties of affirmative action programs, involving different kinds of protagonists, with different kinds of political implications, and with quite different historical trajectories. Looking at this variety from the American experience, we have noted that some affirmative action has given special treatment to whites or to European-descended males. Until after World War II, there was affirmative action for gentiles in many colleges and universities, both for students and faculties. Jews were excluded or admitted in very small numbers. For years, Marian Anderson could not sing at the Met nor in the convention hall of the DAR in Washington. Until 1946 there were no black players among the 400 members of self-named "big league" baseball teams.

What do such items have in common? In each instance, there were already many trained and talented persons from the excluded groups fully qualified as students, professors, singers, or ball players to compete at the highest level. As soon as the barriers were removed, for a combination of civil rights and economic reasons, representation from the excluded ethnic groups expanded rapidly. The abundance of candidates was the result of ethnic institutions and traditions parallel to those of the "exclusive" whites or gentiles.

In other situations, the transition from exclusion to inclusion is not so easy. Some members of the excluded ethnic groups are fully qualified, but many others are not. Careful training and support are needed, but once given and sustained, initial inequalities are quite rapidly reduced. The American armed forces, almost completely segregated and with only the least skilled positions open to blacks before 1949, illustrate this kind of situation. Blacks are now found at all levels from bottom to top, with growing numbers in the most demanding positions. Where needed, remedial and on-the-job training is widely used. In a few decades the United States, through affirmative action, has achieved a major transformation, if not yet a fully completed one.

A third kind of affirmative action program designed to attain equality of opportunity among ethnic groups is the most controversial. The gaps between the average members of ethnic groups, with regard to the skills required, are so large and the inequality in cultural capital so pervasive, that a few months of training, or even a few years, may not be adequate to attain parity. Intensive preparatory training, the accumulation of more cultural capital in families and communities, and changes in the society at large (reduced discrimination in particular) are all required.

It is difficult in a democracy for our political agents to ask long-run as well as short-run questions, but it need not be for the scholar. Is that stretch toward equality that we call "affirmative action of the third kind" best seen as a capital investment, using capital in the strictly economic sense of postponed consumption? Instead of using a shovel to excavate for a new building, we first build a factory that can manufacture scoop shovels and train workers who can use them. It does not strain our sociological imaginations to enlarge the meaning of capital to include the creation of skills, by training and by experience, the major benefits of which occur in the second and later generations.

Modern societies seem culturally better prepared, however, to support the long process of making machine tools that make tools that make parts that are combined to make consumer goods, than they are prepared to accept equivalent processes dealing with the human factor in achieving desired goals.

Nathan Glazer has written that "the reality that many people try to resist is that equality of opportunity and of treatment, insofar as we can measure it, will not automatically lead to an equal outcome for all groups—at least not rapidly."[69] I agree with that observation, although not with its implications, as he sees them. Feinberg, in his well-titled paper, "At a Snail's Pace,"[70] emphasizes that the time to equality as a result of affirmative action programs is long, due to an important degree to structural inertia—affected by such factors as the comparative sizes of groups, the continuously changing pattern of jobs in the occupational structure, and differences among groups in years of experience and tenure. Lieberson and Fuguitt also show that structural effects on job opportunities would persist for several generations, even after the impact of discrimination has been removed. They also indicate, however, that the removal of discrimination would sharply reduce the differences in one generation.[71]

For nearly twenty years after the passage of the Civil Rights Act in the United States, the Supreme Court interpreted it as an indication that the Congress sought not only to prevent individual acts of discrimination but also to attack the structural sources. In *Griggs v. Duke Power Company*, 1971, the Court declared that "Practices, procedures, or tests neutral on their face, and even neutral in . . . intent cannot be maintained if they operate to 'freeze' the status quo of prior discriminatory practices." This principle has been embodied in British legislation dealing with sex discrimination and race relations (although seldom used in practice). It has also been used by the Court of Justice of the European Community as the proper test of the legality of employment provisions.[72]

A second principle designed to attack structural discrimination was formulated in the 1978 *Bakke* case: "It permitted both private and public institutions to give some preference in hiring or admission decisions, to individual members of minority groups in order to help overcome the structural consequences of generations of injustice."[73] "Some preference," however, did not mean quotas, which were unacceptable to the Court, but goals.

In recent years, these two principles have been reversed by the Supreme Court.[74] Affirmative action designed to reduce structural discrimination has been sharply curtailed by decisions that hold the only specific historical discrimination affecting specific individuals is covered by the Civil Rights Act.[75] In my judgment, this change indicates, once again, the inability or unwillingness of the American political system to sustain a long-run view in programs to increase equal opportunity.

deVries and Pettigrew, in a comparative study of affirmative action in the Netherlands and the United States, emphasize the different cultural contexts within which the two systems developed. In the Netherlands, the strong cultural opposition to prejudice and discrimination has led them to emphasize the positive effects of affirmative action. In the United States, attitudes are less favorable, racial prejudices are stronger. This leads to poorly executed programs and a tendency to stress the negative results, which are then used to "prove" that affirmative action is a failure. "The irony is," deVries and Pettigrew conclude, "that it is this same racist legacy that necessitates affirmative action in the first place. Critics of affirmative action blame the program for the problems, when they should point to the origin of these problems that affirmative action, properly administered and governmentally supported, could help to ameliorate."[76]

The Affirmative Action Dilemma

In attempting to maximize (or, more accurately, optimize) liberty and equality of opportunity among ethnic groups with very different historical experiences, societies are faced with a serious dilemma. As soon as you are equally qualified, the liberal moderate (if that is not an oxymoron) says, you will receive equal education and employment. Those who are behind reply, We cannot be equally qualified *until* we receive equal education and employment, because we need training, experience, hope, and models. Affirmative action programs say, in effect, that granted inter-ethnic history and contemporary situations, the latter argument is at this time the more powerful.

Does that imply the need for quotas to guarantee opportunities that have long been denied? No term is more ambiguous—and therefore more politically sensitive—than *quota*. In the past, and to some degree still today, a quota was a ceiling: No *more* than X percent of group A is to be accepted, appointed, or admitted. X sometimes meant, and means, zero percent. As a result, many qualified persons have been excluded.

Today, quota is more likely to be interpreted as a floor: No *less* than Y percent is to be accepted. The result of such a quota, it is often argued, is to bring in unqualified persons.

What happens, then, when a society sets goals rather than quotas? A goal, rather than a quota, is a soft, ambiguous, flexible, and therefore politically more acceptable target. It is criticized from the right for being a full-fledged quota and from the left for being a pious promise without authoritative backing. If one goes simply on the basis of past American experience, the latter judgment seems more nearly correct.

Are societies caught, then, between the devil and the deep blue sea? Probably. We had better learn quickly how to swim and how to foil the devil. This does not mean adopting quotas, but it does mean increasing the intensity of the reviews of goals to see that idle promises are not serving as policies. (It also means not muddying the political waters by calling goals "quotas.") If too few qualified or potentially qualified candidates are available, unqualified persons need not be selected; if more than enough are available, a higher number than the goal can be selected.

If goals are set by reference to population ratios, rather than by reference to those with the necessary qualifications *plus* those who can attain those qualifications on the job or by preparatory training and experience, the failure rate will be high. Costs will be high for those who fail, for the school or the company, and for the affirmative action program.[77] Noting that, one must also ask: What is failure? Who determines it? Has the training been adequate? What are the costs of doing nothing? Have we learned to take the long view?

Another part of the dilemma: So-called privileged groups contain members who also suffer from early and persisting disadvantages. They are likely to have the least seniority, the most shaky preparation—and are therefore most likely to be displaced. New and severe problems are thereby added, by affirmative action, to their already great frustrations.

The well-off among the dominant ethnic groups are quite well insulated against the shifts of opportunity. (If fact, it is when that insulation wears thin for *them* that affirmative action policies are brought under most severe pressure.)

Slowly, societies are learning how to spread the risks of social change—unemployment insurance, labor unions, social security systems, adult education and retraining programs, and the like, are involved—but little serious attention has been given specifically to programs that can spread the risks associated with affirmative action.

The mirror image of this problem is that a large share of the gains from affirmative action has gone to the most advantaged members of the target groups, those best able to compete without such programs. Our picture of the Harijan in India may be of ninety million utterly destitute peasants. That is an incomplete picture. There is a large number, even if a small percentage, in the scheduled castes who are well-trained and well-positioned to take advantage of the opportunities set aside for Harijans. In the United States also, the individuals who are best trained and best organized among the designated ethnic groups gain most from affirmative action. The moral of the story, in my judgment, is not that such programs should be set aside, as some minority as well as majority scholars have suggested, but that greatly increased attention should be given to those in greatest need. Since this will also increase the pressure on those most vulnerable in the dominant groups, their plight must be addressed simultaneously.

The tension between liberty and equality and the narrowing of the circles of fraternity implicit in affirmative action can be reduced, in my judgment, only in a situation where the need for affirmative action is also being steadily reduced by other policies. These would include policies related to poverty, education, nutrition, community planning, and many other issues. The dilemma faced by so-cieties seeking to reduce the inequalities of opportunity among ethnic groups is sharpest when programs related to those issues are being cut back or eliminated at the same time that affirmative action programs are being challenged and curtailed. The least protected in all of the groups involved are thereby thrust into harsh confrontation.

Costs are attached to affirmative action as to any other policy. Opponents and proponents who argue from an unspecified utopian position might better spend their time inventing a frictionless machine, or getting out 100 percent of the energy locked up in a gallon of gasoline, or batting a thousand.

INDOLENCE, CULTURE OF POVERTY, UNDERCLASS, OR WHAT?

Perhaps King Lear was wondering about the same question as he looked out at a group of beggars caught in a raging storm:

> Poor naked wretches, where so e'er you are
> That bide the pelting of this pitiless storm,
> How shall your houseless heads and unfed sides,
> Your loop'd and window'd raggedness, defend you
> From seasons such as these?
> —King Lear to the fool, Act II, iv

How indeed? How do the poor defend themselves from seasons such as these, which is to say, from all seasons? By wrapping themselves in a culture that explains, justifies, even celebrates their plight? By downgrading the value of things and experiences that others pursue, often frantically? By designing little acts of retaliation against those with so much power over them?

Studies of poverty, a term that in wealthy societies necessarily implies inequality, have flowed in a steady stream—perhaps I should say a torrent—for half a century or more. Being poor or well-off and being a member of certain ethnic groups are not, of course, synonymous.[78] In many societies, however, the correlation between income and ethnicity is high. The contrasts in wealth are even greater. This is true in most Latin American countries, in South Africa, in the United States, in many Asian countries, and increasingly

TABLE 6.1
Percentage Distribution of Income to United States Households[79]

	1969	1979	1989	Gain or Loss
Top quintile of households in the United States	43.0	44.2	46.8	+3.8%
Middle 60 percent	52.9	51.7	49.3	−3.6%
Lowest quintile	4.1	4.1	3.8	−0.3%

TABLE 6.2
Median Household Incomes in the United States

	White	Black	Hispanic
Median Income	$35,975	$20,209	$23,446
(Percent of White)		56.2	65.2

in Europe. More importantly for our purposes, the ethnic element plays a part in both theories of poverty and in policies designed to deal with it (or to avoid dealing with it).

I will not take much time here to document the fact that poverty has not only persisted but in recent years has increased in many societies, particularly among racial and ethnic minorities. Here are a few such facts:

In the United States, during the last twenty years, what was already in 1969 a large disparity between the incomes of the top 20 percent and the bottom 20 percent of households (more than 10 to 1) had become by 1989 a disparity of more than 12 to 1.

When these data are given in dollars, based on the 60,000-household sample of 1989 (U.S. Dept. of Commerce, 1990), we see substantial differences among ethnic groups.[80]

The poverty rates tell the same story.

The ratio of the income of the average chairman of the board to that of a blue-collar worker in 1980 was 25 to 1; in 1990 it was 91 to 1.[81] For several decades, unemployment rates for black workers have remained steadily more than twice as high as those for white workers. In 1950 they were no higher. The Hispanic rate has been about 1 ½ that of the non-Hispanic white. The Native American rate is three times as high.

The minimum wage, although it was raised in 1991, is still one-third lower in dollars adjusted for inflation than it was twenty years ago.

TABLE 6.3
Percentages in the United States Falling Below the Poverty Line[80]

	Individuals	Married	Female Headed Household
White	10.0	5.0	25.4
Black	30.7	11.8	46.5
Hispanic origin	26.2	16.2	47.5
Asian or Pacific Islander	14.1	9.4	30.2
Other races	16.4	10.1	39.6

I believe it is clear, without citing other figures, that incomes in the United States have become more inegalitarian in the last twenty years, and that the weight of this change has fallen heavily, but of course not exclusively, on minority ethnic groups.

Public opinion polls indicate that the American inegalitarian income distribution is supported, to a fairly strong degree, by the population, as compared, for example, with the opinions expressed in Germany and Britain. When asked what percentage of income should be paid as taxes by high vs. low income earners, in 1990 84.3 percent in Germany said "much larger" or "larger"; 83.2 percent in Britain made those choices; but only 59.3 percent of American respondents. The percentages believing that government should reduce the income differences between high- and low-income earners were 51.8 percent of Germans, 56.7 percent of Britains, and 33.3 percent of Americans who agreed or strongly agreed. When the wording was changed to "government should reduce income differences between rich and poor," the pattern did not change, although the percentages rose for all three countries: 60.4 percent of Germans said definitely or probably, as did 70.8 percent of Britains and 41.7 percent of Americans.[83]

In a national poll reported by the *Washington Post National Weekly* (May 7–13, 1990, 13), differences between the United States and Austria and Italy were even greater than those between the U.S. and Britain and Germany. In Austria and Italy over 80 percent, but in the U.S. only 29 percent agreed that "it is the responsibility of the government to reduce the differences in income between people with high incomes and those with low income." It seems reasonable to suggest that middle-class respondents, who make up the majority of the American sample, under a threat by upward redistribution of income and a loss of their former share fear equality as a further erosion of their positions.

It is interesting and surprising to note that African Americans are not significantly different from the rest of the population in their responses to these kinds of income questions. The following figures compare black respondents in a special survey taken by the NORC in 1987 with the non-black respondents to the same questions in 1983–1987 polls:

"The way things are in America, people like me and my family have a good chance of improving our standard of living—do you agree or disagree?" On a five-point scale, with five indicating "strongly agree," the mean score for non-blacks was 3.65, for blacks, 3.81. The statement that "Large differences in income are necessary for America's prosperity," also received more support from blacks than non-blacks, 3.16 to 2.90. The same small contrast appeared when those in the samples responded to this statement: "Differences in income in America are too large": blacks, 3.68; nonblacks, 3.48. (On this question, the scoring was reversed, with 1 meaning "strongly agree," and 5 meaning "strongly disagree.")[84]

Such opinion polls give us a hint, but perhaps no more than a hint, that African Americans are quite thoroughly integrated, in opinions and values, on questions of income and government actions with respect to income.

A brief look at the Soviet situation shortly before the country broke apart reveals similar income differentials among ethnic groups. It is difficult to speak with confidence about the ethnicity-poverty connection in the USSR, because the data refer mainly to republics, all of which have ethnically mixed populations to some degree. And the data are somewhat problematic, to be treated with a certain amount of questioning—as indeed are such data for many countries.

Nevertheless, one cannot begin to understand the contemporary ethnic situation in the region of the former USSR without noting, among many other things, the large disparity in incomes among the republics. In table 6.4 the percentage of the total GNP (gross national product) for each of the fifteen republics is compared with the percentage of the population.

Although the situation of each republic is different from the others in history, ethnic mix, resources, degree of urbanization, and size, we gain some insight by clustering them.

Russia and Byelorussia were, as of 1990, much more prosperous, the Baltic republics marginally so, and the remaining ten republics all in deficit, with their share of the total production less

TABLE 6.4

Population and Gross National Product of Soviet Republics, 1990[85]

	Percent of the Population	Percent of GNP
Russia	51.4	61.1
Byelorussia	3.5	4.2
Latvia	1.0	1.1
Lithuania	1.3	1.4
Estonia	0.6	0.6
Ukraine	18.0	16.2
Moldavia	1.5	1.2
Georgia	1.9	1.6
Armenia	1.2	0.9
Azerbaijan	2.4	1.7
Kazakhstan	5.7	4.3
Kirghizia	1.5	0.8
Turkmenia	1.3	0.7
Tadzhikistan	1.8	0.8
Uzbekistan	6.9	3.3

TABLE 6.5

Comparison of Population and Gross National Product of
Clustered Soviet Republics

	Percent of the Population	Percent of GNP	Surplus or Deficit
Russia and Byelorussia	54.9	65.3	+10.4
Latvia, Lithuania, and Estonia	2.9	3.1	+0.2
Georgia, Armenia, and Azerbaijan	5.5	4.4	−1.3
Ukraine, and Moldavia	19.5	17.4	−2.1
Kazakhstan, Kirghizia, Turkmenia, Tadzhikistan, and Uzbekistan	17.2	9.9	−7.3

than their share of the population. Substantial resentment over this disparity is directed at the Russians in their midst, other ethnic groups, the centralized social order that has perpetuated the disparity, and members of their own group who are supporting that order.

Seen more positively, their resentment has led to the formation of many organizations working for democracy that, in many instances, led the campaigns for independence.

The experience of ethnic inequality is well illustrated by Hedrick Smith's comments on Uzbekistan: "Moscow's cotton colonialism not only corrupted Uzbek political life, but contaminated the Uzbek economy and the personal lives of Uzbecks as well. It ravaged the environment, adulterated the region's water supply, poisoned the health of millions, and blighted the lives of Uzbek farm workers, especially the women and children. . . . For years, Uzbek leaders and the Soviet press trumpeted cotton as the 'gold' of Uzbekistan. But very little of that gold trickled down to Uzbek farm workers."[86] According to government statistics, 45 percent of Uzbekian workers earn less than the subsistence wage; 22.8 percent are unemployed.[87]

How can we account for such disparities in income virtually everywhere? In what ways, if any, is the ethnic order implicated in those disparities? Since equality in the literal sense is seldom approved (except in some communes), in examining these questions I shall use "equality" more nearly in the sense of "distributive justice"—the range within which all persons should be included, with precise placement determined by various criteria. Kenneth Boulding has suggested two principles that, in America, underlie judgments of distributive justice: a "principle of alienation"—no person should be left without a claim on resources—and a "principle of desert"—each should get what he/she deserves. Thus Boulding sees two contrasting, yet complementary, judgments.[88]

Alves and Rossi have put this suggestion to an empirical test by asking a representative sample of American adults to state what they considered fair earnings for individuals and households who differed in various ways (occupation, education, marital status, number of children, sex, and ethnicity). These six characteristics were randomly assigned to "vignettes" that described individuals and households in every possible combination (except the extremely anomalous—e.g., physician without a college education). Each was assigned a gross annual income and a net income that indicated taxes ranging from 0 percent to 35 percent. In the ratings, there was a tendency to consider the best paid as overpaid, whatever their qualifications, and those poorly paid to be underpaid. Qualifications, however, were taken into account, as was need, measured by marital status and number of children. Of the "status" characteristics, only being on welfare significantly affected the judgments—those on welfare were seen as overpaid. Sex and ethnicity influenced judgments, but to a statistically insignificant degree.

Perhaps the most interesting finding in the study is the range of "fairly paid" estimates. Comparing the "working poor" with the "best off" among households, one finds that a "fair" difference is considered to be 1.0 to 3.26. The comparison of the "welfare poor" with the "best off" households was 1.0 to 6.17. For one-person households the matching judgments were 1.0 to 3.04 for the working-poor——best off comparison and 1.0 to 13.59 for the welfare-poor——best-off comparison. The latter indicates a severe judgment of "fair" for welfare individuals.[89] Yet even that difference is small compared with reality. If one takes the dollar figures given by Alves and Rossi and multiplies by 2.3 (that is, the amount of inflation, 1975–1990), the comparison of welfare-poor individuals with the best-off is $5,837 to $79,316; the comparison for husband-wife households is $16,585 to $102,272.

Even these largest differences in judgments are small compared with reality in the United States, where million-dollar incomes are no longer rare and are often highly publicized.

Poverty Seen Field-Theoretically

Being poor in a society where almost everyone is poor, and where the few who are not are socially or physically "hidden," is quite different from being poor where many are rich and quite visible and where there is a high correlation between level of income and ethnicity. Three explanations of poverty mingle in the public debate in urban industrial societies where, it seems probable, sufficient resources to eliminate poverty are available.

The first explanation is based on real or alleged individual differences: Some are poor because they are unskilled, lazy, ignorant, or content with their lot. A second explanation stresses the fact that some groups have persistently higher rates of poverty than others because they share poverty-enhancing values and norms—a culture of poverty. The third explanation emphasizes the unequal availability of opportunities, often due to discrimination reenforced by stereotypes. As we shall see, in recent years there has been extensive discussion of *the underclass,* a term by which numerous authors have sought to avoid "blaming the victim" a common outcome of using characterological or cultural explanations. They do so by emphasizing the force of discrimination and the lack of opportunities, while recognizing that some communities and groups bear the injuries dealt by those forces, sometimes with maladaptive responses. (In other uses, however, underclass is used to refer to character and culture, the first two explanations noted above.)

The Culture of Poverty. The major theoretical problem in all of this is where to start. These are interdependent forces. Which one came first? The discussion was given a sharp focus by Oscar Lewis, in a series of works beginning in 1959, in which he sought to show that not all cultures were equally well adapted to the urban-industrial world. Individuals in many parts of the world have been socialized to an ethnic group or a society and its culture based, for example, on family and community, not individual achievement; on traditional ways of doing things, not on endemic change; on a rural subsistence economy, not on a constantly changing occupational system. When they moved into a society emphasizing skill, ambition, individualism, and change, they did not—could not—easily adapt to the new world. They held on to their accustomed ways as a kind of cultural insurance policy.

Although Oscar Lewis surely intended, by his discussions of the concept, to contribute to the sympathetic or at least the objective study of a life-style that seemed to depart significantly from the dominant values and norms, he had another kind of influence as well.[90] Drawing his material primarily from his studies of Mexicans, Mexican Americans, and Puerto Ricans, Lewis sought, by the use of the "cultural of poverty" idea, to describe "in positive terms a subculture of Western society with its own structure and rationale, a way of life handed on from generation to generation along family lines. The culture of poverty is not just a matter of deprivation or disorganization, a term signifying the absence of something. It is a culture in the traditional anthropological sense in that it provides human beings with a design for living, with a ready made set of solutions for human problems, and so serves a significant adaptive function."[91]

If poverty is so deeply rooted in a traditional way of life as Lewis believed, then it imposed, among those socialized to it, a major obstacle to acculturation to the values of a mainly middle-class, competitive, future-oriented society. Those inclined to explain poverty as due not to the structure of society or to discrimination but to the individual characteristics of the poor and their shared values, were attracted to the concept of a "culture of poverty." It was used, for example, by Banfield, first with reference to Italian villagers and then to American cities.[92] It was also in harmony with many aspects of federal American policy in the 1980s and early 1990s.

I will not undertake here a full examination of the culture of poverty "debate."[93] The concept sharply challenges the emphasis on opportunity and the structures of contact that both preceded[94] and followed it.[95] The most highly critical see it as nothing more than blaming the victim. Others see it as a superficial "cultural" explanation of what it is, in reality, a "value-stretch," a "shadow culture," an adaptation to extremely limited opportunities.[96] Thus a point of view that was first expressed to lend support to cultural pluralism and to affirm the dignity of the life-styles of lower classes and minority groups came to be used, according to these critics, to support conditions that perpetuate poverty and discrimination.

Thus some see the lives of those in poverty as the cumulative cultural result of the experience of poverty mingled with various ethnic elements. "Lower class culture is a distinctive tradition many centuries old with an integrity of its own."[97]

Others, however, criticize the concept of a culture of poverty. They emphasize the continuing experience of discrimination and the high chances of failure: Family instability among lower-class African Americans does not so much represent a subcultural style as "the cultural model of the larger society as seen through the prism of failure."[98] Liebow sees the subculture of the street-corner people he studied as a "shadow system"—subsidiary, thinner, less weighty, less thoroughly internalized, and to be understood only in its relationship to the dominant culture.

Rainwater develops a similar perspective: "Norms with their existential concomitants can be regarded as rules for playing a particular game. The game represents one kind of adaptation to the environmental situation in which a group finds itself. . . . If the individual is not allowed in the game . . . [which, Rainwater says, most have a strong desire to play] or if he cannot obtain the resources to play the game successfully and thus experiences constant failure . . . he withdraws from the game. Instead, he will try to find another game to play, either one that is already existing and at hand or one that he himself invents." Rainwater adds an important point: "But what if a good many people cannot play the normative game, are in constant communication with each other, and there is generational continuity among them? In that case, the stage is set for the invention and diffusion of substitute games of a wide variety. . . . The substitute adaptations of each generation condition the possibilities subsequent generations have of adapting in terms of the requirements of the normative games.[99]

I agree substantially with these critics. Students of poverty need to recall, however, the story of the blind men and the elephant. Those who emphasize the presumed culture of poverty and its characterological effects have seized the tail. To say that an elephant is very much like a rope doesn't take us very far; yet we should not forget the tiny truth that it contains. Those who emphasize the structure of opportunities are touching the body of the problem, even if they call it a wall. A full account, however, must take account of many factors. Lest I get tangled even more in this analogy, let me say simply that poverty experienced through several generations, in a context of limited opportunities and discrimination, does influence values and norms. This effect, if the conditions persist, feeds back into the system that produced it, giving it some reenforcement. Current research demonstrates, however, that this effect is surprisingly small. Results and interpretations of the "guaranteed-income experiments" are complex; but there is little disagreement with the finding that the great majority of the poor want to work; they share the work ethic.[100] Hill and Ponza have shown that children raised in families strongly dependent upon welfare are themselves dependent on welfare in only a very small percentage of cases.[101]

Because of its enormous policy implications, a full understanding of the extent to which and the ways in which recently rural, poorly educated, relatively unskilled persons are acculturated to the norms and values of a rapidly changing urban society, with its escalating skill requirements, is of great importance. The present level of public understanding is—to put the best face on it—modest, with the result that current policies ostensibly designed to reduce poverty often instead contribute to its perpetuation.

In his novel *Poor Folk*, Dostoevsky brilliantly described the contrast between the life of poverty and the life of wealth. But when Makar received a gift of one hundred rubles (worth a bit more in 1845 than now), his life, behavior, self-image, and treatment by others all changed drastically. He had not been living out a culture of poverty, but a life-style coerced by poverty.

A century later, Charles S. Johnson, angry (I believe this gentle man could get angry) at the stereotype of the universal laziness and ignorance of black workers, coined a memorable phrase: "pseudo-ignorant malingering." You can insult me, pay me a pittance, cheat me at the company store, but you cannot, at the same time, make me work hard and take care of your tools as if they were my own. This same idea was expressed in the Soviet Union by the quip, "They pretend to pay us and we pretend to work." A decade before perestroika, Lenski noted that with no fear of unemployment and no hope for increasing their income, Soviet workers were frequently absent from work, negligent, and sometimes given to bribes and threats and extravagant consumption of vodka.[102] Recently a Soviet factory manager spoke to Hedrick Smith about "the appalling incompetence of Soviet construction workers and their reckless disregard for deadlines. . . . 'We think it's normal to take fifteen or twenty years to build a factory.' "[103]

Insofar as there is a culture of poverty to which the most disadvantaged members of the most disadvantaged ethnic groups are partially socialized (have I put in enough qualifiers?), it is essential that we see the part played by the non-poor in keeping it alive. The culture of affluence and the activities of those who share it—or hope to—reenforces the cultural and the structure of poverty.[104] This argument is often made with respect to educational systems. Tom Bottomore says of the classic studies of Bourdieu and Passeron: "These investigations connect cultural phenomena firmly with the structural characteristics of a society, and begin to show how a culture produced by this structure in turn helps to maintain it."[105]

In introducing the revised edition of their well-named book, *Reproduction*, Bourdieu and Passeron say that they sought to examine "the mediations and processes which tend, behind the backs of the agents engaged in the school system—teachers, students and their parents—and often against their will, to ensure the transmission of cultural capital across generations and to stamp pre-existing differences in inherited cultural capital with a meritocratic seal."[106] This reference to France is reenforced by such writers as Oakes and Ogbu with reference to the United States.[107]

I would emphasize, however, the numerous exceptions, the failures to transmit cultural capital across generational lines, and the failure to deny such capital to those presumably trapped in a culture of poverty.

Some of us are tempted to believe there is a culture of poverty because it is the reciprocal of the belief that life's rewards are justly correlated with effort and competence. American culture, among others, with its presumption of abundant opportunities, makes it easy to believe that the poor are responsible for their own condition, as Michael Lewis put it.[108] Believing is seeing.

The Underclass

The persistence of poverty, particularly among ethnic minorities, is scarcely to be doubted. The controversy over the phrase "culture of poverty," however, with the implication that it explained poverty, has led to a search for a new term with less ideological baggage.[109] *Underclass* is the term now most widely used.

Is it only a revised, more "politically correct" version of the culture of poverty? Does it deal adequately with the question: How much culture (persistent values and norms) is there among the factors that influence those who are designated part of the "underclass"? Does it deal adequately with the distribution of opportunities and the experience of discrimination? The term is used in such various ways that I believe one can only say yes and no to such questions.

I have contended earlier that words or phrases with strong political and moral connotations are likely to be defined in a wide variety of ways. Their meanings are situational. We can decipher them only in their usages. If *lumpen proletariat* seems disparaging and hostile, Marx sought to make it into a badge of honor. To contrast the "deserving poor" with the "undeserving" is clearly to make a moral (or immoral?) statement. One can try to objectify or neutralize stratification terms, as in the *Yankee City* series of books, by designing a six-class system ranging from upper-upper to lower-lower, but the terms stay neutral only if the human experience on the various levels is pushed into the shadows.

My own preference for a word to designate those who are most seriously disadvantaged in urban-industrial societies is "dispossessed." But that also has political-moral connotations—that some have had their full citizenship and their chances for a decent livelihood taken away. Full citizenship and a decent livelihood were their birthright; but some have lost it even before birth.

Although the widespread use and extensive research on the underclass, especially in the United States, is quite recent, the term itself is not new. A generation ago, in a discussion of persistent unemployment, Gunnar Myrdal saw that it might "trap an 'under class' of unemployed and, gradually, unemployable persons and families at the bottom of society."[110] Some current definitions are close to the one implied by Myrdal: The underclass are "those persons who are weakly connected to the formal labor force and whose social context tends to maintain or further this attachment."[111] Wilson also emphasizes the lack of jobs but adds other elements in his definition: The underclass is "that heterogeneous grouping of families and individuals who are outside the mainstream of the American [or other?] occupational system. Included . . . are individuals who lack training and skills and either experience long-term unemployment or are not members of the labor force, individuals who are engaged in street crime and other forms of aberrant behavior, and families that experience long-term spells of poverty and/or welfare dependency."[112] He explicitly rejects a culture of poverty interpretation by stressing the impact of isolation.

Wilson's definition of underclass is an effort to combine structural with individual factors; but persons with liberal values tend to emphasize the former while conservatives emphasize the latter. In her study of Puerto Ricans in the United States, Tienda finds strong support for a structural explanation:" Rapidly falling employment opportunities in jobs where Puerto Ricans traditionally have worked and the concentration of Puerto Ricans in areas experiencing severe economic dislocation are largely responsible for their disproportionate impoverishment."[113]

The liberal view is that if the concept of underclass is used, it must be a structural concept: "It must denote a new sociospacial patterning of class and racial domination, recognizable by the unprecedented concentration of the most socially excluded and economically marginal members of the dominated racial and economic group. It should not be used as a label to designate a new breed of individuals molded freely by a mythical and all-powerful culture of poverty."[114]

Thus the liberal view affirms that the values and norms and behaviors of the poor are not the central elements in defining or explaining the underclass. Rather, the norms, values, behaviors, and social structures of the non-poor are central. The conservative looks at a different side of the picture. "Much of today's entrenched poverty reflects the fact that poor adults seldom work consistently. The problem cannot be blamed predominantly on lack of jobs or the other barriers to employment, as the chance to work seems widely available. More likely, the poor do not see work in menial jobs as fair, possible, or obligatory, though they want to work in principle. . . . The poor must become workers before they can stake larger claims to equality."[115] (Perhaps the more dedicated liberals are saying under their breath: Yes, you can learn to swim, my darling daughter; but until you do, don't go near the water.)

Charles Murray sees an underclass "several generations deep," with "a population of students—the children of what has become known as the 'underclass'—that comes to the classroom with an array of disadvantages beyond simple economic poverty."[116]

The term *underclass* is now in the public vocabulary. A recent newspaper story is filled with such phrases as these: severe skill shortages, mounting youth disaffection, racial conflict, heavily hierarchical and exclusionary education systems, lack of ambition, large-scale labor shortages combined with mass unemployment, more youngsters dropping out of school.

Do these describe New York or Chicago or the United States generally? No, they refer to London, Berlin, and Paris, to Italy, Sweden, Germany, France, Ireland, Spain, and Britain: "This semipermanent unemployed class could form the nucleus for a new Germany 'underclass.' Even in Paris . . . there is a growing and visible underclass."[117]

What are we to do with a word with such diverse meanings and interpretations, such broad applications? Maria Vesperi sees it as a word that makes it easier to ignore the poor. "Underclass" marks "a profound but subtle change in the way Americans think about their national community." For many, poverty no longer seems remediable. "Instead of focusing on the shortage of good jobs and good job training, we try to convince ourselves that the underclass is unemployable."[118]

Fortunately, we are getting more carefully phrased—indeed, I dare say more objective—definitions,[119] more powerful research, and as a result, more convincing interpretations of the very sharp breaks with historical trends, beginning in the mid-1960s, that have led to what is now often called "the underclass."[120] The term itself, with all of its historical baggage, may well be replaced. We will be left, however, with a keener understanding of difficult and often tragic developments—hitting ethnic minorities with special force—in advanced industrial societies. This may even lead us to reassess our priorities and to adopt policies better designed than those we have now to deal with the sources of these developments.

Prosser speaks of three ways in which the underclass has been defined. If we put the three together, I believe we have a good working definition: "(1) a geographic concentration of individuals with some characteristic associated with the underclass, such as poverty; (2) common occurrences in a given locale of several forms of behavior associated with the underclass—weak labor force attachment, dependency on welfare, teenage pregnancy, dropping out of school, and criminal activity; and (3) the persistence of these behaviors across two or more generations.[121]

It is not an easy task to put these three elements together. The more variables one uses simultaneously, in a definition or in research, the smaller the size of the underclass. (Years ago someone defined Swedes as tall, blond, blue-eyed, and dolichocephalic. When a sample was measured, only 11 percent of the Swedes were Swedes.) In a study by Anne Hill and June O'Neill, using data from the National Longitudinal Survey of Youth, the number in the underclass declined sharply as additional defining variables were added.

TABLE 6.6
Percentages of Youth in the Underclass by Ethnicity[122]

	Black	Hispanic	White
Percentage of Men with			
high proportion of low-work years	26.0	16.1	7.8
and a high-school dropout	9.9	7.2	2.2
and a high-school dropout and ever in jail	3.5	0.9	0.6
Percentage of Women with			
high proportion of low-work years	20.5	10.0	2.7
and a high-school dropout	5.7	3.3	1.2
and a high-school dropout and ever in jail	2.9	1.5	0.6

This study should remind us that sweeping generalizations about the size and characteristics of the underclass on the basis of one or two characteristics reenforce stereotypes rather than enlighten us.

The critical question remains: How can we account for the sharp discontinuities in American experience, beginning a quarter of a century ago, regarding the absorption of ethnic minorities into the urban economy and the social structure generally? One might start with America's love affair with the automobile, an enchantment strongly encouraged by a powerful combination that included not only car manufacturers, but also workers and owners in steel, cement, rubber, oil, asphalt, and other industries that tied into a significant portion of the American economy. Then we must note: highways and cars meant much more extensive urban dispersal.

Jobs as well as people moved out to the suburbs and now to "edge city," for land, tax reduction, and better air. They also moved to the Sun Belt, and overseas. Technical, clerical, and professional jobs became more numerous, while the blue collar jobs, which were the first step on the ladder for earlier migrants to the city, became fewer. An economic slowdown precipitated, among other things, by the "oil shock" of 1973 reenforced these trends. The least protected workers—those with poorer education, fewer skills, less familiarity with city life—were the hardest hit.

A technological revolution in agriculture, starting, one might say for dramatic effect, with the cotton-picking machine, 1939 ff., sent an unprecedented number of rural migrants fleeing their three-dollars-a-day wage, if they had a job, for the promise of ten dollars a day, even at the minimum wage.

What they found, however, was discrimination in housing and jobs, isolation, and deteriorating cities.[123]

This is in sharp contrast with earlier experiences in the United States. Kasarda underlies the contrast by noting the work of the urban sociologists in the Chicago school. "Their field studies vividly described how each migrant group initially concentrated in highly segregated enclaves within deteriorating inner-city zones, where they faced suspicion, distrust, discrimination, and outright hostility from earlier ethnic arrivals. Yet these studies also showed how, with the passage of time, each group was able to carve a niche in the economy, adjust to city life, assimilate into mainstream institutions, climb the socioeconomic ladder, and eventually move to desegregated housing beyond the core ghettos and slums."[124]

This process, however, has been "overwhelmed by fundamental changes in the structure of city economies," as Kasarda puts it. Look at the most critical factor, the change in number and type of jobs, in selected cities and suburbs:

These data tell an astounding story. As ethnic minorities make up larger and larger proportions of the population of central cities, the kinds of entry-level jobs on which they are dependent for a start are disappearing while they increase dramatically in the suburbs. White-collar and professional jobs for which some are qualified, although increasing in the central cities, are increasing much more rapidly in the suburbs, movement to which is inhibited by the mea-

TABLE 6.7

Change in Number of Jobs in Selected Central Cities and Suburban
Rings, by Occupational Sector, 1970–1980[125]

Metropolitan Area	Managerial	Technical	Clerical	Blue-Collar	Total
Boston					
Central city	26,120	30,300	−40,400	−62,500	−46,480
Suburbs	104,660	75,820	69,460	116,440	366,380
Chicago					
Central city	51,560	68,400	−89,760	−118,860	−88,860
Suburbs	156,120	120,660	115,360	237,900	630,040
Cleveland					
Central city	2,900	14,240	−25,280	−34,580	−42,720
Suburbs	30,140	26,160	16,960	23,800	97,060
Detroit					
Central city	4,700	15,840	−35,540	−89,860	−104,860
Suburbs	51,860	62,500	43,240	29,310	186,920
New York					
Central city	90,460	173,780	−187,820	−171,500	−95,080
Suburbs	200,140	210,800	51,060	27,080	489,080
Philadelphia					
Central city	23,040	35,360	−54,060	−75,200	−70,860
Suburbs	50,280	55,880	36,240	29,500	171,900

ger resources of the underclass and the discrimination they face.
Even commuting to work imposes a greater burden on black than on
white workers. 1980 census data indicate a 25 percent longer com-
mute (in time), both for black workers with less than a high-school
education and those who have high-school diplomas, compared
with white workers at the same educational levels.[126]

The Cycle of Poverty. How can we pull together these numerous and sometimes contradictory statements about poverty and inequality, emphasizing what seems to stand up under analysis,
excluding exaggerations and errors, and, above all, fitting the various elements together into a coherent system?

Following the pattern of our earlier discussion of systems of
discrimination and of equality, I attempt in figure 6.2 to describe
what I see as the field of forces within which poverty is experienced.

Each of the elements in figure 6.2 has already been discussed
directly or indirectly. Structural, cultural, and characterological factors are included. We need only to point out the implied time order,
starting with the structural factor. Persons with inclinations that
differ from mine might begin at the right side of this cybernetic sys-

tem. I believe, however, that such a procedure is historically weak, even though the factors on the right are part of the system. In my view they are, in the first instance, effects of structural conditions. When those conditions persist, however, they create new factors— the responses and adaptations of the individuals and groups in poverty—that can reenforce the system.

Segregation is a critical element in the complex of causes. It produces a multiplier effect on the forces creating an underclass. Massey and Denton powerfully document the way segregation, by concentrating poverty, concentrates other conditions associated with it. "Deleterious conditions such as falling retail demand, increasing welfare dependency, growing family disruption, and rising educational failure are all concentrated simultaneously by raising the rate of poverty under a regime of high segregation."[127]

The system outlined in figure 6.2 is drawn as if it were a closed, almost self-perpetuating social process, a system difficult to break, as the contemporary literature on the underclass emphasizes. In fact, however, it is not closed. The "vicious cycle of poverty," as it is often called, is not all-powerful. Numerous influences whose own sources and histories are relatively independent of the poverty cycle, with its ethnic elements, impinge upon that cycle. Education, in particular, is a kind of centrifugal force, helping one to spin away. Racial discrimination, however, can be thought of as a centripetal force, tending to push those affected by it back into the system.[128] The strength of these contrasting influences, of course, is affected by the larger situation of which they are a part.

I have drawn three islands outside the system, with arrows indicating that the designated influences both affect and are affected by the system of poverty. The interactions thus suggested keep the system open to change. They present opportunities, but also the possibility that the system will be reenforced. Most significantly, they are forces to which both analysts and policy makers must give unrelenting attention if we are to deepen our understanding and increase the chances that the dispossessed can reclaim their human inheritance.

FRATERNITY AND THE NEED FOR ENEMIES

Discussions of liberty and equality are incomplete until we pay equally close attention to fraternity, to the boundaries of the cir-

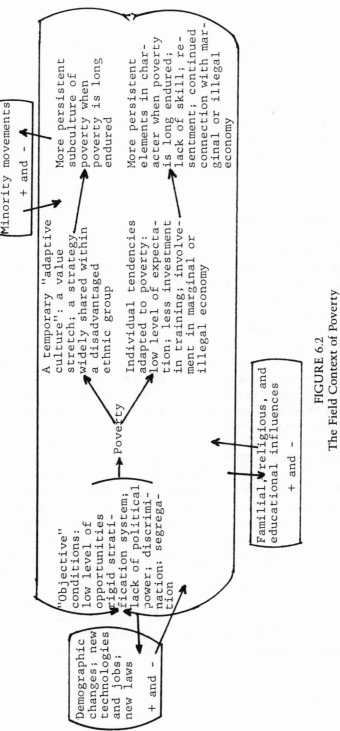

FIGURE 6.2
The Field Context of Poverty
(Adapted from Simpson and Yinger, 1985: 118)

cles within which the values of liberty and equality are being assessed and evaluated. Intricate social and psychological processes are involved in marking boundaries that separate "them" from "us." Those processes define enemies as well as friends.

Recently in the United States it has often been said with reference to our international relations—and not entirely in jest: What are we going to do for enemies, now that the USSR has left the field of battle and can no longer be counted on as "the evil empire"?

Not to worry. We have been well supplied by a series of opponents, often individuals representing a movement or a country: We have had Khadafi, Ortega, Noreiga, and Saddam Hussein. For some Americans, Japan is back onstage in a villain's role, as are some immigrants.

Ethnic groups are equally well supplied with opponents—persons outside a fraternal circle that has been drawn by reference to differences in ancestral background, religion, language, or race. Today we are experiencing a virtual pandemic of ethnic conflict. Some of the lines separating "us" from "them" persist for generations; others shift with remarkable speed.

Do these antagonisms demonstrate a strong "need for enemies," for witches, satans, evil empires, a need that sets serious limits to, or competes strongly with, the forces supporting fraternity? Are there equivalent forces documenting the need for allies, compatriots, brothers and sisters; are there forces that support cooperation, friendliness, altruism?

To answer these questions I will add an analytic element to the more frequent descriptive and ideological approaches to fraternity that I have touched upon. An adequate approach to a theory of fraternity requires, in my judgment, four kinds of inquiry: Are the lines that separate "us" from "them" drawn primarily in our genes, in our socialization (especially during infancy and childhood), in our culture (with its ambivalent values regarding the diameter of the fraternal circle), or in the social structure within which we live (especially with reference to the costs and the benefits that incline us toward particular inclusions and exclusions)?

To no one's surprise, my answer is: All four levels are involved; no one is definitive. I can only begin to suggest the reasoning and the evidence behind this sweeping statement, while hoping that I can at least provoke you into trying out this multi-level, field-theoretical paradigm.[129]

Residents of the twentieth century have no difficulty in agreeing with the statement *Homo homini lupus*. Our wolf-like behavior is agonizingly apparent (although, as many have said, this is probably an insult to wolves). Lorenz has asserted that *Homo sapiens* has a phylogenetically-programmed flowing spring of aggression. Ardrey, Morris, Wilson and others, in various ways, have made similar arguments.[130]

No one can doubt the biological capability for aggression among human beings. But we are not genetically destined to be unfraternal; we are not simply agents of our inheritance. Genes offset each other, for we are also "phylogenetically programmed" for altruism.[131] And the groups within which we interact channel and sublimate our aggressive tendencies.

Although Freud also placed the inclination toward aggression in our inheritance, he was more careful to note that it was channeled and inhibited by socialization and by particular circumstances—at great psychic cost, in his view.

"It is always possible," he wrote, "to bind together a considerable number of people in love, so long as there are other people left over to receive the manifestations of their aggressiveness. . . . It is precisely communities with adjoining territories, and related to each other in other ways as well, who are engaged in constant feuds and in ridiculing each other."[132]

Psychiatrists have documented this view by their studies of the "stranger anxiety" felt by infants when unfamiliar sounds and sights break into the circle of security created by those who nurture them.[133] A fear of strangers laid down in childhood can be transposed into a fear of "enemies" in adulthood. Enemies are more than strangers. They are not only frightening but evil—the more so because they carry our own load of displacement (we cannot fully express our hostility toward those whom we love and are dependent upon) and of projection (we cannot deal directly with our own guilt). Meanwhile, those whom we have turned into "theys" are displacing some of their hostility and projecting some of their guilt onto us.

In conflictful inter-ethnic relations, as in international relations, stereotypes and atrocity stories—along with atrocity realities—help the contending forces deal with their own ambivalences.[134] "A group that feels threatened contaminates the enemy group with its own negative mirror image and involuntary widens its distance from it."[135]

And of course "enemies" are in some measure actual enemies: their values clash with ours; their interests collide with our interests.

Children are not necessarily dominated, however, by "stranger anxiety." It may be a minor inclination in a context of loving parents and a supporting community. An impressive body of research under such titles as "roots of caring, sharing, and helping," "altruism and helping behavior," "positive social behavior and morality," "positive forms of social behavior," "altruistic behavior by children" has documented the conditions that support tendencies to enlarge the circle of helpfulness and friendliness.[136]

While recognizing the constraints imposed on the size of the fraternal circle by biological and psychological influences, sociologists, social psychologists, and anthropologists also (and sometimes exclusively) emphasize cultural, structural, and situational influences.[137] Individual-level approaches cannot answer the question: How are individualized enemies transposed into shared enemies, into threats, not just to me, but to the community, the ethnic group, and the whole society?

To use the current terms for an old problem: How to connect micro and macro levels of influence on human behavior? The "stranger anxiety" may make infants candidates for hostility, but why against group X rather than group Y? Why into a shared choice of enemy, often scarcely known? And then, what converts yesterday's enemies into today's friends? Neither our genes nor our early socialization has changed.

Both cultural and structural factors are involved in determining who "we" are and who "they" are. Mack speaks of "cultural amplifiers"—familiar tastes, sounds, objects, songs that bind one to those who share and furnish those recurring objects and experiences.[138] At the same time, children are often furnished targets for externalization (projecting and displacing) and stereotypes to justify the choice. In the contemporary world, the press, television, and the movies give vivid portrayals, both real and symbolic, of who "they" are.

The negative aspects of ethnic relations are sociologically and psychologically close to witchcraft in more isolated and homogeneous societies. As Kluckhohn said of Navaho witchcraft, it was an effort to develop a defense against fear and feelings of powerlessness by affirming the solidarity of the group and "by dramatically defining what is bad."[139]

The problems were different in seventeenth-century Salem, but the sociological process was similar: The identification and trials of the witches were used, as Erikson convincingly shows, to reconfirm and reestablish threatened cultural and social boundaries.[138]

It is not a long leap into the twentieth century where witch hunts and witch trials abound, although we normally use a different vocabulary. The witches may be a threatening society or an ethnic group speaking a different language, practicing a different religion, or getting a tan more easily or less easily than we. As in the seventeenth century, powerful, poorly understood and potentially destructive forces are loose in the world. Alienation and anomie are widely noted and experienced.

It is difficult to empathize with one's traditional enemies whatever the extent of discrimination against them or the severity of their suffering, which is perhaps as extreme as or more extreme than one's own. We need our enemies, our non-Us, our deviants (as Durkheim would put it), to help us draw less vague and threatening boundaries and to define the good by defining the bad.

How convenient that ethnic groups are found almost everywhere to serve this purpose. Palestinians would have to face more directly their own resentments against fellow Muslims, the ruling elites of the prosperous Arab societies were Israelis not there, acting out their own needs and perceptions in ways that repeatedly confirm the Palestinians' views of them.

Israelis would have to face more directly their own deep divisions—Orthodox vs. secular, Ashkenazi vs. Sephardic, Jew vs. non-Jew—were the Palestinians not there and close by, acting out their own needs and perceptions in ways that repeatedly confirm Israelis' view of them.

Yes, it is convenient to appeal to ethnic sentiments in political conflicts; but the side effects may be disastrous. Are the working-class European-descended whites in the United States going to improve their situation by accepting the invitation to hate the proffered "Willie Hortons"? Will that create more jobs, build more homes, increase support for schools, produce a more equitable tax system? Or is it closer to the truth to say, with Murray Kempton, that "the genius of our politics is the art of distracting the resentments of a cheated middle class and letting them fall upon a worse-cheated lower class,"[141] while noting that adding an ethnic coloration makes the genius seem even brighter—until all the costs are taken into account?

An uncompromising stand against Palestinian claims may seem to protect Israeli interests; but there, too, the costs are heavy. The Palestinian cause allows the Arab states to wave "the flag of the homeless," bringing them at least a superficial unity in opposing the sovereignty and integrity of Israel. An Israeli-Palestinian settlement would help to "restore Israel's democratic reputation, cement the traditional U.S.-Israeli friendship and rekindle the support of troubled American Jews."[142]

In heterogeneous societies, efforts to reestablish solidarity, legitimacy, and eunomia by witchcraft—by the collective displacement and projection of our needs, fears, and guilts onto those defined as inferior, as different, as outsiders—cannot work. In multicultural societies, the great need is for new ideas that can lead to smooth, continuous transitions. The creation of witches that help the dominant groups to patrol their traditional boundaries and to protect their accustomed income, power, and status, is of little value—even for those who dominate. The reality and the interpretations of the threats societies face vary too much. Individuals within societies and societies themselves are too interdependent.

Those "who fear witches soon find themselves surrounded by them."[143] And the fear, with its attached labels and persecution, helps to increase the very thing that is feared, as Erikson goes on to say. Some assert their differences more strongly and harden their own group lines when attacked, acting out the proffered role partly because their convictions are reinforced, but partly out of resentment, partly because it makes them more attractive to other excluded persons, and partly because their options have been narrowed by the designation.[144] Narrowly and tightly drawn fraternal circles, solidified by discrimination, are a tragic element in the crises of the twentieth century.

Failure to understand this lesson will intensify, is intensifying, ethnic conflict in many societies today. Many, probably most, Americans applauded the struggle in Georgia and the Baltic republics for independence from the USSR, or at least from Russian domination. There is much that is rich and strengthening about patriotism (matriotism?), especially among those whose country is being threatened or occupied. It is one of the deepest of human emotions. A PBS documentary (June 24, 1991) alternated scenes of song festivals in the Baltic states with pictures (January 1991) of Soviet armor seeking, violently, to repress a movement for liberty, for independence. The violence did not end the protests. It had the opposite effect: The

Latvian, Estonian, and Lithuanian crowds stood up to the army. Democratic forces in Russia and elsewhere in the USSR saw that they were not immune from such attacks, but they also saw that they had allies. They increased their pressure on the central government of the USSR, which once again shifted to more liberal, or perhaps one should say a more liberating, policy. When that policy was only poorly acted upon, protests mounted again. By December 1991, the USSR came to an end.

Fraternal inhabitants of this small planet, we are all moved by these developments. But I must urge you to follow with equal concern the struggle for pluralism within these newly independent republics. Under some conditions, patriotism turns into nationalism (patriotism felt for the dominant ethnic group), or even into chauvisism (nationalism that is as much anti-Them, the non-Us, whoever they are, as pro-liberation).

Each of the Soviet, republics is multi-ethnic; but in several instances, the dominant groups' leaders tend toward chauvinism. That can be illustrated by the situation in Georgia, where one-third of the population is non-Georgian. In an impudent moment five years ago, I asked Georgian friends in Tbilisi how the Russians, Germans, Muslim Abkhasians and Ossetians, Armenians, Jews—most of them life-long residents—would be integrated into a sovereign Georgian state. Would they, I asked—the Georgians themselves—become the Russians of Georgia? They knew the point of the question immediately, forgave me, smiled at my naiveté, and assured me that friendship and full citizenship for all, regardless of ethnicity, could be counted on. Having been the recipient of the legendary hospitality and generosity of Georgia, I almost believed them. And in their eagerness for independence, they almost believed themselves. Later events, however, suggest a different possibility. More South Ossetians (Georgian Muslims with their own hopes for autonomy) have been killed by Georgian troops than the Soviet troops killed in Tbilisi in 1989. Zviad Gamsakhurdia, who was elected Georgian president, combined religious and nationalistic rhetoric in his speeches. He arrested political rivals as "enemies of the Georgian people," put the press under government control, and called for "the rebirth of the religious and national ideals of our ancestors."[145] Perhaps his need, not just for Georgian friends but also for the dedicated fervor of the zealot, accounted for his chauvinism. It was difficult to turn off, however, when independence was achieved; and it was proving to be even more difficult to erase the costs involved in drawing a narrow fraternal circle. Scores were killed and the major avenue of Tbilisi left in shambles in the violent protests against Gamsakhurdia's authoritarian rule—protests that forced him from office.

In one of the ironies of this ironic time, Gamsakhurdia has been succeeded by Eduard Shevardnadze, who had imprisoned him several years ago for his vigorous anti-communism, a stand that led to his election as Georgia's first president, with 87 percent of the vote. Now it is the old Communist who heads a Council of sixty members. He was elected president in autumn 1992.

Ethnic conflicts did not cease after that election. Protests among the South Ossetians have continued; and secessionists in the Georgian region of Abkhazia have mounted a fierce battle for independence. They have been just as fiercely resisted, with hundreds of casualties on both sides. At least among the dominant voices we hear few calling for a multi-cultural society. Decades of repression within the Soviet Union have caused such views to wither among the contending groups.

Despite such continuing ethnic conflicts, however, perhaps we are entitled to hope that, with his extensive international experience as foreign minister in Gorbachev's government, with a popularity rating that has jumped from 30 to 70 percent, matching the regard in which he is held abroad, Schevardnadze can heal the ethnic wounds. When his years as head of the Communist government in Georgia are noted, Schevardnadze asks: Why can't a politician evolve as artists do? "Picasso had his different periods. . . . I made mistakes, I was sometimes unfair, but what is one supposed to do— to stick to one position to the end, to the death? We have all changed.[146]

The Need for Allies

It is ironic that our need for enemies and our need for allies are bound together in a kind of symbiotic relationship. Having so convincingly created enemies—with their cooperation, their often enthusiastic reciprocity—we find ourselves in need of friends, allies, comrades. The capacity for friendship, I have suggested, is found on the same four levels of influence that support our capacity for aggression and exclusion. I can only hint at some of the psychological and sociological process involved.

In a psychological twist similar to "believing is seeing,"[147] we are often most drawn to those for whom we have sacrificed, suffered, or—more prosaically—for whom we have done favors. We have a kind of investment in those persons and groups. Other things being equal, the greater the favor, suffering, or sacrifice, the larger the investment.

If you want someone to like you or support you, let *him* do *you* a favor. Or as Machiavelli put it: "It is the nature of man to feel as much bound by the favors they do as by those they receive." We rather easily forget favors done us; not so the favors we do. The more people have suffered in protection of their prince, Machiavelli declared, the greater their loyalty, having invested so much in his success.

The blood of the martyrs is the seed of the church; and the blood of the soldiers, Kenneth Boulding observed, is the seed of the state.[148] In the same way, dominant groups that seek to oppress a minority ethnic group may succeed only in strengthening the ethnic loyalty of its members. Oppression creates those essential ingredients: esprit de corps and martyrdom.

Of course the oppression may be so severe, so cruel, so complete that identification is driven underground, disguised in culture and religion, or deflected from more direct expression. Forbidden religious groups, however, can live a hidden existence for generations. Networks of opposition can be held together by underground printing presses and mimeograph machines; letters can be passed from friend to friend, furtively, daringly.

When a policy of *glasnost* is proclaimed, by whatever name, the books, manuscripts, pamphlets, and letters quite suddenly appear to a wider public. Churches, often powerful symbols of ethnic identity, are once again filled. Those who suffered most under oppression are now the heroes or martyrs of the group.

On the whole, esprit de corps and martyrdom have a very good press. Even chauvinism, if it is experienced in a severe conflict situation, is applauded—if Monsieur Chauvin is one of us.

But friends created by suffering and sacrifice may be bound into a circle so tight that the ability to recognize the suffering and sacrifices of others is sharply curtailed. These "others" are caught in the same constriction of imagination. Around the world, almost daily, we see the dreadful consequences of ethnic groups, often in the name of universal brotherhood, reducing the liberty and equality not only of those with whom they contend, but their own as well.

Conclusion. Return for a moment to the three charts describing possible relationships among liberty, equality, and fraternity as they relate to ethnic relationships. Are they mutually supportive, competitive, or independent? My own guess—or more optimistically, my well-based assessment—is that chart 3 (Figure 6.2), picturing the independence of the three values, is least useful. It is difficult to imagine the social conditions under which the weight of one could vary without affecting the weight of one or both of the others.

The jury is out on the other two models. Chart 2 describes a kind of tripartite zero-sum situation in which an increase in any one of the three values inevitably decreases the others (or holds one steady while decreasing the other even further. In the last years of the Soviet Union, many of those who sought perestroika believed that the strong emphasis on equality (in ideological terms, if not in fact) had inevitably meant a loss of liberty for both individuals and groups. Because the emphasis on equality had meant equality-in-poverty (and privileges for the few), it had also greatly reduced the chances for fraternity among the republics.

Chart 2, however, seems to me to be too constrictive. It describes some situations, but not others. Chart 1 is more often the best guide to students of ethnicity. In the societies that I have studied most intensively (the United States, USSR, Israel, South Africa, Yugoslavia, and Britain), levels of liberty, equality, and fraternity are tied quite closely together. In the United States, for example, in the last fifteen years, as we have become significantly more inegalitarian, we have also experienced a reduction of liberty and of fraternity. Or so it seems to me.

Whatever the correctness of that judgment, I hope that I have encouraged you to think deeply about the intricate connections of liberty, equality, and fraternity as they bear on ethnicity. To be indifferent to social processes seriously endangering any one of the three is to endanger all three. The world today is our laboratory for the study of the intricate connections between the ethnic order and liberty-equality-fraternity. The topic is of worldwide significance, both for a science of society and for democratic polity.

Chapter 7

RELIGION AND ETHNICITY

There is a close and, I think it is fair to say, natural affinity between religion and ethnicity. This affinity is strongest where the sense of a primordial attachment to an ancestral group and its traditions is most deeply felt. It is weakest where the ethic boundaries have been only recently drawn, where those boundaries are temporary or situational or markers of a pan-ethnic cluster of related but diverse groups. Almost nowhere, however, can an ethnic order be described and analyzed without reference to a religious factor.

Since definitions of religion tend to be quite diverse, even idiosyncratic (I shall scarcely avoid that problem), let me indicate how I think of it. We need a definition of sufficient generality that it can enclose the wide variety of religions that are related in various ways to ethnicity. I shall be thinking of religion in these terms:

The human individual, blessed (and sometimes cursed) with the power of language, capable therefore of anticipating the future, including a foreknowledge of his own death, able to verbalize ideal states, and to create standards, is continually threatened with failure, with frustration, and with his conception of justice unfulfilled.

These problems tend to loom up as overwhelming or absolute evils. Religion is the attempt to "relativize" those evils by interpreting them as part of some larger good, some conception of the absolute that puts the individual's problems into new perspective, thus to remove or reduce their crushing impact. At the same time, social relations, human societies, are threatened by these same problems. Fear and frustration can lead to disrupting hostilities, until they can be reinterpreted as a part of a shared experience. Additionally, each individual tends to think only of himself or herself, to make his joys and her desires into "absolute goods," threatening the patterns of mutual adjustment that social life requires. Religion is the attempt to relativize the individual's desires, as well as fears, by subordinating them to a conception of absolute good more in harmony with the shared and often mutually contradictory needs and desires of human groups.[1]

Religion, seen in this way, is a system of beliefs and practices by means of which a group of people struggles with the ultimate problems of human life—suffering, injustice, and meaninglessness. It expresses their refusal to capitulate to death, to give up in the face of frustration, to allow hostility to tear apart their human associations (although these may be enclosed in narrow boundaries). The quality of being religious, seen from the individual point of view, implies two things: a belief that evil, pain, bewilderment, and injustice are fundamental facts of existence; and a set of practices and related sanctified beliefs that express a conviction that he or she and all of those with whom one is most fundamentally connected can ultimately be saved from those facts.[2]

Theoretical Background

Several theories of the sources of religion, although developed without reference to ethnicity, square with the assertion of a close religion-ethnicity connection. Georg Simmel, in a famous essay, developed the thesis that one of the sources of religion is human relations that themselves are nonreligious. Faith is first of all a relationship between individuals. Without it, Simmel wrote, society would disintegrate. "In faith in a deity the highest development of faith has become incorporate, so to speak; has been relieved of its connection with its social counterpart."[3]

Noting the persistence of religious faith despite three centuries of growing scientific predominance, Reinhold Niebuhr and Erik

Erikson both take a position similar to Simmel's: Faith is first of all a product of the trust a child learns from loving parents. Religion raises that trust to a social principle that helps one deal with all the tragedies of life. In Niebuhr's words, "Life is full of ills and hazards, of natural and historical evils, so that this childlike trust will soon be dissipated if maturity cannot devise a method of transmuting the basic trust of childhood, based on obvious security, to a faith which transcends all the incoherencies, incongruities, and ills of life."[4]

Although both Freud and Marx took positions somewhat similar to those of Simmel, Erikson and Niebuhr, they gave quite different interpretations. Freud saw the source of religion in the transposition of childhood comfort and protection into a kind of parental surrogate; but he lamented this as a sign of human weakness.[5] Marx, following Feuerbach (Marx advised baptism in the "fire brook"), saw religion as a projection of human capacities and powers onto deities; but he saw this, at least in highly stratified societies, as an expression of a deepening human alienation.[6] Religion became, in his view, an opiate that dulls the efforts of the disadvantaged to oppose injustice. For the advantaged, it thereby sanctifies the beliefs and institutions that protect their superior positions.

Gramsci's concept of "hegemony" expands the quite rigid Marxist view in a useful way. Reenforcing the system of direct domination, hegemony, to Gramsci, is the "spontaneous" consent given to rulers by the general population.[7] Religious leaders, intellectuals, and others are the "deputies" of the dominant groups, giving them a softer face.

But "spontaneous consent," or legitimacy, as it might be called, can be weakened or lost. It can be awarded to groups challenging the dominant order. Thus, contrary to the Marxist view, religion can be seen as a major engine of change, able to capture the allegiance and readiness to sacrifice required to transform a society. (Whether or not the transformation is to be celebrated or lamented depends, of course, on one's values and one's status.)

These theories that connect religion with family and clan and socialization suggest a religion-ethnicity connection but do not develop it. Durkheim's *The Elementary Forms of the Religious Life* is a much more instructive guide to the connection between ethnicity and religion. For him, society is the object of religious veneration and the basic source of "the sacred." "So everything leads us back to this same idea: before all, rites are means by which the social group reaffirms itself periodically. . . . Men who feel themselves united, partially by bonds of blood, but still more by a community of interest and tradition, assemble and become conscious of their moral unity."[8]

Fortes makes skillful use of the Durkheimian perspective in his interpretation of the Tellensi (West African) ancestor cult. "It is the religious counterpart of their social order, hallowing it, investing it with a value that transcends mundane interests. . . . The ancestor cult is the transposition to the religious plane of the relationships of parents and children; and that is what I mean by describing it as the ritualization of filial piety."[9]

Religious Change and Social Change

Although political, military, and economic affairs receive most of the headlines, religious developments of recent years have also been of major significance, particularly where an ethnic factor is involved. Indeed, in many countries, political, military, and economic trends cannot be understood without full attention to challenging or supporting ethno-religious trends. A primary theme of anthropology and sociology, that societies can be understood only by focusing on the complex interactions among all of their institutions, is given continuous documentation. Religion is not simply a part of a dependent "superstructure," as Marxists would say. Nor is it separate and autonomous, unaffected by the secular context. Interaction and interdependence are the central processes.

The belief, widely held in the West in the 1960s, that religion was fading from the scene has been sharply challenged by evidence of powerful religious currents flowing from both the "Right" and the "Left."

Conservative religious movements, often attached to an ethnic revival, gain strength among those who see the world they have come to depend upon, in both its religious and its secular aspects, utterly threatened by what they see as secularism, by technology, by contact with other world views. Some people gain power and status by these trends. But others, who see them only as the road to disaster, may support a religiously inspired counterrevolution, as in Iran and more generally in the Islamic world, in an effort to reverse the social trends. In religiously pluralistic societies such as the United States, those who are dismayed by the secular trends may strengthen or shift their allegiance to fundamentalist churches.

Some will support conservative political movements that promise to protect the threatened values and statuses. A few of their leaders will enter politics directly or seek, by full use of the technology of the world they deplore, to influence politics.

Other people, however, are not dismayed by the speed of change in the modern world. They are dismayed by the absence of necessary drastic adaptations to those changes by the established religious and secular institutions. When many people of common ethnic identity share this perception, a religious movement can emerge—religion not as opiate but as stimulant. In many parts of Central America and South America, local grassroots congregations have been formed, inspired by a "liberation theology" that seeks to tie religious thought and action closely to questions of justice and equality. For generations the Catholic Church had been seen as a strong supporter, indeed an integral part of the political and economic structures of power in Latin America. Now, significant numbers—doubtless a minority, but a large and active minority—both of laymen and of religious leaders appeal for change in the status structure, with the strong class and ethnic lines that run through it, in the name of liberation theology.[10]

Ethno-Religious Movements among Native Americans

The nature of religious challenges to the ethnic order of a society vary widely, depending upon the religious traditions involved and the structures of power connecting the ethnic groups. When the use of the aboriginal language declines in an ethnic group, when what is felt as a cultural invasion by powerful outsiders persists—often bringing nearly irresistible technologies and even customs—then ancestral religious forms and new but indigenous religious movements come to the fore. They have a heavier share in the task of ethnic definition and self-preservation. Such developments have been important among Native Americans for many generations.

I will not refer here to the numerous pre-Columbian religions, which were quite similar in their world views despite many differences.[11] These comments address some of the ways that Native American-European American relationships have influenced and have been influenced by religion.

The Peyote cult, now known as the Native American Church of North America, has not sought to restore a lost dominance but to secure an accepted place as a fundamentally Indian religious form, despite its use of the mildly disorienting drug of the peyote cactus button—now legally excluded from prohibitions against drug use. At the same time it has become acculturated to many Christian beliefs and practices. It is a kind of pan-Indian religion of the reservations, tying together some 250,000 Native Americans from many tribes in an affirmation of their shared cultural identity.[12]

Of wider influence, however, are the pervasive and controversial relationships between Christian churches and missions and Native Americans. At first coercively acculturative, at least a few white Christians have begun to look on the blending of Indian and Christian elements as not only possible, but desirable.[13] Native American responses range from reassertion of ancestral religions, to declarations, somewhat similar to black theology, that Christianity is most truly found in its Indian forms, for "God is red," to reaffirmation of a multi-ethnic Christianity. These themes are all expressed in the thought of Vine Deloria, Jr.:

> Tribal religions . . . face the task of entrenching themselves in a contemporary Indian society that is becoming increasingly accustomed to the life-style of contemporary America. While traditional Indians speak of reverence for the earth, Indian reservations continue to pile up junk cars and beer cans at an alarming rate . . . [And yet] within the traditions, beliefs, and customs of the American Indian people are the guidelines for mankind's future. . . . Who will find peace with the lands? . . . Who will listen to the trees, the animals and birds, the voices of the places of the land? As the long-forgotten peoples of the respective continents rise and begin to reclaim their ancient heritage, they will discover the meaning of the lands of their ancestors. That is when the invaders of the North American continent will finally discover that for this land God is Red.[14]

The Ghost Dance. Although the Ghost Dance, an earlier religious movement among Native Americans, is more strikingly different from the dominant religions than those we have mentioned, it may be of more value in helping us to understand the reciprocal influence of religion and inter-ethnic situations. If I may stretch the meaning of the concept almost to the breaking point, I believe it is possible to draw important lessons by looking at the Ghost Dance as a kind of liberation theology. These lessons concern not only Native American-dominant American relationships, but also the religion-ethnicity connection more generally. They deal with the way protest movements are shaped out of religious materials.

In thinking of the Ghost Dance as liberation theology one does not, of course, forget the wide, even enormous differences in the language, the religious metaphors, the traditions and myths among diverse religious movements. The similarity among them lies in the nature of their resistance to oppressive regimes.

It is not surprising to find among Native Americans a series of religious movements, alongside many other types of response, resulting from the enormous disorganizing pressures to which they have been subjected. The nature of these ethno-religious movements has been shaped by generations of contact with Christianity, by the enormity of white domination, and by a widespread myth of a culture hero who would appear to lead them into a terrestrial paradise.[15]

Among the large number of messianic movements that developed in this context, the Ghost Dance was the most dramatic and widespread. In it one sees a powerful religious effort to reestablish the validity of Indian cultures, to oppose the overwhelming power of the white man, and to overcome personal confusion and frustration. It spread first in the early 1870s among the tribes of the Far West, stemming from the vision of a Paiute shaman, Wodziwob. He prophesied that all the dead Indians would come back, brought to life by the dance. Although his own tribe did not become very excited, his message was amplified and spread by other missionaries: Those who believed, who danced, would see their relatives in a very few years; the white people would disappear.

Some tribes were unconvinced by Wodziwob or his followers. "But elsewhere the doctrine seemed better at third hand than at first hand, and it ran like a powder train," spreading through several tribes in California, Oregon, and Nevada, receiving fresh interpretation and variations as it moved. "As it traveled, it appears that the tribes which took up the cult most hungrily were those suffering the greatest deterioration in their former ways of life, while those which were lukewarm or flatly rejected the dance were the ones who had had the least disturbance."[16]

After a few years the Ghost Dance began to decline, with its promise of an immediate restoration of the Indian to his old place unfulfilled. In 1890, however, another Paiute, Wovoka, received a vision that was the starting point for a new wave of the dance. The nature of the vision is not entirely clear, for Wovoka proclaimed some Christian ethical views (live at peace with one another and the whites; avoid lying, stealing, and war). Yet in a letter to the Arapaho and Cheyenne tribes he repeated the idea that there would be a reunion on earth with the dead Indians, that the dance that God had given him would prevent the whites from interfering with the Indians any more. While Ghost Dance doctrine forbade war, it foresaw the annihilation of the white man.[17]

The dance spread quickly, not through the tribes that had taken it up twenty years earlier, nor among the then-prosperous Navahos or the self-contained Pueblos, but across the Rocky Mountains among the Plains Indians—the Cheyenne and Arapaho, the Pawnee and Sioux. The revival can be understood only against the background of white domination, cultural confusion, the loss of the buffalo, with all that it meant for the Plains Indian economy and way of life, and the inability to carry out the old rituals. The Ghost Dance represented a renaissance of Indian culture to the Pawnee, "the very flame of new hope to the Sioux."

"Into this situation of cultural decay and gradual darkness, the Ghost Dance doctrine shown like a bright light. Indian ways were not gone, never to be recovered. Indian ways were coming back. Those who had lived before in the "golden age" were still carrying on the old ceremonies, old dances, old performances, and old games in the beyond. They were coming back; they were bringing the old ways and the buffalo. Dance, dance, dance. The white man would be destroyed by a great wind. The Indian would be left with the buffalo, with his ancestors, with his old friends and his old enemies. Cast aside the white man's ways like an old garment; put on the clothes of the Indian again. Get ready for the new day and the old times."[18]

The Ghost Dance was a last desperate attempt to reestablish the native values and to recover a sense of the worthwhileness and meaning of life while incorporating new values from the surrounding society. Among the Sioux it led to tragedy, for it precipitated the complicated series of events that brought about the Battle of Wounded Knee, where more than two hundred Native Americans and sixty United States soldiers were killed. And with them died the Dance among the Sioux.

No matter how dramatic or traumatic this episode in American ethnic history, of what significance can it be for us today? If we climb the abstraction ladder (while not forgetting the many differences that we have set aside, the details we have omitted), we can use the Ghost Dance as a parable for many ethno-religious movements. Look at different histories, myths, and metaphors, but at somewhat similar experiences of oppression and cultural disarray, and we see religion playing an important part in many "revitalization movements," in ethnic resurgence, and in "ethnogenesis"—the creation of a new ethnic group from among those sharing a common set of defining experiences.

After his intensive study of the 1890 Ghost Dance, Mooney climbed the abstraction ladder even higher than I have suggested; but I believe he helps us to see similarities between events around us and events of widely scattered places and times. History does not repeat itself; but neither does it leave us uninstructed about our own times. Here is Mooney's sweeping interpretation of the Ghost Dance as one of a universal species of religious movements, often ethnically based, that seek to recapture a lost Arcadia: "The lost paradise is the world's dreamland of youth. What tribe or people has not had its golden age, before Pandora's box was loosed? And when the race lies crushed and groaning beneath an alien yoke, how natural is the dream of a redeemer, an Arthur, who shall return from exile or awake from some long sleep to drive out the usurper and win back for the people what they have lost. The hope becomes a faith and the faith becomes the creed of priests and prophets, until the hero is a god and the dream a religion, looking to some great miracle of nature for its culmination and accomplishment. The doctrines of the Hindu avatar, the Hebrew Messiah, the Christian millennium, and the Hesunanin of the Indian Ghost Dance are essentially the same, and have their origin in a hope and longing common to all humanity."[19]

Even when we find Mooney's interpretation too extravagant, he helps us to see contemporary ethno-religious movements in a clearer light. We need to study much more carefully how a society and the various groups within it get from here to there culturally, how values evolve, and who suffers in the process. In commenting, in 1980, on the overpowering success of the Ayatollah Khomeini in winning support for his harsh repression, not only of Christians and Bahais, but of Sunni and Kurdish Muslims, Martin Marty observed that the Ayatollah had the Shah, "who imported but hoarded the best features of technology and left the oppressed with nothing except trampled customs and disintegrating culture."[20]

Where we find fervent, zealous, even fanatical ethno-religious movements, we will be wise in trying to understand them, and by chance to respond to them more creatively, to ask: What past ways of life have been lost, what new ways, tantalizingly in view, have been denied? Thus we may gain an essential insight not only into Iran, but also into Northern Ireland, Lebanon, Nigeria, India, Palestine, Israel, the United States, Sri Lanka, and many other societies divided by ethno-religious boundaries.

To be sure, several factors qualify the ethnicity-religion connection. It is perhaps too easy to assume that ethnic divisions in a society are matched—and reenforced—by religious divisions. That is often true. For example, almost all Malays are Muslims; very few Malaysians of Chinese background are Muslims; the Moluccans in Holland are Muslims, most of the Dutch are Christians; ethnic lines in Yugoslavia are highly correlated with religious differences. It is also true, however, that in many situations, religious lines cut across ethnic lines. In the United States, persons of German background are Protestants, Catholics, and Jews; there are a few more Irish-descended Protestants than Catholics; although most black Americans are Protestant, five percent are Catholic, one percent or more are Muslim, and several thousand are Jews; and at least twenty percent of the twenty million American Hispanics are Protestant, with most of the rest being Catholic. Most of the republics of the former Soviet Union are religiously heterogeneous. In Israel, there are Christian as well as Muslim Palestinians sharing the land with the Jewish majority.

The fact that each of several ethnic groups in a society is religiously divided does not mean that religion is of little importance in inter-ethnic relations. It does mean, however, that one must distinguish carefully between situations in which tightly knit ethno-religious groups interact from situations where the religious identities in some measure crosscut the ethnic identities. In some instances, religious differences within an ethnic group heighten the influence of the religious factor. That the Southern Baptist Conventions claims 2,300 Hispanic pastors, compared with fewer than 2,000 Hispanic Catholic priests, is an important item in the American ethnic order, with probable impact on Hispanic-Anglo relations, on social mobility, and on integration.[21]

Religious differences within an ethnic group can be the result of historical factors, such as the migration 300 and more years ago of thousands of English and Scottish Protestants to Ireland. I will not discuss here the "reasons of state" that propelled this often coercive migration, but want only to note its impact not only on Ireland, but also on the United States by the fact that, in effect, it created two Irelands. Over forty million Americans claim an Irish ancestry, with many claiming a second or third ancestry as well. Of these latter, Scots-Irish is the most common (much more common than Irish-Scots), suggesting to Lieberson and Waters that those who thus report themselves to the census can well be regarded as an ethnic group separate from those who call themselves as Irish only.[22]

In addition to such historical factors, individual choice also loosens the connection between ethnicity and religious identity. Some drop out, others shift (conversion, to the receiving group, apostasy to the group that is left)—processes that we shall comment on.

Religion among African Americans

The close connection between religion and ethnicity is nowhere more clearly shown than in the history of African Americans. In its earliest years the experience of slavery powerfully affected their religion; and as it developed, their religion powerfully affected the experience of slavery. The resulting beliefs, practices, institutional structures, and patterns of leadership have been continuous and dominating influences, even as they have been adapted to freedom, industrialization, and urban life.

They have also been enormously influential, one must emphasize, in the churches and the lives of European Americans. Their doctrines and practices have been shaped in a variety of often unintended and sharply conflicting ways by the nature of black-white relations in the United States. It takes a great deal of energy and emotion to deal with the fact of segregation in a universalist religion.

"Religious gatherings were the first forms of association permitted under the slave system, and the first black leaders were religious teachers. The doctrines and practices were a subtle mixture of adaptation to the enormous power of the planters and of attack on that power."[23]

Early studies emphasized what I shall call the "shield element" in African Americans religion. It developed as a way of protecting its adherents from the cruel blows of slavery. As Powdermaker interpreted it, black religion developed partly as a way of deflecting and controlling the hostility that was instigated so powerfully by the slave experience. It was also a way of attempting to rescue victory from defeat: suffering is only a prelude to ultimate victory and reward; power comes from suffering.[24] (This is a basic theme in many religions.)

This emphasis was even more strongly represented in the teachings of the Christian missionaries of pre-Civil War days. They emphasized the rewards for humility and the glories of the future life. This message came partly from their own doctrines and partly from the insistence of planters that they preach only that kind of religion.[25]

More recent studies of early African American religion have emphasized not only the adaptive, but also the aggressive elements in black religion. It was a sword as well as a shield. There developed a distinctive blend of African and American elements into what Raboteau interpreted as a "distinctive form of Christianity."[26] The religious lives of slaves helped them to survive as "autonomous human beings with a culture of their own within the white master's world," and at the same time armed them with the ability to protest, for "We must be struck by the appearance of one or another kind of messianic preacher in almost every slave revolt on record."[27]

One must emphasize also the religious lives of the several hundred thousand free African Americans, some of them former slaves, all of them targets of discrimination, because they too developed a religion of sword and shield.

After emancipation, the church developed into the cornerstone of black community life.[28] The protest theme was muted in the churches of small towns and rural areas, but among the growing urban population it became more and more prominent. Beginning in the 1950s it became a vital part of the civil rights movement, not only through the lives of the major leaders, but through the sustained courage of thousands of nameless participants.[29]

Ethno-religious protest has also taken a theological form in the work of those who redefine Christianity in terms of black experience almost exclusively. "Black theology affirms that the church of the Oppressed One must be a black church."[30] This is the analog of nationalism when one is looking at ethnicity from a political perspective. Others develop it in a less extreme way: "Black theology will need to give full expression to the particularity of the black experience while not neglecting the universal character of religion."[31]

In my view, the more adaptive aspects of black religion, strongly activist but equally strong for conciliation, reflect not only the realities of black experience but also express the inclusive element in Christianity.

In religion, as in politics, it is vastly difficult to be universalistic when one is on top. Some of those on bottom, however, also find it difficult, in politics as well as religion. They proclaim, with scriptural authority, that the last shall be first; we must turn the world upside down; Nietzsche saw this as an indication that religion is an expression of the repressed resentments of the powerless. It is their attempt to enchain their masters by symbolic means in face of the failures of other methods to break their control. Weber later emphasized that it was suffering, not resentment, with which religion was primarily concerned. This played no part in Nietzsche's thinking. He also missed the fragile but vital universal themes that have been forged out of life's most difficult experiences.

We would be wise to recognize the blending, in varying proportions in different settings, of the effects on African American religion of resentment (often muted and disguised), of suffering (so overwhelming in their experience), and of universalism (the belief that all persons, whatever their race, are children of God.) These are the bedrock of black churches down to the present. These churches remain the defining institution of many if not most African Americans as an ethnic group.

Black churches have been influenced by the integrative elements in the civil rights movement and in other aspects of American society. Although churches are still largely racially divided, they are no longer the most segregated institution in the Untied States, as has often been asserted.

Since World War II there has been a slow increase in the level of integration in local congregations. Nearly four of ten Whites attend church with Blacks, according to data from the General Social Survey.[32] For the most part this indicates the presence of a few black families in a congregation. Less than 35 percent of those who lived in segregated neighborhoods attend integrated churches, compared with nearly 60 percent of those who live in integrated neighborhoods.

In the late 1950s many Protestant and Catholic churches began to move from very modest to more active involvement in the civil rights movement. One aspect of this development was an increased willingness and interest in expanding the number of African American ministers and church leaders. Most, but not all, of the increase has been on the denominational not the congregational level. Few black pastors or priests serve integrated congregations.

Of the growing number of black bishops (e.g., in 1990, eleven Catholic, ten Episcopal, fifteen Methodist), several serve as administrators of areas containing both white and black churches. On the whole, however, black ministers and bishops in partially integrated denominations serve primarily black constituents.

What are some of the consequences of this modest amount of church integration? The continuing existence and importance of African American churches is not in doubt. Despite the large increase in the number of black government officials, academicians, artists, physicians, lawyers, and other professionals, black clergy remain among the most influential leaders in African American communities, on the personal, local, and societal levels. At the same time, the greater openness of predominantly white churches (most of the black churches have always been open) reenforces secular trends toward equality.

In my judgment, church integration is of greater importance for the white than for the black congregants. It is the white parishioners who have paid the biggest price for segregated churches. Their stereotypes, their ethnic parochialisms, have been reenforced. Their understanding of the complex ethnic issues of society has been constrained, and thus their ability and willingness to deal with those issues has been reduced. To be sure, only as other sources of segregation and of ethnic inequality have been reduced will churches become extensively integrated. Meanwhile, we can regard the small steps already taken as an integral and perhaps an essential part of the process of change toward a more unified yet diversified society.

The Black Muslims. Ethnically based protest movements in the United States have not been limited to the Christian tradition. Beginning in the 1930s, the Black Muslims carried the protest against discrimination into a separatist, black improvement, anti-white movement.[33] Over several decades, part of it has developed into a more conciliatory and more orthodox or standard Muslim movement, with Malcolm X opening the door in his last years by his denunciation of black racism and his embrace of Muslim orthodoxy. "He has become a hero to quite contrasting kinds of people, because in his lifetime he stood for sharply contrasting kinds of goals and means. But above all, he stood for unmitigated attack on racial discrimination; he challenged 'whitey'."[34]

Wallace Muhammad, son of the founder, has carried that trend further by seeking reconciliation with black Christians, disbanding the quasi-miliary Fruit of Islam, and seeing the American Muslim Mission as a branch of Sunni Muslim orthodoxy.[35]

Thus some part of the Black Muslim movement is moving from sect to church, to use the well-known concepts of Troeltsch. With a growing black middle class, the partial success of the civil rights movement, the appearance of new leaders, the growing prosperity of the religious organization, and other contextual changes, their harsh separatism has been significantly modified. Rather than *Muhammad Speaks*, the official publication of the American Muslim Mission is now *Bilalian News*, named for Bilal, an Ethiopian who had been the caller to prayer in the Prophet Muhammad's first Muslim community.[36] In addition, African American Muslim mosques in major American cities repudiate the separatism of the Black Muslims, emphasizing instead Islamic tolerance.

That is not the end of the story, however. A new schism, or an old schism never fully repaired, is an important part of the African American Muslim picture. With Louis Farrakhan as its most prominent leader, the Nation of Islam is seeking to return to the earlier doctrines. There have been few economic gains for the majority of black Americans since 1970; the pace of educational and political gains has been slow; unemployment remains at more than twice the level of that among white Americans. Such circumstances give strength to Farrakhan's persistent emphasis on separation and alienation from American society. The ethno-religious line is sharply drawn, with support from many of the most disprivileged of urban African Americans.[37]

He could see the reasons for the changes being made by Wallace Muhammad, Farrakhan has remarked, "if the white man had improved just a little. But the devil hasn't changed. If anything, he's gotten worse."[38] Farrakhan continues to offend American liberal sensibilities by antisemitic remarks, by declaring that Hitler did many good things for Germany and that Khadafy and Khomeini are his brothers in Islam.

It remains to be seen whether the United States will be able to draw the Durkheimian lesson from this harsh religious movement: Deviants, "witches," even "terrorists" can help a society to reaffirm, to rediscover, its basic values. The simplest thing is to attack Farrakhan as an uncivilized man. The wisest thing may be to see him as an early (or even late) warning signal—a kind of fever marking the course of a serious illness in American society. The conditions that produced the original Black Muslims are still widespread. The Farrakhan schism may not persist, but similar angry religious and other kinds of protest will surely occur if these conditions are not removed.

> Gloucester, 'tis true that we are in great danger;
> The greater therefore should our courage be. . . .
> There is some soul of goodness in things evil,
> Would men observingly distill it out. . . .
> Thus may we gather honey from the weed,
> And make a moral of the devil himself.
> —Shakespeare's King Henry V
> Before the battle of Agincourt,
> Act IV, Scene I

RELIGIOUS SHIFTS, RELIGIOUS CHANGE, AND ETHNIC IDENTITIES

Despite the close connection between one's most basic and intimate relations and religion, in the modern world many people move to another denomination, convert to a different religion, drop out, or become inactive. Although many ethnic groups have strong religious identities—one might say that they are anchored in religion—we cannot say that an ethnicity-religion connection is unbreakable. Intermarriage, changes in social class, family tensions, generational life-style changes, language shifts, secular aculturation and integration, changes or lack of changes in the religions available—all can influence the religion-ethnicity connection.

Many subtle distinctions have been made in discussions of this topic.[39] With reference to religious shifts, I will make brief comments only on those that are most directly related to ethnicity.

Those denominations or religions that have the strongest connections with an ethnic group are least likely to lose members to another religion. (They are not necessarily less likely, however, to have fewer dropouts or inactive members.) Most switching is to a religion or denomination that is quite similar to the one being left. Ethnically based religions tend to be more clearly distinguished from others than are those without a clear ethnic connection.

Switching and dropping out do not have the same implications for ethnicity. A person can "drop out of religion and still keep the quasi-ethnic ties of family neighborhood, language, and culture that also formed part of the affiliation."[40] Dropping out or switching can reflect a weakening ethnic attachment, however; or it can be a contributing cause of such weakening.

A change of membership is not identical with conversion. There can be several different reasons to join a new religious organization: to unite a family; to participate in nonreligious activities; to have a church connection despite the unavailability of one's own; to try to improve one's social standing. Conversion, however, represents a more drastic change of belief and behavior. It requires what Thomas Kuhn called, with reference to scientific theories, a paradigm shift in the way experiences are interpreted.[41]

When persons of a different background are converted to a new religion it is not only they who are changed. Christianity, for example, has been acculturated by converts and potential converts as well as acculturating them. Its numerous denominations reflect the enormous variety of ethnic and racial groups and the wide range of circumstances within which it has developed. Its history has been imprinted on its doctrines, beliefs, and rituals.

Within Buddhism, the Mahayana, Theravada, and Tantric traditions express the different environments within which they developed. Almost as many variation on those themes are found as there are societies or people among who Buddhism has developed. In Hawaii, Buddhist children sing in their Sunday schools, "Buddha loves me, this I know."

Although Judaism has a strong universalistic quality, it is also quite clearly an ethnic religion. Like the other universalist religions it has been shaped by its various environments. Jews in Bombay, Buenos Aires, Algiers, New York, Moscow, and Tel Aviv share a common faith and tradition; but they differ in significant ways as well. Out of the highly assimilationist setting of Germany in the nineteenth century came Reform Judaism. The more open environment of the United States has given rise to Conservative Judaism. Orthodoxy, which is found in varying strengths in most environments, is being powerfully influenced by the creation of the state of Israel and the challenge it brings to reconcile the universalism of Judaism with affairs of state. Max Weber's assertion that where religious values collide with the demands of statehood, religion will lose, is being strongly tested. In Weber's words: "The state's absolute end is to safeguard (or to change) the external and internal distribution of power; ultimately, this end must seem meaningless to any universalist religion of salvation. . . . It is absolutely essential for every political association to appeal to the naked violence of coercive means in the face of outsiders as well as in the face of internal enemies."[42]

We do not find much reason in the events during the seventy-five years since that was written to question Weber's judgment, whether with respect to Israel, which did not exist when he wrote, or many other states—Christian, Muslim, and Hindu. The Hinduism of India when it was a British colony changed when it became the majority religion in an independent multi-religious state. As the state of India struggles to maintain a secular democratic society, a minority of Hindus move toward ethnic chauvinism in conflict with Muslim fundamentalists.

In another comparison, the Hinduism of Bali seems almost lighthearted, shaped by the indigenous, Muslim, and Buddhist religious influences around it and by the history and culture of Indonesia. And the Indians of Trinidad and Fiji (most of them Hindus) have begun to learn the political give-and-take needed to live peacefully in societies closely divided between religiously defined ethnic groups.

Until recently, perhaps, most Americans and West Europeans have thought of Muslims as quite closely united in an Islamic civilization. We learned something of Egypt through ancient history, something of Turkey and the Ottoman Empire through early modern and modern history down through World War I, and then of the oil-producing states of the Arabian peninsula as the world developed into a highly interdependent economic system.

Since World War II, however, event after event has taught us that in fact there are scores of ethnic groups defined by their Muslim identities, but also by the variety of their circumstances and locations.

There are several states wtih Muslim majorities, ranging in size from Indonesia, the largest, to Bangladesh, Pakistan, Iran, Egypt and the other states of Mediterranean Africa, Turkey, the six Islamic republics of the former Soviet Union, and the several states around the Persian Gulf. All of them contain non-Muslim ethnic groups and several Muslim groups that are ethnically distinct due to lingual, doctrinal, and other cultural differences and different histories. There are nearly ninety million Muslims in India. Although less than 10 percent of the population, they are a potent political force. Perhaps half (or more) of Nigeria's eighty-five million population is Muslim. (We cannot be sure, because the issue of the balance of Christians and Muslims is too sensitive for the Census.) And by now we are aware that Germany, France, Holland, Britain, and other

West European states have over ten million Muslims. There are two million or more in the United States.

All of this is to say that a religious element is involved in the ethnic orders of most of the societies I have mentioned. And in my judgment, religion is not a mere epiphenomenon, a symbolic representation of the "true and basic causes" of ethnic conflict—for the earth's oil or for control over territory. Particularly for those whose lives are most difficult, religious values and structures are involved in defining the terms of the struggles.

RELIGION, ETHNICITY, AND CONFLICT

The intricate connections among religions, ethnicity, and conflict revealed themselves almost continuously during the last several decades, and nowhere more clearly than in the Near East and Middle East. It has been a story of Lebanon and the decay, after 1975, of what had seemed its miraculous, if tenuous, balance among several Christian and Muslim groups; a story of Israelis and Palestinians and the struggle to protect a Jewish homeland entangled with a struggle to find a Palestinian homeland. It is a story of Iraq and Iran, with their mixtures of Sunni, Shi'ite, and Kurdish Muslims (not to mention small groups of Christians, Jews, and Bahais) fighting a catastrophic war for dominance over the region. It is also a story of Iraq's attack on Kuwait, in some ways a continuation of the Iran-Iraq conflict and the struggle for hegemony in the Persian Gulf area, but more directly a struggle over oil, and thus of greater concern to the Western powers, as well as to the other Arab states. And it is a story of a thirteen-year struggle in Afghanistan that on the surface is a conflict between a left-leaning government (for nine years strongly supported by the USSR) and a variety of rebel groups who were getting military support from the U.S. through Pakistan, but is also a conflict among several ethnic groups with harshly contrasting ideas about what they want Afghanistan to be.

The Kurds, Enclosed by Arabs, Turks, and Iranians. To illustrate the ethnic-religious forces in this region, I will refer briefly to the Kurds, an ethnic nation and would-be state (Kurdistan) of more than twenty million people scattered mainly through the contiguous areas of five states: Turkey (9 million), Iran (5 million), Iraq (4 million), Syria (800,000), and the Caucasus, formerly part of the U.S.S.R. (300,000). They claim the right to an area as large as France, the largest part in eastern Turkey. To the Turks, however, they are "mountain Turks"; and there is little support for Kurdistan in any of the other states beyond some promises of greater autonomy.

To begin to understand the Kurdish situation we must recall the Ottoman Empire, which dominated most of this area for four hundred years, and the course of events following its dissolution in the years following World War I.

After the collapse of the long and harsh rule of the Ottoman Empire, European states, especially Britain, took the lead in reorganizing the region, mainly in an effort to protect their own geopolitical interests and their security. They hastily created "states" out of the variety of ethnic groups by "lines drawn in the sand"; and ". . . once a nation-state was declared to have been established, the ethnic or religious groups that did not belong to the ruling group could find themselves excluded from the political community and viewed (however long their ancestors might have lived in the region) as strangers.[43] Iraq, for example, included three former Turkish provinces: the Kurdish-dominated northern region, Sunni-Muslim Baghdad, and Shi'ite-Muslim Basra, divisions that became tragically visible to Europe and America in 1991, but which had been the source of extreme violence for many years. Since the boundaries were often believed to be arbitrary and unjust by those who were thus enclosed in the new states, controversy was inevitable. Authoritarian and violent rule became the norm as the reigning groups have sought to impose their central control over peoples who felt no loyalty or affection for them.

The Kurds are the largest of the ethnic groups in the area that have been deprived of political control over their own lives. "When empires fall, not everyone emerges with a state of his own," as a *New York Times* headline put it (April 14, 1991). One must add, however, that even if by some miracle Kurdistan were to come into being it would not be a nation-state. Turks, Iraqis, Iranians, and others live in the areas that are predominantly Kurdish. The task of creating a just state, with security for all of its members, would remain.

The contemporary Kurdish story can be hinted at—and through it, the current situation in the Middle East—by a series of headlines from New York, Washington, Geneva, Ankara, Tokyo, Baghdad, Silopi-Turkey, and Cairo, dating from April 1991 to January 1993:

Iran deluged with 1.5 million Kurdish refugees.
Long memories make the Kurds distrust Hussein.

Baghdad hopeful on Kurdish pact but insists on control
of oil center.
Iraqi Kurds reject autonomy pact as an allied plan stirs
new hope.
U.N. says Kurds take most parts of an Iraqi city.
Turks bomb, strafe Kurds in Iraq.
Kurds versus Kurds.
Two Kurdish parties agree to merger.
Kurds in Turkey firebomb store; 11 people killed.
300,000 Kurds may have been killed in Iraq.
Iraq, a case of genocide.

This glimpse of one twenty-month period (refugees driven out, refugees coming back; Turkish-Iraqi confrontation even as they separately attack the Kurds and are attacked by them; Kurdish hopes for autonomy up and down; Kurds disagreeing among themselves) lead up to the last headline: "The Arab world comes to the end of illusions."

The dream of a unified and politically stable Arab world cannot be realized so long as multi-ethnic states try to act like nation-states (or tribal fiefdoms), while millions of their non-Arab citizens, such as the Kurds, are denied human rights. Nor can the dream be realized when it is difficult to speak of a "brotherly Arab world," for it is still a world within which inter-state boundary and resources conflicts remain unexamined. They can no longer forge even a superficial unity by sharing a common hatred of Israel, because the costs of such a policy—in particular the neglect of attention to their internal problems—are now becoming apparent. (Of course, the reciprocal of that can be applied to Israel.)

The dream of a unified and politically stable Arab world will not be realized so long as there are sharply different views of what it means to be Muslim, not just Arab.

In an overly simplified scheme, one can say that there are three often harshly conflicting, views of how contemporary Arab states can remain Muslim while responding to the challenges of the current situation. The relationships among the three are pictured in Figure 7.1

No state can be fully characterized by any one of the three views. Indeed, all three are doubtless found in every society. But the balances among them are different, because of their varying histories, resources, populations sizes, neighbors, and ethnic mixtures. In

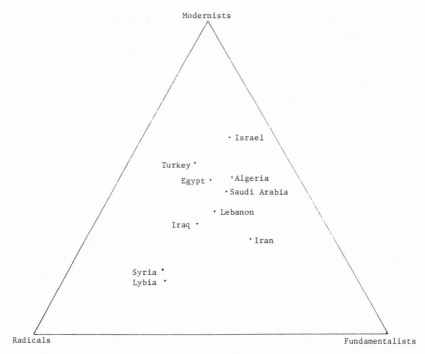

FIGURE 7.1
Three Responses to Change and Crisis in the Middle East

figure 7.1, I have included some non-Arab states for comparisons. My guesses should be taken only as points of departure in thinking about the Middle East.

The radical states, or the most radical voices in those states, profess that they want a redistribution of power. So far this has been expressed mainly with respect to outside forces. The current leaders have taken few steps toward more open and participatory practices in their own societies.

Modern states are fully defined, not simply by the level of technological development, but also by the steps taken toward the rule of law and the protection of human rights. The more modern of the states of the Near East and Middle East may have somewhat better records on human rights, but they are far from meeting exacting standards.

Religious fundamentalists see fully Islamic states as the true and basic response to a cultural and not just a political crisis. That emphasis leaves little room for ethnic conciliation and individual-human rights.

How deep is the cultural crisis among the Arabs? In Hourani's view, "defeat goes deeper into the human soul than victory." Having lost the Ottoman Empire—their last, if cruel, protection from the cultural invasion from Europe—the Arab people, in this view, have built a cultural barrier of their own, a rigid barrier defended with uncompromising zeal. One of the most powerful of the political movements, the Ba'ath (rebirth) movement, has given birth mainly to repressive regimes, as in Iraq and Syria.[44]

Can there develop a blend of a muted modernism (perhaps one that can teach an "over-developed" West that continued technological growth is not the cure for all human ills), a softened radicalism focused more on what it is for (societies with expanded human rights?) than on what it is against, and a fundamentalism that recaptures the classical Muslim universalism so often obscured in contemporary ethnic nationalisms?

A supreme task. It requires not only the wisdom and dedication of the Arab world, but also the support of all of those—now both friends and foes—with whom they are so interdependent.

Lest this WAIF (White American International Folk) sounds too critical and unsympathetic to the Arab world, let me remind Western readers that we are not free of intolerant fundamentalism and chauvinism. There is little radicalism; but we see the obverse, a trend away from the small steps we had taken toward a living wage for all, as the rich get richer and the poor poorer, especially in the United States. And our record on human rights remain shaky, at least as judged by heroic standards. To be sure, the American record looks better when seen against not uncommon practices around the world.[45]

Religious Universalism and Ethnicity

If religion primordially gives unity and solidarity to a group, what happens when several groups, with different religions, are brought together in a single state? And what happens when universal religions challenge the close connection of religion and society, religion and ethnic group?

Few topics show a more sharply contrasting set of images to the student of ethnicity than religion, seen in the light of such questions. After reading the studies of interreligious contact, or even scanning a few days' headlines, one is struck with a sense of sad recognition of the truth in an Edward Sorel cartoon.[46] In the cartoon we see a series of sketches of a man listening to the news on TV. These are the captions beside the sketches:

Scene 1: Another day of religious conflict between Hindus and Muslims has resulted in over a hundred deaths in India.

Scene 2: Violence between Catholics and Protestants claimed the lives of twelve in Belfast today.

Scene 3: A protest by Jerusalem Muslims ended with sixteen deaths when Jews and Druze opened fire.

Scene 4: Over thirty died today when Maronite Christians and Muslims clashed in a new attempt to wrest control of Lebanon.

Scene 5: Jews in Moscow say increased attendance at Russian Orthodox churches has meant an increase in antisemitic vandalism.

Scene 6: Two mosques in Algiers were bombed today and police suspect rival Muslim fundamentalists.

Scene 7: Religious leaders met with President Bush at the White House and later expressed their belief that religion alone holds the key to peace.

Scene 8: [The man in utter bewilderment exclaims]: Are they crazy?!

We would share that bewilderment if we neglected reference to the enormously complex and ambiguous range of beliefs and practices in the universalistic religions regarding ethnic divisions. One needs little documentation of the scriptural emphasis on one human community. It appears in many forms. "Be loving towards strangers, for by this some have entertained angels without being aware of it" (Hebrews, 13:2). The *Quran* and the Hadith interpretations are filled with references to an ultimate message to all of mankind. The Dalai Lama opened a speech in the United States in 1991 with an expansive "brothers and sisters." Martin Luther King, Jr. spoke of universal fraternity as the highest of human relationships.

Neither the headlines of religious-ethnic conflict nor the words of universalism, however, are adequate for our purposes. It is common to distinguish a religion—as expressed in its most sacred texts and doctrines—from the practices and prejudices within the societies where that religion predominates. Both Islam and Christianity appeared in relatively colorblind environments and adhered to the doctrine of the unity of mankind. Yet both gave birth to slave-holding societies and to severe ethnic prejudices.[47] Davis puts this in historical context: "Like Judaism and Christianity, Islamic religion emerged at a time when chattel slavery was as universally accepted as human warfare. If all three religions sought to regulate and ameliorate slavery, Islam was most explicit in its conviction that freedom is the natural and presumed status of mankind."[48] Yet prejudice against Blacks and their exclusion from full fraternity and liberty were the predominant fact in the Islamic world by the end of the seventh century.[49] Adherents of other religions, regardless of race, were also in practice kept outside the circle of fraternity. The same kind of exclusion, of course, was widespread, indeed almost universal, in Christianity.

On a moment's thought, it must seem that monotheism—one God for all of humankind—must soften the lines of division among us. On second thought we realize that, in practice, it has hardened as well as softened those lines. Monotheism has proved to be a two-edged sword; or, more correctly, it has had influences ranging from "the brotherhood of all under one God" to "kill the infidel who does not believe in, and is not supported by, the one true God—ours."

How we approach the analysis of this contradiction is strongly influenced by our assumptions. If a religious group and its tradition are, in one's mind, a unique, mystical, supernatural or transcendental event, one is almost certain to defend its intrinsicality, to lament change, and to resist those who believe differently. If a religious group and tradition, however, are seen as a natural, human product, and its beliefs, myths, and metaphors (I do not use these terms pejoratively) are seen as the product of given times and places, change is regarded as normal; other groups and traditions can be accepted as partners in a shared guest. (Here, I shall assume the latter to be the appropriate choice for a scholarly, comparative study; but I do not assert it as manifestly "true" in some more ultimate sense.)

Within the major religions, persistent ecumenical efforts are an expression, although incomplete and partial, of the universal side of religion, an effort to give it a stronger institutional locale. Ecumenism has its smallest beginnings in toleration; but it can move up through conversation, to cooperation (World Fellowship of Buddhists), federation (National and World Councils of Churches), and integration (the unions of various Protestant churches).

Even the smallest beginnings of ecumenism, however, are difficult in the relationships across major religious lines. Despite their unity on some basic primordial level, the major world religions are separated by their different histories, world views, myths, and metaphors. They are anchored in different civilizations; in many instances their adherents live in sharply contrasting conditions.[50] Even Judaism, Christianity, and Islam, which a visitor from Mars might see as closely related, are more often characterized at this stage of history, as at many other times, by confrontation, not cooperation or even toleration. Divisions within the major faiths are scarcely less common. Moderates or those insufficiently zealous are isolated and sometimes killed (Malcolm X, Sheik Hassan Khaled, Salmon Rushdie).

Much of this confrontation, to be sure, is rooted in inter-state conflicts. A religious cloak is used to cover economic, status, and geopolitical struggles, perhaps giving them an ardor, an intractable, uncompromising quality that more explicitly secular disputes would lack. It may also win the support of those who have no such mundane interests, whose interests, indeed, are severely injured by the conflicts.

All of this is to say that the universal element in religion keeps breaking down, dis-integrating. *Gott mit uns*, but not with them. Saddam Hussein was quick to declare the Persian Gulf war a "holy war," with God on Baghdad's side in the battle against invading Western infidels. King Fahd of Saudi Arabia also saw a holy war, but with holiness utterly lacking in Iraq. President Bush came about as close as an American president can get to declaring a "holy war." In multi-credal America, such declarations must be of "just wars" that transcend all creeds. President Bush drew on the fifth-century (and pre-gunpowder) doctrine of St. Augustine in his reference to a "just war"; and at a prayer breakfast he declared, "I should have made more clear that God is our rock and our salvation."[51]

I do not make these references to "holy war" in order to say A plague on all your houses. There are major differences among states in their support for human rights, in the readiness to use cruel punishments, in the persistence of attacks on minority ethnic and religious groups. There are, however, fewer differences in the depth of their concerns for their own economic and power interests. It is difficult to keep a clear eye on the former when attention is sharply focused on the latter.

If religio-secular conflicts are writ large on the inter-state level, many of the same questions appear in connection with intra-state ethnic clashes:

At least eight dead in Nigerian city as Muslim-Christian riots go on.

Indian myth sharpens reality in religious strife.

Europe's bishops unable to heal rifts [between Roman Catholics and other Christians].

The Sudan forces 400,000 to desert [They were Christians and traditional African believers].

Two dissident Mongol groups are suppressed by Chinese.[52]

Religious Conflict in Northern Ireland. Ethnic conflicts with a religious aspect develop when two or more groups have radically different views of how their shared society ought to be organized. Protestant unionists in Northern Ireland want to remain British; Catholic nationalists want to be united with the Irish Republic; (many in the uneasy center are ready for accommodation and compromise). Although the Northern Ireland ethnic division is rooted in history and religion, the contemporary conflict stems from uneven economic development, political inequalities, separation punctuated by violent contact, and a kind of self-perpetuating cycle of revenge for revenge for revenge—no one remembering who struck the first blow. The minority Catholics, with fewer economic and political resources, have been the more violent since 1969 (nearly three thousand have been killed), seeking to destroy the ordinary rhythms of life, in England as well as in Northern Ireland, and to force a drastic change in the social order. They fear a state that seems to keep them in perpetual minority status. Their Protestant opponents fear not only losing their advantages, but also being absorbed into a state, the Irish Republic, that seems to them to be most clearly defined by its religious emphasis and the special status granted to the Church. (This itself is part of Irish history, the Catholic Church having been the major defender of the Irish majority against British domination. Yet, ironically, the Church opposed Irish independence from Britain in the nineteenth century, fearing that an independent state might dominate the Church or weaken its "church universal" theme.) In this kind of confrontation, the violent few can prevent the uncertain many from taking the small but essential first steps toward accommodation and, perhaps, pluralistic tolerance.[53]

India's Struggle to Maintain a Religiously Pluralistic State. The poignancy, the harshness, the difficulty in imagining the final act of the religio-ethnic drama being played in Northern Ireland can help us to think about somewhat similar dramas being played on other stages—in India, Sri Lanka, and in the Nagorno-Karbakh region of Azerbaijan. In these and many other societies, religion is one of the critical lines of division, in both substantive and symbolic ways. No study of ethnic relations in such societies would be adequate without analysis of the religious factor.

In the months following India's independence, in 1947, a vast refugee movement, with millions of Muslims fleeing from Hindu-dominated areas and millions of Hindus fleeing Muslim-dominated areas, resulted in hundreds of thousands of deaths. A few months earlier, Mahatma Gandhi had been killed by a Hindu "nationalist" who protested against Gandhi's goal of a non-sectarian, religiously pluralistic India. That continued to be the goal of Jawaharlal Nehru and Indira Gahdhi, his daughter, who, after two years, succeeded him as president. But in 1984 she too was murdered, a victim of her opposition to religio-ethnic groups who were demanding communal recognition. In this case the violence came from Sikhs. Five hundred years ago the Sikhs had developed, as a middle way between Hindu and Muslim, a blending of faiths. But Indian independence and persistent communal violence has produced a Sikh version of uncompromising fundamentalism.

In 1991 tragedy struck again, with the assassination of Indira Gandhi's son, Rajiv Gandhi, whether by Punjab separatists, Hindu nationalists, or persons supporting an independent Hindu province in Sri Lanka (a project he had at first supported and then sought to stop).

In the election following the assassination of Rajiv Gandhi, a Hindu nationalist party won control over Uttar Pradesh, India's largest state, and became the second largest party in Parliament, behind only a weakened Congress party.

Perhaps the subtitle of V.S. Naipaul's book on India says it correctly: "A Million Munities Now." Communal, religio-ethnic violence is endemic. The headlines, all from the early 1990s, tell that side of the story: "Indian election campaigning ends amid political violence"; "India is going off a cliff"; "Democracy and religion clash again in India"; "Peace plea fails; 22 die in Punjab."

The three murders are the violent thunderclaps in a continuing storm of religious conflict. The Indian army is seen as an occupying force in Kashmir, India's only state with a Muslim majority. That Kashmir must remain an integral part of India is basic government policy. The Indian military has acted with harsh repression to enforce that policy, as in January 1993, when forty persons were killed by fire and gun. In April more than 100 were killed in a crossfire of violence and arson that destroyed large sections of Srinigan, the Capital. The Muslim majority have responded, through the years, with violence against Hindu merchants and administrators. The death toll is over one thousand, including several hundred militants fighting for independence or union with Pakistan.[54]

In the Punjab, Sikh militants, seeking separation from India, have killed scores of people. The factions among them add fratricidal rebellion to the interreligious violence.

In this context, an intensified Hindu nationalism was almost inevitable. Clashes between Hindus and Muslims have left several hundred dead. This nationalism is built upon the long-standing resentment among some Hindus of the domination of India, as they saw it, by outsiders (beginning nine hundred years ago!). This is the kind of historical memory that furnishes justification and makes vivid the resentments and frustration of more current events, such as the concept of a secular state built into the independence movement and the significant increase in the prosperity of some Muslims.[55]

The most serious conflict in recent years was started December 6, 1992, when Hindu militants destroyed a mosque built over four hundred years ago by Mogul emperor Babur. The mosque, which Hindu fundamentalist had protested for years, stood on what they regarded as a sacred site, the birthplace of the god Ram. Riots raged for several days in many parts of the country, as the Hindu militants proclaimed, in words and deeds, "India is ours" (sounding not unlike extreme nationalists elsewhere).

The federal government, seeking to uphold its standard of a religiously pluralistic, non-sectarian society, banned Hindu and Muslim fundamentalist groups; but the ban is difficult to enforce in regions where their views predominate. Hundreds were jailed, officials were removed, and thousands arrested. But the rioting went on for several days. Before it was over, two thousand people, mostly Muslim, had been killed.

Bordered by Pakistan and Bangladesh, close to Iran and Afghanistan, Muslim states with strong fundamentalist movements, and living in a world where religions, in many areas, have been politicized in the service of ethnic causes, India's tragic outbreak of religious violence is not surprising. Nevertheless it is a peril to the

Indian state. Its non-sectarian principles did not develop simply as a way of holding together within one polity the large Hindu and Muslim populations. There are also Sikhs, Buddhists, Christians, Jews, Jains, agnostics. Hinduism itself is highly diverse. Seeing it ". . . as one religion, in fact, is a comparatively recent development."[56]

The threat to India as a multi-ethnic, multi-religious state is most easily seen in the Muslim-Hindu conflicts, especially the rise of Hindu nationalism in several settings and Muslim nationalism in Kashmir. The ruling Congress Party, fearful of losing votes to the fundamentalist Hindu parties, has been tentative in its efforts to suppress the violence and intolerance. (One inclined toward comparative study might note that it would not take much transposition to apply this comment to other democratic societies.) In the long run, however, the greater threat may be the fact that India's secularism rests, not so much on tolerance, as on a kind of balance of intolerances among the several communities, as Sen observes.

And yet, the world's largest democracy is still holding free elections. The majority support the Gandhi-Nehru vision of a secular state. This view, however, is being sorely tested. With a population as large as that of Europe, east and west, including Russia, plus the United States—a population probably as religiously and linguistically complex as all of those societies put together—India is indeed riven by ancient differences and animosities. But this may, sadly, be more expressive of the human condition in this period than of anything peculiarly Indian.

The Ethno-Religious Clash in Sri Lanka. In the early 1980s, a separatist movement began to develop in that part of the island-state of Sri Lanka occupied primarily by ethnic Tamils. This was in part a response to legal constraints and economic pressures that had been building in the central government for a generation. Although most of the Tamils were from families that had been in Sri Lanka (Ceylon) for many generations, they had only recently begun to move into occupational "niches" in competition with the Sinhalese majority and to press for political power in proportion to their numbers (about one eighth of the total of 17 ½ million). India, with its sixty million Tamils, is just across the Palk Strait.[57]

Despite relatively peaceful ethnic-religious relationships over several centuries, in Sri Lanka we have had during recent years an almost "classic" setting for the development of ethnic violence:

- A long-established majority population (c. ¾) and a vigorous minority building up over a period of two centuries, as well as other smaller minorities.
- Mainly Buddhist Sinhalese, mainly Hindu Tamils, plus a few Muslims and Christians.
- Language difference—Sinhala vs. Tamil.
- Regional concentration of the minority, but with some dispersion through the southern regions.
- An enormous ancestral state nearby for the minority Tamils (India).
- A world where ethnic nationalisms seem almost to ricochet from region to region, from continent to continent: Lebanon, the Sudan, Burma, Ethiopia, the Philippines, Ireland, Spain, Bangladesh, India, Yugoslavia, Iraq, Turkey.
- A majority unwilling to grant full rights to a minority, in part out of what seems a blind ethnocentrism and in part out of fear of cultural extinction when they think of the sixty million Tamils in India.

Headlines suggest the flow of events:

Fighting in Sri Lanka dims hope for ethnic peace (April 22, 1984)

Tamil leaders reject offer from Sri Lanka in peace negotiations (Nov. 9, 1986).

Sri Lanka arises as issue in Indian State [Tamil Nadu] vote (Oct. 9, 1988).

Blood, alienation and chauvinism accompany Sri Lankans to polls (Dec. 18, 1988).

Sinhalese militants threaten to paralyze government and divide the nation (Aug. 27, 1989).

Sri Lankan army is closing in on a citadel of resistance by Tamil rebels (Aug. 26, 1990).

Muslims in Sri Lanka flee violence of civil war (Sept. 2, 1990). Brutal rebellion pushing northern Sri Lanka back to pre-industrial era (Aug. 29, 1991).

100 Muslims die in ethnic attack in Sri Lanka (Oct. 16, 1992).
Suicide bomber kills President of Sri Lanka (May 2, 1993).[58]

Early in this period, as the tentative gestures of negotiations
led to modest results, the most impatient Tamils created a fighting
force, the Liberation Tigers, in an effort to win by violence, at increasing levels of intensity, a seperate Tamil state. Many moderate
Tamils were killed. To the Liberation Tigers they were traitors.
Thus those among the Tamil who were least ready to work for accommodations and compromises within a multi-religious state began to dominate the action. They now nearly control the charred
and battered northern region of the country.

As an inevitable reciprocal, some of the Sinhalese shifted to
terror. They opposed the Sri Lankan-Indian peace agreement of
1987, which would have created a single Tamil-dominated administrative area, as a sellout to India and an excessive concession to
the Tamils (having opposed, one should add, more moderate conces-
sions earlier). In this context, the army has become the critical
force. The contending religio-ethnic groups remain unreconciled. In
a decade, some 17,000 have been killed—another demonstration of
the effects, in a diverse society, of basing politics on religion and ethnicity. And the world, with few policies regarding such events and
fewer ways to become involved, watches in dismay.

The Clash of Religions in Nagorno-Karabakh. As the Soviet
Union, with its capacity for oppression and its willingness to use it,
fell apart, long-inhibited animosities within many of the republics
were released. Among the most tragic is the violent confrontation
between Muslim Azerbaijanis and the Christian Armenians who
make up 80 percent of the Nagorno-Karabakh region within
Azerbaijan.

In the distant background are the shared yet different experiences of Armenia and Azerbaijan with the Persian, Turkish, and
Russian empires. Perhaps they learned some skills in protecting
themselves, despite the overwhelming power of these empires,
since their culturally distinctive qualities and their identities persist. This is partly due to the way they were play against each other
by the imperial powers. Within the Soviet Union, they expressed not
only an acceptable "official nationalism," a kind of permissible patriotism, but also a dissident nationalism, focused on human rights
and in a few cases the goal of separation, and among their own eth-

nic minorities various counter-nationalisms, expressing opposition to perceived discrimination.[59]

During the last forty years or more both republics have become more homogeneous ethnically, due to a combination of out-migration of persons of other ethnic backgrounds, in-migration from elsewhere of fellow Armenians or Azerbaijanis, and differential birthrates. Thus the number of Azerbaijanis in Armenia in 1989 (85,000) was 2.57 percent; in 1959 it had been 6.11 percent. The number of Armenians in Azerbaijan in 1989 (390,000) was 5.56 percent; in 1959 it had been 11.96 percent.[60]

About forty percent of the 390,000, it should be noted, were in Nagorno-Karabakh, where Armenians make up about 80 percent of the population. The region is within Azerbaijan but close to the Armenian border. Encouraged by the liberal developments in the Soviet Union, in the winter of 1987 the Armenians in Nagorno-Karabakh were demanding union with Armenia. The Azerbaijani response: scores were killed. When Gorbachev declared that the region would remain as part of Azerbaijan, in March 1988, the violence resumed. By the end of the year thousands of people on both sides had become refugees. Armenia, already suffering from the effects of a major earthquake, found itself cut off from many of its supply lines by an Azerbaijan blockade.

There was a period of several months of unstable peace, enforced by the Soviet armed forces, but with the breakup of the USSR, the conflict was renewed with even greater ferocity, powered by weapons bought or stolen from military bases of the Commonwealth of Independent States. If Armenians had been the main victims at first, it was Azerbaijanis—particularly those resident in Nagorno-Karabakh who were now hit the hardest. Unable to protect them, President Ayaz Mutalibov resigned in March 1992.

In four years of conflict at least two thousand persons have been killed and hundreds of thousands have fled from areas where they were in the minority ethnic group. The sadly familiar cycle of revenge for revenge for revenge continues. As of this writing, peace talks continue; so also does the killing.

THE ISRAELI-PALESTINIAN CONFLICT

These brief references to Ireland, India, Sri Lanka, Nagorno-Karabakh, and elsewhere may help us to keep in mind how frequently religious elements enter into ethnic struggles. No society faces a more severe ethno-religious conflict than Israel; and I will examine it somewhat more fully. Because of its historical depth, the severity of the disagreements, and the ways in which it involves the interests and concerns of other societies, the experience of Israel takes us into the central questions of religiously defined ethnic conflicts.

Religion, I have suggested, is both substantive and symbolic. Sharp disagreements divide Palestinians and Israelis on questions of power and status. At the same time, both sides emphasize traditional, even scriptural justifications for their positions. Their world views are in sharp contrast. At the very least, fundamentalists on both sides hold strategic balance of power positions, guaranteeing that religious themes will be critically involved as Israel, and indeed many other societies, seek to find a way to build accommodation and toleration, if not reconciliation between two groups claiming the same land.

Complicating this situation is the strongly felt need among Israeli Jews to attain some measure of assimilation between the pioneer Ashkenazic Jews and the more recent and very heterogeneous Sephardim, along with the absorption of hundreds of thousands of immigrants from the former Soviet Union. Of course not all of the Sephardim, or Oriental and Asian Jews, are recent migrants.[61] In any event, it is their cultural, even their religious, difference, more than the time of their arrival in Israel, that is crucial for the process of assimilation. Black Jews from the United States, tens of thousands of Ethiopian Jews—most of them part of a community that has been substantially isolated from the mainstreams of Jewish life for two thousand years—as well as the more numerous Jews from the African Mediterranean states and the Middle Eastern Arab states all present Israel with enormous educational, language, occupational, and political problems, complicated by stereotypes and discrimination.[62] The Ethiopian Jews have been startled to discover that there are Jews who identify mainly with a secular state, not with Judaism, while at the same time the most Orthodox of Israeli Jews regard the Ethiopians themselves as not truly Jewish.

The wide variety of immigrants places Israel on the list of states—perhaps at the head of the list—seeking to create cohesive, tolerant, and just societies out of populations with diverse cultural backgrounds. This effort is severely limited, however. Israeli Palestinians have been pushed to the margins and denied full citizenship.

Americans look at Israel in the context of their own experience, in which ethnic diversity has played a continuing part. Most see diversity as central to the very strength and definition of America as well as the source of persistent problems. We're still trying to get it right; we manage two steps forward only to fall one step back. So Americans tend to be sympathetic, if also impatient, with Israel as it responds to its own multi-culturalism, most recently with reference to the 1989–1992 wave of Jewish immigrants from the Soviet Union and the powerful *intifada* protest from the West Bank.

This enormous migration from the collapsing Soviet Union (about 450,000 1989–1992, with perhaps many more in the next several years) is itself a source of controversy. Many Israeli Palestinians see it as an effort to reduce their already small influence in a state where their hold on citizenship is tenuous. Palestinians in the occupied West Bank and Gaza see it as an additional threat to their hopes for autonomy or independence.

At the same time, Israeli Jews are divided in their expectations regarding Soviet Jews. Some hope to find the majority of them to be supporters of a more orthodox Judaism and a more clearly Jewish state. Others hope, and believe, that they will give greater support to the idea of a secular state and a more open ethnic policy.

Assessment of this range of views, however, has not yet been taken. Many of the new immigrants face serious occupational, residential, and social problems. One may say, "I remain a person of Russian culture. . . . I am a stranger here." And another, "For me this is a rebirth. I only know one country which is mine, Israel."[63] Some Soviet Jews bring much-needed skills and are quickly absorbed into the work force. Others try to enter an already overcrowded field, only to find themselves unemployed and poorly housed.

In the years ahead these facts may prove to be of importance, for the immigrants themselves, for Israel and for the world situation. Scarcely half of the Soviet Jews are from Russia. The relationships among those from Ukraine, Bylerussia, Georgia, Tajikistan, the Central Asian republics, and Russia may be influenced by developments in their countries of origin. A competition may develop—has already developed—between Israel and the United States and other countries for those with technical skills, particularly those related to nuclear power. Even if Israel's portion is thus reduced, it "will be absorbing much of the educated elite of a superpower."[64]

What it means to be a Jew will continue to be a subject of controversy between the more orthodox Israelis and the more secularized, the latter including many of the Soviet migrants, who "have a clear interest—both personal and collective—in a secular Israel in which they will not have to conform to religious laws they don't believe in."[65]

The slight majority of Sephardic Jews before 1989 is being reduced and perhaps reversed by this newest wave of migrants, virtually all of whom are Ashkenazis. The slow economic and political gains of the former may be threatened. At least in the short run, stereotypes of the "Asiatics" may be reenforced.

Such factors as these are of great importance for Israel today. How their impact is felt, however, is strongly influenced by the more visible struggle between Palestinian and Jewish Israelis and the political debate, both international and within the state, over the status of Palestinians in the occupied West Bank and Gaza. The continued threat of, indeed the fact of, multi-state involvement is severe, complicating every decision. Although the USA-USSR aspect of this issue has been removed or sharply curtailed, the Arab world and the Muslim world more generally, the United States, and much of Europe continue to see their vital interests as being deeply involved in the outcome of the Israeli-Palestinian struggle.

The Changing Situation for Israel

By 1991 several significant developments not only in Israel, but in the Arab world, Eastern Europe, the USSR, and the United States seemed to have opened a window of opportunity, or at least to have cast doubt on long-held assumptions.

1) An Arab state has become, or is perceived to be, a serious threat to others. It is difficult to maintain a united Arab front on policies toward Israel when North African Muslims, for example, condemn the Saudi, Syria, and Kuwaiti support for the United Nations (United States?) battle to drive Iraq out of Kuwait. They saw such action as support for "imperial aggression against a brother Arab nation," as an attack on "the brother Iraqi people," and an act intended "to prevent the renaissance of the Arab nation".[66] Thus the dearly held beliefs in pan-Arab unity and pan-Islamic brotherhood have been seriously weakened.

2) States in the Middle East no longer need to adapt to, nor can they exploit, the USA-USSR confrontation that had, since World

War II, vitally affected that region, as well as most other strategic areas in the world.

3) Some Arab states have found themselves beholden to the United States as a result of its massive military support. Or perhaps I should say: That part of their ambivalent interests that pulled them toward the United States has become more powerful. As they look out at the world in the early1990s they doubtless sense the probability that further support from America and other non-Arab states will be needed, in the form of weapons and diplomacy, if not of military action.

4) Internal divisions within several of the Muslim states of the Middle East further contribute to the fluidity, the unpredictability, of the situation. Since the Khomeini revolution of 1979, nervous rulers throughout the area have wondered when fundamentalism within their own countries would challenge their rule. The possibilities are there, in Algeria, Tunisia, Morocco, the Sudan and Egypt, Lebanon, Jordon, Yemen, and Saudi Arabia.

Wealthy Saudis have supported fundamentalist movements with hundreds of millions of dollars. Until recently this has been with the acquiescence of the Saudi government, which saw such support as a way to win allies for its conservative regime. The Persian Gulf crisis of 1991 (and ff?) however, proved otherwise. What was seen as the hypocrisy of the Saudi elite was condemned, especially in Egypt. "Most Islamic movements in the Arab world, from Morocco to Egypt, supported Iraq's invasion of Kuwait and Baghdad's call for the overthrow of the Saudi royal family. . . . Saudi Arabia's government is beginning a quiet campaign to convince wealthy Saudis who give money to Islamic causes to beware of financing radical fundamentalist movements."[67] King Fahd is creating a new Consultative Council, a small step toward a more pluralistic base of authority and, perchance, a safeguard against fundamentalist challenges.

5) Islamic movements are often seen as "outlets" for the poverty stricken and repressed masses, a way of expressing their resentment against the wealthy few. If "outlet" is regarded, however, as a religious surrogate for deeply felt needs, it may be a poorly conceived term. A religious movement can focus resentment.

Such resentment can be displaced onto historically and ethnically visible targets. Israeli society, Hertzberg writes "is increasingly troubled by the knowledge that the deepest tide running in the region is the anger of the have-nots. Even after

Saddam Hussein is gone, America, Israeli, and the Arab national leaders will have to reckon with tens of millions of Arabs who will be increasingly hungry, and increasingly angry. . . . Resources will have to be redistributed in the Middle East, or more and more of the hungry and resentful will try to arm themselves with the terrible weapons that Saddam Hussein is now brandishing. . . . The real threat to Israel is no longer the PLO; it is the pan-Arabism of the poor."[68]

Disunity among the Arabs may, for a time, postpone the full impact of such a situation, but one hesitates to challenge Hertzberg's judgment that Israel's very life depends upon making peace with the Palestinians and thereby creating an opening to the Arab world and helping the people throughout the region "to achieve more decent lives."

What is true of Israel is equally true of the Arab regimes. Some may continue to try to displace the hostilities of the poor onto Israel. Developments we have referred to in their own societies, however, and those in Israel, the United States, and elsewhere, may be making this more difficult to do. Egypt, the largest and perhaps the poorest of the Arab states, has developed a *modus vivendi*, if not a full relationship with Israel.

Saddam Hussein convinced many of the poorest Arabs that he was fighting for them. For several decades, the urbanizing, industrializing process has been bringing more and more of them into contact with a wider world, increasing their frustrations but also their sense of other possibilities. The dramatic changes in Eastern Europe and the Soviet Union have highlighted the vulnerability of authoritarian rule. Some religious leaders have used the energy generated by these kinds of experiences to win support for fundamentalist movements and regimes. Others, more secularized, have used them to solidify their mass support for authoritarian states, even while appealing to fundamentalist sentiments. Other expressions of protest, however, are more nearly popular uprisings against disfranchisement and poverty, often expressed in the language of nationalism.

Such is the movement of the young Palestinians in the West Bank and the Gaza strip, the intifada, that seeks to force Israel out of those territories. Along with impassioned nationalists, there are fanatics among them, more effective in shattering the uneasy acceptance of Israeli occupation than in moving toward any new goal. But their slingshots, stones, and Molotov cocktails challenged the status quo and forced Israel into a more open debate on its policies. The intifada protest, which started in 1987, has been forcefully, often brutally, suppressed by Israel, with hundreds killed and thousands imprisoned. Forty years before the "Palestinian uprising," terrorists among the Jews, including some who later became Israeli leaders, were fighting to obtain a homeland. The intifada's own brutality has often been most powerfully shown in attacks on other Palestinians accused of betrayal, of supporting the Israeli occupation. The Associated Press tally lists 679 killed in 1987–1992. The most lasting effect for Israel is likely to be "the deep crisis within Israeli politics and society, which will never be the same again."[69] 1,003 Palestinians have been killed by Israeli forces; 112 Israelis have been killed by Palestinians.

By 1991 the intifada seemed to be a spent force. More moderate Palestinians began to appear, or reappear after Saddam Hussein, hailed as a hero by the more radical Palestinians, lost some of his luster and after the internal violence against other Arabs became ever more serious. This may be a premature judgment. The killing of several Israeli soldiers, the deportation, without trial, of 415 Palestinians to a no-man's land in Southern Lebanon—an action condemned by the United Nations—raised the level of violence again in December 1992.[70] Scores of Palestinians and Israeli Jews were killed in the first few months of 1993.

6) Many forces supporting positive change, however, continue. The loss of strong supporters in Eastern Europe has strengthened the voices of moderates in the PLO. In 1988, its executive council finally recognized the sovereignty of Israel over land within its pre-1967 borders and to Israel's right to exist. In 1991 the PLO dropped Abu Abbas, one of its more intransigent members and widely regarded as a terrorist, from its ruling executive council. And in 1992 it began, somewhat ambiguously, to accept a Middle Eastern peace process, to which it objected and to which it had not been admitted. Other Palestinians have submitted a plan for elections in the disputed occupied territories. Like Israel's ambiguous offer of elections in 1988, the 1992 Palestinian plan is scarcely more than a nod of recognition that diplomatic movement is underway. Yet it is one more small light shining through the window of opportunity.[71]

7) Since its founding in 1948, Israel has had the strong support of the United States government and a large majority of the Amer-

ican people. This expresses not only the fact that the United States is home for almost half of the world's Jews, but also the widely shared belief that the creation of a Jewish state was the right response to the horrors of the holocaust, the strongest guarantee that no such tragedy could again occur.

Almost from the beginning, a few Americans emphasized that many Palestinians also lived in the area that had become Israel. The enormity of the pressures against the new state, however, was the dominant fact as seen from the United States. Private and governmental support remained strong through the several Arab-Israeli wars. A volatile mixture of cold war, Arab resentment, maximalist Zionist dreams, the strategic importance of oil, and the need for enemies on all sides prevented any major shifts in policy for thirty years. A small light appeared in 1979 when the governments of Anwar Sadat of Egypt and Menachem Begin of Israel, nurtured by President Jimmy Carter, came to the Camp David agreement: Israel returned the Sinai to Egypt; Egypt signed a peace treaty with Israel.

The volatile mixture of forces was still there, however. Sadat was killed; widespread Arab condemnation of the very fact of Israel persisted; and Israel continued its search for security through military power and uncompromising policies.

This brief and doubtless overly simple description of the years after 1948 began to need revision in the late 1980s. And among the forces both reflecting and affecting that need for revision are the changes in American attitudes and policies. These changes occurred among the general public, including Jews, and in the activities of the government.

For several years the General Social Survey of the NORC has asked a carefully selected sample of the American population to indicate how much they liked various countries. Choices ranged along a ten-point scale from "like very much" to "dislike very much." The rating of Israel in 1974 was 6.6; in 1985 it was 6.4. By 1987, however, it had fallen to 5.7, where it remained in 1990.[72] Although still on the positive side of the mean of the scale (5.5), the 1990 ranking was a significant decline from a few years earlier.

In 1991 the United States government began to increase its pressure on Israel to stop building residences on the West Bank. Israel was requesting a ten billion dollar loan guarantee to help it finance just such building, among other projects. When the building continued in 1992, the American warnings against the project became stronger. Since more general aid to Israel has continued, even increased, the "loan guarantee," which involved no direct exchange of funds, had become a symbolic struggle—the United States seeks to strengthen its ties to what it sees as more moderate Arab states, while Israel rushes to complete more West Bank settlements to have in place a *fait accomplis* (irreversible "facts on the ground," as Moshe Dayan has called them) as peace talks get underway. A *Wall Street Journal*/NBC poll in January 1992 found that the general American public agreed with the United States government policies: 73 percent opposed the loan guarantees so long as the West Bank building continued; 18 percent favored them.[73]

American Jews are prominent among those seeking to break the impasse in Israeli-Palestinian relations. Two-thirds support an exchange of territory for peace, a policy that was firmly rejected by the Likud government, but has been supported, albeit somewhat tentatively, by the Labor government. Controversy between the American Israel Public Committee (the major lobbying group in the United States in defense of Israel) and important Jewish organizations (such as the American Jewish Committee, the American Jewish Congress, and the Anti-Defamation League) has become more open and vigorous. The Jewish Peace Lobby has been founded. It favors a Palestinian state, but one without major weapons. *Tikkun*, a magazine strongly supporting the end of the occupation of the West Bank and Gaza by Israel ("The Occupation: Immoral and Stupid") has been founded. Open letters from Jewish American academics, journalists, and religious leaders abound, rebuking the Israeli government, lamenting the loss of moral purpose, and expressing the fear that serious, perhaps fatal blows to Israel will result if present policies are not changed.

I cannot give a quantitative estimate of the strength of these developments; but to this observer they appear to be a major change over the last five years. They add up to the fact that perhaps two-thirds of American Jews now favor reconciliation with the Palestinians, the exchange of land for peace, and a return in Israel to the essential process of full democracy and peaceful development. This is one more element in the mixture of contemporary events creating the possibility of political-moral-diplomatic movement in the Middle East.

8) Reflecting and affecting all of these developments are the changes—and the resistance to the changes—within Israel. The Likud Party of Prime Minister Yitzhak Shamir, with the support of the several members of fundamentalist religious parties, had held fast to the belief that permanent control of the West Bank and Gaza was essential to the safety and development of Israel. Shamir made some gestures toward offering autonomy to the 1.7 million Palestinians in the occupied territories and joined in the first stages of peace negotiations. In January 1992, however, these gestures proved to be too much for the five parliament members from the far right. They withdrew their support from the government, leaving Shamir without a majority and setting the stage for an election.

While Shamir was in office the most visible source of conflict between the Palestinians and the Israeli government was the building of settlements for Jewish Israelis on the West Bank. To Shamir, "The settlements are an indication of the rightful claim of the Jewish people to the territories." "We are convinced," Shamir has stated, "we are owners of these territories and the land belongs to us."[74]

A different view is expressed by Abba Eban, former Foreign Minister of Israel. He laments the militant ethnic-nationalism of the Likud Party; he believes it sharply contradicts the dreams of the founders of Israel. To Eban, the central task of the Israeli government is not simply to assert its own rights, but also to be concerned with a harmony of rights that includes all of those involved. Without such harmony, Israel cannot be safe, but more importantly, it cannot fulfill its dreams.[75]

The June, 1992 election was a clear victory for Yitzhak Rabin and the Labor Party. The tone of the peace talks began to change. Rabin has expressed a willingness to return part of the Golan Heights to Syria. And the Israeli-Syrian negotiators began to define the agenda of a peace agreement. Three major questions were identified: What will peace mean—exchange of embassies, trade? How much of the Golan Heights will be returned? What kind of security arrangements will be put in place along the common frontier? To agree on the questions is the first, but short, step toward the answers.

For years, the ideologies of the Israelis and Palestinians, perhaps more sharply conflicting than those of Israel and Syria, have created contrasting pictures of what has happened and what should happen. Believing is seeing. The sharp cleavage in Jerusalem has been made "deeper and more dangerous by the fusion, on both sides, of nationalist and religious metaphors. . . . Many Palestinians maintain the illusion that if they are only steadfast enough, the Israelis will one day vanish into thin air. Many Israelis cling to a parallel misapprehension that if economic conditions among Arabs of Jerusalem improve, they will, in the end, prefer freedom of religious worship under a relatively benevolent Israeli regime over the rigid, repressive authoritarianism common today in Arab societies."[76]

Even wise and moderate leaders find it difficult to reach common ground when powerful historical memories and ideologies furnish the defining terms. In responding to comments about Jerusalem made by Professor Avishai Margalit, Mayor Teddy Kollek wrote: "I am not comfortable if someone merely says, 'In 1967 Israel conquered East Jerusalem'. . . . Twenty-five years later, I feel it is important to state that this was the result of a war not of Israel's choosing but a war of aggression initiated by all our Arab neighbors that, had our enemies had their way, would have been a war of extermination. . . . I protest the assumption hidden behind much Arab argumentation that there need be no penalty for attacking Israel repeatedly." In his letter of response, Margalit wrote: "The Palestinians have paid in very hard currency for that war. Who knows better than he [Mayor Kollek] that 150,000 Jews (the number is his own) have been settled on the other side of the Green Line, on Palestinian land? . . . . In the balance of terror the Palestinians are clearly on the lighter side of the scales."[77]

It is a sad fact that after the poignant exchange of letters between these two wonderfully informed and articulate people—able to walk in each other's shoes for quite a ways—we find them, in the end, taking different roads.[78]

What do these several developments mean if Israel will withdraw from none of the disputed territory and the PLO demands nothing less than an independent state?

Awesome problems lie behind these mutually contradictory requirements: questions of citizenship, of boundaries, of the status of Jerusalem, of security, of self-determination. These are made more severe by the competing claims over historical, even scriptural, rights to a nation-state in the same territory (or substantially overlapping territories). History has linked Palestinians and Jews and their national movements, "Neither can make the other disappear, and neither can achieve peace without fulfilling some of the most deeply held aspirations of the other."[79]

Gottlieb believed that, despite the harsh words, "The softer subtext suggests that Israel will be ready to offer maximal self-rule and political rights for the Palestinians in the West Bank and Gaza, the formula called 'self-rule plus,' and that the Palestinians will be prepared to accept a 'demilitarized state' linked to Jordan."[80] In his view, state and homeland are separate concepts; "The national rights of a people can be exercised in different fashions in different parts of the homeland."[81] The emerging European community, he believed, may offer a valuable model. Four years later, however, we have to note the negative model of the collapsing Soviet Union, where one ethnic group after another has demanded a state to coincide with and to protect its homeland. These demands are urgent in spite of, or perhaps because of, the fact that each of the states is multi-ethnic. Thus what is seen as a homeland state (a nation-state) for some is seen as another version of a potentially coercive state by the ethnic minorities within it.

In recent years the qualified optimism for accommodation and peace has been subdued by the stronger assertion of uncompromising fundamentalism among both Jews and Muslims. Even if this is a minority view, as I would judge it to be among Israelis, if less certainly in the Muslim societies, those who affirm orthodoxy or fundamentalism can hold a strategic balance-of-power position that blocks negotiations.

It is more difficult to hear the words of Rabbi David Hartman, who holds that the Jewish tradition not only allows pluralism, it requires it. Palestinians' "fundamental human desires" must be recognized or Israel will become a society dominated by force.[82] Under the pessimistic title "A Lost Chance for Peace," Hertzberg takes a very similar position in reference to American policies toward Israel: "Jews as a minority in the United States have spent the last century demanding equality for themselves. They have achieved it against the opposition of American nationalists, who insisted that Christians should have more rights than Jews. American Jews cannot now convincingly join the Israeli government in denying equality to Palestinians in the name of Jewish nationalism."[83]

A similar strain is found on the Muslim side. The most zealous Palestinians fear peace because it will require that they give up their urgent desire that Israel should somehow disappear. It of course will not, just as the several million Palestinians will not disappear. They are aided by the increasingly visible Muslim fundamentalists in several countries, and by more secularized and politicized Muslims who seek to maintain what is often a tenuous hold on power by alliances with the fundamentalists.

In such contexts, those who see both interests of state and Muslim doctrines requiring a search for peace work under severe constraints.

Amidst these social forces shaping a severe communal conflict are intense personal experiences. "Palestinians still see Jews as despoilers who have stolen their home and their pride. . . . For Jews to acknowledge Palestinians, they have to acknowledge that they took someone's land, that they live in someone's home and that they have to reach an accommodation with them."[84] And how can Jews feel friendly toward Palestinians who supported Saddam Hussein, longtime foe of Israel? Who is the owner of this shared national home, and who is the guest?

Thus the conflict is a national struggle, but "it is also a very personal encounter between two sets of people who, despite decades of contact and confrontation, do not know each other very well but fear each other intensely. It is the accumulation of thousands of incidents—large and small, earth-shaking and trivial, achingly complicated and brutally simple. Together they form a vast mountain of anger, damage and dread that could easily bury the fragile, halting process underway in Washington."[85]

How will these various social and personal forces play themselves out during the next several years? In 1989 Gidon Gottlieb could write that, despite the harsh and bitter rhetoric, small steps had been taken to close the great divide between Israeli and Palestinian claims and expectations: The Camp David accord of a decade earlier; King Hussein's readiness to relinquish claims to the West Bank; the PLO, in declaring Palestinian independence, renouncing terrorism and—rather ambiguously—accepting Israel's right to exist; the Likud-Labor coalition government of Israel initiating the prospect of elections on the West Bank leading to transitional self-rule (within the state of Israel).[86]

By 1993 the several other developments in Israel and abroad that I have mentioned have, at the least, exposed the tragic possibilities in the present impasse. In a more optimistic interpretation, however, using a religious frame appropriate to this chapter, we may be seeing at least a small shift in the balance of the ethnic-universalistic polarity.

Conclusion

Almost everywhere in the Middle East, religion and politics seem closely connected. Only two states with written constitutions—Lebanon and Turkey—have no established religion. All are experiencing, however, the pull of modernization, which to the devout is virtually a synonym for secularization. Powerful movements in several of the countries "share the objective of undoing the secularizing reforms of the last century, abolishing the imported codes of law and the social customs that came with them, and returning to the holy law of Islam and the Islamic political order. . . . Even nationalism and patriotism, which, after some initial opposition from pious Muslims, had begun to be generally accepted, are now once again being questioned and even denounced."[87] As Lewis emphasized, historically speaking "there are no lords spiritual for Muslims, or for that matter for Jews, no political churchmen like Richelieu or Wolsey." Today, however, one can see "Muslim and Jewish men of religion who, forsaking traditional values, have become both political and ecclesiastical."[88]

After the Reformation several primarily Protestant societies invented the separation of church and state, designed to prevent the state from extending its power by claiming religious sanction and churches from imposing their doctrines on others with the aid of secular authority. The melding of authority, the cooptation of one by the other, was long seen as a Christian, not a Muslim or Jewish problem. "Looking at the contemporary Middle East, both Jewish and Muslim, one must ask whether this is still true—or whether Jews and Muslims may perhaps have caught a Christian disease and might therefore consider a Christian remedy."[89]

Max Weber would surely answer: Yes they have, and yes they should, for present trends can only bring terrible harm to the classical religious views and make state policies rigid and coercive. And we must add that mainly Christian societies would equally benefit by employing and developing better models of their own invention. When this happens the universalism in these religions will be released from its political bondage, freeing them to serve as arbiters in the religio-ethnic conflicts now tearing apart many societies.

Chapter 8

LANGUAGE AND ETHNICITY

Wer fremde Sprache nicht kennt
weiss nichts von seiner eigenen.
—*Goethe*

Considering the vital importance of language to culture as a whole, perhaps without distorting his meaning we can extend Goethe's statement to say Those who know no foreign culture know nothing of their own.

Opponents of such a sentiment, however, are more likely to say:

That society is most fortunate
Where all speak the same language.
Those divided by language risk
Cultural disarray and insufficient loyalty.

A great deal of history revolves around the issue, from the empires of ancient Greece and Rome to the recent struggles over language policy in the Soviet Union and India. And of course the United States, Canada, and many other countries on every continent face the language dilemma.

The subtitle of LaPierre's excellent study of *Le pouvoir politique et les langues* is *Babel et Leviathan*. Societies continue to search for ways to avoid the horns of the dilemma: a meaningless, utterly confusing babel of tongues (and, let me add again, of cultures) on one side set against a coercive, authoritarian Leviathan demanding the supremacy of its own language on the other. Is it possible to attain *e pluribus unum:* a society that is indeed both plural and unified?

LANGUAGE POLICIES IN MULTI-ETHNIC SOCIETIES

One of the most important aspects of any society is its language structure. Is it basically monolingual or multilingual? Within a language, are there distinctive dialects (major language variations) or accents (minor language variations)? These can be ranged along a continuum from minimal (I think I detect a trace of an accent) to maximal (He might as well be speaking Greek to me).

We need to distinguish between language use (she speaks English at school and on the job but Spanish at home) from language identification (her native language is Spanish) and both of these from what can be called language memory (all four of her grandparents spoke only Spanish).

The ethnic order in virtually every society is entwined with its language structure. Somewhere there may be a monolingual society, with no accents or dialects that, nonetheless, has distinctive ethnic groups, based on different ancestries, religions, or races. Far more common, however, are societies where variation in language use and identification is highly correlated with, and causally interdependent with, ethnic variation.[1] The sharper the language divide, other things being equal, the clearer are the ethnic lines of division. Since other things are seldom equal—groups may vary by class, region, religion, race—dialect or accent may be stronger markers of ethnicity than a major language difference.

"Standard speech"—the variety of a language, the "center" one might say, around which the other forms are heard to revolve— is typically the speech pattern of the dominant ethnic group, especially of its middle and upper classes. They do not hear themselves as speaking a dialect. As someone has said, a language pure and simple is a dialect with an army and navy. The variations closest to the "center" vary mainly by accent, a little by vocabulary, only slightly by grammar.

The language policies of a society are part of the larger political process. They reflect the comparative powers of linguistic groups as well as more general political institutions and values. These most often reenforce the strength of the dominant groups, but in democratic societies there are some built-in restraints that set limits to linguistic dominance. These include minority linguistic communities, laws, a culture of pluralism, and international ties.

For several decades the language situation in the Soviet Union indicated the stronger acculturative pull of the largest, most dominant Republic. Some Russian speakers learned the language of another Republic, especially if they resided in that Republic. A much larger proportion of non-Russians, however, learned Russian. In 1959, 87.6 percent of the non-Russians reported their native language as their first language. By 1989, this had fallen to 84.1 percent. In the same thirty-year period, those naming Russian as their first language increased from 10.8 percent to 14.6 percent. Considering the vigorous Russification policy, this shift seems quite small. To it we need to add, however, the more rapid increase of the use of Russian as a second language—an increase from less than a third to nearly half by 1989.[2]

With the breakup of the Soviet Union and the increase in ethnic tension, including hostility toward Russia, this language shift is likely to be slowed and perhaps even reversed. It seems likely that English and German will become the languages most frequently studied as second languages in many of the newly independent republics. In some, Turkish, Arabic, or Persian (Farsi) may grow in influence.

LaPierre contrasts, in a typological sense, unitary-centralized policies and federal policies.[3] The former seek to build a nation-state, to minimize linguistic and cultural variation, to bring newcomers into the mainstream—or perhaps one ought to say the only stream. One language is preeminent; its mastery is essential for full acceptance or status improvement.

Few societies fit this type precisely. France might be most often cited as closest to it, while being praised for the variety of the peoples it has admitted and criticized for its intensity in trying to establish a unitary language and cultural dominance. There may be more than a little stereotyping in this appraisal, however.[4] At least we have to note that such a policy has been only partially successful; several distinct languages and dialects continue; and with the addition of four or more million newcomers to the French population in the last few decades, adding great variety to the linguistic and religious picture, a unitary-centralized policy faces a continuous challenge. The fact that many of the newcomers speak French, to be sure, eases the problem.

Many other newcomers, however, do not speak French, or speak it poorly. And the intrusion of English words and phrases, along with the increase in the use of English in international business and political discourse, has heightened the anxiety of those who fear that the dominance of French is threatened. Expressive of this fear is this addition to the Constitution by the French Parliament in the Spring of 1992: "The language of the Republic is French." (In contrast, one should note some increase in tolerance for regional languages, even some government support, reflecting the emerging influence of the European Community.)[5]

A federal policy, following LaPierre's typology, imposes limits on central governments. Linguistic rights are protected; and smaller ethnic groups are guaranteed some autonomy and proportional influence at the federal level. Switzerland is readily cited as close to the federated model. Although nearly three-fourths of the population is German speaking, the one-fifth who are French-speaking and the one-twentieth who speak Italian face no language handicaps or barriers. This federal policy works well partly because so much power is decentralized to the Cantons, each with one clearly dominant language. However, with newcomers from a variety of language backgrounds making up nearly 15 percent of the population, the pluralistic language policy faces a major challenge.

A federal language model is made explicit in articles 7 and 8 of the European Convention for the Protection of Minorities. "Any person belonging to a linguistic minority shall have the right to use his language freely, in public as well as in private. . . . whenever a minority reaches a substantial percentage of the population of a region or of the total population, its members shall have the right, as far as possible, to speak and write in their own language to the political authorities of this region or, where appropriate, of the state." The authorities, in turn, "shall have a corresponding obligation."[6]

It is often true that the dominant ethnic groups, even when they have a clearly formed unitary-centralized or a federal linguistic policy, may have other policies and engage in other activities that hinder or even undermine their policies regarding language. If some ethnic groups face persistent discrimination that blocks integration and acculturation, they may develop an intense, partly reflexive ethnicity within which their distinctive language or dialect is emphasized. This can be the effect, not of the activity of the central government or of the majority, but of an opposition group. Thus Le Pen and his followers in France, while seeking to maintain the dominance of the French language, also express such hostility to newcomers that both the opportunity and the desire to master French are sharply reduced. The concentration of newcomers in urban ghettos and suburban shantytowns where they find family, friends, and others who speak their native language—along with nearly segregated schools—contributes to this result.

As long as it was assumed that the newcomers were "guest workers" who would return to their homelands after a few years, failures of integration and lack of facility in French were not seen as serious problems. In fact, they could be seen as desirable insofar as they made the return more likely. As it became apparent, however, that millions of "guests" were becoming immigrants—by the mid-1970s—France began to emphasize again the need for integration. A similar shift occurred in Germany and the other states with large numbers of newcomers.[7] Yet the policy conflict continues. Some German conservatives favor Turkish language instruction for children of Turkish background, hoping to prevent assimilation and thus to encourage their return "home."

Unfortunately the educational-legal gap is not easily removed even without policy disagreements. Just as educational competence becomes increasingly important, deficits increase for those lacking "linguistic capital." Those who start behind quickly fall further behind.[8] Only a policy backed by major resources can break such a cycle.

The United States, with its own large group of non-English speaking "guest workers" and immigrants, faces a similar situation. They have entered a country where one language is dominant. This is not so much the result of a unitary-centralized policy, to use LaPierre's term, as of social forces working on the stream of individual and family migrants. Native Americans were, for several generations, a major exception to this generalization. They did not, of course, migrate to the United States in search of a new life. So long as they could maintain separate communities their native languages remained viable, along with increasing knowledge of English as a second language. The situation has drastically changed, however, during the last several decades; and native-language use has dropped sharply as a result. Integrated schools, the small size of many communities, the deterioration of the rural Indian economy, urbanization, intermarriage have all led to the increased use of English. Native Americans can now be included in the generalization that the learning of English has not been primarily due to official policies. As Heath has put it: "For speakers of other languages, the primary mandate for English has come from societal forces working on an individual's desire to secure education and employment, move into English-speaking circles, and negotiate daily interactions with the bureaucratic and commercial mainstream."[9]

One cannot exclude public policies entirely from the list of forces mandating English. There is no constitutional language requirement; nor were there any laws for over a century. In the early 1900s, however, laws were passed that made literacy in English a requirement for naturalization "apparently in an attempt to limit new immigrants' access to the political process";[10] or to put this somewhat more generously, in an attempt to increase the likelihood that the rights and responsibilities of citizenship were more fully understood.

The Language of Intergroup Conflict

When asked what he would do if he had the power to bring order to the world, Confucius replied, "First I would straighten out the language." In a day of "spin-doctors" in the media, of "newspeak," of calculated double entendres, we can only wish he had had the power. Blaga Dimitrova, vice president of Bulgaria, is speaking of his own country and Eastern Europe, but his words resonate the world over when he writes: "Now, in a turbulent time, we are witnessing a new, comic performance of that old joker, our own language. The old totalitarian attitudes and stereotype are being thrown away and are being replaced, by what? By the same attitudes and stereotypes, only now turned in the opposite direction: Newspeak, version two, one might say.

"Emotional exaggeration. Truth handed down from the highest authority. Aggressiveness. Disdain for conventional opinion. Black and white judgments without nuance or shading. Demagogy. Ceaseless repetition. Cliches. Only a sense of humor, even a coarse one, can bring something fresh and revitalizing into our lives."[11]

Dimitrova is referring to people who speak "the same" language. It is one thing if a German cannot communicate accurately with a Turkish immigrant, a Frenchman with a Vietnamese, an American with a Haitian, or an English speaker with a Zulu speaker in South Africa.[12] But the language in inter-ethnic conflict is often a single language forged into a weapon. It is a language of stereotypes, of aggressiveness, of demagogy, of "black and white judgments without nuance or shading." Having discussed stereotyping in chapter 4, I will here only repeat that it is not an innocent judgment. It is a pre-judgment, a judgment ahead of the facts. Since in many instances believing is seeing, prejudices produce the selectivity in our observations necessary to confirm our already fixed opinion.

Violent language against a group often precedes or accompanies violent action. In wartime, in genocidal attacks, in episodes of inter-ethnic violence, atrocity stories and dehumanizing descriptions are readily believed. They help to push our doubts and guilts out of mind.[13]

Words are not enough. Actions may be taken to make (or attempt to make) the opponents into what the attackers need them to be if their actions are going to seem just and wise. Enemies can be made more vile by degradation, starvation, discrimination, sometimes the result of deliberate policy, sometimes the long-run effect of ideology. Concurrently, the victimizers themselves may be dehumanized, by atrocity stories, stereotypes, and violence.[14] Thus language can create a filter through which contending ethnic groups see each other only in distorted images.[15]

Is Black Vernacular Converging or Diverging from Standard English?

It is widely believed that as conditions of life converge, as opportunities become more equal and contact more frequent, differences in dialects between two or more ethnic groups will be reduced. In the United States, public schools have reduced differences in accents. Persons from the whole spectrum of ethnic groups are members of the same mass audience for movies, radio, and television, and are therefore, presumably, hearing and learning common speech patterns.

All of those things may be true. It is also true, however, that there are dialect-preserving and even dialect-making effects in ethnic social isolation, discrimination, and conflict, among other social forces continually remaking language. The effects of schools and the mass media are small compared with the influence on speech patterns of the immediate family and friends. The balance of the forces of convergence and divergence in language usages may be one of the most accurate indices of the extent of equality and the levels of ethnic conflict.

A generation ago linguists debated whether vernacular black English was primarily a variation of the English brought by the migrants from England, "the same as, or only slightly different from the dialects of disadvantaged southern whites," or whether it was primarily "a development from plantation Creole with a strikingly different structure from English."[16] Those who believed the latter to be true recognized that the black dialect was being modified by contact with American English, although they disagreed on the extent to which or the conditions under which such modification was taking place.

Recently several linguists, William Labov in particular, have argued, on the basis of evidence from the speech of African Americans in several cities, that the vernacular of the inner city is increasingly different from the dialects of whites nearby. "In all of the cities concerned, we find the cities splitting into black and white components. . . . Our reports are not only of blacks moving off in their own direction, but also of whites moving off in their own direction."[17] There is a great deal of evidence, Labov notes, of convergence between black and white dialects among the growing middle class of African Americans; but among the most disadvantaged and isolated blacks, "all of the social and economic conditions for divergence were there."[18]

Not surprisingly, on a topic of such complexity and sensitivity several linguists qualified, doubted, or disagreed with Labov's findings. Vaughn-Cooke emphasized in particular the lack of a time dimension in the studies of Labov and his associates. Without a comparison of language use at two periods of time, one cannot speak confidently about changes in accent, vocabulary, or grammar. Such an argument does not disprove Labov's thesis but requires that we reserve our judgments. The fact that the studies cited by Vaughn-Cooke are mainly based on data from small towns and cities makes her criticism less powerful. Using age differences as a kind of methodological surrogate for a time dimension, Bailey found language differences among the generations, a fact that supports Labov's thesis. He also noted the greater social isolation in the densely settled inner-city black communities than in the more segregated but less isolated experience in rural areas and small towns.

Spears would give less emphasis to isolation and more to what he sees as "independent cultural (including linguistic) development" in the large black communities. He believes, with Labov, that inner-city black vernacular speech—and also white vernaculars—have been moving away from the standard English, but attributes this less to segregation from white English speakers than to the lack of contact with middle-class African Americans.[19]

The disagreements on the causes and the extent of language change among inner-city African Americans are based not only on different assessment of the facts, but also on values and strategies related to inequality and discrimination. The judgment of this non-linguist, but interested student is that contemporary American urban conditions are, on balance, increasing the linguistic differences between the most disadvantaged blacks and whites, and between both of them and those who speak standard English. Black children from the inner city are particularly at a disadvantage, as are those from the English-speaking (Creole-speaking) Caribbean. Their teachers, both black and white, speak a dialect quite different from their own. This affects the learning of mathematics as well as those subjects that are more obviously dependent on language.[20]

Of course, there are many factors besides language that reinforce the racial divide in America. It is important to listen to Arthur Spear's question: "After all, what would happen if all black people in the United States suddenly woke up tomorrow morning speaking English like President Reagan's or Queen Elizabeth II's, for that matter? Would the economic problems of black people be set on a steady path toward solution?"[21]

Language divergence may, in the first instance, be an effect of historical experiences, of job and housing discrimination, of prejudice; but here, as in many aspects of social life, effects enter into a cycle of interacting factors, reinforcing the system which produced them. It is in this sense that Labov's findings are important. "We're in danger of forming a permanent underclass, and our linguistic findings reflect that danger."[22]

Counter-Language. Divergent dialects help to define group boundaries. Under some conditions there may be persons motivated to draw those boundaries with such clarity that no one can fail to see, and to hear, who we are and who they are. They may develop a counterculture that seeks to turn the dominant values and norms upside down. A group that is utterly deprived and isolated, blocked from any chance for success by following the usual routes, feeling itself completely walled off from the society around it, with no way to breach or climb the wall, may create a "counter society" within which they can succeed. Achievement seems more likely because the members define success on their own terms, and they select their own means to attain it—the values and norms of a counter-culture. One aspect of such a society can be an "oppositional identity," to use John Ogbu's term, and a counter-language that turns the usual proprieties and rules upside down. It is a language designed to oppose, confuse, offend, or separate the group from the dominant society.[23]

Groups of many sorts can develop counter-languages that are used not to communicate directly but to offend and attack. Halliday describes the "pelting speech" of the "counterculture of vagabonds" in Elizabethan England, the argot of the Calcutta underworld, and what he calls the anti-language used in Polish prisons—surely a diverse list—to note how they are alike in developing a language of opposition, of reversal.

The appearance and persistence of a counter-language in a minority ethnic group (most fully among its youth) is an important indicator of conflictful ethnic relations. If we listen carefully we can hear a counter-language in the ghetto English vernacular. It affirms a societal identity in opposition to one proffered by the larger society. The power structure of the dominant society is revealed and supported by its language, so a counter-language is used by the oppressed to construct a new reality.

Since the significance of the ghetto vernacular for black-white relations is a matter of some controversy, several comments on the use of the term *counter-language* in reference to it seem desirable:[24] (1) Counter-language is not a pejorative term. If the reality to which it is opposed is repugnant, one assesses the value of the counter-language by seeking to discover the degree to which it is successful in changing that reality or protecting members of the anti-society from its injustices. (That is, to be sure, a difficult task—one that I shall not undertake here.) (2) Counter-language is not a synonym for nonlanguage. It is probably no longer necessary to emphasize that nonstandard modes of speech are full and complex languages.[25] (3) Empirically, counter-languages are often mixed with subcultural dialects, and the protest elements are difficult to separate from the traditional elements. A subcultural dialect is "somebody's mother tongue." "An anti-language, however, is nobody's 'mother tongue'; it exists solely in the context of resocialization, and the reality it creates is inherently an alternative reality . . . a *counter*-reality, set up in *opposition* to some established norm."[26] It follows that if a counter-language is deemed abhorrent, it is of little value simply to try to teach a "nice" language. The effort should be directed toward changing the abhorrent reality of which the counter-language is one manifestation.

The black English vernacular is composed of several elements, mixed in different proportions among different groups: standard speech, a traditional dialect forged on the plantation and in the city, and a counter-language. This last ingredient indicates the effort among the most alienated and deprived to create a counter-reality, freed from the inevitable entanglement of the dominant reality— within which they suffer—with dominant language usages.

Labov's discussion of sounding or playing the dozens, the trading of ritual insults, in some black communities shows clearly that their language practices cannot fully be understood unless relationships with the dominant society are taken into account:

"Obscenity does not play as large a part as one would expect from the character of the original dozens. Many sounds *are* obscene in the full sense of the word. The speaker uses as many 'bad' words and images as possible—that is, subject to taboo and moral reprimand in adult middle-class society. . . . The meaning of the sounds and activities would be entirely lost without reference to these middle-class norms. Many sounds are 'good' because they are 'bad'—because the speakers know that they would arouse disgust and revulsion among those committed to the 'good' standards of middle-class society. . . . Sounds derive their meaning from the opposition between two major sets of values: their way of being 'good' and our ways of being bad."[27]

What are we to say when millions of white adolescents applaud, and buy the records of, Afro-Euro-American Michael Jackson when he sings "I'm bad," and when, more generally, they adopt a "shocking" argot? Perhaps we can say that generational conflicts have something in common with ethnic conflicts. There is a difference, however: in a few years one is no longer an adolescent. The "deprivations" against which many fifteen-year-old white youths, male and female, protest by such counter-language diminish or fade away. Ethnic discrimination and deprivation, vastly more corrosive, remain.

To give up one's counter-language at the urging of a school teacher or a pleading parent would be to capitulate to a society that is seen as utterly unfair and, in any event, inaccessible. Better to drop out of school and seek security in one's gang where everyone is ten-feet tall.

Because of their experiences of an ethnic identity above all others, the most deprived may misread their options; they may be blind to new openings; they may stereotype members of the dominant group and thereby miss the chance for support in expanding their opportunities. The reciprocal of this is that many in dominant groups are likely to see such attitudes as willful disregard of real options or as signs of inferiority. Neither private feelings nor public policies are well designed to breach such vicious circles. Because they are reinforced, in some measure, by linguistic differences they are made the more difficult to break.

MULTILINGUALISM IN THE UNITED STATES

Compared with India or the former Soviet Union (or Russia today), the United States seems to many to be quite homogeneous linguistically. Although there is no official language, newcomers must be able to speak and write English if they wish to be naturalized. A very high proportion of the children and grandchildren of the fifty million immigrants, and many of the immigrants themselves, have adopted English as their language of choice.

That is not a complete picture, however, with reference either to history or the current situation. America has been multi-lingual from the beginning. When persons of Spanish, Portuguese, English, French, Dutch, and German background began to settle in the "new world," they came in contact, not only with each other, but with Native Americans who spoke some three hundred different languages. It is easily seen why many languages would persist during the early years of the United States: contact between language groups was reduced by the low rates of literacy, slow transportation, the scarcity of nationwide media, and the presence of many small rural communities whose residents were almost entirely of one ethnic group.

Even under urban conditions, the heavy rates of immigration in the late nineteenth and early twentieth centuries often led to ethnic communities large enough to sustain schools, churches, and publications within which the language of the countries of origin was used.

Thinking the current situation is something new, we may have a tendency in the United States to forget the complexity of the language pattern in the past. Here is the way the *New York Herald Tribune* saw it in 1909:

"Tammany Hall is going after the votes in twenty different languages this year. If the Democratic organization does not get its share of the great cosmopolitan vote it won't be because it didn't try. Spellbinders have been engaged to disseminate doctrine in Yiddish, Hungarian, Bohemian, Greek, Italian, Polish, Russian, Swedish, Norwegian, Chinese, Danish, French, German, Armenian, and Boweryese, among other tongues."[28]

Joshua Fishman and his associates have documented how extensive the community resources of ethnic languages were even in the recent past (1985), and doubtless still are today. In their inventory, they found such resources to be available in ninety-one languages. These included 1,031 publications, 2,590 broadcasting outlets, 6,553 schools, and 13,638 religious groups, a total of nearly fourteen thousand. Non-English language resources are found in every state of the union. Groups whose period of mass migration was three or more generations ago are among the users. For some languages there is a single source (Bengali, Amharic, and Maori, for example); for others there are thousands (Hebrew, 5,824; Spanish, 4,395; Pennsylvania German, 2,303).[29] Most users of these non-English resources doubtless speak English; indeed they may regard it as their first language. These indications of American language diversity are primarily signs of additive acculturation, not of substitution, and of an interest in acculturation more generally, especially among the Hispanics.

Fishman emphasized that the Yiddish, French, German, and Spanish publications in the United States all show much more interest in ethnicity than in language preservation. The interest of the Spanish-language press in particular is more negative than positive in its references to Hispanic identification. It is concerned primarily with problems of the foreign-born minority still searching for the "American dream." One should note also that the press is mainly owned by non-Hispanic whites.[30]

Since World War II, however, and especially after 1965, the issue of language diversity has once again become a matter of sharp public debate. This is a result primarily of the dramatic increase in our Spanish-speaking population and, in smaller but still significant numbers, of immigrants from Asia, Europe, Africa, and the Caribbean for whom English is not the mother tongue. The civil rights movement, concurrently, has emphasized the need for a language policy that would protect the educational and other civil rights of these millions of non-English speaking newcomers. Although they make up a smaller proportion of the population than did immigrants in the late nineteenth and early twentieth centuries, their absolute number is greater.

Because it is the largest of the dozens of groups for whom English is not the native tongue, I will refer primarily to the Spanish-speaking population of the United States. For several reasons it also raises the policy issues and the political debate in the most acute form. These reasons include easy access to their various homelands in Mexico, Central America, the Caribbean, and South America; the steady replenishment of Spanish speakers; the traditionally strong family and community patterns; increased acceptance of and accommodation to use of Spanish in the United States, including job opportunities that do not require English; at the same time, existing obstacles to economic and educational advancement; and the large concentration of Spanish speakers in some areas.

These factors together have proved powerful enough to create a social movement to preserve not only the Spanish language but also the culture and community life on which a shared language would be the most cohesive influence. It is not clear, however, that this movement is a strong attraction among third- and later-generation Americans. Nor is it the dominant view among immigrants.

We must be wary of generalizations about the Spanish-speaking population in the United States. It contains a variety of attitudes about the retention of Spanish and about the influence of language on their adaptation to the United States. The 2,800 respondents to the Latino National Political Survey, 1989–1990 (which included persons of Mexican, Puerto Rican, and Cuban background) were strongly in favor of bilingual education. Especially those who are United States citizens, however, were overwhelmingly in favor of using the program to teach English, or English and Spanish, rather than seeking to preserve the Spanish language and culture.[31]

In Puerto Rico, we should note, disagreements over language policy differ quite sharply from those on the mainland. For many years, both Spanish and English were official languages; but in 1991 a Spanish-only law was adopted, expressing a strong desire to protect "Puerto Rican nationality." In 1993, however, a new government on the island, stressing the advantages of U.S. citizenship within a Commonwealth status, re-established English as an official language, along with Spanish. Such shifts in language policy reflect the political and cultural ambivalence of many Puerto Ricans—their desire to be Americans, but their desire also for cultural autonomy.

Many, probably most, Latinos in the United States learn English by the third generation, some substituting it for Spanish, but others adding it to their language repertoire. A score or more of Spanish-speaking countries are represented in the immigrant population of the United States. Their reasons for migrating, the nature of their pre-migration economic and political experience, their primary region of residence in the United States, the dialect of Spanish spoken, and other factors produce a diverse pan-ethnic cluster more than a distinct ethnic group.

Bilingual Policies and Programs in the United States

Through the centuries, language supremacy and the "purity" of the dominant language have been focal points of struggle over power and over national or ethnic group identity in many lands—in France, Germany, Turkey, Canada, India, the Soviet Union, and Malaysia, for example. The patterns of stratification are often clearly revealed, and reinforced, by variations in dialect and language and by the policies adopted with reference to those variations.[32]

In the United States in recent years attention to the language-ethnicity connection has been most sharply focused on bilingual education. The term is now most likely to be used to refer to programs that have been developed in many schools in response to the fact that among their students are a large number who do not speak English or who speak it only poorly.[33]

There is a long history of bilingual training in the United States and elsewhere, some of it connected with schools, but in the past more often connected with ethnic churches or other ethnic institutions.[34] Those receiving such training have not necessarily been at risk educationally nor economically disadvantaged. Although I shall be discussing the ways in which ethnic inequality and conflict are connected with language and dialect differences, it is well to remember that there are several varieties of bilingual individuals who may not fit that pattern. Cazden and Snow distinguish among three types of bilingual individuals. The first they call "transient"—persons who are monolingual in a foreign language at home before going to school, and monolingual in English twelve years later, having moved through a period of bilinguality. Another type they call "natively bilingual"—persons whose parents regularly use two languages or who live in communities where two languages are in common use. The third type they call "elite"—persons whose family resources and interests assure access to a second language.[35]

American policies, and debates on the policies, do not deal with the relatively non-problematic kinds of bilingualism. They are concerned with questions of inequality or, oppositely, the dangers of separatism. Some see continued barriers to their integration if current programs of bilingual training, or something similar, are not available. Others see a fragmented America if they are continued. (And in each group there are some who see loss of privilege or status if their preferred policies are not in place.)

Hornberger distinguishes three orientations to the multilingual situation: 1) Language-as-problem. How can we incorporate those in linguistic minorities into the mainstream? 2) Language-as-right. How can we maintain the human and civil right to speak one's mother tongue? 3) Language-as-resource. How can we conserve and develop the country's linguistic resources?[36]

The range of views on these orientations can perhaps best be shown by reference to bilingual programs in American schools and to the English-only movement that has developed primarily, I believe it is fair to say, in an effort to refute and to stop those programs.

Three policies, not usually clearly articulated, compete in the public arena:[37]

1. Resist the growth of bilingual training in the schools. This is a one-language country, to everyone's advantage.
2. Recognize as a temporary fact that for some students, English is not a native language. Bilingual policy should be to create a bridge over into English.
3. Accept bilingualism as a fact of life in the United States and as an advantage to the country. Pluralism in language as in other cultural qualities is desirable. In areas where many persons are non-English speakers, other languages should be given some kind of official standing.

One could describe a number of variations on these three themes, but the brief comments may indicate the range. Since the Bilingual Education Act of 1968, indeed on a state and local basis for several years before then, official policy has approximated statement two. Agreement on goals, however, has not increased; nor has agreement on the consequences of bilingual education. Indeed, it may have decreased, as bilingual education has become a major civil-rights issue among some groups even while resistance to it has also grown, as in California, Texas, Florida, and New Jersey.[38] Fifteen states have passed some kind of "English as the official language" legislation. But twenty or more have defeated such proposals.[39]

Part of the resistance to bilingual education is fiscal. Several language groups (out of the ninety or more home languages, with as many as twenty in large cities) may make claims on the resources of a school district. Part is opposition to the separatism (pluralism to its supporters) that is seen by some to be involved. Although most of the descendents of recent immigrants are shifting to English at a rate similar to earlier groups—English predominating by the third generation—some Spanish speakers "may be electing to bypass the process of acculturation and assimilation that turned previous immigrant groups into English-speaking Americans."[40]

Opposition to bilingual education is most visible in the activities of "U.S.English," an organization founded by the late United States senator S. I. Hayakawa and others. In a form letter seeking public support, U.S.English declares: "English has long been the main unifying force of the American people. But now prolonged bilingual education in public schools and multilingual ballots threaten to divide us along language lines." (Most supporters of bilingual programs, of course, believe that bilingual training is the best, and essential, way to prevent us from being divided along language lines.) U.S.English has been promoting a constitutional amendment that declares English to be the official language of the country, in the belief that it will help to mend the fractures that it sees developing.[41]

Bilingual training, in the judgment of some if its opponents, segregates limited-English children, provides them with an inferior education, and often dooms them to unskilled jobs as adults.[42] They see such training as more likely to keep non-English speaking children as "separate and unequal minorities" rather than speeding their integration and opening new opportunities. They believe that bilingual programs have shifted from temporary assistance for limited-English children to a tool for creating or protecting the influence and status of ethnic adults. As Imhoff puts it: "When ethnic leaders try to preserve their power by maintaining the separate identity of their ethnic group, the bilingual-education movement becomes just another arm of a much wider power struggle. When the bilingual-education establishment controls jobs and separate em-

pires within school districts, non-English-speaking children are reduced to pawns in their game."[43]

Thomas Pettigrew presents evidence that sharply challenges
this interpretation of the politics of bilingualism. In a study of California voting patterns, by county, he found a very high correlation
(+.80) between votes for an English-only referendum and anti-
minority votes (e.g., opposition to busing). This finding supports the
view that the English-only movement is not so much pro-
integration as it is anti-minority. It expresses the sentiment that
"we had to learn English without special help; so should they."[44]

Supporters of the bilingual program emphasize different issues
and challenge the claims of its opponents that it has become an instrument for the perpetuation of ethnic separation. Raul Yzaguirre,
the head of the national council of La Raza, holds that bilingual education is the accepted means of reversing the poor performance of
Hispanic students. "I was around when bilingual education was
born," he writes. "The impulse wasn't driven by any need to preserve language. It was driven by a yearning for solutions to help the
most under-educated minority in the country. . . . We have found a
way to achieve educational parity and, by the way, to have people
who are competent in two languages."[45]

In 1974 the Supreme Court ruled (9–0) in *Lau v. Nichols,* a case
involving a Chinese student, that it is a violation of civil rights to
teach pupils in English if they do not understand the language.
"There is no equality of treatment merely by providing students
with the same facilities, textbooks, teachers and curriculum; for
students who do not understand English are effectively foreclosed
from any meaningful education."[46]

It is not enough, proponents of bilingual training declare, to become proficient in English if this is accomplished only by such intense concentration on learning the new language that students fall
behind in their other subjects. Some programs, recognizing this
problem, teach some subjects other than English in the students'
first language. There is some evidence that mastering the first language helps one to learn English.

Dialects, Languages, Inequality, and Conflict

As our earlier discussion of counter-languages may have suggested,
dialect differences are, in many ways, less easily dealt with in
schools and elsewhere than are language differences. Non-standard

dialects are more often clear signs of ethnic and socioeconomic differences; fewer people grant them authenticity as languages.[47] With the increase in the number of pupils whose "native language" is a non-standard dialect, however, and with more school integration, dialects are much more in evidence in American schools. Early students such as Basil Bernstein stressed, however sympathetically, the limiting influence of what they saw as restricted dialects on cognition.[48] Language deprivation equals cognitive deprivation. Especially in his early work Bernstein failed to distinguish adequately between the cognitive and the pragmatic aspects of a dialect in a particular setting.

His critics believe that he missed the richness of non-standard dialects, with their own syntax, grammar, and vocabulary.[49] These critics sometimes failed to note that dialects adapted to restricted settings may not be good media if one wants to move freely in wider circles. Nor did they note that to some degree they were anti-languages, in Halliday's sense, designed to oppose the larger society while establishing one's identity with and communicating with one's group.

Ought dialect differences be a part of or treated alongside language differences in bilingual programs? Federal Judge Charles Joiner ruled that the Ann Arbor School Board had violated the civil rights of eleven black students by not recognizing their different manner of speech as a fact to be dealt with in teaching, not a criterion for judging the quality of students. Responses to his decision varied widely. Carl Rowan believed that the ruling was "dubious at best," an invitation to an alibi, until we "do something about the absences from school, until we make more black parents understand the value of reading in the home, until more teachers force ghetto students to read newspapers and magazines and at least try to resist peer-pressures to downgrade standard English."[50] William Raspberry saw it differently. He read the decision to say, "What we are talking about is teaching children to read without turning them off, without teachers deciding on the basis of their speech patterns that they cannot learn."[51]

The latter interpretation seems to be closer to Judge Joiner's intent. He sought to remove a barrier to learning—an often unconscious negative attitude of teachers toward the home language of some of their black students. They need to recognize the existence of that language "and to use that knowledge," he wrote, "as a way of helping the children to learn to read standard English."[52]

Rowan's fears may be justified; or Judge Joiner's hopes may prove to be well founded. And of course both may be right with reference to particular individuals and specific situations. What we need to know is the possible outcomes, under different conditions, of various policies toward dialects and languages that are closely correlated with minority backgrounds and deprivation. Is it possible to deal with language differences in such a way that they even become, in the process of reduction, integrative and positive?

In discussing bilingualism, it is important to remember that it is one thing to teach "English as a Second Language" (there are numerous ESL programs) by providing supplementary training in English. It is something else to teach bilingualism, on the premise that maintaining and improving competence in the first language is a goal complementary to the goal of mastering English.

This contrast prompts us to ask several questions: To what degree do language differences and different competencies in English stand as barriers to integration both among and within schools? Do bilingual programs set groups apart, emphasizing their differences; or do they furnish greater opportunities for communication and interaction? How do various kinds of bilingual programs affect the school performance, self-concepts, persistence in schools, job opportunities, and life chances generally for persons from different classes and communities with different lingual mixes?[53]

Wise and effective policies regarding bilingualism depend upon a clear choice of goals (which may be a mixture, achieved through political discourse) and upon effective research that yields information in which we have confidence.[54] In the United States today, the collision of two rather sharply contrasting goals have had the effect of producing a mixture, but more by a pragmatic balance than by political discourse. Supporters of such groups as U.S.English oppose the very basis of current bilingual educational programs. "Bilingual education is rooted in a social theory of cultural pluralism and a belief in the institutional racism of American schools. U.S.English advocates an emphasis on the commonalities between Americans rather than on the divisions between ethnic and cultural subgroups. It advocates English-language training leading to rapid classroom integration rather than to long-term language-based segregation within schools. Politically, advocacy of bilingual education comes primarily from Hispanic organizations whose continued power depends upon maintaining strong ethnic solidarity and separatism and from defining Hispanic Americans as a minority rather than as an immigrant group."[55]

It is instructive to compare Imhoff's statement with the first paragraph of Fishman's chapter on "Positive Bilingualism." " 'Modern' man, and even modern social science (including modern linguistics), has had difficulty conceiving bilingualism positively. The overwhelming majority of references to this phenomenon are in terms of poverty or disharmony or disadvantages and debits of other kinds. The reasons for such a negative view of bilingualism are not hard to find. They derive from monolingual economic, political, cultural, and ideological investments or establishments and from the self-serving world views that they have fostered. Opponents who differ greatly in other respects—e.g., unreconstructed capitalists and equally unreconstructed communists—come together with amazing agreement as to the purported evils of bilingualism, each seeing in it a stumbling block to the image of progress, peace, and plenty that each consciously or subconsciously subscribes to and that each would (or does) consciously or subconsciously benefit from.' "[56]

The emphasis of U.S.English on "the commonalities between Americans" tends to hide the reality of wide differences in opportunity and wide differences in the cultural capital—particularly the command over standard English—that children bring to school. When these differences are disregarded, the children thus disadvantaged fall progressively further behind. Rather than "rapid classroom integration" we get tracking, labeling, and steering that may magnify differences.[57]

One can applaud Fishman's emphasis on "positive bilingualism," as I do, while also noting the need to develop programs that nourish differences in such a way that all are enriched by expanded cultural resources rather than divided into antagonistic groups.

In my view, the need for bilingual education in American schools, and in many other countries, is unquestionable. But of what kind should it be? Toward what goals should it be directed? Any given program will have different effects on different students, depending on their facility with language, their home situations, their friends, the ethnic mix of schools, the strength of the bilingual training of teachers, and other aspects of the school experience.

There is wide agreement on one of the goals of bilingual programs. They are designed to speed up the learning and to improve the use of standard English. There is less agreement on a second goal, to protect and improve the use of another language. Some people fear that this latter goal has been neglected; others fear that it has been given priority. To attain equal opportunity and to maintain a valuable language resource, those who speak a "non-state" language require training in the language of their intimacy and the language of their functional polity, as Fishman has put it. Needless to say, those who speak the "state language" natively would also profit, and society would profit, if they learned a second language.

The expectation is that a bilingual program will increase the rate of high-school graduation and college attendance, resulting in improved occupational chances and performance. Such a program, of course, is only one of many influences on students whose native language is not English. We must emphasize, with Cazden and Snow, that "no decision about the language of instruction can alone solve the social problems—such as poverty, discrimination, and drugs—that face many of these students outside school. It is simply one decision schools can make—in fact, cannot avoid making one way or another."[58]

Will the availability of the home language during the early years of education retard the learning of English? Using the standard techniques of demographic projection, Veltman estimates that the language preferences of Americans of Spanish-speaking background will be about the same at the end of this century as they are now or as they were in the mid-1970s, despite the likelihood of large numbers of newcomers. Taking account of the mix of generations and the current rates of learning English, he estimates that by the beginning of the twenty-first century, 45 percent of Hispanics will be English-bilingual; 36 percent will be Spanish-bilingual; and 19 percent will not use English on a regular basis.[59]

What opponents call a "bilingual establishment," mainly Spanish-speaking, in my judgment is not a major factor in the extent of language shift or language preservation. Whether or not there is such an establishment, some demographic and cultural forces in the United States may slow down somewhat the shift to English as the nearly exclusive choice of Hispanics. There are now some twenty-two million persons of Spanish-speaking background. They make up a majority or a large minority of students in many school districts. There are numerous communities of Hispanics large enough to maintain ethnic institutions. And the 9 percent of the United States population that is now of Hispanic background will, if present trends continue, grow to about 12 percent by the year 2020. These are forces on which those who hope for the continuation of Spanish-speaking communities can ride (creating a kind of U.S. Quebec, as some opponents think of it).

Structural forces and individual choices affecting the acquisition of English, however, are much stronger. Full access to the political process requires English. Job opportunities in a Spanish-speaking niche are limited in range and number. The Spanish-background population is divided ethnically and in its aspirations for integration and acculturation.

Throughout most of the world, as Heath points out, the established pattern of language learning has been additive. Individuals keep their native language while learning another. The pattern in the English-speaking world, however, has more commonly been substitutive.[60] If, with respect to its Spanish speaking members, the United States moves toward additive language acculturation, the country will be well served. Among native English speakers, Spanish has replaced French and Latin as the most commonly learned second language, thus to some degree additive acculturation is working both ways. One can hope that it will increase among those of English-speaking background, with further additions not only to those who have learned Spanish, but to those who speak French, German, Italian, Hindi, Russian, Chinese, Japanese, Hebrew, Arabic, and the many other languages that are crucial to communication in this interdependent world as well as in the ethnically heterogeneous United States.

The general question can be raised with respect to societies all over the world: Can we have it both ways? Can we have pluralism, the reduction of prejudice and discrimination, expanded access to equal educational and occupational opportunities, and the preservation of treasured languages and cultures? (Not all the elements of any culture, in my view, are treasured. Perhaps a tolerant pluralism among ethnic groups can help us to see, and to get rid of the aberrations—the sexism, racism, and gross inequalities—that tarnish most cultures.) And at the same time, can we expand the command over a society-wide language that underlines our mutual interests and interdependencies, a shared language that opens options and expands contacts? At this time in world history, bilinguality or multilinguality that includes English, which is the second language in many societies, may be of special value internationally as well.

The current critical debate over bilingualism, and the related debate over the appropriate range of topics and sources for schools and colleges, have documented serious division in the United States. The division is likely to continue; but if the United States is to continue to take the lead in creating an international society, it must design policies—not yet visible—that narrow the gap.

Chapter 9

ETHNICITY: SOURCE OF STRENGTH? SOURCE OF CONFLICT?

Out of timber so crooked
as that from which man is made
nothing entirely straight can be built.
—Immanuel Kant

"Aus so krummen Holze, als woraus der Mench gemacht ist, kann nichts ganz Gerades gezimmert werden."[1] We are readily persuaded, in the late twentieth century, that mankind is built out of *krummen Holze*. Although the world has escaped a potentially obliterating war for nearly half a century, civil wars, most of them involving an ethnic factor, are tearing apart scores of societies, with little hope, in the short run at least, that the underlying sources of the conflicts can be removed.

Many other societies in little danger of civil wars—such as the United States, Britain, Canada, most of Western Europe, and Japan—are nevertheless torn by ethnic strife. In many ways they are more seriously divided along ethnic lines, marked by racial, lingual, religious, and national differences, than they were a generation ago. To some degree they are faced with a technical-economic problem: What are the most effective ways to reduce ethnic tensions, and where will we find the resources to employ those ways? Much more seriously, however, they face a social-moral problem: What kind of a society do we want? To what degree is our ethnic diversity a resource to be cultivated, to what degree a problem to be solved?

Many Americans, including some candidates for high office, have been saying that the machinery of government is broken. They want to take it apart, to repair it, rebuild it, or replace it. No doubt major changes are needed, in the United States and elsewhere; but poorly operating governmental machinery is more a symptom than a cause. If we believe that our major problems are technical and economic and devote our resources and talent primarily to attempt to repair the machinery, we shall surely be gravely disappointed. It is of little value to have a smoothly running, powerful machine if some of the riders want to go north, others south; if some want everybody to have a seat, others have a rather exclusive guest list.

When we define our problems in the first instance as moral-political problems, we see conflicting desires, different goals, zero-sum choices to be made. The major task of a society, and its government, is to negotiate those conflicts, to emphasize shared goals and interdependence, and to seek to optimize the quality of life. That means to attain the maximum level of life's satisfactions for all, including generations to come, when competitive and even conflicting values and interests are taken fully into account. This is a task at once delicate and enormously complicated. But once a society has put its moral and political problems first on the agenda, the technical and economic problems can be much more effectively dealt with.

The moral problem is the more serious because both dominant ethnic groups (or the core groups of these societies) and minority ethnic groups are themselves divided. Let us develop a tolerant pluralism, say some of the dominants, for we have become an international society. No, others reply, let us preserve and protect the ways of our founding fathers, to maintain a unified society. And from the minority ethnic groups we hear a kind of echo—in counterpoint: Let us preserve our cultural birthrights. No, let us accept and learn the established ways of our new-found homes.

Although I am dismayed at this tangle of moral judgments and distressed at the violence which it engenders, I cannot suppress an optimistic note. The Chinese characters for conflict, I am told, combine the concepts of crisis and opportunity. Or, to play with Kant's statement, one can note that "crooked timber" might be stressed maple, from which beautiful furniture can be made. And to say that "nothing *entirely* straight can be built" (*"kann nichts ganz Gerades gezimmert werden"*) is to imply that something substantially straight *can* be built.

If these sentences suggest a reasonable point of view, there are opportunities in the current crises, but utopian thinking may prevent us from seeing them. Utopias have their value; "nothing so wonderfully expands the imaginative horizons of human potentialities—but as guides to conduct they can prove literally fatal."[2] The pursuit of culturally homogeneous societies, in this interdependent and mobile world, is in almost all cases utopian—with all of the quick attractiveness but the deeper errors that mode of thought entails. This is true when one speaks of dominant groups who seek to Americanize, Germanize, or Russianize. It is also true when one speaks of less powerful, perhaps seriously disadvantaged, ethnic groups within which movements have developed that seek undivided loyalty, unmindful of larger and smaller circles of shared values, reciprocities, and interests.

The dominant groups may only recently have come to power. A strong impulse of the newly empowered in some states is to drive out, or to deprive of even the barest minimum of life's necessities, or to withhold full citizenship from those who only yesterday were comrades in a struggle for equity within or independence from an imperial state. The urgent desire to strengthen their tenuous hold on power and to establish the identity of the new state leads to acts of "purification." They may as seriously constrain linguistic, religious, and national "deviants" as they themselves were constrained in the recent past.

The urge to purify is also strengthened among some members of the dominant ethnic groups in well-established states. Some feel culturally threatened by rapid social changes, by increasing numbers of newcomers and by newly visible long-time residents. Others feel economically and politically threatened. Movements develop that are designed to purge the society of "foreigners," of those who are ethnically different. Although not now of great influence in stable democracies, some 10 or 15 percent, as we have noted earlier, give support to parties or leaders who are anti-Arab, antisemitic, anti-Turk, anti-African, or anti-Asian American—the targets varying with the setting.

Behind such movements is the utopian dream: If we were only more alike, if all were truly French, or German, or American, our problems would be sharply reduced. It would be foolish to deny the need for a set of shared understandings and values. It is not self-evident, however, that some particular groups should select and interpret those understandings and values. Nor is it clear that diversity, in rapidly changing societies, is a threat; it may be an essential resource.

Perhaps a metaphor based on evolutionary theory can give us a hint regarding the place of ethnic diversity. Organisms evolve in a series of transactions with their environments. Intricate interdependencies may develop, such that a small change in the environment proves devastating to some species. Those that are the least specialized can best survive environmental changes or adapt to the widest range of circumstances.

Homo sapiens is biologically a very unspecialized species. It is genetically programmed, one might say, for flexibility. Its members can adapt to a very wide range of environments, because it has few if any instincts (depending on how strictly one defines instinct). By its lack of instinctive responses (which evolve as answers to recurring events), it is better able genetically to deal with new, nonrecurring events.

Let me press the biological metaphor a bit further, drawing on the poetic words of Loren Eiseley. He described the evolution of a deviant fish, the snout, at a time some 300 million years ago when waters were receding from many parts of the planet. With his stubby fins and mutant lung, he was not a very successful fish, so long as water was everywhere; but in the changing environment, more elegant fish were dying of oxygen starvation in the "primeval ooze." However, descendants of the snout, that poor bog-trapped failure, dominated the earth millennia later, for "among those gasping, dying creatures, whose small brains winked out forever in the long Silurian drought, the Snout and his brethren survived."[3]

Thus some individuals inherit, by random variation or by mutation, "a capacity to resist a new environmental threat or to exploit a new environmental opportunity superior to more 'normal' members of the species. Animals with long necks may get nothing for their pains if most of the foliage is near the ground; but if low bushes are destroyed by environmental change or taken over by competitors, it pays to be a giraffe. The trouble is that the environment may continue to change; and the giraffe, who has his neck stuck out for good, can then be in trouble."[4]

What has all this to do with ethnicity, you may ask. Without taking the analogy too seriously, think of culture as the human functional equivalent of instinct. Culture has to be learned, but it is deeply implanted in most of us. It furnishes us with cognitive, aesthetic, and moral standards that we take almost for granted. Those differently trained seem to us to be strange, naive, immoral. Culture thus conceived has both the advantages and the disadvantages of instinct. It furnishes us ready-made answers and responses to the recurring events of life. By the same token it furnishes only weak guidelines when a society or some part of it is experiencing important changes—in size, resources, or contacts.

Contemporary societies and ethnic groups may be in serious need of cultural "snouts," those poor, bog-trapped failures, to use Eiseley's phrase, who perchance can furnish cultural resources of value in a rapidly changing world.

It is doubtless most appropriate for me to illustrate this point by reference to the United States. I am an inordinately enthusiastic American, yet I must continually ask myself: Is the dominant American culture—now sometimes challenged from abroad and also, to some degree, by our variety of ethnic cultures—well designed to deal with the threats and the opportunities of the years ahead? America, I find it easy to believe, is the most admired country in the world, although that admiration may rest more on its power and wealth than on its contributions to the quality of life, at home and abroad. Despite America's great strengths and accomplishments, are the values and norms that support military nationalism, environmental conquest, ethnic discrimination, the inequities faced by women, the enormous and increasing gap between rich and poor, the easy acceptance of greed, the feeble support for the health and education of its children—are these not in need of strong and steady competition from cultural alternatives?

Needless to say, in all societies minority ethnic cultures are equally in need of continuous revision, having developed under circumstances vastly different from those their adherents now face. In particular, the impulse to separation and purity is an obstacle to cultural adaptation. Those seeking statehood by violence may find that the tradition that justified and energized their struggle is an inadequate blueprint for their new situation. Most will enclose ethnic minorities, whom they may regard as the devious occupants of Trojan horses, within their new boundaries. They will thereby lose the chance to examine cultural alternatives and perhaps to develop hybrids of greater strength and beauty.

Some of those seeking equity and cultural freedom within a polity also stress separation. For example, *The Economist* has recently noted and criticized this trend among African Americans in predominantly white universities. Separate fraternities and academic ceremonies have become popular even among those most strongly opposed to apartheid elsewhere. "They live in a mainly white country, just as South African whites live in a mainly black one. Integration is the best hope for both. Black separatism is like the free East Germans choosing to rebuild the Berlin Wall."[5]

This is to put the matter too strongly, in my judgment. Such separation expresses the feeling—exaggerated, but with strong supporting evidence—that since they are already separated out by many whites, they may as well make virtue of necessity. It may also furnish an opportunity to pull back from persistent minority status for a time, to build morale, to be recreative.

Nevertheless, separation has many unwanted side effects, for minority ethnic groups as for the majority. What is inadequate, in my judgment, in *The Economist's* statement is the inference that change can be self-willed by an ethnic minority. Patterns of separation are embedded in a complex system of discrimination. All elements in the system must be changed, with the first steps, perhaps as far as the second mile, taken by the most advantaged.

Ethnicity and "The End of History"

The analysis of ethnicity has been a vital topic for scholars and policy makers for many decades. Efforts to draw just and stable state boundaries after World War I and again after World War II, the tasks faced by the empires trying to govern multi-ethnic populations, heavy rates of immigration, the claims and the imperfect efforts of the Soviet Union to create a stable multi-ethnic society (even while believing that ethnic groups would fade away), persistent racial discrimination in the United States along with a continuous debate over the extent and sources of immigration—these are among the factors that have kept ethnicity on many public agenda going back a century or more.

Shortly after World War I, Randolph Bourne remarked that many of the immigrants to the United States were not simply those who missed the Mayflower: when they did come, they took a *Maiblume*, a *Fleur de Mai*, a *Fior di Maggio*, or a *Majblomst*. Americans still need to remember Bourne's observation, changing it only to note that our newcomers now arrive by plane, train, truck, bus, makeshift sailboat, and on foot, as well as by ship; and that they come in larger numbers from Latin America and Asia than from Europe. Looking at America from the perspective of 1920, Bourne declared that in a world that has dreamed of nationalism, "We find that we have all unaware been building up the first international nation."[6]

Despite important pioneering scholarly work, however, recognition of the significance of the ethnic factor in many societies has been forced on us more by events than by research. The civil rights movement in the United States, the increased number of immigrants and their changing origins after 1965, the growing diversity of Western European populations, the vast number of refugees in many parts of the world, the rapid decolonization of many societies in Asia and Africa, the breakup of the Soviet Union and the release of its satellites in Eastern Europe—exposing the ethnic divisions that had been kept in the shadows—the aftershocks of all these earth-shaking events in Yugoslavia, in the Middle East, in Asia, in Africa, within societies whose ethnic orders had been held together by only fragile legitimacy—such a rush of events has vastly increased the interest in and the importance of ethnic relations.

Not unexpectedly, interpretations of the causes and consequences of these events vary widely. In particular, they have been influenced by two contrasting assumptions. An earlier tendency on the part of many writers to assume that in the long run, at least, ethnicity would fade as a decisive influence is now often replaced by an assumption that it is a persistent, perhaps permanent, aspect of social life. The earlier assumption surely led to hypotheses that could not be disconfirmed, for who can refute a statement that ethnic lines will eventually disappear? Predictions based on arguments from "eventuality" are like the epitaph on the grave of the hypochondriac: "You see, I really was sick." Neither medical nor social diagnosis is advanced by arguments that something will "eventually" occur.

On the other hand, we are not any better served by the many contemporary assertions that ethnicity is a primordial fact, not simply tenacious but virtually indestructible. The assumption of the inevitability of ethnicity, like the assumption of its ultimate disappearance, affects definitions, observations, and interpretations. Ethnic groups have disappeared. Under some conditions they are minimally important. Other situations bring them to the fore, making them rallying points for a campaign for freedom and equality or sources of an ideology justifying chauvinism and violence.

We will be wise, in my judgment, to set aside both preconceptions and to ask: Under what conditions does the ethnic factor explain a large part of social process and human behavior; when is it of minor importance?

The moral and policy questions are as vital as the research questions. How and in what manner should we try to combine particularism and universalism as organizing principles of society? Of course the question is as relevant for inter-state as for inter-ethnic relations. How the world answers it with respect to one arena has important consequences for the other.

If we are to have international stability and peace, we shall have to learn to live with diversity; we shall have to extend the concept of pluralism beyond the frontiers of states. When communism fell apart as the governing ideology in the USSR and Eastern Europe, most of us in the West applauded and breathed a sigh of relief. Capitalism had taken a long step toward becoming a universal principle. We had won the cold war. It was the "end of history," since humankind had struggled its way, after many detours, to the best and final political economy, democratic capitalism.[7] The combination of science, the uniquely efficient economic organization, the market, and a democratic polity, says Fukuyama, has ended the debate.

Well, perhaps not quite. To believe so is to deprive ourselves of the opportunity, during this fluid period in history, to make some of the adjustments that are required lest the slogan "end of history" takes on a tragic rather than a celebratory meaning.

Seeing the West's victory in the cold war with the "totalitarian Left" and the collapse or serious weakening of the "authoritarian Right" (a politically correct distinction for those who needed to find a difference between oppressive regimes we supported and those we opposed), Fukuyama argued that liberal democracy may constitute the "end point of mankind's ideological evolution . . . the final form of human government. . ."; and in that sense it can be seen as "the end of history." Earlier forms of government "were characterized by grave defects and irrationalities that led to their eventual collapse," but "liberal democracy was arguably free from such fundamental internal contradictions." Of course he recognizes serious problems in democratic societies, but he holds that "these problems were ones of incomplete implementation of the twin principles of liberty and equality on which modern democracy is founded, rather than of flaws in the principles themselves."[8]

I have no desire to disagree with the affirmation that the ideal of liberal democracy is a noble one. Before we put a cap on history, however, we need to ask why even the most advantaged and advanced societies are so far from attaining it, and why their attempts to achieve the ideal have so often created barriers in the way of others seeking similar goals. Until we approach an answer to those questions, the ideal remains a utopia, unencumbered by attention to problems that seriously retard or block its attainment.

The following are some of the reasons why the near-utopian proclamation of the end of history is an inadequate guide to the future.

Most people have not yet found out about the alleged triumphant last act. They live in authoritarian societies with weak market economies. We must hope that they do not believe that history has come to an end, that the good society has been invented so that they need only learn how to apply the lessons. For societies and especially the less powerful ethnic communities within them, with annual incomes of two hundred dollars per capita, the image of societies with incomes of twenty thousand dollars per capita—one hundred times their own—cannot stand as models. They will be writing different histories. The few such societies that join the affluent world in the next several decades will probably also write different chapters of their own.

The future stretches out quite a ways. Has human experimentation with its social orders come to an end? Are there societies today where the majority of the population says: We have some tidying up to do, but no longer are great changes required? I know of none.

The world is still militarized. We spend over one trillion dollars a year (over a quarter of that by the United States and another quarter by the other liberal democracies). States with troublesome neighbors or neighbors who control desired land and resources, if they also have good bank accounts or good credit, have no difficulty in securing the most technologically advanced weapons. Often their neighbors have the same opportunities.

The world population is growing about one billion per decade, adding a number equivalent to the population of the United States, Western Europe, Japan, Russia, and Brazil every ten or eleven years. Most of this growth is occurring in societies where democratic cap italism is only a remote possibility for the next several decades. Meanwhile, the newcomers arrive on a planet progressively less able to sustain its present population except by "drawing down" non-renewable resources.

What kind of a free market capitalism has been attained at the end of history? What do we wish the newly freed or the newly cre ated societies to emulate? A market economy with a persistently high level of unemployment, especially among ethnic minorities? A society where many hidden costs are not reflected in the pricing system? In the United States oil costs about twenty dollars a barrel. That does not include the costs of maintaining friendly relations with oil producing states, the cost of military equipment related to the protection of oil supplies, the costs of cleaning up oil spills, of suffering the consequences of polluted water and air, or of retarding the development of an energy policy needed for long-run planning for a sustainable supply of energy when the world's oil supplies are exhausted. This list of costs not included in the pricing of oil is doubtless incomplete and distorted by my values. I think it is adequate to illustrate, however, that some rather drastic changes are needed in even the most advanced contemporary markets before we can acclaim them as the end of the historical quest for the best possible economic system.

Should the less developed societies emulate the more advanced in the number of renegade banks, in the enormity of the contrast in incomes between the wealthiest 10 percent and the poorest, especially in the United States? Hedrick Smith recently reported the rather sorrowful question of a Moscow businessman: How can we get privatization without cowboy capitalism?[9] Countries everywhere need an answer before we close the books on history.

A "free market" decides, as any economic system must, what goods and services shall be produced, in what amounts; the techniques of combining human and natural resources; who gets what is produced, and in what amounts; whether to use wealth now or later. Those who defend this system most ardently, however, often don't want it, at least as applied to themselves. They want protection from the market. And many factors reduce the possibility of the Adam Smithian utopia, which envisaged a very fluid system: easy entry into and exit from markets, universal and speedy knowledge of market conditions, no guild restrictions (today Smith might revise his 1776 magnum opus to write about ethnic barriers as the economic equivalents of guilds).

Among the barriers to the attainment of such a market are widespread oligopoly and sometimes monopoly; inadequate consumer knowledge; insufficient labor mobility and of opportunities for retraining—serious weaknesses in a highly dynamic economy; laws, regulations, and subsidies that mainly benefit the wealthy; and discrimination—barriers to access put in the way of the members of some ethnic groups, whether as buyers or sellers. One can doubt that history has come to an end, settling down into the pattern of current "free enterprise" systems at a time when such distortions block the operation of purely market influences.

Many values are often acclaimed in speeches but less often included in budgets. These are values that are not easily included within the mechanisms of markets. Every child needs good education and health care; but not all can afford it, nor can the communities within which they live. If private resources and taxes cannot support a strong school system in districts inhabited mainly by ethnic minorities, the impersonal market says, in effect: That's a pity, but there is little economic demand. The human demand is high, however, and everyone pays the cost of failure to measure that demand by mechanisms other than the market.

One additional question must be posed to those who see the current dominance of the rather rough-hewn democratic capitalist societies as the final stage in the development of political-economic systems: What has happened to the search for recognition, the desire to be somebody? "We do not want only to satisfy our needs for food, shelter, sex, and comfort; we much more powerfully wish to establish ourselves as people to be reckoned with. . . . Mankind is much more powerfully driven by the desire for recognition than by desire for a high standard of living."[10] Fukuyama also raises this issue; but it is nearly lost, it appears to me, by his tendency toward utopian thinking. Ryan's statement may be an exaggeration; but the world-shaking events of the last few years, particularly the struggles by ethnic groups for nationhood or for full civil rights—events that have in many instances slashed standards of living in the name of non-economic goals—are testimony to centripetal forces that are writing new chapters, whether for better or worse, of the human story.

UNIVERSALISM VERSUS PARTICULARISM

Two major principles and ideologies, embodied in many social orders, compete for allegiance in the world today. In fact they have been competing for millennia, but perhaps never before with such intensity. The antinomy, labeled here as universalism vs. particularism, has been expressed in many different but related ways: Using the physical terms, we can speak by analogy of centrifugal and centripetal forces. With reference to social forces, one might refer to globalism and localism. Using related terms, in previous chapters I have analyzed sources of assimilation vs. dissimilation, the one enlarging the circle of social interaction and cultural sharing, the other intensifying or maintaining social and cultural differentiation.

These various pairs of terms are not synonyms, but in common they focus our attention on the forces and ideologies that expand the range of human contacts, expressing our interdependencies and our common needs and experiences, while at the same time emphasizing the cultural and structural boundaries that separate the members of human groups from each other.

Each of these ideologies rests upon a base of facts and experiences. When we think of the earth in universalistic terms we see the rapid growth of a world economy, a communication network that has sharply reduced isolation, and a growing recognition that many crucial resources are not renewable. (States fight to maintain or increase their shares; but grandchildren have no vote.) We are all dependent on air, water, and soil; and almost all of us are busily polluting them—particularly those of use who live in the "most highly developed" societies. By the end of the century a score or more of states are likely to have nuclear weapons or the capacity to make them. Who can doubt: if we don't hang together we shall hang separately.

The facts and experiences related to particularism, in our case ethnicity, are no less powerful even if more subtle. In most societies one need only look around to see and hear people who speak a different language, or one's own with an accent, practice a different religion, and trace their ancestry to a different homeland. When these differences combine with a need to belong to a group where one is recognized as a comrade, even if of lowly status, a group that connects with one's family line—although the connection can be very slight or mythical—then boundary lines are readily drawn. Those boundaries may be lightly traced. Under conditions of value confusion, however, of anomie, of economic change with its related opportunities and hardships, of political upheaval that casts doubt on the legitimacy of larger circles of authority, then ethnic boundaries are drawn more heavily.

Both universalism and particularism have a noble side and a destructive, coercive side. Naipaul, in commenting on the slow development of a universal civilization (built on religious, economic, and political structures), noted that "the expansion of Europe gave it for at least three centuries a racial tint, which still causes pain." Now, however, he sees "immense changes," an extraordinary attempt of this civilization to accommodate the rest of the world, and all the currents of that world's thought."[11] He speaks of the beauty of the Golden Rule and of the idea of the "pursuit of happiness" as a universal right.

The positive aspects of universalism—equal respect and human rights for all; each person is a child of God, thus all are brothers and sisters—are still discolored by the "racial tint" of which Naipaul wrote, or a political or religious tint in some of its manifestations. Circles of interaction have often been enlarged and maintained by force. In the eighteenth century, Johann Herder gave the highest place to the ideals of cultural self-determination, non-aggressive nations, peaceful coexistence, and variety. For him, Alexander the Great, Caesar, Charlemagne, Christian knights, British empire builders, missionaries were villains because their universalism was based on dominance and uniformity. One has little difficulty in adding twentieth century representatives to Herder's list, as in Isaiah Berlin's observation that Stalin kept down the ethnic Babel, but at terrible cost. "Universalism, by reducing everything to the lowest common denominator which applies to all men at all times, drained both lives and ideals of that specific content which alone gave them point."[12]

Must we leap, then, to the side of particularism? If everyone were as peaceful and tolerant as Herder we might land on solid ground. In contrast to domineering empires, he saw peaceful coexistence of diverse nations as the ideal. In the late twentieth century, however, we scarcely need to emphasize that particularism, like universalism, has its dark side. "Herder's *Volksgeist* became the Third Reich. And today the Serbian *Volksgeist* is at war with the Croatian *Volksgeist*."[13] The wounds of authoritarian humiliation or of discrimination in democratic societies can turn the desire for cultural self-determination within a larger, peaceful polity into nationalistic aggression.[14]

All of this is to say that multi-ethnic societies are faced with a serious dilemma: Under assimilative pressure, cultures may be lost that contain elements needed for adaptation to a changing world— the loss of a kind of cultural gene pool. (Is there, in additive acculturation, something akin to hybrid vigor?) At the same time, individuals can experience the loss of a sense of attachment highly needed in this enormously complex world.

Yet under pluralistic and separatist pressure, cultural forms may be preserved that are maladaptive and unjust—sexist, racist, harshly stratified, and militarized. Conflict expressed along ethnic lines is often harsher, more intractable, because it carries a high emotive component.

While we study the proliferation of ethnic groups and their claims to statehood, growing to an important degree out of the decline of empires and the creation of new, multi-ethnic states, we need to be aware of an opposite trend: the growth of multi-state organizations and interdependencies. There is a complex network of activities sponsored by the United Nations, such as WHO and UNESCO. Many of these are scarcely visible to the general public, when compared with its political and peacekeeping activities; but they are testimony to increasingly important shared needs and interests.

For thirty years or more, the European Community has been taking form, with a decisive step due to be taken in 1993. From the Treaty of Rome, in 1957, to the Treaty of Maastricht in 1991, the European Community moved from an association of states to a confederation or, as *The Economist* put it, toward a "not-quite-federation." The Treaty of Masstricht allows some flexibility, leaves the members some options, to make it possible for twelve or more central and north European states to join. "It is the way to make Maastricht's deeper community compatible with a much wider one."[15]

Many questions remain to be answered, however, before we can know the size and strength of the European Community. By the end of the century will the member states have yielded the last of their sovereignty to the Community—perhaps most decisively marked now by their separate currencies and their separate war-making powers? Will all or some of the Scandinavian and east European states be added to the current list of twelve members? Will each of the states belonging to the union become, in effect, ethnic-groups within a complex confederation? Although all twelve of the founding states had ratified the Treaty on European Union by May, 1993, major policy questions remain.

In 1993 one reads conflicting estimates of the probable depth and width of the Community: "The 21st century belongs to Europe"; but "Europe is getting jittery about arranged union." In several of the states, ethnic tensions are among the major sources of the nervousness. As borders separating the states are eliminated, permitting migration from one to another, the ethnic mix of all the countries is of interest to each of the members. With a tide of asylum seekers and immigrants, particularly into Germany and France, questions regarding ethnicity will remain prominent on the public agenda.

Meanwhile, the rudiments of a North American Community can be seen, with trade agreements among Canada, Mexico, and the United States bringing their economies closer together. At the same time the American population of Mexican origin continues to increase and the steady rate of migration, in both directions, across the Canadian-United States border suggests the slow development of an ethnically-diverse North American population.

Such developments are based on rapidly expanding communication, transportation, cultural, and economic networks across state lines. For the most part, these developments influence the lives of the elites, the highly trained and professional groups. The working classes, Frankel suggests, have little experience with and perhaps can expect few gains from these supra-state developments.[16] As their states become more diverse, they are likely to feel less closely identified with them, more fearful of the "foreigners" who are their neighbors. Their strongest identity may be with their ethnic groups.

This possibility is documented by the collapse of the Soviet Union that for seventy-four years had been a kind of Euro-Asian Community. A set of closely interacting factors account for the fact that, among other divisive forces, it was torn apart by serious ethnic conflict. In the background is the cruelty of an authoritarian central government, often acting in direct violation of its own nationalities policies. There was persistent Russian nationalism. The drive for empire through most of its history claimed resources badly needed for internal development. A deteriorating economy led to harsher competition. The breakup of other empires was visible worldwide, weakening the legitimacy or acceptability of patterns of ethnic domination.

Although the experience of the USSR has unique elements, the world should find in the highly disruptive sequence of events important lessons of wide applicability. As new multi-ethnic states seek for stability and legitimacy and old states find their population more and more diverse, they can readily see that larger or more dominant ethnic groups, or even a multi-ethnic elite, cannot attain or maintain for long a stable and secure society based on ethnic discrimination and repression. The costs of attempting to maintain an unjust and inegalitarian ethnic order are enormous.

The great need, strong voices are beginning to declare, is to develop structures that at the same time are based on universal principles, with the full recognition of interdependence, and on pluralism, the recognition of cultural differences. Mikhail Gorbachev has called for "a common European home" that encloses the great variety of peoples within an international system of agreements and reciprocities. Vaclav Havel, president of the Czech Republic, has written: "I certainly do not want . . . to suppress the national dimension of a person's identity. . . . I merely reject the kind of political notions that attempt, in the name of nationality, to suppress other aspects of the human home, other aspects of humanity, and human rights. . . . A civic society, based on the universality of human rights, best enables us to realize ourselves as everything we are—not only members of our nation, but members of our family, our community, our region, our church, our professional association, our political party, our country, our supranational communities—and to be all of this because society treats us chiefly as members of the human race."[17]

Darras, a French poet, creates the same image for us, this time from Brussels, a multi-cultural city of long-standing. Looking out over La Grand-Place (Grote Markt) from a tavern several stories above, "overlooking and overhearing the bubbling, babbling Babel of tongues below," he remarks: "It is almost as though one were in the midst of a Bruegel canvas, the very image of a multi-cultural Europe united in a common enthusiasm for diversity. . . . Perhaps we can both [England and France] learn from that great sloping Grote Markt . . . where we can walk and talk and sit and eat and drink and dance and buy flowers, all the while surrounded by the visible reconciliation of historical conflict."[18]

Other writers who also think in terms of a mixture of universal principles and cultural diversity are, however, more qualified in their support of the diversity element in the mix. "The genius of America," Schlesinger writes, "lies in its capacity to forge a single nation from peoples of remarkably diverse racial, religious, and ethnic origins. . . . Our task is to combine due appreciation of the splendid diversity of the nation with due emphasis on the great unifying

Western ideas of individual freedom, political democracy, and human rights."[19]

Berlin takes a similar stand: "I believe that the common culture which all societies deeply need can only be disrupted by more than a moderate degree of self-assertion on the part of ethnic or other minorities conscious of a common identity.[20]

Nearly thirty years ago I expressed the belief that the way in which the affiliation or rejection of ethnic, religious, and racial minorities is worked out within societies will strongly influence our ability to build a world order in which similarities are not coerced and differences do not divide. We are dealing here with one of the great intellectual and moral questions of the day.[21]

I see no reason to change that statement today; but I am more concerned than I was then about the romanticism sometimes attached to the emphasis on ethnicity. (With Irving Babbitt I think of something as romantic if it is wonderful rather than probable.) Current romanticism matches that attached to earlier notions of the melting pot. There is something warm and supportive and rich about ethnic attachments, as there can be about love of country. But there is also something small-minded, mean, and constricting. If we do not yet have a personalized noun to match on the ethnic-group level the use of the name of Monsieur Chauvin on the societal or state level, we do have some matching words and actions. I do not think that civilization will be advanced by listening to one's blood or by encouraging people to respond to the instincts of their flesh.[22] Lothrop Stoddard, Madison Grant, Houston Stewart Chamberlain, et al (not to mention more vicious forms of ethnocentrism) are going to be no better the second time around.

In the sometimes harsh debate over the impact of ethnic diversity—its value or its divisiveness—the proponents of diversity emphasize how cultural variation adds richness to a society and how assimilation stifles creativity and denies civil rights. They say little about the costs of self-imposed segregation, the freezing of the "real culture," to use Linton's term again, in maladaptive practices, or the reduction of individual liberty. Ironically, if ethnic groups coerce their members into orthodoxies in the name of solidarity in the pursuit of freedom for the groups, they reduce the liberty of individuals to build for themselves more complex cultural repertoires.

Proponents of a strong central culture are inclined to define it in ideal terms, using the noble historical documents and the glorious oratory of their leaders or would-be leaders. They say little about the real culture—the departures from heroic standards, the frequent, even systematic discrimination against ethnic minorities, who may as a result find it difficult to feel uplifted by references to "the great unifying Western ideas of individual freedom, political democracy, and human rights."

To attain the stereoscopic vision needed to view in depth the complicated phenomena of ethnicity we need to look from the perspectives of both insiders and outsiders. Each person can be an insider in one context, an outsider in another. It is difficult to be both at once; but we must aspire to approach such 20-20 vision. As an illustration, one can think of insiders as those who are bearing the brunt of a discriminatory system; outsiders, in this case, are members of the dominant group. One can argue that the outside position allows greater objectivity and perspective. Insiders may "know" about a problem as a patient knows about a toothache; but that is not sufficient qualification for diagnosis and treatment. Others can argue that those without the ache cannot truly understand; their knowledge is superficial, lacking in realism. Merton, in his seminal article on "Insiders and Outsiders" observes that the pain, humiliation, and frustration experienced by those in a minority ethnic group may be so built into social structures and euphemistic words that they become almost invisible to outsiders.[23] Yet insider status by itself scarcely furnishes adequate credentials. Shared ex-

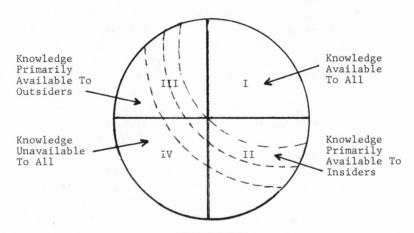

FIGURE 9.1
Insider and Outsider Knowledge
Adapted from Simpson and Yinger, 1985:9.

periences can furnish insight, but group loyalties can also blind us, as Francis Bacon emphasized long ago.

Without implying the comparative value of the various perspectives in any particular situation, Figure 9.1 may suggest the need to combine the strengths of different experiences and points of view and, beyond that, the need to enlarge the body of shared knowledge, as noted by the successive dotted lines.[24]

We need to distinguish between "acquaintance with" and "knowledge about" a difference that my be drawn less clearly in English, as Merton notes, than in other languages: *noscere* and *scire, kennen* and *wissen, connaître* and *savoir.* And having made the distinction, we need to blend the insights that can come from acquaintance with and knowledge about.

CONCLUSION

Ethnic lines will not disappear in the foreseeable future. In many parts of the world strong forces are drawing those lines more sharply. Ethnic groups in conflict mutually reenforce their antagonistic identities. In the midst of collapsing states and empires, old dreams of their own nation-state become vivid for many long-suffering ethnic minorities. In less conflictful settings, the continuing need for a more personal identity in a culturally complex and rapidly changing world persists.

Even in the most open and tolerant societies, where forces of assimilation are strong, "symbolic," "affective," "sidestream" "emergent," or "situational" ethnicity, to note the variety of terms that have been used to refer to a more open, flexible, even changeable identity, will continue.[25] In spite of identity shifts and high rates of intermarriage in some settings and extensive acculturation and integration in many settings, some ethnic lines will remain sharp and some individuals will think first of their ethnic group when they appraise their own identities. At this period in history, at any rate, it is not a matter of assimilation versus ethnicity, but of assimilation and ethnicity.

Although we cannot fail today to recognize ethnicity as an important fact of life, should we celebrate that fact as a source of great humanistic strength or lament it as an unfortunate necessity or take a position somewhere between those poles?

There is ample evidence "that strong networks of private associations, based on the ideal of pluralism, do not weaken the cohesion of a democratic society but actually strengthen it. Such networks serve both to relate an individual, through groups that are close and meaningful to him, to the large, complex society, and also to protect him from excessive encroachments on his freedom by that society."[26] The task is to keep identities derived from such networks in balance with individual and humanwide identities. Czeslaw Milosz is speaking of Poland and Lithuania, but suggests a larger principle when he writes: "Perhaps those sardines fighting each other in the mouth of a whale are not untypical of the relations between humans when they search for self-assertion through ethnic values magnified into absolutes."[27] Will we be swallowed up by humanwide problems while identifying with parochial groups?

Devereux makes an opposite point—too strongly for my taste, but an essential point—when he calls attention to the strain between individual integrity and ethnicity: "Sane and mature persons do not hypercathect their ethnic identity or any other class identity. . . . The current tendency to stress one's ethnic or class identity, its use as a crutch, is prima facie evidence of the impending collapse of the only valid sense of identity: one's differentness, which is replaced by the most archaic pseudo-identity possible."[28]

We need to be aware of the causes and consequences of various mixes of individual, ethnic, societal, and humanwide identities. A society is wise, in my judgment, that creates an environment where the right to ethnicity is fully protected and mutual respect is strongly supported, while at the same time it works to strengthen those conditions (greater political and economic equality, low levels of prejudice and discrimination, universal human rights) that tend to make ethnic identity a relatively small part of most person's identities. That society is most fortunate where ethnicity continues as a minor melody, serving as counterpoint to major themes of individual identity on one hand and identity with the larger society and the world on the other.

Human beings have not learned well how to get from here to there culturally, how to add new elements that enrich rather than confuse or disappoint us with unforeseen and unwanted side effects, or how to set aside customs that are inherently unjust and cruel or at the least poorly adapted to a world that has been so drastically changed.

This is not a new situation for humanity; but the outcomes of error are likely to be much more severe than in earlier times. The present crisis of meaning and the sharp disputes over values are now generations old, and many people feel, with Matthew Arnold, that they are

> "wandering between two worlds, one dead
> the other powerless to be born."[29]

In our no-person's lands, between two worlds, we look for a path that avoids the minefields scattered so profusely across our cultural landscapes. None is more explosive today than ethnic intolerance and ethnic nationalism.

What can we expect to emerge out of the present turmoil as we move into the twenty-first century? My own hope—perhaps my own utopia—is quite clear: First, I envisage a world populated by states with democratic polities, with the gross inequalities in political access now so prevalent sharply reduced. Mainly market economies would be the rule, but their present serious inadequacies would be curtailed, their weaknesses dealt with by public policies, not simply denied or overlooked. Those needs and values not represented in market forces would be fully considered. This last requisite might be approached by picking up on Franklin Roosevelt's request to Congress that they find ways and means to implement "a second bill of rights." Added to freedom of speech, freedom of religion, and the other traditional rights would be such rights as those to a job, nutrition, education, safety, and a healthful environment.

These ideas were not new in 1944. Something very similar was expressed by an eloquent voice in 1908, drawing on an emerging European view: "I do not agree with those who say that every man must look after himself, and that intervention by the State in such matters as I have referred to will be fatal to his self-reliance, his foresight, and his thrift. . . . It is a great mistake to suppose that thrift is caused only by fear; where there is no hope, be sure there will be no thrift."[30] These are the words of Winston Churchill.

Among the industrial states, the United States has probably gone least far in that direction. There is room for argument about how these rights can best be assured, but little room, in my view, about their essential quality in a democratic society.

To these economic and political elements I would add cultural elements. The belief that the nation-state, as I have defined it, is possible and desirable would become rare, softened by a growing conviction that pluralism and tolerance among ethnic groups is essential. At the same time, the conviction that one's identity is most truly and fully defined by one's ethnicity would also become rare. It would be nested in a group of larger and smaller identities, out of which cross-cutting memberships and contacts would appear, reducing ethnocentrism, helping to create civil societies where all persons are equal in citizenship despite differences in ancestry.[31]

Conflicts often spring from the demands of ethnic minorities for equal access to all the rights of citizenship. If those rights are seen to be beyond reach, non-negotiable, embroiled in conflict, the demands are not likely to shrink, but to grow. Disguised for a time and repressed below the surface of awareness of those in power, they can appear with what seems to be startling speed. Their seeds, however, have been planted decades, even centuries, ago.

Historically, ethnic groups caught in absolutist or semi-autocratic regimes "rooted in one ethnic majority," did not, could not—because of discrimination and isolation—merge into a group of freely associating individual citizens, that is, could not merge into civil societies. As is now utterly clear, ethnic identities of ancient origin have persisted into the late twentieth century, "outlasting not only the Hapsburgs, Romanovs, and Hohenzollerns, but state socialism as well."[32] And, we must add, outlasting the European-crafted statehoods of the Middle East and Africa, and the unequal distribution of the rights of citizenship in democratic societies.

Now, to our dismay, in many lands the struggle for independence and justice is releasing passions that threaten to duplicate the cruelties of authoritarian and colonial regimes. *Chacun prend à l'adversaire, qu'il le veuille ou non.* (One takes on the face of his adversary whether or not he wishes to.) The corroding effects of imperialism are not destroyed by the violent assertion of ethnic rights and identities above all others. One group's claim to sovereignty becomes to another group a threat of oppression. In Edward Said's words: ". . . to accept nativism is to accept the consequence of imperialism, the racial, religious, and political divisions imposed by imperialism itself." The assumption that each person has one absolute and essential identity—black or white, Serb or Croat, Hindu or Muslim, Georgian or Ossetian, Palestinian or Jew—has ". . . the power to turn human beings against each other; often this abandonment of the secular world [I would prefer to say abandonment of civil society] has led to a sort of millenarianism if the movement has a mass base . . . or into an unthinking acceptance of stereotypes, myths, animosities, and traditions encouraged by imperialism."[33]

The conflicts and cruelties in multi-ethnic societies do not result from their diversity of backgrounds nor from inter-group contact. They come from isolation, from segregation and its attendent attitudes and actions. "Ethnic cleansing," whether in a brutal form, seeking by violence to create a homogeneous land, or in a more limited form, seeking to expel or to deny entrance to those who are ethnically different, leaves not cleansed but weaknened and corrupted societies.

Even if ethnic homogeneity were to be attained, the major problems of justice, equity, and adaptation to competing interests would remain, except that the fracturing of society would occur along different fault lines.

In his seminal essay on "Science as a Vocation," Max Weber quoted Leo Tolstoy's belief that " 'Science is meaningless because it gives no answer to our question, the only question of importance to us: What shall we do and how shall we live?' " Weber believed Tolstoy's judgment to be indisputable, "except in discussing the means for a firmly given and presupposed end." If your goal is clear, this is what you need to know in order to attain it. This is an importance exception. Weber goes on to observe that science is of use in helping us to put the questions correctly.[34]

I will follow Weber's suggestion, hoping that I can help to put the major questions regarding ethnicity correctly. To end this long essay on a series of questions, to be sure, is like ending a symphony on an unresolved minor chord. Such conclusions imply unfinished business. If they are successful they may say to the listener (reader): What does all this mean? How should I finish it? I shall think deeply about it, for the resolution is of great significance; a diligent search for the answers is an urgent task.

A question well asked can clarify a problem; it can send a person in the right direction in the search for understanding, if not for problem-closing answers.

Although I have essayed tentative answers here and there, questions regarding the strength but also the conflict potential of ethnicity press in on us, ever more strongly in recent years. The basic analytic question is this: To what degree, in what ways, under what conditions, and with what consequences do ethnic groups occupy an important place in a society; and under what conditions are they relatively less salient? Smaller, but still huge, questions are needed to help us think about that basic question. Here are a few possibilities:

How can the present connections between the ethnic orders of most societies and discrimination be broken, the inequalities significantly reduced, opening the possibilities for a tolerant pluralism?

What is needed to keep our ethnic identities subordinate to our human-wide identities, our identities as persons, and identities as members of multi-ethnic societies? When ethnic identities dominate thought and action, they are divisive and often tragic. It may be that a society is not injured when some few make ethnicity their "vocation." It surely suffers, however, when cross-cutting memberships are destroyed and subgroup memberships become preeminent for large numbers.

How can support for cultural diversity be maintained without encouraging the tendency in each group to treat its traditional ways as sacrosanct, which, ipso facto, tends to make the traditional ways of others repugnant? Ethnic variation brings richness to a society and to individuals if it occurs in a context that also brings unity to a society and to humankind and allows freedom of choice to individuals. Cultures contain many glorious elements; but they may also be encumbered with the flotsam and jetsam of the historical passage. If the ethnic structure freezes each group in "the good old ways"—ethnocentric at best; sexist, racist, and chauvinistic at worst—we shall certainly not be able to adapt to life on this small and crowded planet.

Societies struggling for wise and just policies to deal with the effects of ethnic differences among their people are having a dress rehearsal for an even larger epic drama on the world stage. The world has become so small, so interdependent, so vulnerable to our incredibly destructive weapons and our archaic beliefs that wars can be won, that all societies are becoming, in effect, ethnic groups in an emerging world order. Let us hope that we are learning, in this dress rehearsal, the value of, indeed the necessity for, tolerance, the art of compromise, and the knowledge needed to create just societies, for tomorrow we shall have the even larger task of designing a multi-societal, multi-cultural planet based on principles of peace and justice.

NOTES

CHAPTER 1

1. See Tom Smith, 1980, 1982.

2. Stein and Hill, 1977; see also Nash, 1989; Sandra Wallman in Rex and Mason, 1986:226–45.

3. The next several pages have been adapted from my chapter in Coser and Larsen, 1976:197–216.

4. See, e.g., Dubow, 1989 on South Africa.

5. See Kivisto, 1989.

6. Gerald Berreman in DeVos and Romanucci-Ross, 1975:71–105; Greeley, 1974.

7. Efforts to draw the boundaries of ethnicity must recognize the seamless web of social life. Lines drawn for analytic purposes are sharper than reality. One might add, for example, a model that refers to quasi-ethnicity. It would be closest to model 2 in figure 1.1. An imperial power expands its hegemony (preponderant influence) over other states, usually those closest to its own borders, proclaiming them to be part of its sphere of influence. These states retain some technical autonomy or sovereignty but can be seen also as suppressed ethnic groups. Although I will not explore this issue, I suggest that a theory of ethnicity might inform the history and sociology of, for example, USSR-East European relations and USA-Central American relations.

8. Lieberson and Waters, 1988:264.

9. Alba, 1990; Waters, 1990. A similar development is occurring in Canada; see Pryor et al, 1992.

10. See Baltzell, 1964; Christopher, 1989; Brookhiser, 1991.

11. *WASP* is generally seen as a derogatory or derisive term. Rather than feeling abused, however, I prefer to treat it with a bit of whimsy. *WASP* is not a very precise term. It has taken on not only multi-ethnic meaning, but class and, in some cases, gender meanings: WASP = upper class white male. As a result I no longer feel well identified by any of the possible labels—English, British, north European, or WASP. I am, in fact, a WAIF (White American International Fellow)—a male with several European ancestral lines. There are, of course, White American International Females. With the males, they all are White American International Folk. WAIFS are such a diverse lot, however, with the usual mix of scoundrels and heroes, that I am seeking to join an emerging ethnic group, the Honorable Universal Mix of Ancestors and Neighbors (HUMAN).

12. Linton, 1937:427–29; see also Holloway, 1990.

13. See Bricker, 1975.

14. Novak, 1971:60

15. Blackwell, 1975.

16. See, for example, Liah Greenfield's *Nationalism: Five Roads to Modernity*, 1992. She skillfully examines the growth of "nationhood" in England, France, and the United States, seeing it as the development of a strong sense of a common identity across lingual and cultural lines. A "universalistic" view of citizenship, she argues, was a major factor in detaching feelings of nationhood from diverse ancestral lines. For lack of a universalistic view of citizenship, however, Germany and Russia have not been nearly so successful in melding a shared nationhood out of their multiethnic populations.

Even though I use the terms differently, there are many precedents for using *nation* and *nationhood* in this way. One does not quarrel with definitions used so consistently and skillfully. She does neglect, however, the abundant evidence that the United States, England, and France have granted less than full citizenship—"equal participation in nationhood," to use her phrase—to many of their ethnic groups, down to the present day.

17. See Foster, 1980; Bertelsen, 1977.

18. Linz in Tiryakian and Rogowski, 1985; Woolard, 1989.

19. See Tilly, 1990: chap. 1; Newman, 1987; Eugen Weber, 1991 and 1976; Rogers Brubaker, 1992; Richard Bernstein, 1990; Colley, 1992; Goulbourne, 1991.

20. See Wolf, 1982; Anthony Smith, 1989; Hobsbawm, 1990.

21. See Douglass, 1988; Meadwell, 1989; Robert Clark, 1987; Fox, 1990.

22. Anthony Smith, 1984, 1988; see also Armstrong, 1982. Brumberg, 1992, makes an excellent analysis of the contemporary blending of historical grievances with the "grandeur" of national myths in Ukraine.

23. Connor, 1984, 1990; Hechter, 1987; Avineri, 1990.

24. Studlar and McAllister, 1988.

25. Hechter, 1987; see also Anthony Smith, 1984.

26. Hechter, 1977; Stone, 1979.

27. Anthony Smith, 1988:9.

28. Geertz, 1963:108; see also Giddens, 1985.

29. See Frankel, 1990; Mark Katz, 1993.

30. Said, 1991:162.

31. See Wheeler, 1962; Janowsky, 1945; Allworth, 1977; Azrael, 1978; W. J. Kolarz in Lind, 1955: chap 9; Rakowska-Harmstone, 1977; Connor, 1984.

32. van den Berghe, 1978:xv.

33 See, e.g., Stone, 1977; van den Berghe, 1983; Eisinger, 1980; Steinberg, 1981; Williams, 1975; Benson, 1981; Banton, 1983.

34. Benedict, 1940:127–28.

35. DuBois, 1897:7.

36. Cornacchia and Nelson, 1992:121.

37. Wolf, 1982:380–81.

38. Omi and Winant, 1986.

39. Merton, 1972; see also Suttles, 1990:38–42.

40. Williams, 1975:126.

41. Wilson, 1978, 1987.

42. Ronald Taylor, 1979:1401; see also Roosens, 1989.

43. Dobzhansky, 1962.

44. See, e.g., Dominquez, 1986; U.S. Bureau of the Census, 1981; Segal, 1991; F. James Davis, 1991; see also Degler, 1991, for a valuable history of the ways in which biological influences have been interpreted in American thought. For ancient attitudes toward racial differences, see Snowden, 1983.

45. Leonard Thompson, 1985.

46. United Nations, 1952:490.

47. Wagley and Harris, 1958:10.

48. Wirth, in Linton, 1945:347. None of these anthropological and sociological definitions of minority is based on a numerical criterion.

49. See Horowitz, 1985.

50. See Ronald Taylor, 1979; Clifton, 1990.

51. *Economist*, April 11–17, 1992:48. Italics mine.

52. For a sampling of tribal studies and commentaries, see Morgan, 1964 (1877); Firth, 1957; Malinowski, 1922.

53. See Katz, 1992; Dresh, 1989.

54. See, e.g., Nabakov, 1991; Spicer, 1982; Cornell, 1988; J. Milton Yinger and Simpson, 1978; Lyon, 1974.

55. See Applegate, 1990; Brustein, 1988; Reed, 1983; Himes, 1991; Woolard, 1989; Garreau, 1982; LaCoste, 1986.

56. J. Milton Yinger, 1982:4. There is an enormous literature on various aspects of this topic. See, e.g., Durkheim, 1947, 1947a; Mauss, 1954; Malinowski, 1932; Clark and Wilson, 1961; Parsons, 1937:89–114; Homans, 1961; Blau, 1964; Gluckman, 1963; Marshall Sahlins, 1972; Colson, 1974; Emerson, 1976; Weiner, 1992; Cook, 1987.

57. Macy, 1991:808.

58. See Olson, 1965; Hardin, 1968; Ostrom, 1990; Macy, 1991.

59. Backman, 1981:241.

60. Berger, Rosenholtz, and Zelditch, 1980:479; see also Berger and Zelditch, 1985; E. G. Cohen, 1982; Dovidio and Gaertner, 1981; Laumann, 1973; Zerubavel, 1991.

61. Allport and Postman, 1945:61–81.

62. Neier, 1991:295.

63. United States Army Western Defense Command, 1943:33–34 italics mine.

64. See Kearney, 1989; Moch, 1992.

65. Tandon, 1973:7.

66. Iacovetta, 1991; *The New York Times*, July 8, 1990:E–2.

67. *Population Today*, Jan. 1991; see also Dreyer, 1976.

68. Laber, 1990.

69. Karklins, 1986; Akiner, 1986; Martha Olcott in Hajda and Beissinger, 1990:253–80.

70. See Heisler and Heisler, 1986; Dignan, 1981; Martin, 1980; Schechtman, 1962.

71. See U.S. Dept. of Justice, 1992; Kalish, Nov. 1992; Portes and Rumbaut, 1990; Simon, 1986; Reid, 1986; Hofstetter, 1984; Crewdson, 1983. We need to treat administrative racial categories rather lightly. Imagine how the 1990 racial distribution would change if the U.S. census had used the instructions given in 1890: carefully distinguish among blacks, mulattoes, quadroons, and octoroons. (See the NYT, April 9, 1993:E3.) Instead of 12.1% black, we might have, to give a rough guess: black, 3.1%; mulattoes, 6.0%; quadroons, 2.0%; octoroons, 1.0%. Racial and ethnic classifications are much more nearly social than biological constructs.

72. See United Nations, Centre for Human Rights, 1992:62–123; Tarzi, 1991.

73. U.S. Dept. of Justice, Immigration and Naturalization Service, 1987 and 1989.

74. See United Nations, 1992; Carl Haub and Nancy Yinger, 1992.

CHAPTER 2

1. Havel, 1990, 6.

2. Derrida, 1978; see also Rorty, 1989; chap. 1.

3. Young, 1976; Glazer and Moynihan, 1975; Blauner, 1972.

4. Pettigrew, 1969; Kuper, 1977.

5. Lieberson, 1963, 10.

6. DeVos and Romanucci-Ross, 1975:v.

7. Basham and DeGroot, 1977:423.

8. Francis, 1976: chap. 20; Simpson, 1968.

9. This section has been adapted and revised from J. Milton Yinger, 1981 and 1985a.

10. See Richardson, 1974; Lieberson, Dalto, and Johnston, 1975; Richard Pipes in Glazer and Moynihan, 1975:453–65.

11. See John Goshko, *Washington Post National Weekly*, July 22–28, 1991:19; Kenneth Noble, *The New York Times*, April 13, 1991:1,3.

12. See Neil Henry, *Washington Post National Weekly*, July 15–21, 1991:16.

13. *Cleveland Plain Dealer*, June 2, 1991:3–C.

14. Yinger and Simpson, 1978.

15. Wirth, 1945.

16. Gambino, 1975; Greeley, 1971, 1974; Novak, 1971; Gordon, 1964; Epstein, 1978.

17. Pierre van den Berghe in Rex and Mason, 1986:250. See also van den Berghe, 1981. Horowitz, 1985, chap. 2, emphasizes kinship more for its cultural than its biological elements.

18. J. Milton Yinger, 1986b:20.

19. Gordon, 1964:29; see also Schooler, 1976.

20. Epstein, 1978:xi.

21. Greeley, 1971:26.

22. Parthé, 1992:63; see also Wendy Griswold, 1992; Benedict Anderson, 1983.

23. See Young, 1976:489–501.

24. See Orlando Patterson in Glazer and Moynihan, 1975:305–349.

25. *Anomie* is a state of normlesness, of value conflicts. In a state of anomie, Durkheim wrote, ". . . the most reprehensible acts are rendered pure by success. . . . The limits are unknown between the possible and the impossible, what is just and unjust, legitimate claims and hopes and those which are immoderate. Consequently there is no restraint on aspirations." (Durkheim, 1951:253).

There are dozens of definitions of alienation. I think of it as the experienced loss of a relationship, the loss of a sense of participation and control, as, for example, with reference to government or society as a whole. (See J. Milton Yinger in Knutson, 1973: chap. 7; and 1965b: chap. 9).

26. See Greeley, 1971: chap. 13; Parsons in Glazer and Moynihan, 1975:68–69; Kilson in Glazer and Moynihan, 1975:260.

27. Novak, 1971:229; see also DeVos and Romanucci-Ross, 1975:25.

28. See Abner Cohen, 1974 and 1974a; Nisbet, 1975; Daniel Bell in Glazer and Moynihan, 1975:141–74; Young, 1976; Despres, 1975; Enloe, 1973; Léons, 1978; Yancey, Ericksen, and Juliani, 1976.

29. Cohen, 1974:39.

30. Hechter, 1974.

31. Bell in Glazer and Moynihan, 1975; see also Young, 1976: chap. 4.

32. Parsons in Glazer and Moynihan, 1975:63–67.

33. Hechter, 1974:1151.

34. Bell in Glazer and Moynihan, 1975:145.

35. Nisbet, 1975:9–12.

36. Abner Cohen, 1969:2.

37. See Johnston and Yoels, 1977; George Scott, 1990; Gans, 1992.

38. Fallows, 1974:1–2.

39. William J. Wilson, 1978.

40. See Patterson, 1977.

41. Porter in Glazer and Mohnihan, 1975:293.

42. The political and military dominance by states may prove to be a brief period in history. Such dominance is now beginning to be challenged from above by inter-state alliances and organizations and from below by ethnic groups seeking autonomy or independence. (Most of those attaining independence soon find themselves also challenged from above and below.)

43. For comments on various combinations of these variables, see Hurh, Kim, and Kim, 1979; Simpson, 1968; Murgúia, 1982; Melville, 1983; Blau, Blum, and Schwartz, 1982; Joó, 1991: Drobizheva, 1991; Stevens, 1992.

44. On such processes, see Schelling, 1978.

45. Several paragraphs in this section have been adapted from Yinger, 1985b.

46. Davis, Haub, and Willette, 1983:151; see also Bean and Swicegood, 1985. It is essential to distinguish among the diverse Latino, or Hispanic, groups. Americans of Mexican, Puerto Rican, and Cuban descent—to cite only the three largest—vary in historical background, relationships to the United States, class distributions, location, and in many other ways. See Shorris, 1992; see also the Latino National Survey, 1992.

Edmonston and Passel estimate a growth in the Hispanic population between 1990 and 2040 from 9 to 18 percent of the projected total population of 356 million. The Mexican proportion will almost surely increase, perhaps to two-thirds of the 64 million Hispanics, or nearly 43 million persons.

In these projections, the Asian-origin population will have increased from 3 to 10 percent (to 34.5 million), African Americans from 12.1 to 12.4 percent (to 44.1 million), and the non-Hispanic European-origin population will have fallen from 75 to 59 percent (210.5 million).

Among the Hispanics, approximately one-third will be foreign-born, one-third second generation, and one-third of third or later generation. The U.S.-born proportion will have increased from 59% to 67%. (See Edmonston and Passel, 1992:6–7).

Of course these fifty-year projections can be strongly affected by international and national developments.

47. Phillip Vargas, *Washington Post National Weekly*, April 8–14, 1991:27.

48. See *General Characteristics of the Population*, 1951, and *Statistical Abstracts* of the U.S. Bureau of the Census, 1950.

49. *The New York Times*, June 20, 1991:8.

50. Mittelbach and Moore, 1968; see also Salgado de Snyder and Padilla, 1982. Intermarriage is discussed in chapter 4, herein.

51. Murgúia, 1982; see also Bureau of the Census, March 1977.

52. See Massey, 1987; Browning and de la Garza, 1986; Massey et al., 1986.

53. See the chapters by Shirley Brice Heath, Reynaldo F. Marcias, and Joshua Fishman in Connor, 1985; also Stolzenberg, 1990; Resnick, 1988; Yolando R. Solé, 1990; see also chapter 8 herein.

54. Fuentes, 1992; 410.

55. Stolzenberg, 1990; Keefe and Padilla, 1987; Mirande and Enriquez, 1980.

56. See Chavez, 1991; Rodriquez, 1983.

57. Griffith, Frase, and Ralph, 1989.

58. *Ibid.:* 23.

59. Adapted from Nelson and Tienda, 1985:61.

60. Educational Testing Service, *The Reading Report Card, 1971–1988,* 1990; see also Valdivieso and Davis, 1988.

61. Turner, Fix, and Struyk, 1991:28–29; see also Surace, 1982; Melendez, Rodriquez, and Figueroa, 1991; Defreitas, 1991.

62. Turner, Struyk, and Yinger, 1991:36; J. Yinger, 1993.

63. John Yinger, 1991:xii; see also Massey and Denton, 1989; Munnell et al, 1992.

64. See Schuman, Steeh, and Bobo, 1985; T. W. Smith, 1990.

65. See Ashmore and DelBoca, 1976; Kinder and Sears, 1983.

66. Data from the U.S. Census, 1990, reported in *The New York Times,* Jan. 19, 1992:12; see also Stolzenberg, 1990.

67. *The New York Times,* Jan. 27, 1991:E–4.

68. Kalish, May, 1992; and see the chapters by Nathan Glazer, Rodolfo de la Garza, and Harry P. Pachón in Connor, 1985; Moore and Pachón, 1985; Portes and Bach, 1985; Janowski, 1986. For discussion of an earlier period, see Grebler, Moore, and Guzman, 1970.

69. For a map of the district, see Kalish, May 1992:3.

70. *Ibid.*

71. One might wonder—and the courts will surely inquire—whether the 1992 redistricting did not in some cases caricature the Voting Rights Act. The Act was intended to guarantee minority voting rights, presumably including the right to vote for friendly non-minority candidates, not to segregate minority voters in order to reduce their potential impact. (I wrote this statement in the spring of 1992. A year later the Supreme Court declared that such bizarre districts may violate the constitution. The 5-4 decision was made more in the defense of white than of black voters.)

Chapter 3

1. Gordon, 1964:71; 1978:169.

2. See, e.g., Alba, 1976; 1985; Gregory, 1976; Patterson, 1977.

3. Spicer, 1968.

4. See Herskovits, 1938; Linton, 1940.

5. Padilla, 1980; Hurh et al, 1979; Holloway, 1990.

6. The next several paragraphs have been adapted and revised from J. Milton Yinger, 1981.

7. Sen, 1993:30.

8. Levine, 1973; chap. 2.

9. See Stayman and Deshpande, 1989.

10. See Polgar, 1960; Charles Valentine, 1971; Hannerz, 1969; Naka-mura, 1988; DuBois, 1953 (1903).

11. The concept of 'marginal man' has been used mainly to refer to the personal consequences of standing at the margins of two cultural worlds; but the extensive literature on this topic also enriches the discussion of additive vs. substitutive acculturation. See, e.g., Stonequist, 1937, Wright and Wright, 1972; MacGregor, 1946; Spindler and Spindler, 1971; Tax, 1978; Murguía, 1975; Poggie, 1973, Burke, 1981; Simpson and Yinger, 1985, 123–27.

12. Triandis, 1976, 183.

13. Triandis, 1976, 179; see also Naroll, et al., 1971.

14. See Ramirez and Castaneda, 1974.

15. Carroll, 1988.

16. See *The New York Times*, April 25, 1990; see also Elder, 1971.

17. *Dances with Wolves* was given mixed reviews. For some, the over-whelming violence, especially during the first several minutes, and the re-verse stereotyping (most whites were villains) were the defining—and negative—elements. At best it was seen as glamorized entertainment. The Lakota Sioux, however, saw a depiction of themselves and their ancestors that seemed real and supportive. To quote the *Lakota Times*, Nov. 27, 1990, a tribal newspaper: "Costner and co-producer Jim Wilson have created a first. They tell a story woven among Plains Indians filled with honor and respect to Lakota people. As Lakota movie-goers emerge from the film we are happy. And sad. We are validated simply because someone told the truth. And in a beautiful way."

18. Ivanov, 1984. See also Beals, 1967:215; Hallowell, 1957:207; Yinger and Simpson, 1978:142–44. Acculturation, much of it additive, has been going on between Native Americans and Europeans for half a millennium. In recent scholarship, encounter, not discovery, and frontiers as zones

of interaction call attention to cultural exchange. See Axtell, 1992; Elliott, 1993; Pagden, 1993; Weber, 1992; White, 1991.

19. Smolicz, 1988:393.

20. Richard Bernstein, 1990b.

21. *Ibid.:* 3.

22. Alterman, 1990:584–85.

23. New York State Dept. of Education, 1989.

24. See Troyna and Carrington, 1990.

25. Quoted by Hacker, 1990:19

26. Ogbu, 1978.

27. Hacker, 1990; Sleeper, 1990, esp. chap. 8.

28. Schlesinger, 1991.

29. Schlesinger, 1992:125–26, 101–02; and see 45–72.

30. J. Yinger, 1993; Massey and Denton, 1993; Turner, Fix, and Struyk, 1991; Turner, Struyk, and Yinger, 1991; Munnell et al., 1992; Alba and Logan, 1991; Orfield and Ashkinaze, 1991, chap. 4. To job and housing discrimination we need to add reference to what has been called environmental racism: the frequent use of minority communities as the repositories of toxic wastes, as the location for environmentally damaging industries, as the place where lead-paint-encrusted schools and houses are most commonly found. See Bullard, 1992; Commission for Race and Justice of the United Church of Christ, Chavis and Lee, eds., 1987.

31. Pollitt, 1991, 330–332; Marx, 1992.

32. Naipaul, 1991a:22.

33. Maran, 1989.

34. Triandis, 1976b:184; See also William J. Wilson, 1987; BettyLou Valentine, 1978; Stack, 1974; Suttles, 1968; and Liebow, 1967.

35. See Robin M. Williams, Jr., 1977:95.

36. Breton, 1964; Haug and Portes, 1979; Turner and Bonacich, 1980.

37. See Furnivall, 1948; Smith in Kuper and Smith, 1971: chaps. 2 and 13.

38. Gurr and Scarritt, 1989, 378.

39. See Gurr and Scarritt, 1989; Claude, 1976.

40. United Nations, Centre for Human Rights, 1991. Some societies deviate from the U.N. standards in their legal and customary views as well as in their practices.

41. United Nations, Centre for Human Rights, 1991, 7; see also Banton, 1990 and 1991.

42. United Nations, 1991, 159.

43. Since the Maastrich Treaty was signed in 1991, additional issues have slowed the movement toward integration within the European Community. Among them are these: a sluggish economy in most of western Europe; the persistent pressure felt due to the large number of refugees; the weakness, so far, of direct democratic influence, since most actions are in the hands, not of a legislature, but in the bureaucracies that administer the several agencies; a lingering fear of Germany's dominance; and continuing opposition from those who believe they will lose more than they can hope to gain. See Hoffmann, 1992 and 1993.

44. *Japan Times*, Tokyo, Nov. 18, 1991:2.

45. Honolulu *Star-Bulletin and Advertiser*, March 1, 1987:B–3, quoting a professor of law, Univ. of Tokyo.

46. For several views and some historical background, see Watkins, 1990; Marrus, 1985; Heisler and Heisler, 1986; Peach, 1990; Miles and Singer-Kérel, 1991; Castles, Booth, and Wallace, 1984; Moch, 1992.

47. U. S. Dept. of Labor, 1980:10.

48. *The New York Times*, Sept. 22, 1991:8.

49. Jan. 28, 1990:6.

50. Sullivan, 1988.

51. On the Basques and indigenous ethnic groups more generally, see Clark, 1987; Heiberg, 1989; Rousseau and Zariski, 1987; Sahlins, 1989; Douglass, 1988; Linz, 1985; John Sullivan, 1988; McCrone, 1984; Morgan, 1981; Kearney, 1989; Woolard, 1989; Conversi, 1990; Davies, 1989.

52. U.S. Department of Labor, 1980:17.

53. On split labor markets see Cain, 1976; Marshall, 1974; Bonacich, 1972.

54. Schmitter, 1983:313.

55. Hechter, 1977.

56. Sayari, 1986:96–97.

57. See Schmitter, 1983; Heisler, 1985.

58. Robinson, 1990:283–84; see also Robinson, 1988.

59. Tove Skutnabb-Kangas in Edwards, 1984:17–48.

60. Malhotra, 1985; for comments on the situation in France, see Solé, 1985.

61. Safran, 1986, 103.

62. U.S. Department of Labor, 1980:19.

63. Safran, 1986; 107.

64. *Ibid.:* 108.

65. *Ibid.:* 111.

66. Ash, 1990a:15.

67. *Ibid.*

68. Quoted in Judith Miller, 1991:81.

69. Heilig et al., 1990.

70. Dahrendorf, 1967; see also Schmitter, 1980.

71. U.S. Department of Labor, 1980:18.

72. Fisher, 1991:10.

73. *The New York Times*, Oct. 1, 1991:1; Nov. 24, 1991:10.

74. Fisher, 1991.

75. *The New York Times*, Sept. 29, 1991:1, 11.

76. Ash, 1990c; 13.

77. *The New York Times*, Oct. 1, 1991:1, 6. By mid-1993 several immigrants, most of them Turkish, had been killed.

78. Ash, 1990a:13.

79. Ash, 1991:22.

80. *The New York Times*, Aug. 11, 1991:6.

81. *Washington Post National Weekly*, Oct. 14–20, 1991:17.

82. Cleveland *Plain Dealer*, Dec. 25, 1992:3–C.

83. Ash, 1990a:14–15.

84. See Hitchens, 1992; Glenny, 1992, 1993.

85. To put this in sociological terms: historical memory is not just an individual's record of the past; it is a social product. It can be understood only by reference to present groups and interactions within which it is embedded. See Halbwachs, 1992.

86. Ignatieff, 1993:3.

87. *Ibid.*; see also Glenny, 1992; Rusinow, 1988.

88. Ignatieff, 1993:3. For background see Djilas, 1962; Djilas, 1991.

89. See Eugen Weber, 1976; Sahlins, 1989; Richard Bernstein, 1990.

90. Dignan, 1981.

91. *The New York Times*, Nov. 11, 1991:6. This is scarcely a new development in France, although the targets of ethnic hostility have changed. See, e.g., Arendt, 1946, on antisemitism; and Soucy, 1972, on the career of Maurice Barrès.

92. *The New York Times*, Oct. 19, 1990:A–8.

93. *The New York Times*, June 23, 1991:7.

94. Quoted by *The New York Times*, June 23, 1991:7; see also Husbands, 1991; Singer, 1991.

95. *The New York Times*, March 3, 1990:5.

96. See, e.g., Richmond, 1951; Banton, 1959; Glass, 1961; Watson, 1977; Rex and Tomlinson, 1979; Tambs-Lyche, 1980.

97. Heilig, Büttner, and Lutz, 1990.

98. *Nation*, Dec. 23, 1991:815; Miller, 1991:80.

99. See Jenkins and Kposowa, 1990; Finnegan, 1992; Krymkowski and Hall, 1990; Cohen and Kilson, 1992.

100. *Washington Post National Weekly*, July 15–21, 1991:16.

101. *Washington Post National Weekly*, Jan. 6–12, 1992:24.

102. Quoted by *Japan Times*, Nov. 4, 1991:5.

103. *The New York Times*, Sept. 9, 1991:3; *Washington Post National Weekly*, Oct. 21–27, 1991:16.

104. *The New York Times,* Oct. 6, 1991:E–3.

105. *The New York Times,* Jan. 19, 1992:3.

106. *The New York Times,* Aug. 8, 1988:E–1.

107. *Washington Post National Weekly,* Sept. 5–11, 1988; 17–8.

108. *The New York Times,* Nov. 15, 1990:A–4.

109. See Murphree, 1988.

110. Kauffmann, 1991:7.

111. *Ibid.*

112. Christopher Wren in *The New York Times,* June 23, 1991, E–3.

113. Wren, 1990:32.

114. This section has been adapted from "The Research Agenda: New Directions for Desegregation Studies," in *Advancing the Art of Inquiry in School Desegregation Research,* Jeffrey Prager, Douglas Longshore, and Melvin Seeman, Editors. New York: Praeger, 1986, pp. 229–254.

115. See Kozol, 1991.

116. J. Milton Yinger, 1965b.

117. For reviews and commentaries see Richard J. Hill, 1981; Eagly and Himmelfarb, 1978; Schuman and Johnson, 1976; Fishbein and Ajzen, 1975; and the papers by Schuman, Fishbein, Maynes, and Kelman in Yinger and Cutler, 1978, 373–420.

118. A. W. Smith, 1981.

119. Jacobson, 1978.

120. Ogbu, 1978; Prager, Longshore and Seeman, 1986, 21–45.

121. Suttles in Prager, Longshore and Seeman, 1986:47–74. See Smelser, 1991, on the British experience.

122. Gutman, 1976:468–69.

123. Schelling, 1978:93–94.

124. Sieber, 1981:216.

125. Schmidt, 1989; John Yinger, 1980.

126. See, e.g., Rosenberg, 1989, 1979; Rosenberg and Simmons, 1972; Taylor and Walsh, 1979; Phyllis A. Katz, 1976, chap. 4; Goering, 1972; Heiss

and Owens, 1972; McCarthy and Yancey, 1971; Drury, 1980. For general reviews and commentaries and some confirmation of earlier findings, see Porter and Washington, 1979; Barry D. Adam, 1978; Williams and Morland, 1976; Porter, 1971; Asher and Allen, 1969; Smelser, Mecca, and Vasconcellos, 1989.

127. Rosenberg in Prager, Longshore, and Seeman, 1986:175–203.

128. Taylor and Walsh, 1979.

129. See Hughes and Demo, 1989; see also Jackson and Gurin, 1987.

130. Hunt, 1977: Granovetter in Prager, Longshore, and Seeman, 1986, 81–110.

131. Clark and Clark, 1947; Elkins, 1959; Stampp, 1965; Basil Bernstein, 1966.

132. Genovese, 1974; Fogel and Engerman, 1974; Gutman, 1976; Labov, 1972; Jules-Rosette and Mehan, in Prager, Longshore, and Seeman, 1986:212.

133. McCarthy and Yancey, 1971b, 591.

134. Barry D. Adam, 1978, 49, 51.

135. Pettigrew, 1978, 60.

136. Weinberg, 1975; Bradley and Bradley, 1977.

137. E.g., Kanter, 1977; S. E. Taylor, 1981; Epps, 1975; Willie, 1976.

138. Harrington, 1975.

139. Henry, 1980; Metz, 1978; Blalock in Prager, Longshore, and Seeman, 1986:111–141; Grant, 1981.

140. Braddock, 1990; Alexander, Cook, and McDill, 1978; Kerckhoff, 1986; Rist, 1970; Frederick Erickson, 1975; Rosenbaum, 1976; Riehl, Natriello, and Pallas, 1992; Matsueda, 1992. McDermott, 1977; Oakes, 1985; Shavit, 1984. Kilgore, 1991, finds more positive effects; Gamoran, 1992, finds mixed effects.

141. Lacy and Middleton, 1981; Summers and Wolf, 1977.

142. Wilkerson, 1991.

143. Robinson and Preston, 1976; Blalock in Prager, Lonshore, and Seeman, 1986.

144. Granovetter, 81–110 in Prager, Longshore and Seaman, 1986.

145. Granovetter, 1982.

146. Schofield, 1979.

147. Suttles in Prager, Longshore, and Seeman, 1986; see also Heyns, 1978; Entwisle and Alexander, 1992; Silverman and Shaw, 1973; Yinger et al., 1977.

148. Clotfelter, 1979:366.

149. John Yinger, 1979:459.

150. *Ibid.*

151. See, e.g., Waldron, 1989; *Civil Rights Update,* December, 1980; Taeuber, 1979; Rossell, 1978; Finger, 1978; Loewen, 1979.

152. See, e.g., Coleman, Kelly, and Moore, 1975; Pettigrew and Green, 1976; Farley, 1976; Sly and Pol, 1978.

153. See Long and DeAre, 1981.

154. Farley, Richards and Wurdock, 1980.

155. Orfield, 1978.

156. *The New York Times,* Dec. 12, 1992:B–7.

157. 418 U.S., 1974; see also Orfield, 1978; Henderson and von Euler, 1979.

158. See Natriello, McDill, and Pallas, 1990; Jaynes and Williams, 1989: chap. 7; Hochschild, 1984.

159. Heyns, 1978; Entwisle and Alexander, 1992.

160. J. Milton Yinger, Ikeda, Laycock, and Cutler, 1977.

CHAPTER 4

1. A student speaking to David Remnick. See *Washington Post National Weekly* Jan. 13–19, 1992:16.

2. Several paragraphs in this section have been adapted from J. Milton Yinger, 1981. See also Weinreich, 1986.

3. Hallowell, 1963; Heard, 1973.

4. See David Gonzales, *The New York Times,* Nov. 15, 1992:E–6; see also Shorris, 1992.

5. Lieberson and Waters, 1988:33; see also Farley, 1991.

6. Quoted by Lieberson, 1985:171.

7. Quoted in the *Washington Post National Weekly*, Feb. 11–17, 1991:12.

8. See Harris, 1992.

9. Goulbourne, 1991. This is an indication of the social influence on identity. Social identity theory explores the way group memberships shape identity choices. In many situations, ethnic groups foster the social identity of their members. They seek to maintain or increase the salience of membership and to give it a positive quality. See Tajfel and Turner, 1985, 1979; Louw-Potgieter, 1988; Pettigrew and Martin in vanOudenhoven et al, 1989:169–200.

10. Adapted from Horowitz, 1991:50–53.

11. Lieberson and Waters, 1988:47–49.

12. Royce, 1982:187.

13. *Ibid.*

14. *Cleveland Plain Dealer*, citing Grant McCracken, Aug. 4, 1990:7.

15. Stayman and Deshpande, 1989.

16. DeVos, 1975:30; Connor, 1985: chap. 1.

17. DeVos, 1975:31–32; see also Kozol, 1991.

18. J. Milton Yinger, 1982:273–74.

19. *The New York Times*, April 16, 1989:14, quoting Joyce Ladner.

20. *Ibid.*, quoting Ernest White, founder of the mentor program.

21. See Connor, 1985: chap. 1 for reference to the variety of ways that Mexican Americans identify themselves and the importance of the differences for behavior.

22. On the accumulation of roles, see Stephen R. Marks, 1977; Sieber, 1974. See also Allport on concentric circles of identity, 1954:43–46.

23. Nisbet, 1975:12; see also Marty and Appleby, 1991.

24. Steele, 1990:xi; see White, 1991, for factors influencing identity among African Americans; see also Cornell, 1990; Helms, 1990; Jaynes and Williams, 1989:191–200.

25. See Antonovsky, 1956; Stonequist, 1937; Willie, 1975.

26. DuBois, 1953.

27. Shattuck and Ka, 1990:18–20; Senghor, 1964, 1971, 1977, three volumes under the general title *Liberté*; see especially Vol. 3.

28. Tricarico, 1989:24–26.

29. Horowitz in Glazer and Moynihan, 1975:137; see also Schöpflin, 1991.

30. Lieberson, 1985:168.

31. Stein and Hill, 1977.

32. Gans 1979.

33. See Marty and Appleby, 1991.

34. Alba, 1985:12.

35. Waters, 1990:156.

36. *Ibid.*

37. Novak, 1971.

38. Waters, 1990:157.

39. *Ibid.*

40. Erik Erikson, 1963:285–87.

41. Waters, 1990:151.

42. Sapir, 1931:13–14.

43. Bellah et al, 1985; Bellah et al, 1991.

44. In addition to the works cited in this section, the following sampling of references may indicate the range of discussion of the concept of identity generally and of specific ethnic identities: Weigert, Teitge, and Teitge, 1986; Erik Erikson, 1968; Zurcher, 1977; Tajfel, 1982; Woolard, 1989; Alba, 1985; Karklins, 1986; Kivisto, 1989; Bracewell, 1991; Fugita and O'Brien, 1991.

45. Several paragraphs in this section have been drawn from J. Milton Yinger, 1981 and Yinger, 1985a.

46. Stuckert, 1976:135–39; see also Williamson, 1980:188–91; Davis, 1991.

47. See Gist and Dworkin, 1972; Karklins, 1986: chap. 6; Spickard, 1989; Adams, 1937.

48. Myrdal, 1944:124; see also Higginbotham, 1978.

49. These data come from Kalish, Dec., 1992.

50. Karklins, 1986:156.

51. Gist and Dworkin, 1972; Lifton, 1975; Hiroshi Wagatsuma in Rotberg, 1978:119–29; Burkhardt, 1983.

52. Jiobu, 1988.

53. Keith and Herring, 1991.

54. Dobzhansky, 1962.

55. See Gist and Dworkin, 1972; Solaun and Kronus, 1973; Shaefer, 1980.

56. On biological aspects of race see Simpson and Yinger, 1985: chap. 2.

57. S. M. Cohen, 1977; Roy, 1962; White and Chadwick, 1972.

58. See Spickard, 1989:235–311; Lillian Smith, 1949.

59. See Ikeda, 1991.

60. For a discussion of this issue, see J. Milton Yinger, 1968a.

61. Adapted from Peter R. Jones, 1984:400.

62. The bibliography on this topic is very large. See, e.g., Kalmijn, 1991; Hwang and Saenz, 1990; Alba, 1990, 1985, 1985a; Alba and Golden, 1986; Alba and Kessler, 1979; Lieberson and Waters, 1988; Spickard, 1989; Rytina, Blau, Blum, and Schwartz, 1988; Stevens and Swicegood, 1987; McRae, 1983; Blau, Becker, and Fitzpatrick, 1984; Jiobu, 1988:149–77; Heer, 1980; Blau, 1977; Gurak and Fitzpatrick, 1982; Murguia, 1982; Peach, 1980; Porterfield, 1978; Robinson, 1980; Kim Bok-lim, 1977; Farber, Gordon, and Mayer, 1979; J. Milton Yinger, 1968a, 1968b, Kennedy, 1952; Romanzo Adams, 1937; Snipp, 1989; Wilkinson, 1975; Root, 1992.

63. One rate can be transposed into the other by use of the following formulas, with x as the group rate and y the individual rate:

$$y = \frac{100\,x}{200 - x} \qquad x = \frac{200\,y}{100 + y}$$

See Rodman, 1965.

64. Lieberson and Waters, 1988:173. For study of earlier rates of inter-marriage among European Americans, see Pagnini and Morgan, 1990.

65. See Lieberson and Waters, 1988:171–75.

66. Reported by the U.S. Census, 1993. See also Kalish, Dec., 1992; Root, 1992.

67. J. Milton Yinger, 1968a.

68. These data are drawn from Steinfels, 1992. They indicate higher rates of intermarriage and lower rates of conversion to Judaism than do the data reported by Stephen Cohen, 1990:9–10.

69. Adapted from Tom Smith, 1991:54.

70. *Ibid.:* 55.

71. See Spickard, 1989:305.

CHAPTER 5

1. Pettigrew and Taylor, 1986:502; see also Pettigrew, 1985; Cambridge and Feuchtwang, 1990; Burt, 1992, esp. chap. 5.

2. Hamill, 1988, 92.

3. The next several pages are adapted from J. Milton Yinger, 1983.

4. See, e.g., Buroway, 1976; Kaufman, 1983.

5. See Katznelson, 1973; William J. Wilson, 1978; Form, 1985; Semyonov and Lewin-Epstein, 1989.

6. Adorno *et al.*, 1950.

7. See, e.g., Ackerman and Jahoda, 1950; Kirscht and Dillehay, 1967; Rokeach, 1960; Simpson and Yinger, 1985: chap. 4; Tajfel, 1969; Bagley and Verma, 1979; Bagley *et al.*, 1979; Seeman, 1981; Apostle, et al., 1983.

8. Hamilton, 1981; Miller, 1982.

9. Sumner, 1906, 13–16; Lanternari, 1980; Brewer and Campbell, 1976; Levine and Campbell, 1972.

10. See Catton, 1961–62.

11. See Brewer and Campbell, 1976; Scheepers, Felling, and Peters, 1989.

12. See, e.g., Adam and Giliomee, 1979; Glaser and Possony, 1979. William Cohen, 1991, shows how deeply racial discrimination was entrenched in the United States after the Civil War; see esp. chap. 8.

13. See Della Fave, 1980; Barry D. Adam, 1978; Hughes and Demo, 1989; West, 1993: chap. 1.

14. Coleman, 1971:82.

15. Rotter, 1966.

16. Perlmuter and Monty, 1977:759–65.

17. Seeman, 1972; J. Milton Yinger, 1973.

18. Graham and Gurr, 1969.

19. Coleman, 1971:97–98.

20. The nature and extent of contact are among the most important situational influences. See, e.g., Allport, 1954: chap. 16; Pettigrew, 1969; Williams, Dean, and Suchman, 1964: chap. 7; Robin M. Williams, 1977:264–80; Simpson and Yinger, 1985:390–97; Amir, 1969; Miller and Brewer, 1984.

21. Wispe, 1972, 1991; Oliner and Oliner, 1988; Hinde and Groebel, 1992.

22. See Etzioni, 1988; Campbell, 1975; Myrdal, 1944; Lernoux, 1982; Levine, 1981; Wuthnow, 1991; Piliavin and Hong-wen Charng, 1990.

23. Rosenberg, 1979; Louden, 1981; Jaynes and Williams, 1989, Chap. 4.

24. Coles, 1967.

25. Genovese, 1974; Gutman, 1976; Patterson, 1982; Stampp, 1965.

26. Srinivas, 1966; Schermerhorn, 1978; Beteille, 1965, 1991.

27. Naipaul, 1991.

28. Danigelis, 1977:41.

29. Geertz, 1962.

30. Light, 1977.

31. For background discussions, see Davidson, 1991; Pakenham, 1991; Brown, 1966; Carter, 1980; Kuper and Smith, 1971; van den Berghe, 1978; Dubow, 1989.

32. *Washington Post National Weekly*, July 27, 1987:16. Items along the way on this topic: Wilhelm Verwoerd, grandson of Hendrik Verwoerd, architect of apartheid, has joined the African National Conference, seeking to help bring blacks and whites together. A few young Afrikaners are defying the call to military service—a strong declaration that they seek a multiethnic South Africa. See the London *Observer*, July 25, 1992; Cleveland *Plain Dealer*, Sept. 6, 1992.

33. *The New York Times*, Aug. 3, 1986:1.

34. Horowitz, 1985a:22; see also Adam and Moodley, 1986.

35. *The New York Times*, Spring Survey of Education, April 26, 1981. We should note that this was written more than a decade ago.

36. Sparks, 1990, 376.

36. Horowitz, 1991, 234.

37. Horowitz, 1991, 234.

38. Sparks, 1990, 153–161; Moodie, 1974.

39. Leonard Thompson, 1985.

40. *The New York Times*, Nov. 10, 1985, 12; *Cleveland Plain Dealer*, Nov. 7, 1990, 3–A.

41. *Christian Science Monitor*, Nov. 13, 1990, p. 6. See Prozesky, 1990.

42. Sparks, 1990, 278–297; Takatso Mofokeng in Prozesky, 1990, chap. 3.

43. J. Milton Yinger, 1970, chaps. 21–22.

44. *Christian Science Monitor*, Oct. 15, 1990, 4.

45. *The New York Times*, June 6, 1991, 13.

46. *The New York Times*, June 23, 1991, E–3.

47. St. Petersburg *Times*, March 19, 1992:1; Associated Press, Nov. 11, 1992.

48. van den Berghe, 1965:511.

49. Adam and Giliomee, 1979:25–32.

50. For a range of interpretations of the goals and strategies of black South Africans, see Frederikse, 1990; Pogrund, 1991; Kuper, 1957 and 1974:255–74; Sparks, 1990:233–77; Horowitz, 1991; Mallaby, 1992.

51. Associated Press, Nov. 26, 1992; *The New York Times*, Nov. 20, 1992:1.

52. Sparks, 1990:314.

53. See Associated Press release, Jan. 2, 1993; *The New York Times*, Dec. 20, 1992; Dec. 19, 1992; June 22, 1991; Feb. 10, 1991.

54. From a trenchant review of Scott, 1990, by Bob Scribner, AJS, vol. 97/3 (Nov., 1991): 861–62.

55. See Starr, 1990; Scott, 1990.

56. There is a substantial literature on ethnic mobilization. See, e.g., Adam and Giliomee, 1979; Burstein, 1991; Coleman, 1971; Gamson, 1975; Gamson, Fireman, and Rytina, 1982; Genovese, 1974; Kriesberg, 1979; Leifer, 1981; McCarthy and Zald, 1977; Olzak, 1983; Srinivas, 1969; Tilly, 1978; Zald and McCarthy, 1979.

57. Laumann and Pappi, 1976.

58. Jackson, 1976:13.

59. See Geschwender, 1978.

60. Faustinine C. Jones, 1981.

61. McCarthy and Zald, 1977.

62. Coleman, 1971, 1.

63. Simpson and Yinger, 1985:416; see also Coleman, 1987; Bruce Fireman and William Gamson in Zald and McCarthy, 1979:15–18.

64. Simpson and Yinger, 1985, 417.

65. *The New York Times*, Sept. 3, 1991, A18.

66. As a sample, see Osgood, 1962; Deutsch, 1973; Boyle and Lawler, 1991; Katz, 1991; Barash, 1991; and the many valuable articles in the *Journal of Conflict Resolution*.

67. Shepard, 1969, 1.

68. For discussions of the impact of forestry, mining, agricultural, and industrial practices on ethnic minorities, see *Cultural Survival Quarterly*, e.g., Vol. 6, no 1 and 2; Vol. 5, no 3 (1981 and 1982); see also Bullard, 1992; Commission For Race and Justice, 1987; Čapek, 1993.

69. See Catton, 1980.

70. O'Hare et al., 1991.

71. Quoted in *Washington Post National Weekly,* Sept. 2–8, 1991, p. 37.

72. Clifford Krauss in *The New York Times,* May 5, 1991, E–4. On the opportunities and problems in Namibia and Ethiopia, see Campbell (chap. 5) and Ottoway (chap. 6) in Katz, 1991.

73. See Dillingham, 1981; Moore, 1981; Pettigrew, 1981.

74. Lieberson, 1980.

CHAPTER 6

1. Quoted in Hofstadter, 1959:51.

2. Cooley, 1909:53.

3. Weber, 1946: chap. 7.

4. Myrdal, 1944:lxxii.

5. Gans, 1988; Lucas, 1985; Rieder, 1985.

6. Williams, 1970:452–500.

7. Rokeach, 1973:64; see also Lipset, 1990; Stoetzel, 1983.

8. Karklins, 1986; Lapidus, 1989; Lenski, 1978; Zaslavskaya, 1990.

9. Zaslavskaya, 1990.

10. *New York Times,* March 11, 1973:E–15.

11. Stinchcombe, 1968:122.

12. Mill, 1937:201. In a compelling argument, Patterson traces the origin of the great emphasis on the value of freedom in the modern West to a kind of dialectic by which "the very idea and valuation of freedom was generated by the existence and growth of slavery." (Patterson, 1991:xiv).

13. Berlin, 1969:162–63.

14. *Ibid.:* 163.

15. See Mill, 1937: chap. 1.

16. See Mount, 1981; Waters, 1990: chap. 7; Lukes, 1973; Bellah et al, 1985; Selznick, 1992.

17. See Foner, 1990.

18. Tawney, 1931:147.

19. Laski, 1948:406.

20. *Ibid.*, 1948:718.

21. Quoted by Schumacher, 1973:32; see also Kahn, Brown, and Martel, 1976.

22. J. Milton Yinger, 1982:219. See Commoner, 1971; Schumacher, 1973; Stavrianos, 1976; Roszak, 1978; Catton, 1980.

23. Lasch, 1991.

24. Those effects, however, may become even greater. Blau and Blau (1982) have shown decisively, for example, that levels of criminal violence are not significantly associated with poverty. It is economic inequality between races, the experience of *relative* disadvantage that raises levels of criminal violence.

25. Quoted by Cooper, 1991.

26. McWilliams, in *The Idea of Fraternity in America*, 1973.

27. Markham, 1927:265.

28. Dostoyevsky, *The Brothers Karamazov*, Part II, Book VI, Chap. 2, 1950.

29. Reich, 1991a, 1991b.

30. Reich, 1991b:42–43.

31. Ladd and J. Yinger, 1989.

32. In addition to Reich, 1991a and Ladd and Yinger, 1989, see William J. Wilson, 1987 and 1989; Phillips, 1990; Ellwod, 1989; Lemann, 1991.

33. Dahrendorf, 1990.

34. Michnik, 1990:7.

35. *Ibid.*, 1990:7; see also Graubard, 1990.

36. We would be wise, I believe, to keep steadily in mind Michnik's final paragraph: "Just as France showed two faces during the Dreyfus trial, two faces are now being shown in Eastern and Central Europe. Even then, however, the forces of good and evil were not neatly divided along the lines separating leftist republicans and rightist national conservatives. It is never that simple. For that reason we must always be prepared to understand and acknowledge the values of our opponents, even those we are fighting

against. Only then are we truly Europeans." Or, we can add, only then are we truly human. See also Glenny, 1993.

37. Sinyavsky, 1990:239.

38. Frank, 1991:43. For valuable discussions of the tension between individualism and "corporate" identities more generally (not simply with reference to ethnicity), see Etzioni, 1988; Capps and Fenn, 1992; Fenn and Capps, 1992.

39. Kluegel and Smith, 1983; see also Carter, 1991.

40. See Fried, 1991; Richard A. Epstein, 1992. For a variety of views on affirmative action see also Orlans and O'Neill, 1992; Rosenfeld, 1991.

41. Tawney, 1931:128.

42. Lim, 1985:250.

43. See Lynch, 1969; Corbridge, 1989.

44. Wills, 1991:16; see also Ezorsky, 1991; Coontz, 1992: chap. 4.

45. See Turner et al., 1991.

46. Cross et al., 1990.

47. John Yinger, 1991:xii; see also 1993.

48. Dovidio and Gaertner, 1981; see also Ashmore and DelBoca, 1976.

49. Joleen Kirschenman and Kathryn M. Neckerman in Jencks and Peterson, 1991:221.

50. See, e.g., Schuman, Steeh, and Bobo, 1985; Steeh and Schuman, 1992; Jaynes and Williams, 1989: chap. 3.

51. Tom Smith, 1990.

52. Dovidio and Gaertner, 1981:200.

53. *New York Times*, April 29, 1991:E–5.

54. Griswold, 1979:57–58.

55. *Ibid.:* 57.

56. *New York Times*, May 3, 1981:15.

57. U.S. Department of Health and Human Services, 1980.

58. Bundy, 1978:16.

59. *Washington Post National Weekly,* May 27–June 2, 1991:33; *The New York Times,* May 19, 1991:E–5.

60. *Washington Post National Weekly,* July 8–14, 1991:29 (Italics mine.)

61. Edsall, 1991:7.

62. *Ibid.*

63. Kenworthy and Edsall, 1991:14.

64. *Ibid.*

65. Steele, 1990:116.

66. Julian Bond, *The New York Times,* 6–24–90:E–21.

67. Schlonio Katz, 1967, 74.

68. Simpson and Yinger, 1985, 132.

69. Glazer, 1983:216. See also Glazer in Phyllis Katz and Taylor, 1988:329–39.

70. Feinberg, 1984.

71. Lieberson and Fuguitt, 1977.

72. See Dworkin, 1991.

73. *Ibid.:* 26.

74. *Wards Cove Packing Co. v. Alioto,* 1989; *City of Richmond v. Croson, 1989.*

75. For a defense of this reversal, see Fried, 1991.

76. deVries and Pettigrew, 1993 (pagination from ms.). See also Pettigrew and Martin, 1987; Shadid, 1991.

77. Carl Hoffman, 1985.

78. The correlation, however, is high. *In re* the black-white contrast in the United States, see Hacker, 1992; Jaynes and Williams, 1989: chap. 6; Blauner, 1989; Massey and Denton, 1993.

79. United States Dept. of Commerce, Bureau of the Census, 1990:5. On the complex issues related to the definition and measurement of poverty, see p. 15. See also Danziger and Gottschalk, 1993.

80. U.S. Dept of Commerce, Bureau of the Census, 1990. Quintile comparisons vary somewhat, depending on whether or not they refer to pre-tax and pre-transfer incomes. Tax rates and such transfers as food stamps reduce the contrasts somewhat.

81. *Ibid.*, pp. 8–9.

82. *Harper's Index*, Jan., 1991.

83. General Social Survey *News*, Sept., 1991.

84. National Opinion Research Center, 1989.

85. Adapted from *The New York Times*, Sept. 1, 1991, 2E.

86. Hedrick Smith, 1990:310.

87. *Ibid.*

88. See Boulding, 1962; see also Alves and Rossi, 1978; Rawls, 1971; Bell and Robinson, 1978; Coleman, 1974; Hochschild, 1981.

89. Alves and Rossi, 1978.

90. See Oscar Lewis, 1959, 1961, 1966a, 1966b.

91. Oscar Lewis, 1966b:19.

92. Banfield, 1958, 1968.

93. See Simpson and Yinger, 1985: chap. 6.

94. Allison Davis and Havighurst, 1947; Sutherland, 1942.

95. Michael Lewis, 1978; Charles Valentine, 1968; Waxman, 1977; Abell and Lyon, 1979.

96. William Ryan, 1971; Rodman, 1963; Liebow, 1967; Coward, Feagin, and Williams, 1974; Della Fave, 1974a; Suttles, 1968; BettyLou Valentine, 1978; Roach and Gursslin, 1967; Sanders, 1990.

97. Walter Miller, 1958:18.

98. Liebow, 1967:221.

99. Rainwater, 1970:142–43; see also Graves, 1974.

100. Kershaw and Fair, 1976; Watts and Rees, 1977a, 1977b; Haveman, 1977; Covello, 1980.

101. Hill and Ponza, 1983.

102. Lenski, 1978.

103. Hedrick Smith, 1990:185.

104. Gans, 1962.

105. Bottomore in Foreword to Bourdieu and Passeron, 1990:xvii.

106. *Ibid*, 1990:ix.

107. Oakes, 1985; Ogbu, 1978.

108. Michael Lewis, 1978.

109. One should not forget that the largest number, although not the largest percentage, are white. This has long been true. See Jaqueline Jones, 1992.

110. Myrdal, 1962:34; see also Rainwater, 1969; Glasgow, 1980; Michael Katz, 1993.

111. Van Haitsma, 1989:28.

112. Wilson, 1987:8.

113. Tienda, 1989:105.

114. Wacquant and Wilson, in Wilson, 1989:15.

115. Lawrence Mead, in William J. Wilson, 1989:156.

116. Murray, 1984.

117. Joel Kotkin in the *Washington Post National Weekly*, Sept. 23–29, 1991:23–24.

118. Vesperi, St. Petersburg, FL *Times*, Feb. 17, 1991, 1, 5.

119. Ricketts and Sawhill, 1988; Mincy, Sawhill, and Wolf, 1990; Van Haitsma, 1989.

120. For a diversity of views, see William Wilson, 1987, 1991, 1989; Prosser, 1991; Jencks and Peterson, 1991; Jencks, 1991; Auletta, 1982; Field, 1989; Kasarda, 1989; Phillips, 1990; Lemann, 1991; Murray, 1984; Danziger, 1989; Kuttner, 1991; Danziger and Gottschalk, 1987; Coombes and Hubbuck, 1992; Carole Marks, 1991; O'Hare, 1991; Rex, 1988; Westergaard, 1992; Massey and Denton, 1993; Duster, 1988; Michael Katz, 1993.

121. Prosser, 1991:3.

122. Adapted from Prosser, 1991:4.

123. Turner, Struyk, and Yinger, 1991; Turner, Fix, and Struyk, 1991; John Yinger, 1986; Massey, 1990.

124. Kasarda, 1989:27; see also Lieberson, 1980.

125. Adapted from Kasarda, 1989:29. Data from the U.S. Dept. of Commerce, Bureau of the Census.

126. *Ibid.:* 41.

127. Massey and Denton, 1993:146; see especially chaps. 4 and 5. See also Galster, and Keeney, 1988; Galster, 1991.

128. See Blau and Duncan, 1967, esp. chap. 5; Duncan, 1968.

129. J. Milton Yinger, 1965b.

130. Lorenz, 1960; Ardrey, 1966; Desmond Morris, 1967; E. O. Wilson, 1975.

131. Montagu, 1975; Caplan, 1978; Sahlins, 1976; Berkowitz, 1962; Tinbergen, 1969; Trivers, 1971; Mazur and Robertson, 1972; Durkheim, 1973; Barkow, 1978.

132. Freud, 1962:61.

133. Spitz, 1965; Harry Sullivan, 1953.

134. Dower, 1986.

135. Volkan, 1988:100; see also DeMause, 1991.

136. See e.g., Bryan and London, 1970; Krebs, 1970; Staub, 1972; Macauley and Berkowitz, 1970; Mussen and Nancy Eisenberg-Berg, 1977; Wispe, 1991, 1972; Campbell, 1975.

137. Kelman, 1973.

138. Mack, 1983, 1984.

139. Kluckhohn, 1944.

140. Kai Erikson, 1966.

141. *New York Times Book Review,* Feb. 2, 1982, p. 8.

142. Perlmutter, 1989–90, 132. I discuss this topic more fully in Chapter 7.

143. Kai Erikson, 1966, 22. See also Bergesen, 1977.

144. J. Milton Yinger, 1982, 244.

145. Brumberg, 1991.

146. *The New York Times,* April 20, 1992, A–8.

147. Hamilton, 1981.

148. Boulding, *New Republic*, Oct. 7, 1967, p. 7.

CHAPTER 7

1. J. Milton Yinger, 1957:15–16.

2. See J. Milton Yinger, 1970:3–16.

3. Simmel, 1905:360.

4. Niebuhr in Cutler, 1968:x; see also Erik Erikson, 1968; Spiro, 1987, 177–178; J. Milton Yinger, 1970: chap. 3.

5. Freud, 1928.

6. See Marx, 1935; Feuerbach, 1957.

7. Gramsci, 1971.

8. Durkheim, 1947:387.

9. Fortes, 1959:29–30.

10. See Adriance, 1991; Lernoux, 1982; Navarro, 1991; Christian Smith, 1991; Candeleria, 1990; Martin, 1990.

11. See, e.g., Hultkrantz, 1979; Powers, 1977; Wallace, 1970.

12. See Aberle, 1982; Bowden, 1981; Hazel Hertzberg, 1971.

13. Bowden, 1981.

14. Deloria, 1973:66, 260, 300–301.

15. The following several paragraphs have been adapted from J. Milton Yinger, 1970:319–324.

16. Howells, 1948, 270; see also Mooney, 1965; Aberle, 1959; Wallace, 1956; Thornton, 1981; Hultkrantz, 1979; Neihardt, 1979; Underhill, 1965; LaBarre, 1972, Nabokov, 1991.

17. Howells, 1948:270.

18. Lesser, 1933:112.

19. Mooney, 1965:1.

20. Martin Marty, *Saturday Review*, May, 1980.

21. *The New York Times*, May 14, 1989: p. 1.

22. Lieberson and Waters, 1988:13–14.

23. Simpson and Yinger, 1985:318.

24. Powdermaker, 1943.

25. Simpson, 1978:219–21; chaps. 7 and 8.

26. Raboteau, 1978.

27. Genovese, 1970, 34–35; see also Harding, 1969; Wilmore, 1973; Lincoln and Mamiya, 1990; Baer, 1988; Baer and Singer, 1988.

28. DuBois, 1903; Frazier, 1963; Johnson, 1941; Lincoln and Mamiya, 1990.

29. See King, 1958; 1963; 1968, see also Jacobson, 1992.

30. Cone, 1970; see also Cleague, 1968; Lincoln, 1974, 135–52.

31. Roberts, 1974, 47.

32. The next few paragraphs are based on "Black Americans in Predominantly White Churches," a memorandum I prepared (1987) for the National Research Council of the National Science Foundation. The NRC bears no responsibility for my interpretations. Most of the data have been obtained from research departments of the national offices of American churches and from the G.S.S.

33. Lincoln, 1961; Essien-Udom, 1962.

34. Simpson and Yinger, 1985, 321; see also Malcolm X, 1966; Goldman, 1979.

35. Muhammad, 1980; Mamiya, 1982; Whitehurst, 1980.

36. Mamiya, 1982, 139.

37. *Ibid.*, 1982. It should be noted, however, that only a small proportion of Black Muslims are followers of Farrakhan.

38. *Cleveland Plain Dealer*, Nov. 15, 1978, A27.

39. Bromley, 1988; Hoge, 1981; Crippen, 1988; Hadaway and Roof, in Bromley, 1988, 29–46; Babchuk and Whitt, 1990; Sandormirsky and Wilson, 1990; Heirich, 1977; Snow and Machalek, 1980; Turner, 1979.

40. Sandormirsky and Wilson, 1990, 1213.

41. See Kenneth Jones, 1978; Heirich, 1977; Sherkat and Ellison, 1991.

42. Weber, 1946, 14.

43. Partner, 1990, 25; see also Esman and Rabinovich, 1988; Hourani, 1991; Glass, 1990; Kedourie and Haim, 1982; Razi, 1990; Miller, 1993; Arjomand, 1984.

44. See Partner, 1990.

45. One thinks of a story told by James Zogby, president of the Arab-American Institute. As leader of the political-action group for Arab Americans, he was having difficulty, although a Democrat, making contact with candidate Bill Clinton's campaign. So Zogby called Senator Lieberman, an Orthodox Jew, who arranged a contact for him with George Stephanopoulos, Clinton's communication director, through whom he secured a meeting with Clinton, to everyone's satisfaction. As reported by David Broder: "Zogby made the obvious point: 'Only in America would an Arab-American spokesman call a Jewish-American senator to call a Greek Orthodox campaign operative to let us help a Southern Baptist get elected President.' " *Cleveland Plain Dealer*, Dec. 13, 1992:D–3.

46. *Nation*, July 1, 1991:7.

47. See Wood, 1990; Lewis, 1990; Hodgson, 1974.

48. Davis, 1990, 36.

49. Lewis, 1990.

50. See Tillich, 1963.

51. *St. Petersburg Times*, Feb. 2, 1992, 3–E.

52. These headlines appeared in a seven-month period in *The New York Times*, July 28, 1991 to February 22, 1992.

53. See O'Brien, 1988; Hickey, 1984; See, 1986.

54. *The New York Times*, Jan. 7, 1993:A–6; April 14, 1993:A1.

55. See Desmond, 1992; Srinivasan, 1989; Malik and Vajpeyi, 1989; Brass, 1991; Béteille, 1991.

56. Sen, 1993:26.

57. See Silva et al, 1988; Sabaratnam, 1987; McGowan, 1991; Tambiah, 1986.

58. These headlines are from *The New York Times*.

59. Suny, 1990, 241.

60. *Ibid.*, 237.

61. Shafir, 1990.

62. See, e.g., Yishai, 1984; Yogev, 1987; Peled, 1990.

63. *USA Today*, Dec. 27, 1990.

64. Margalit, 1991:20.

65. *Ibid.:* 22.

66. *Washington Post National Weekly*, Feb. 4–10, 1991, 19.

67. *The New York Times*, March 1, 1992, 6.

68. Arthur Hertzberg, 1990, 47; see also Razi, 1990; Grossman, 1992.

69. Elon, 1988, 101; see also Grossman, 1988; Kimmerling and Migdal, 1993; Hilterman, 1991; Hunter, 1991.

70. Associated Press, Cleveland *Plain Dealer*, Dec. 20, 1992:4–A.

71. On the PLO see Wallach and Wallach, 1990; see also MacLeod, 1989 and 1991.

72. Tom Smith, 1991:57.

73. See Arthur Hertzberg, 1992:20.

74. Quoted in the *Washington Post National Weekly*, Oct. 7–13, 1991:24. The 100,000 or more Jewish settlers on the West Bank are among the strongest—indeed zealous—supporters of this view. They are not all of one mind, however. Some are primarily religious in orientation, some are Jewish nationalists, and others are profiteers. See Friedman, 1992.

75. Eban, 1992.

76. Amos Elon in the *New York Review of Books*, Aug. 17, 1989:38. See also Yiftachel, 1992; Smooha, 1990; Grossman, 1992.

77. From letters in the *New York Review of Books*, March 2, 1992, 57–58.

78. In addition to references already cited on the Israeli-Palestinian conflict, see Romann and Weingrod, 1991; Heller and Nusseibeh, 1991; Aronson, 1990; McDowall, 1990; Kimmerling, 1989; Esman and Rabinovitch, 1988; Semyonov and Lewin-Epstein, 1987; Benny Morris, 1987; Shipler, 1986; Smooha, 1987; Dawisha, 1986; Ben-Raphael and Sharot, 1991. For discussions of the Arab-Israeli conflict a generation ago, see Den-Dak and Azar, 1972.

79. Kimmerling and Migdal, 1993:280; see also Melman, 1992.

80. Gottlieb, 1989:110.

81. *Ibid.:* 117.

82. Hartman, 1990; see also Sprinzak, 1992; Lustick, 1980; Ruether and Ruether, 1989.

83. Hertzberg, 1992:20.

84. Frankel, 1992:12, quoting Jonathan Kuttab, an Israeli liberal.

85. Frankel, 1992:10.

86. See Gottlieb, 1989.

87. Lewis, 1992:52.

88. *Ibid.:* 52.

89. *Ibid.:* 52.

CHAPTER 8

1. See Edwards, 1984; Fishman, 1989; Grimshaw, 1981; Lieberson, 1981; Christina Paulston in Cazden and Snow, 1990, 38–47; Maynard *et al*, 1991. Roger Sanjek in Casson, 1981:305–28.

2. Anderson and Silver, 1990:95–127; Lapierre, 1988:218.

3. See LaPierre, 1988: chaps. 2–5.

4. Eugen Weber, 1976; Dignan, 1981.

5. See *NYT,* May 3, 1993:1, 6.

6. Levinson, 1992:551.

7. See Tove Skutnabb-Kangas in Edwards, 1984:17–48.

8. Bourdieu and Passeron, 1990.

9. Heath, 1985:259.

10. MacKaye, 1990:145.

11. Dimitrova, 1992:18; see also Herman, 1992.

12. See Chick, 1985.

13. See Kuper, 1982; Dadrian, 1975.

14. See Kuper, 1989.

15. See Gumperz, 1983.

16. Fasold, 1987:3.

17. Labov, 1987:6.

18. *Ibid.:* 6.

19. See *American Speech: A Quarterly of Linguistic Usage*, Spring, 1987, edited by Ralph Fasold, for the papers on "Are Black and White Vernaculars Diverging" by William Labov, Fay Boyd Vaughn-Cooke, Guy Bailey, Arthur Spears, and others. See also Labov, 1972; Kochman, 1972; Abrahams and Szwed, 1975; J. L. Dillard, 1972; Orr, 1987; Baugh, 1983; Hewitt, 1986 (on black and white speech in England); and Abrahams, 1972.

20. See Orr, whose book is aptly titled *Twice as Less*, 1987.

21. In Fasold, 1987:55; see also Hacker, 1992; Terkel, 1992; Jaynes and Williams, 1989: chap. 6.

22. William Labov, quoted in the *Washington Post National Weekly*, May 6, 1985:10.

23. See Ogbu, 1978; Adams, 1977; Babcock, 1978; Halliday, 1976; J. Milton Yinger, 1982, chap. 7.

24. The following few paragraphs have been adapted from J. Milton Yinger, 1982:161–64.

25. Labov, 1972.

26. Halliday, 1976:575.

27. Labov, 1972:324.

28. Quoted by Connor, 1985:283.

29. Fishman, 1985: chap. 7; Fishman, 1980.

30. Fishman, 1985:346–357.

31. Heath, 1985:261; Elías-Olivares et al, 1985; see also *Cleveland Plain Dealer*, Dec. 17, 1992:103.

32. See, e.g., Das Gupta, 1970; Nayar, 1969; Sanjek, 1977; Rubin and Jernudd, 1971; Gumperz, 1971; Barbara Anderson and Brian Silver in Hajda and Beigsinger, 1990, 95–127; Swietochowski, 1991; Woolard, 1989; Edwards, 1984; Edwards and Shearn, 1987; McRae, 1984, 1986; Wardhaugh, 1983; Lieberson, 1981; Gareth Jones, 1983; LaPierre, 1988.

33. See Calderon, 1990; Ramirez and Castaneda, 1974; Hornby, 1977.

34. See Hornberger, 1990; Fishman, 1985: chap. 11; Romaine, 1989; Miller, 1983.

35. Cazden and Snow, 1990:9.

36. Hornberger, 1990:24.

37. Several paragraphs in this section have been adapted from J. Milton Yinger, 1986a.

38. See Heath, 1985; Burke, 1981.

39. Hornberger, 1990:15. Considering the speed with which English has become the language of choice for newcomers to America, I find it difficult to see any need for an "official language" for the country. Such a declaration would be unlikely to speed the shift to English. It would be offensive to many—as the state laws have been. And the campaign to bring it about is likely to continue to misdirect the energies of its supporters and its opponents away from important questions: How can we establish the most effective methods for teaching English? How can we improve the chances for knowledge of other languages, among native English speakers as well as among those learning English as a second language?

40. Nunis, 1981:29.

41. See Judd, 1987; Madrid, 1990; Donahue, 1985; Imhoff, 1990.

42. See Porter, 1990; Chavez, 1991.

43. Imhoff, 1990:61.

44. Pettigrew, Dec. 1992 (personal correspondence).

45. Raul Yzaguirre, quoted by Bernstein, 1990a:48; see also Y. R. Solé, 1990.

46. United States Supreme Court in *Lau v. Nichols;* cited in Hornberger, 1990:18.

47. This is illustrated in a report of the Conference on the Teaching of English in London Elementary Schools, issued by the London County Council, 1909. "The Cockney mode of speech, with its unpleasant twang, is a modern corruption without legitimate credentials, and is unworthy of being the speech of any person in the capital city of the Empire." (Quoted by Matthews, 1938:157.)

48. See Basil Bernstein, 1966:1971–75; Atkinson, 1986.

49. See Labov, 1972; Gumperz, 1971: chap. 17.

50. Quoted by Newell, 1981:27.

51. *Ibid.*, 29.

52. Quoted by Newell, *Ibid.*: 28.

53. See Lopez, 1976; Cafferty, 1982.

54. For reviews of research on bilingual education see Walter Secada and Frederick Mulhauser in Cazden and Snow, 1990:81–106, 107–118; Lopez, 1983.55. Imhoff, 1990:48; see also Crawford, 1992a and 1992b.

56. Fishman, 1985:445; see also Baron, 1990.

57. See Alexander, Cook, and McDill, 1978; Frederick Erickson, 1975; Shavit, 1984; McDermott, 1977; Rist, 1970; Rosenbaum, 1976.

58. Cazden and Snow, 1990, 11.

59. Veltman, 1990a, 1990b; see also Stevens, 1992.

60. Heath, 1985:259; see also Lieberson, Dalto, and Johnston, 1975.

CHAPTER 9

1. See Berlin 1991, who has chosen part of this sentence for the title of his book on the history of ideas: *The Crooked Timber of Mankind.* The translation is Berlin's.

2. O'Brien, 1991:54.

3. Eiseley, 1957:52–53.

4. J. Milton Yinger, 1982:289.

5. *Economist*, March 30, 1992:12.

6. See Bourne's discussion, 1920:266–298; see also Thomas and Znaniecki, 1927, 2 vols. (1918–21, 5 vols.). For the story of the millions who have crossed the Pacific, not the Atlantic, see Takaki, 1989.

7. See Fukuyama, 1992.

8. Fukuyama, 1992:xi; See also Alan Ryan, Nov. 19, 1992. Although I will not examine the issue, I call attention to the fact that 150 years before Fukuyama, Karl Marx also pronounced the end of history, but his utopian road led in a very different direction. The history of all previous societies, he declared, has been the history of class struggles—struggles that at the

end of history would lead to the classless society. The Soviet Union and other societies picked up this theme—ideologically—, but they were soon saying that intermediate stages were inevitable. They could well have used Fukuyama's phrase that there were problems of "incomplete implementation."

Through the years many writers have examined Marx's ideology closely and have modified and challenged it in various ways. Still today, however, about one-quarter of the world's population live under rulers who embrace the Marxist utopian "end of history"—although much more in dogma than in practice.

For a variety of views see Marx, 1956; Gramsci, 1971; Lukacs, 1971; Horkheimer, 1972; Sinyavsky, 1990: chap. 2.

9. Hedrick Smith on PBS, Feb. 2, 1992. For a cogent analysis of markets—their strengths and their limits, see Lane, 1991; see also Stark, 1992.

10. Ryan, 1992, 7.

11. Naipaul, 1991a, 25.

12. Berlin, 1991, 245.

13. Gardels, 1991, 19. A year after Gardels wrote, Bosnia would have been cited as well.

14. See Berlin, 1991.

15. *Economist*, Dec. 14, 1991, 14.

16. Frankel, 1990, 16.

17. Vaclav Havel in *New York Review of Books*, Dec. 5, 1991, 49.

18. Darras, 1990, 14, 20.

19. Schlesinger, 1992, 134, 138.

20. Isaiah Berlin in Gardels, 1991, 21.

21. J. Milton Yinger, 1965a:xi. Tilly (1990) has skillfully examined the way in which, even as states have become the almost universal structures of political power, they are wedged between interstate organizations and sub-state loyalties. To blend these three levels of organization may be the central task of the twenty-first century.

22. See Novak, 1971; Gambino, 1975.

23. Merton, 1972.

24. The design of the figure suggests that the earlier and larger gains are likely to be in sectors II and III. Knowledge that already exists can be

shared in interaction among insiders and outsiders. That interaction can be the source of new knowledge, expanding sector IV.

25. See, e.g., Gans, 1979; Pettigrew, 1978; Fishman, 1985; Yancey, Ericksen, and Juliani, 1976; Okamura, 1981; Galaty, 1982.

26. J. Milton Yinger, 1962–63:398.

27. Milosz in DeVos and Romanucci-Ross, 1975:352. Since that was written Milosz seems to have shifted toward a more supportive view of national independence movements. See Milosz, 1991.

28. Devereux in DeVos and Romanucci-Ross, 1975:67–68.

29. Arnold, 1907, 321.

30. Winston Churchill, quoted by DeSchweinitz, 1943, 7–8.

31. See Marshall, 1960; Bendix, 1964; Barbalet, 1988; Dahrendorf, 1988; Maxim Silverman, 1991.

32. Seligman, 1992:162.

33. Said, 1993:228–29.

34. See Weber, 1946:129–56. Permit me a speculative aside on this issue. To say that science cannot tell us how to live is not to say that scientists lack values. A kind of universalism, egalitarianism, support for free inquiry and, particularly, the value of the pursuit of verifiable truth come readily to scientists as part of their ethos. (See Merton, 1968: chap. 12; for a discussion of some of the opposition to that ethos, see Yinger, 1982:96–113). Nor is acceptance of the "indisputable truth" of Tolstoy's statement to suggest, as he and many others have done, that artists, humanists, and theologians have some special claim to be the source and the protector of values. It is only to say that even a verified truth is no guarantee that something of value, beyond its intrinsic worth, will follow. In my view, an open contest among persons of different points of view, different conceptions of the road to truth, is likely to be of greatest benefit to humanity as we pursue our continuing—indeed our permanent—effort to answer Tolstoy's question: What shall we do and how shall we live? *Truth* and *Value* may be beyond our reach; but truths and values approaching universal acceptance may emerge from manifold efforts.

BIBLIOGRAPHY

Please note the following abbreviations for journal titles:

AA   *American Anthropologist*
AE   *American Ethnologist*
AER   *American Economic Review*
AJS   *American Journal of Sociology*
Annals *Annals of The American Academy of Political and Social Science*
ARS   *Annual Review of Sociology*
ASR   *American Sociological Review*
DEM   *Demography*
ERS   *Ethnic And Racial Studies*
IRS   *International Migration Review*
JSI   *Journal of Social Issues*
JSSR   *Journal For the Scientific Study of Religion*
NYRB   *New York Review of Books*
NYT   *New York Times*
RRR   *Review of Religious Research*
SF   *Social Forces*

Abell, Troy and Larry Lyon. "Do the differences make a difference? An empirical evaluation of the culture of poverty in the United States." AE 6 (Aug. 1979): 602–20.

Aberle, David. *The Peyote Religion among the Navaho.* Chicago: Univ. of Chicago Press, 1982.

———. "The prophet dance and reactions to white contact." *Southwestern Journal of Anthropology* 15 (1959): 74–83.

Abrahams, Roger D. *Language and Cultural Diversity in American Education.* Englewood Cliffs, NJ: Prentice-Hall, 1972.

———and John F. Szwed. "Black English: An essay review." *AA*, 77 (June, 1975): 329–35.

Ackerman, Nathan W. and Marie Jahoda: *Anti-Semitism and Emotional Disorder: A Psychoanalytic Interpretation*. NY: Harper and Row, 1950.

Adam, Barry D. "Inferiorization and 'self-esteem.' " *Social Psychology* 41 (March, 1978): 47–53.

Adam, Heribert. "Racist capitalism versus capitalist non-racialism in South Africa." *ERS* 7 (April, 1984): 268–82.

———and Hermann Giliomee. *Ethnic Power Mobilized: Can South Africa Change?* New Haven, CN: Yale Univ. Press, 1979.

———and Kogila Moodley. *South Africa Without Apartheid: Dismantling Racial Domination*. Berkeley: Univ. of California Press, 1986.

Adams, Robert M. *Bad Mouth: Fugitive Papers on The Dark Side*. Berkeley: Univ. of California Press, 1977.

Adams, Romanzo. *Interracial Marriage in Hawaii: A Study of The Mutually Conditioned Processes of Acculturation and Amalgamation*. NY: Macmillan, 1937.

Adorno, T. W., Else Frenkel-Brunswik, D. J. Levinson, and R. N. Sanford. *The Authoritarian Personality*. NY: Harper and Row, 1950.

Adriance, Madeleine. "Agents of change: The role of priests, sisters, and lay workers in the grassroots Catholic church in Brazil." *JSSR* 30 (Sept., 1991): 292–305.

Akiner, Shirin. *Islamic Peoples of The Soviet Union*, rev. ed. London: KPI, 1986.

Alba, Richard. *Ethnic Identity: The Transformation of White America*. New Haven: Yale Univ. Press, 1990.

———, ed. *Ethnicity and Race in The U.S.A.: Toward The Twenty-First Century*. London: Routledge and Kegan Paul, 1985.

———. *Italian Americans: Into the Twilight of Ethnicity*. Englewood Cliffs, NJ: Prentice-Hall, 1985a.

———. "Social assimilation among American Catholic national-origin groups." *ASR* 41/6 (Dec., 1976): 1030–46.

———and Reid Golden. "Patterns of ethnic marriage in the United States." *SF* 65 (Sept., 1986): 202–223.

———and Ronald Kessler. "Patterns of interethnic marriage among American Catholics." *SF* 57 (June, 1979): 1124–40.

———and John Logan. "Variations on two themes: racial and ethnic patterns in the attainment of suburban residence." *DEM* 28 (Aug., 1991): 431–53.

Aldrich, Howard E. and Roger Waldinger. "Ethnicity and entrepreneurship." *ARS* 16 (1990): 111–36.

Alexander, Karl L., Martha Cook, and Edward L. McDill. "Curriculum tracking and educational stratification: some further evidence." *ASR* 43 (Feb., 1978): 47–66.

Allen, Walter R. and Reynolds Farley. "The shifting social and economic tides of black America, 1950–1980." *ARS* 12 (1986): 277–306.

Allport, Gordon. *The Nature of Prejudice.* Boston: Beacon Press, 1954.

Allport, Gordon and Leo Postman. "The basic psychology of rumor." *Transactions of The New York Academy of Sciences,* Series II, no. VIII, 1945: 61–81.

Allworth, Edward, ed. *Nationality Group Survival in Multi-Ethnic States: Shifting Support Patterns in the Soviet Baltic Region.* NY: Praeger, 1977.

Alterman, Eric. "Not so great." *Nation,* Nov. 19, 1990: 584–85.

Alves, Wayne M. and Peter H. Rossi. "Who should get what? Fairness judgments of the distribution of earnings." *AJS* 84 (Nov., 1978): 541–64.

Amersfoort, Hans van and Boudewijn Surie. "Reluctant hosts: immigration into Dutch society, 1970–1985." *ERS* 10 (April, 1987): 169–85.

Amir, Yehuda. "Contact hypothesis in ethnic relations." *Psychological Bulletin,* May, 1969: 319–42.

Anderson, Barbara A. and Brian D. Silver. "Some factors in the linguistic and ethnic russification of Soviet nationalities: Is everyone becoming Russian?" In Hajda and Beissinger, 1990: 95–127.

Anderson, Benedict. *Imagined Communities: Reflections on The Origin and Spread of Nationalism.* London: Verso, 1983.

Antonovsky, Aaron. "Toward a refinement of the 'marginal man' concept." *SF* 35 (Oct., 1956): 57–62.

Apostle, Richard A., Charles Y. Glock, Thomas Piazza, and Marijean Suelzle. *The Anatomy of Racial Attitudes.* Berkeley: Univ. of California Press, 1983.

Applegate, Celia. *A Nation of Provincials: The German Idea of Heimat.* Berkeley: Univ. of California Press, 1990.

Archdeacon, Thomas J. *Becoming American: An Ethnic History.* NY: Free Press, 1983.

Ardrey, Robert. *Territorial Imperative.* NY: Atheneum, 1966.

Arendt, Hannah. In *Essays on Antisemitism*, K. S. Pinson, ed. NY: Conference on Jewish Relations, 1946: 173–217.

Arjomand, Said Amir. ed. *From Nationalism to Revolutionary Islam.* London: Macmillan, 1984.

Armstrong, John A. *Nations Before Nationalism.* Chapel Hill: Univ. of North Carolina Press, 1982.

Arnold, Matthew. *Poetical Works.* London: Macmillan, 1907.

Aronson, Geoffrey. *Israel, Palestinians and The Intifada: Creating Facts on The West Bank*, rev. ed. London: Kegan Paul, International Institute of Policy Studies, 1990.

Ash, Timothy Garton, "Germany at the front." *NYRB*, Jan. 17, 1991: 21–22.

———. "Germany unbound." *NYRB*, Nov. 22, 1990c: 11–15.

Asher, S. R. and V. L. Allen. "Racial preference and social comparison processes." *JSI* 25 (1969): 157–66.

Ashmore, Richard D. and Frances K. DelBoca. "Psychological approaches to understanding intergroup conflict." In *Towards the Elimination of Racism*, Phylis A. Katz, ed., 1976: 73–123.

Atkinson, Paul. *Language, Structure and Reproduction: An Introduction to The Sociology of Basil Bernstein.* NY: Tavistock, 1986.

Auletta, Ken. *The Underclass.* NY: Random House, 1982.

Avineri, Shlomo. "Toward a socialist theory of nationalism." *Dissent*, Fall, 1990: 447–457.

Axtell, James. *Beyond 1492: Encounters in Colonial North America.* NY: Oxford Univ. Press, 1992.

Azrael, Jeremy, ed. *Soviet Nationality Policies and Practices.* NY: Praeger, 1978.

Babchuk, Nicholas and Hugh P. Whitt. "R-order and religious switching." *JSSR* 29 (June, 1990): 246–54.

Babcock, Barbara A., ed. *The Reversible World: Symbolic Inversion in Art and Society.* Ithaca, NY: Cornell Univ. Press, 1978.

Backman, Carl. "Attraction in interpersonal relations." In *Social Psychology: Sociological Perspectives.* Morris Rosenberg and Ralph H. Turner, eds. NY: Basic Books, 1981: 235–68.

Baer, Hans A. "Bibliography of social science literature on Afro-American religion in the United States." *RRR* 29 (June, 1988): 413–30.

Baer, Hans S. and Merrill Singer, special eds. "Black American religion in the twentieth century." *RRR* 30 (Dec., 1988).

Bagley, Christopher. "Lies, damned lies and Indian ethnicity in the Canadian census." *ERS* 11 (April, 1988): 230–33.

Bagley, Christopher and Gajendra K. Verma. *Racial Prejudice, The Individual and Society.* NY: Saxon House, 1979.

Bagley, Christopher, Gajendra K. Verma, Kanka Mallick, and Loretta Young. *Personality, Self-Esteem and Prejudice.* NY: Saxon House, 1979.

Baltzell, E. Digby. *The Protestant Establishment: Aristocracy and Caste in America.* NY: Random House, 1964.

Banfield, Edward C. *The Unheavenly City: The Nature and Future of Our Urban Crisis.* Boston: Little, Brown, 1968.

———. *The Moral Basis of a Backward Society.* Chicago: Univ. of Chicago Press, 1958.

Banton, Michael. "International action against racial discrimination: a briefing paper." *ERS* 14 (Oct., 1991): 545–56.

———. "The international defence of racial equality." *ERS* 13 (Oct. 1990): 568–83.

———. *Racial Theories.* NY: Cambridge Univ. Press, 1987.

———. *Promoting Racial Harmony.* NY: Cambridge Univ. Press, 1985.

———. *White and Coloured.* London: Alden Press, 1959.

———. *Racial and Ethnic Competition.* NY: Cambridge Univ. Press, 1983.

Barash, David P. *An Introduction to Peace Studies.* Belmont, CA: Wadsworth, 1991.

Barbalet, J. M: *Citizenship: Rights, Struggle, and Class Inequality.* Minneapolis: Univ. of Minnesota Press, 1988.

Barkow, Jerome H. "Culture and sociobiology." *AA* 80 (March, 1978): 5–20.

Baron, Dennis, *The English-Only Question: An Official Language for Americans?* New Haven, CN: Yale Univ. Press, 1990.

Barth, Fredrik. *Ethnic Groups and Boundaries.* Boston: Little, Brown, 1969.

Basham, Richard and David DeGroot. "Current approaches to the anthropology of urban and complex societies." *AA* 79 (June, 1977): 414–40.

Baugh, John. "A survey of Afro-American English." *ARS,* 1983: 335–54.

Beals, Alan R., with George and Louise Spindler. *Culture in Process.* NY: Holt, Rinehart, and Winston, 1967.

Bean, Frank D. and Gary Swicegood. *Mexican American Fertility Patterns.* Austin: Univ. of Texas Press, 1985.

———and Marta Tienda. *The Hispanic Population of The United States.* NY: Russell Sage, 1987.

Bell, Daniel. "Ethnicity and social change." In Glazer and Moynihan, 1975: 141–74.

Bell, Wendell and Robert Robinson. "An index of evaluated equality: measuring conceptions of social justice in England and the United States." *Comparative Studies in Sociology,* Vol. 1 (1978): 235–70.

Bellah, Robert N., Richard Madsen, William M. Sullivan, Ann Swidler, and Steven M. Tipton. *Habits of The Heart: Individualism and Commitment in American Life.* NY: Harper and Row, 1985.

———, *The Good Society.* NY: Knopf, 1991.

Bendix, Reinhart. *Nation Building and Citizenship: Studies of Our Changing Social Order.* NY: Wiley, 1964.

Benedict, Ruth. *Race, Science, and Politics.* Bridgeport, CT: Modern Age Books, 1940.

Ben-Rafael, Eliezer and Stephen Sharot. *Ethnicity, Religion, and Class in Israeli Society.* NY: Cambridge Univ. Press, 1991.

Benson, S. *Ambiguous Ethnicity: Interracial Families in London.* NY: Cambridge Univ. Press, 1981.

Berger, Joseph, Susan J. Rosenholtz, and Morris Zelditch, Jr. "Status organizing processes." *ARS* 6 (1980): 479–508.

———, Morris Zelditch, Jr., and Associates. *Status, Rewards, and Influence: How Expectations Organize Behavior.* San Francisco: Jossey-Bass, 1985.

Bergesen, Albert J. "Political witch hunts; the sacred and the subversive in cross-national perspective." *ASR* 42 (April, 1977): 220–33.

Berkowitz, Leonard. *Aggression: A Social Psychological Analysis.* NY: McGraw-Hill, 1962.

Berlin, Isaiah. *The Crooked Timber of Humanity: Chapters in The History of Ideas.* Henry Hardy, ed. NY: Knopf, 1991.

———. *Four Essays on Liberty.* NY: Oxford Univ. Press, 1969.

Bernstein, Basil. *Class, Codes, and Control,* 3 Vols. London: Routledge and Kegan Paul, 1971–75.

———. "Elaborated and restricted codes: their social origins and some consequences." In *The Ethnography of Speaking. AA* 66, Part 2, Dell Hymes, ed. (1966): 55–69.

Bernstein, Richard. *Fragile Glory: A Portrait of France and The French.* NY: Knopf, 1990.

———. "In U.S. schools: a war of words." *NYT MAGAZINE,* Oct. 14, 1990a): 34ff.

———. "The arts catch up with a society in disarray." *NYT,* Sept. 2, 1990b, sect. II: 1 ff.

Bertelsen, Judy A., ed. *Nonstate Nations in International Politics.* NY: Praeger, 1977.

Beteille, André. *Caste, Class and Power: Changing Patterns of Stratification in a Tanjore Village.* Berkeley: Univ. of California Press, 1965.

———. *Society and Politics in India.* London: Athlone Press, 1991.

Blackwell, James E. *The Black Community: Diversity and Unity.* NY: Harper and Row, 1975.

Blau, Judith R. and Peter M. Blau. "The cost of inequality; metropolitan structure and violent crime." ASR 47 (Feb., 1982): 114–29.

Blau, Peter. *Inequality and Heterogeneity.* NY: Free Press, 1977.

———. *Exchange and Power in Social Life.* NY: Wiley, 1964.

———, Carolyn Becker, and Kevin Fitzpatrick. "Intersecting social affiliations and intermarriage." *SF* 62 (1984): 585–606.

———, Terry C. Blum, and Joseph E. Schwartz. "Heterogeneity and intermarriage." *ASR* 47 (Feb., 1982): 45–62.

————and Otis D. Duncan. *The American Occupational Structure.* NY: Wiley, 1967.

Blauner, Robert. *Racial Oppression in America.* NY: Harper and Row, 1972.

————. *Black Lives, White Lives: Three Decades of Race Relations in America.* Berkeley: Univ. of California Press, 1989.

————. "Internal colonialism and ghetto revolt." *Social Problems* 16 (Spring, 1969): 393–408.

Bonacich, Edna. "Advanced capitalism and black/white relations in the United States." *ASR* 41 (Feb., 1976): 34–51.

————. "A theory of ethnic antagonism: the split labor market." ASR 37 (Oct. 1972): 547–59.

Boulding, Kenneth E. "Social justice in social dynamics." In *Social Justice,* Richard Brandt, ed. Englewood Cliffs, NJ: Prentice-Hall, 1962: 73–92.

Bourdieu, Pierre and Jean-Claude Passeron. *Reproduction in Education, Society, and Culture,* rev. ed. London: Sage Publications, 1990. (Trans. by Richard Nice.)

Bourne, Randolph. *History of a Literary Radical.* NY: B. W. Huebsch, 1920.

Bowden, Henry Warner. *American Indians and Christian Missions: Studies in Cultural Conflict.* Chicago: Univ. of Chicago Press, 1981.

Boyle, Elizabeth Heger and Edward J. Lawler. "Resolving conflict through explicit bargaining." *SF* 69 (June, 1991): 1183–1204.

Bracewell, Wendy, guest ed. "National identity in Eastern Europe and the Soviet Union." *ERS* 14 (Jan., 1991).

Braddock, Jomills H. II. *Tracking: Implications For Student Race-Ethnic Subgroups.* Baltimore MD: The Johns Hopkins Univ. Center for Research on Effective Schooling for Disadvantaged Students. Report no. 1 (Feb., 1990).

Bradley, Lawrence A. and Gifford W. Bradley. "The academic achievement of black students in desegregated schools." *Review of Educational Research* 47 (Summer, 1977): 399–449.

Brass, Paul. *Ethnicity and Nationalism.* Newbury Park, CA: Sage, 1991.

Breton, Raymond. "Institutional completeness of ethnic communities and the personal relations of immigrants." *AJS* 70 (Sept., 1964): 193–205.

Brewer, M. B. and Donald T. Campbell. *Ethnocentrism and Intergroup Attitudes: East African Evidence.* Beverly Hills, CA: Sage, 1976.

Bricker, Victoria Reifler, ed. "Intra-cultural variation." *AE* 2 (Feb., 1975).

Bromley, David G. ed. *Falling From The Faith: Causes and Consequences of Religious Apostasy.* Newbury Park, CA: Sage, 1988.

———and Anson Shupe, eds. *New Christian Politics.* Macon, GA: Mercer Univ. Press, 1984.

Brookhiser, Richard. *The Way of The Wasp: How it Made America, and How it Can Save it, So to Speak.* NY: Free PRESS, 1991.

Brown, Douglas. *A Study of White South African Attitudes.* London: Collins, 1966.

Brown, Peter G. and Henry Shue, eds. *Boundaries: National Autonomy and Its Limits.* Totowa, NJ: Rowman and Littlefield. 1981.

Browning, Harley L. and Rodolfo O. de la Garza. *Mexican Immigrants and Mexicans: An Evolving Relationship.* Austin: Univ. of Texas Press, 1986.

Brubaker, Rogers. *Citizenship and Nationhood in France and Germany.* Cambridge, MA: Harvard Univ. Press, 1992.

Brubaker, William R., ed. *Immigration and The Politics of Citizenship in Europe and North America.* Lanham, MD: University Press of America, 1989.

Brumberg, Abraham. "Not so free at last." *NYRB,* Oct. 22, 1992: 56–64.

———. "Russia after perestroika." *NYRB,* June 27, 1991: 53–62.

———., ed. *Chronicle of a Revolution: A Western-Soviet Inquiry into Perestroika.* NY: Pantheon, 1990.

Brustein, William. *The Social Origins of Political Regionalism: France, 1849–1981.* Berkeley: Univ. of California Press, 1988.

Bryan, J. H. and P. London. "Altruistic behavior by children." *Psychological Bulletin* 73 (1970): 200–211.

Bullard, Robert D., ed. *Confronting Environmental Racism: Voices From The Grass Roots.* Monroe, Maine: South End Press, 1992.

Bundy, McGeorge. "Beyond Bakke: What future for affirmative action?" *Atlantic* 242 (Nov., 1978): 69–73.

Burke, Fred G. "Bilingualism/biculturalism in American education: an adventure in wonderland." *Annals* 454 (March, 1981): 164–77.

Burkhardt, William R. "Institutional barriers, marginality, and adaptation among American-Japanese in Japan." *Journal of Asian Studies* 42 (May, 1983): 519–44.

Burowoy, Michael. "The function and reproduction of migrant labor: comparative material from Southern Africa and the United States." *AJS* 81 (March, 1976): 1050–87.

Burstein, Paul. "Legal mobilization as a social movement tactic: the struggle for equal employment opportunity." *AJS* 96 (March, 1991): 1202–25.

Burt, Ronald S. *Structural Holes: The Social Structure of Competition.* Cambridge, MA: Harvard Univ. Press, 1992.

Cafferty, Pastora San Juan. "The language question: the dilemma of bilingual education for Hispanics in America." In *Ethnic Relations in America.* Lance Liebman, ed. NY: Prentice-Hall, 1982: 101–27.

Cain, Glen G. "The challenge of segmented labor market theories to orthodox theories: a survey." *Journal of Economic Literature* 14 (Dec., 1976): 1215–57.

Calderon, Margarita. *Cooperative Learning for Limited English Proficiency Students.* Baltimore: Center for Research on Effective Schooling for Disadvantaged Students, Johns Hopkins Univ. Report no. 3 (March, 1990).

Cambridge, Alrick X. and Stephan Feuchtwand, eds. *Anti-Racist Strategies.* Avebury, Eng.: Gower Publ., 1990.

Campbell, Donald T. "On the conflicts between biological and social evolution and between psychology and moral tradition." *American Psychologist* 30 (Dec., 1975): 1103–26.

Candeleria, Michael R. *Popular Religion and Liberation: The Dilemma of Liberation Theology.* Albany: State Univ. of New York Press, 1990.

Čapek, Stella M. "The 'environmental justice' frame: a conceptual discussion and an application." *Social Problems* 40/1 (Feb., 1993): 5-24.

Caplan, Arthur, L., ed. *The Sociobiology Debate.* NY: Harper and Row, 1978.

Capps, Donald and Richard K. Fenn, eds. *Individualism Reconsidered: Readings Bearing on the Endangered Self in Modern Society.* Princeton, NJ: Center for Religion, Self, and Society, 1992.

Carroll, Raymonde. *Cultural Misunderstandings: The French-American Experience.* (Trans. by Carol Volk) Chicago: Univ. of Chicago Press, 1988.

Carter, Gwendolen. *Which Way is South Africa Going.* Bloomington: Univ. of Indiana Press, 1980.

Carter, Stephen. *Reflections of an Affirmative Action Baby.* NY: Basic Books, 1991.

Casson, Ronald W., ed. *Language, Culture, and Cognition: Anthropological Perspectives.* NY: Macmillan, 1981.

Castles, Stephen, with Heather Booth and Tina Wallace. *Here for Good: Western Europe's New Ethnic Minorities.* London: Pluto Press, 1984.

Catton, William R., Jr. *Overshoot: The Ecological Basis of Revolutionary Change.* Urbana: Univ. of Illinois Press, 1980.

———. "The functions and disfunctions of ethnocentrism: a theory." *Social Problems* (Winter, 1961–62): 201–11.

Cazden, Courtney B. and Catherine E. Snow, special eds. "English plus: Issues in bilingual education." *Annals* 508 (March, 1990).

Chavez, Linda. *Out of the Barrio: Toward a New Politics of Hispanic Assimilation.* NY: Basic Books, 1991.

Chick, J. Keith. "The interactional accomplishments of discrimination in South Africa." *Language in Society* 14 (Sept., 1985): 299–326.

Christopher, Robert C. *Crashing the Gates: The De-Wasping of America's Power Elite.* NY: Simon and Schuster, 1989.

Clark, Burton. *Educating the Expert Society.* San Francisco: Chandler, 1962.

Clark, Kenneth B. and Mamie P. Clark. "Racial identification and preference in Negro children." In *Readings in Social Psychology.* T M. Newcomb and E. L. Hartley, eds. NY: Holt, 1947: 169–78.

Clark, P. B. and J. Q. Wilson. "Incentive systems; A theory of organizations." *Administrative Science Quarterly* 6 (1961): 129–66.

Clark, Robert P. "Rejectionist voting as an indicator of ethnic nationalism: The case of Spain's Basque Provinces." *Ethnic and Racial Studies.* 10 (Oct., 1987): 427–47.

Claude, Richard P. *Comparative Human Rights.* Baltimore: Johns Hopkins Univ. Press, 1976.

Cleague, Albert B., Jr. *The Black Messiah.* NY: Sheed and Ward, 1968.

Clifton, James A., ed. *The Invented Indian: Cultural Fictions and Government Policies.* New Brunswick, NJ: Transaction Publishers, 1990.

Clotfelter, Charles. "School desegregation as urban public policy." In *Current Issues in Urban Economics.* P. Mieszkowski and M. Straszheim, eds. Baltimore, MD: Johns Hopkins Univ. Press, 1979: 359–87.

Cohen, Abner, ed. *Urban Ethnicity.* London: Tavistock Publications, 1947a.

——. *Two-Dimensional Man.* Berkeley: Univ. of California Press, 1974.

——. *Custom and Politics in Urban Africa: A Study of Hausa Migrants in Yoruba Towns.* London: Routledge and Kegan Paul, 1969.

Cohen, E. G. "Expectations states and interracial interaction in school settings." *ARS,* 8 (1982): 209–35.

Cohen, Mitchell and Martin Kilson, special eds. "Africa: Crisis and Change." *Dissent,* 39/3 (Summer, 1992): whole issue.

Cohen, Ronald. "Ethnicity: Problems and focus in anthropology." *Annual Review of Anthropology* 7 (1978): 379–403.

——. "Altruism: human, cultural, or what?" *JSI* 28 (1972): 39–57.

Cohen, Steven M. "The public perspective." *Roper Center Review,* Nov.–Dec., 1990: 9–10

——. "Socioeconomic determinants of interethnic marriage and friendship." *SF* 55 (1977): 997–1010.

Cohen, William. *At Freedom's Edge: Black Mobility and the Southern Quest for Racial Control, 1861–1915.* Baton Rouge: Louisiana State Univ. Press, 1991.

Coleman, James S. "A review essay on Rawls, John: inequality, sociology, and moral philosophy." *AJS* 80 (Nov., 1974): 739–64.

——. "Free riders and zealots." In *Social Exchange Theory.* Karen Cook, ed. Newbury Park, CA, 1987: 59–82.

——. *Resources for Social Change: Race in The United States.* NY: Wiley, 1971.

——. *The Adolescent Society.* NY: Free Press, 1961.

——, Sara D. Kelly and John Moore. *Trends in School Desegregation, 1968–1973.* Washington: Urban Institute, 1975.

Coles, Robert. *Children of Crisis.* NY: Dell, 1967.

Colley, Linda. *Britons: Forging the Nation 1707–1837.* New Haven, CN: Yale Univ. Press, 1992.

Colson, Elizabeth. *Tradition and Contract: The Problem of Order.* Chicago: Aldine, 1974.

Comaroff, Jean and John Comaroff. "Christianity and colonialism in South Africa." *AE* 13 (Feb., 1986): 1–22.

Commission for Race and Justice. *Toxic Wastes and Race in the United States.* (Benjamin Chavis, Jr., Executive Director; Charles Lee, Director.) NY: United Church of Christ, 1987.

Commoner, Barry. *The Closing Circle: Nature, Man, and Technology.* NYH: Knopf, 1971.

Cone, James H. *A Black Theology of Liberation.* Philadelphia: Lippincott, 1970.

Connor, Walker. "When is a nation?" *ERS* 13 (Jan., 1990): 92–103.

———, ed. *Mexican-Americans in Comparative Perspective.* Washington: Urban Institute Press, 1985.

———. "Eco- or ethno-nationalisms? *ERS* 7 (July, 1984) 342–59.

Conversi, Daniele. "Language or race? The choice of core values in the development of Catalan and Basque nationalisms." *ERS* 13 (Jan., 1990): 50–70.

Cook, Karen S., ed. *Social Exchange Theory.* Newbury Park, CA: Sage, 1987.

Cooley, Charles Horton. *Social Organization.* NY: Scribners, 1909.

Coombes, Mike and Jim Hubbuck. "Monitoring equal employment opportunity at the workplace: the crucial role of the 1991 census." *ERS* 15 (April, 1992): 193–213.

Coontz, Stephanie. *The Way We Never Were: American Families and the Nostalgia Trap.* NY: Basic Books, 1992.

Cooper, Sandi E. *Patriotic Pacifism: Waging War on War in Europe, 1815–1914.* NY: Oxford Univ. Press, 1991.

Corbridge, Stuart. "Tribal politics, finance and the state: the Jharkhand Indians, 1900–1980." *ERS* 12 (April, 1989): 177–207.

Cornacchia, Eugene J. and Dale C. Nelson. "Historical differences in the political experience of American blacks and white ethnics: revisiting an unresolved controversy." *ERS* 15 (Jan., 1992): 102–24.

Cornell, Stephen. "The transformation of the tribe; organization and self-concept in native American ethnicities." *ERS* 11 (Jan., 1988): 27–47.

———. "Land, labour and group formation: Blacks and Indians in the United States." *ERS* 13 (July, 1990): 368–88.

Coser, Lewis A. and Otto N. Larsen, eds. *The Uses of Controversy in Sociology.* NY: Free Press, 1976.

Covello, Vincent T., ed. *Poverty and Public Policy: An Evaluation of Social Science Research.* Cambridge, MA: Schenkman, 1980.

Coward, Barbara E., Joe R. Feagin, and J. Allen Williams, Jr. "The culture of poverty debate: some additional data." *SF* 52 (June, 1974): 621–34.

Crawford, James. *Hold Your Tongue: Bilingualism and The Politics of "English Only."* Redding MA: Addison-Wesley, 1992a.

———, ed. *Language Loyalties: A Source Book on The Official English Controversy.* Chicago: Univ. of Chicago Press, 1992b.

Crewdson, John. *The Tarnished Door: The New Immigrants and the Transformation of America.* NY: New York Times Books, 1983.

Crippen, Timothy. "Old and new gods in the modern world: toward a theory of religious transformation." *SF* 67 (Dec., 1988): 316–36.

Cross, H. G., J. Mell, and W. Zimmerman. *Employer Hiring Practices: Differential Treatment of Hispanic and Angle Job Seekers.* Washington: Urban Institute, 1990.

Cutler, Donald R., ed. *The Religious Situation, 1968.* Boston: Beacon Press, 1968.

Dadrian, Vahakn N. "A typology of genecide." *International Review of Modern Sociology,* 1975: 201–12.

Dahrendorf, Ralf. *Reflections on the Revolution in Europe.* NY: Times Books/Random House, 1990.

———. *The Modern Social Conflict: An Essay on The Politics of Liberty.* London: Weidenfeld and Nicolson, 1988.

———. "Recent changes in class structure of European societies." In *A New Europe.* Stephen Graubard, ed. Boston: Beacon Press, 1967: 291–336.

Danigelis, Nicholas A. "A theory of black political participation in the United States." *SF* 56 (Sept., 1977): 31–47.

Danziger, Sheldon, issue ed. "Defining and measuring the underclass." *Focus* 12 (Spring-Summer, 1989). Institute for Research on Poverty, University of Wisconsin.

———and Peter Gottschalk. "Earnings inequality, the spacial concentration of poverty, and the underclass." *AER* 77 (May, 1987): 211–15.

———&———, eds. *Uneven Tides:* Rising Inequality in America. NY: Russell Sage Foundation, 1993.

Darras, Jacques, with Daniel Snowman. *Beyond the Tunnel of History.* Ann Arbor: Univ. of Michigan Press, 1990.

Das Gupta, Jyotirindra. *Language Conflict and National Development: Group Politics and National Language Policy in India.* Berkeley: Univ. of California Press, 1970.

Davidson, Basil. *Africa in History,* 4th ed. London: Macmillan, 1991.

Davies, Charlotte Aull. *Welsh Nationalism in the Twentieth Century: The Ethnic Option and the Modern State.* NY: Praeger, 1989.

Davis, Allison W. and Robert J. Havighurst. *Father of the Man: How Your Child Gets His Personality.* Boston: Houghton Mifflin, 1947.

Davis, Cary, Carl Haub, and JoAnn Willette. "U. S. Hispanics; changing the face of America." *Population Bulletin* 38 (June, 1983): whole issue.

Davis, David Brion. "Slaves in Islam." *NYRB,* Oct. 11, 1990: 35–39.

Davis, F. James. *Who is Black? One Nation's Definition.* University Park, PA: Pennsylvania State Univ. Press, 1991.

Dawisha, Adeed I. *The Arab Radicals.* NY: Council on Foreign Relations, 1986.

DeFreitas, Gregory. *Inequality at Work: Hispanics in the U.S. Labor Force.* NY: Oxford Univ. Press, 1991.

Degler, Carl N. *In Search of Human Nature: The Decline and Revival of Darwinism in American Social Thought.* NY: Oxford Univ. Press, 1991.

Della Fave, L. Richard. "The meek shall not inherit the earth: self-evaluation and the legitimacy of stratification." *ASR* 45 (Dec., 1980): 955–71.

———. "The culture of poverty revisisted." *Social Problems,* June, 1974: 609–21.

Deloria, Vine, Jr. *God is Red.* NY: Dell, 1973.

DeMause, Lloyd. "The gulf war as mental disorder." NATION, March 11, 1991: 289–308.

Den-Dak, Joseph E. and Edward E. Azar, guest eds. "Research Perspectives on the Arab-Israeli Conflict: A Symposium." *Journal of Conflict Resolution* 16/2 (June, 1972): whole issue.

Derrida, Jacques. *Writing and Difference.* Chicago: Univ. of Chicago Press, 1978.

DeSchweinitz, Karl. *England's Road to Social Security.* Philadelphia: Univ. of Pennsylvania Press, 1943.

Desmond, Edward W. "Storm over India." *NYRB,* May 14, 1992: 37–40.

Despres, Leo A., ed. *Ethnicity and Resource Competition in Plural Societies.* The Hague: Mouton, 1975.

Deutsch, Morton. *The Resolution of Conflict: Constructive and Destructive Processes.* New Haven, CN: Yale Univ. Press, 1973.

Devereux, George. "Ethnic identity: its logical foundations and its dysfunctions." In DeVos and Romanucci-Ross, 1975: 42–70.

DeVos, Georg and Lola Romanucci-Ross, eds. *Ethnic Identity.* Palo Alto, CA: Mayfield Publishing Co., 1975.

deVries, Sjiera and Thomas Pettigrew. "A comparative perspective on affirmative action: *Positieve Aktie* in the Netherlands." *Journal of Basic and Applied Social Psychology* (in press).

Dignan, Don. "Europe's melting pot: a century of large-scale immigration into France." *ERS* 4 (April, 1981): 137–52.

Dillard, J. L. *Black English: Its History and Usage in the United States.* NY: Random House, 1972.

Dillingham, Gerald L. "The emerging black middle class: class conscious or race conscious." *ERS* 4 (Oct., 1981): 432–51.

Dimitrova, Blaga. "The new newspeak." *NYRB,* March 5, 1992: 18.

Djilas, Alexsa. *The Contested Country: Yugoslav Unity and Communist Revolution, 1919–1953.* Cambridge, MA: Harvard Univ. Press, 1991.

Djilas, Milovan. *The New Class: An Analysis of The Communist System.* NY: Praeger, 1962.

Dobzhansky, Theodosius. *Mankind Evolving.* New Haven, CN: Yale Univ. Press, 1962.

Dominquez, Virginia R. *White by Definition: Social Classification in Creole Louisiana.* New Brunswick, NJ: Rutgers Univ. Press, 1986.

Donahue, Thomas S. "U.S. English: Its life and works." *International Journal of the Sociology of Language* 56 (1985): 99–112.

Dostoyevsky, Fyodor. *The Brothers Karamazov.* NY: Modern Library, 1950.

Douglass, William A. "A critique of recent trends in the analysis of ethnonationalism." *ERS* 11 (April, 1988): 192–206.

Dovidio, John F. and Samuel L. Gaertner. "The effects of race, status, and ability on helping behavior." *Social Psychology Quarterly* 44 (Sept., 1981): 192–203.

Dower, John W. *War Without Mercy: Race and Power in the Pacific War.* NY: Pantheon Books, 1986.

Dresh, Paul. *Tribes, Government, and History in Yemen.* Oxford: Oxford Univ. Press, 1989.

Dreyer, June Teufel. *China's Forty Millions: Minority Nationalities and National Integration in the People's Republic of China.* Cambridge, MA: Harvard Univ. Press, 1976.

Drobizheva, L. M. "The role of the intelligentsia in developing national consciousness among the people of the USSR under *perestroika.*" ERS 14 (Jan., 1991): 87–99.

Drury, D. W. "Black self-esteem and desegregated schools." *Sociology of Education* 53 (1980): 88–103.

DuBois, W. E. B. *The Souls of Black Folk.* Greenwich, CN: Fawcett, 1953 (1903).

———. "The conservation of races." American Negro Academy, Occasional Paper, no. 2. Washington: American Negro Acedemy, 1897.

Dubow, Saul. *Racial Segregation and the Origins of Apartheid in South Africa, 1919–36.* London: Macmillan, 1989.

Duncan, Otis D. "Inheritance of poverty or inheritance of race?" In *On Understanding Poverty: Perspectives from the Social Sciences,* Daniel P. Moynihan, ed. NY: Basic Books, 1968.

Durkheim, Emile. *Moral Education: A Study in the Theory and Application of the Sociology of Education.* (Trans. by Everett Wilson and Herman Schnurer.) NY: Free Press, 1973.

———. *Suicide* (Trans. by John A. Spaulding and George Simpson). NY: Free Press, 1951.

———. *The Elementary Forms of the Religious Life.* (Trans. by Joseph W. Swain.) NY: Free Press, 1947a.

———. *The Division of Labor in Society.* (Trans. by George Simpson.) NY: Free Press, 1947b.

Duster, Troy. "Social implications of the 'new' black urban underclass." *Black Scholar* 19/3 (1988): 2–9.

Dworkin, Ronald. "The Reagan Revolution and the Supreme Court." NYRB, July 18, 1991: 23–28.

Eagly, Alice H. and Samuel Himmelfarb. "Attitudes and opinions. *Annual Review of Psychology* 29 (1978): Palo Alto, CA: Annual Reviews: 517–54.

Eban, Abba. *Personal Witness: Israel Through My Eyes.* NY: G. P. Putnam's Sons, 1992.

ECONOMIST, March 30, 1991: 11–12, 17–21. "America's wasted Blacks."

Edmonston, Barry and Jeffrey S. Passel. "U.S. immigration and ethnicity in the 21st century." *Population Today* (Population Reference Bureau), Vol. 20/10 (Oct., 1992): 6–7.

Edsall, Thomas B. "A political powder keg." *Washington Post National Weekly,* Jan. 14–20, 1991: 6–7.

Edwards, John, ed. *Linguistic Minorities, Policies, and Pluralism.* London: Academic Press, 1984.

———and Clare Shearn. "Language and identity in Belgium: perceptions of French and Flemish students." *ERS* 10 (April, 1987): 135–48.

Eisenger, Peter K. *The Politics of Displacement: Racial and Ethnic Transition in Three American Cities.* NY: Academic Press, 1980.

Eiseley, Loren. *The Immense Journey.* NY: Random House, 1957.

Elder, Glen H., Jr. "Intergroup attitudes and social ascent among Negro boys." *AJS* 77 (Jan., 1971): 673–97.

Elías-Olivares, Lucía, Elizabeth Leone, René Cisneros, and John Gutierrez, eds. *Spanish Language Use and Public Life in The USA.* NY: Mouton de Gruyter, 1985.

Elkins, Stanley M. *Slavery: A Problem in American Institutional and Intellectual Life.* Chicago: Univ. of Chicago Press, 1959.

Elliot, J.H. "The rediscovery of America." NYRB, June 24, 1993: 36–41.

Ellwood, David. *Poor Support.* NY: Basic Books, 1989.

Elon, Amos. "From the uprising." *NYRB,* April 14, 1988: 10–14.

Emerson, Richard M. "Social Exchange Theory." *Annual Review of Sociology.* Palo Alto, CA: Annual Reviews, Vol. 2 (1976): 235–62.

Enloe, Cynthia. *Ethnic Conflict and Political Development.* Boston: Little, Brown, 1973.

Entwisle, Doris R. and Karl L. Alexander. "Summer setback: race, poverty, school composition, and mathematics achievement in the first two years of school." ASR 57 (Feb., 1992): 72–84.

Epps, E. "Impact of school desegregation on aspiration, self-concepts, and other aspects of personality." *Law and Contemporary Problems* 39 (1975): 300–313.

Epstein, A. L. *Ethos and Identity: Three Studies in Ethnicity.* London: Tavistock, 1978.

Epstein, Richard A. *Forbidden Grounds: The Case Against Employment Discrimination Laws.* Cambridge, MA: Harvard Univ. Press, 1992.

Erickson, Frederick. "Gatekeeping and the melting pot." *Harvard Educational Review* 45 (Feb., 1975): 44–70.

Erikson, Erik. "The development of ritualization." In *The Religious Situation, 1968.* Edited by Donald Cutler. Boston: Beacon Press, 1968: 711–32.

————. *Childhood and Society,* 2nd ed. NY: W. W. Norton, 1963.

Erikson, Kai T. *Wayward Puritans: A Study in The Sociology of Deviance.* NY: Wiley, 1966.

Esman, Milton J. and Itamar Rabinovich, eds. *Ethnicity, Pluralism, and the State in the Middle East.* Ithaca, NY: Cornell Univ. Press, 1988.

Essien-Udom, E. U. *Black Nationalism.* Chicago: Univ. of Chicago Press, 1962.

Etzioni, Amitai. *The Moral Dimension: Towards a New Economics.* NY: Free Press, 1988.

European Communities. *Encyclopedia and Directory.* London: Europa Publications, 1992.

Ezorsky, Gertrude. *Racism and Justice: The Case for Affirmative Action.* Ithaca, NY: Cornell Univ. Press, 1991.

Fallows, Lloyd A. *The Social Anthropology of the Nation State.* Chicago: Aldine, 1974.

Farber, Bernard, Leonard Gordon and Albert J. Mayer. "Intermarriage and Jewish identity: the implications for pluralism and assimilation in American society." ERS 2/2 (April, 1979): 223–30.

Farley, Reynolds. "The new census question about ancestry: what did it tell us." *Demography* 28 (Aug., 1991): 411–29.

————. "Is Coleman right." *Social Policy* 6 (Jan.-Feb., 1976): 1–10.

————and Walter Allen. *The Color Line and The Quality of Life in America.* NY: Russell Sage, 1987.

————, T. Richards, and C. Wurdock. "School desegregation and white flight: an investigation of competing models and their discrepant findings." *Sociology of Education* 53 (1980): 123–29.

Fasold, Ralph W., William Labov, et al. "Are black and white vernaculars diverging?" *American speech: A Quarterly of Linguistic Usage* 62 (Spring, 1987): 3–80.

Feagin, Joe R. "The continuing significance of race: antiblack discrimination in public places." ASR 56/1 (Feb., 1991): 101-16.

Fein, Helen, ed. *The Persisting Question: Sociological Perspectives and Social Contexts of Modern Antisemitism.* Berlin: Walter de Gruyter, 1987.

Feinberg, William E. "At a snail's pace: time to equality in simple models of affirmative action programs." *AJS* 90 (July, 1984): 168–81.

Fenn, Richard K. and Donald Capps, eds. *The Endangered Self.* Princeton, NJ: Center for Religion, Self and Society, 1992.

Feuerbach, Ludwig. *The Essence of Christianity.* (Trans by George Eliot). NY: Harper and Row, 1957.

Field, Frank, *Losing Out: The Emergence of Britain's Underclass.* Oxford: Basil Blackwell, 1989.

Finger, J. A., Jr. "Why busing plans work." *School Review* 84 (1976): 364–72.

Finnegan, William. *A Complicated War: The Harrowing of Mozambique.* Berkeley: Univ. of California Press, 1992.

Firth, Raymond, *We The Tikopia,* 2nd ed. London: Allen and Unwin, 1957.

Fishbein, Martin and Icek Ajzen. *Beliefs, Attitudes, Intentions, and Behavior: An Introduction to Theory and Research.* Reading, MA: Addison-Wesley, 1975.

Fisher, Marc. "Hitting the wall: Germans come face to face with their real divisions." *Washington Post National Weekly,* May 20–26, 1991: 10–11.

Fishman, Joshua. *Language and Ethnicity in Minority Sociolinguistic Perspective.* Clevedon, Eng.: Multilingual Matters, 1989.

———. "The ethnic revival in the United States." In *Mexican Americans in Comparative Perspective*. Walker Connor, ed. Washington: Urban Institute Press, 1985: 311–54.

———. "Ethnic-community mother-tongue schools in the USA: dynamics and distributions." *International Migration Review* 14 (Summer, 1980): 235–47.

———. *Bilingualism in the Barrio*. Bloomington: Univ. of Indiana Press, 1971.

Fogel, Robert and Stanley Engerman. *Time on the Cross*, two vols. Boston: Little, Brown, 1974.

Foner, Eric. "The romance of the market." *Nation*, Dec. 24, 1990: 796–800.

Form, William. *Divided We Stand: Working Class Stratification in America*. Urbana: Univ. of Illinois Press, 1985.

Fortes, Meyer. *Oedipus and Job in West African Religion*. Cambridge: Cambridge Univ. Press, 1959.

Foster, Charles R. *Nations Without a State: Ethnic Minorities in Western Europe*. NY: Praeger, 1980.

Fox, Richard G., ed. *Nationalist Ideologies and the Production of National Cultures*. Washington: American Anthropological Association, 1990.

Francis, E. K. *Interethnic Relations: An Essay in Sociological Theory*. NY: Elsevier, 1976.

Frank, Joseph. "The triumph of Abram Tertz." (a.k.a. Andrei Sinyavsky) NYRB, June 27, 1991: 35–43.

Frankel, Glenn. "A triangle of ethnic struggle." *Washington Post National Weekly*, Feb. 17–23, 1992: 6–11.

———. "Is the nation-state headed for the dustbin of history?" *Washington Post National Weekly*, Nov. 19–25, 1990: 16.

Frazier, E. Franklin. *The Negro Church in America*. NY: Schooken Books, 1963.

Frederikse, Julie. *The Unbreakable Thread: Non-Racialism in South Africa*. Bloomington: Univ. of Indiana Press, 1990.

Freud, Sigmund. *Civilization and its Discontents*. (Trans. and edited by James Strachey) NY: W. W. Norton, 1962.

———. *The Future of an Illusion*. (Trans. by W. D. Robson-Scott) NY: Horace Liveright and the Institute of Psychoanalysis, 1928.

Fried, Charles. *Order and Law: Arguing the Reagan Revolution—A First-hand Account.* NY: Simon and Schuster, 1991.

Friedman, Robert I. *Zealots for Zion: Inside Israel's West Bank Settlement Movement.* NY: Random House, 1992.

Fuchs, Lawrence H. *The American Kaleidoscope: Race, Ethnicity, and the Civic Culture.* Hanover, NH: University Press of New England, 1990.

Fuentes, Carlos. "The mirror of the other." *Nation,* March 30, 1992: 408–10.

Fugita, Stephen S. and David J. O'Brien. *Japanese American Ethnicity: The Persistence of Community.* Seattle: Univ. of Washington Press, 1991.

Fukuyama, Francis. *The End of History and the Last Man.* NY: Free Press, 1992.

Furnival, J. S. *Colonial Policy and Practice.* London: Cambridge Univ. Press, 1948.

Galaty, John C. "Being 'Massai'; being 'people-of-cattle'; ethnic shifters in East Africa." *AE* (Feb., 1982): 1–20.

Galster, George. "Housing discrimination and urban poverty of African-Americans." *Journal of Housing Research* 2/2 (1991): 87–124.

Galster, George C. and W. Mark Keeney. "Race, residence, discrimination, and economic opportunity: modeling the nexus of urban racial phenomena." *Urban Affairs Quarterly* 24 (1988): 87–117.

Gambino, Richard. *Blood of My Blood: The Dilemma of the Italian-Americans.* NY: Doubleday, 1975.

Gamson, William A. *The Strategy of Social Protest.* Homewood, Ill.: Dorsey Press, 1975.

———, Bruce Fireman, and Steven Rytina. *Encounters with Unjust Authority.* Homewood, Ill.: Dorsey Press, 1982.

Gans, Herbert J. "Second generation decline: scenarios for the economic and ethnic futures of the post-1965 American immigrants." *ERS* 15/2 (April, 1992): 173–92.

———. *Middle American Individualism: The Future of Liberal Democracy.* NY: Free Press, 1988.

———. "Symbolic ethnicity: the future of ethnic groups and cultures in America." *ERS* 2 (Jan., 1979): 1–20.

———. *The Urban Villagers: Group and Class in the Life of Italian-Americans.* NY: Free Press, 1962.

Gardels, Nathan. "Two concepts of nationalism: an interview with Isaiah Berlin." *NYRB*, Nov. 21, 1991: 19–23.

Garreau, Joel. *The Nine Nations of North America.* NY: Avon, 1982.

Geertz, Clifford, ed. *Old Societies and New States: The Quest for Modernity in Asia and Africa.* NY: Free Press, 1963.

———. "The rotating credit association: a 'middle rung' in development." *Economic Development and Cultural Change* 10 (1962): 241–63.

Genovese, Eugene. *Roll, Jordan, Roll: The World the Slaves Made.* NY: Pantheon, 1974.

———. "American slaves and their history." *NYRB*, Dec. 3, 1970: 34–43.

Geschwender, James A. "On power and powerlessness: or with a little help from your friends." In Yinger and Cutler, 1978: 439–54.

Giddens, Anthony. *The Nation-State and Violence.* Berkeley: Univ. of California Press, 1985.

Gist, Noel P. and Anthony G. Dworkin, eds. *The Blending of Races: Marginality and Identity in World Perspective.* NY: Wiley, 1972.

Glaser, Kurt and Stefan T. Possony. *Victims of Politics: The State of Human Rights.* NY: Columbia Univ. Press, 1979.

Glasgow, Douglas G. *The Black Underclass: Poverty, Unemployment and Entrapment of Ghetto Youth.* San Francisco: Jossey-Bass, 1980.

Glass, Charles. *Tribes with Flags: A Dangerous Passage Through the Chaos of the Middle East.* NY: Atlantic Monthly Press, 1990.

Glass, Ruth. *London's Newcomers: The West Indian Migrants.* Cambridge, MA: Harvard Univ. Press, 1961.

Glazer, Nathan. *Affirmative Discrimination: Ethnic Inequality and Public Policy,* 2nd ed. Cambridge, MA: Harvard Univ. Press, 1987.

———. *Ethnic Dilemmas 1964–1982.* Cambridge, MA: Harvard Univ. Press, 1983.

———and Daniel P. Moynihan, eds. *Ethnicity: Theory and Experience.* Cambridge, MA: Harvard Univ. Press, 1975.

Glenny, Misha. "Bosnia: the last chance?" *NYRB*, Jan. 28, 1993: 5–8.

414   Bibliography

———. *The Fall of Yugoslavia: The Third Balkan War.* NY: Penguin, 1992.

Gluck, Ken. "The new Russian imperialists." *Nation,* Sept. 14, 1992: 243–46.

Gluckman, Max. *Order and Rebellion in Tribal Society.* London: Cohen and West, 1963.

Goering, J. M. "Changing perceptions and evaluations of physical characteristics among blacks, 1950–70." *Phylon* 33 (1972): 231–41.

Goldman, Peter. *The Death and Life of Malcolm X,* 2nd ed. Urbana: Univ. of Illinois Press, 1979.

Goldstone, Jack A., Ted R. Gurr, and Farrokh Moshiri, eds. *Revolutions of the Late Twentieth Century.* Boulder, Colorado: Westview Press, 1991.

Gordon, Milton M. *Human Nature, Class, and Ethnicity.* NY: Oxford Univ. Press, 1978.

———. *Assimilation in American Life: The Role of Religion, Race, and National Origin.* NY: Oxford Univ. Press, 1964.

Gottlieb, Gidon. "Israel and the Palestinians." *Foreign Affairs* 68 (Fall, 1989): 109–26.

Goulbourne, Harry. *Ethnicity and Nationalism in Post-Imperial Britain.* Cambridge: Cambridge Univ. Press, 1991.

Graham, H. D. and Ted R. Gurr, eds. *Violence in America.* NY: Praeger, 1969.

Gramsci, Antonio. *Selections from the Prison Notebooks.* (Edited and trans. by Quintin Hoare and Geoffrey N. Smith). NY: International Publishers, 1971.

Granovetter, Mark. "The strength of weak ties; a network theory revisited." In *Sociological Theory* (Randall Collins, ed.) San Francisco: Jossey-Bass, 1983.

Grant, Gerald. "The character of education and the education of character." *Daedalus* 110 (1981): 135–49.

Graubard, Stephen R., ed. "Eastern Europe . . . Central Europe . . . Europe." *Daedalus* 119/1 (Winter, 1990): whole issue.

Graves, Theodore D. "Urban Indian personality and the 'culture of poverty.'" *AE* 1/1 (Feb., 1974): 65–86.

Grebler, Leo, Joan Moore, and Ralph C. Guzman. *The Mexican American People: The Nation's Second Largest Minority.* NY: Free Press, 1970.

Greeley, Andrew M. *Ethnicity in the United States: A Preliminary Reconnaisance.* NY: Wiley, 1974.

———. *Why Can't They Be Like Us?* NY: E. P. Dutton, 1971.

Greenawalt, Kent. "The implications of *Regents of California v. Bakke* for university admissions and hiring." *Equal Opportunity Review,* Feb., 1979: 1–8.

Greenfield, Liah. *Nationalism: Five Roads to Modernity.* Cambridge, MA: Harvard Univ. Press, 1992.

Gregory, James R. "The modification of an interethnic boundary in Belize." *AE* 3 (Nov., 1976): 683–708.

Griffith, Jeanne E., Mary J. Frase, and John H. Ralph. "American education: the challenge of change." *Population Bulletin* 44 (Dec., 1989).

Grimshaw, Allen D. *Language as Social Resource: Essays by Allen Day Grimshaw.* (Selected and introduced by Anwar S. Dil) Stanford, CA: Stanford Univ. Press, 1981.

Griswold, Erwin N. "The Bakke problem—allocation of scarce resources in education and other areas." *Washington University Law Quarterly* (Winter, 1979): 58–80.

Griswold, Wendy. "The writing on the mud wall: Nigerian novels and the imaginary village." *ASR* 57/6 (Dec., 1992): 709–24.

Grossman, David. *Sleeping on a Wire: Conversations with Palestinians in Israel.* (Trans. by Haim Watzman) NY: Farrar, Straus & Giroux, 1992.

———. *The Yellow Wind.* (Trans. by Haim Watzman). NY: Farrar, Straus, and Giroux, 1988.

Gumperz, John J., ed. *Language and Social Identity.* NY: Cambridge Univ. Press, 1983.

———. *Language in Social Groups.* (Essays selected and edited by Anwar S. Dil.) Stanford, CA: Stanford Univ. Press, 1971.

Gurak, Douglas T. and Joseph P. Fitzpatrick. "Intermarriage among Hispanic groups in New York City." *AJS* 87 (Jan., 1982): 921–42.

Gurevitch, Z. D. "The other side of the dialogue: on making the other strange and the experience of otherness." *AJS* 93 (March, 1988): 1179–99.

Gurr, Ted R. and James R. Scarritt. "Minorities rights at risk: a global survey." *Human Rights Quarterly* 11 (1989): 375–405.

Gutman, Herbert G. *The Black Family in Slavery and Freedom, 1750–1925.* NY: Pantheon, 1976.

Hacker, Andrew. *Two Nations: Black and White, Separate, Hostile, Unequal.* NY: Scribners, 1992.

———. "Trans-national America." *NYRB* 37 (Nov. 22, 1990): 19–24.

Hadaway, C. Kirk, David G. Hackett, and James F. Miller. "The most segregated institution: correlates of interracial church participation." *RRR* 25 (March, 1984): 204–19.

Hajda, Lubomyr and Mark Beissisnger, eds. *The Nationalities Factor in Soviet Politics and Society.* Boulder, COL.: Westview Press, 1990.

Halbwachs, Maurice. *On Collective Memory.* (Edited and trans. by Lewis Coser.) Chicago: Univ. of Chicago Press, 1992.

Halliday, M. A. K. "Anti-Languages." *AA* 78 (Sept., 1976): 570–84.

Hallowell, A. Irving. "American Indians, white and black: the phenomenon of transculturalization." *Current Anthropology* 4 (Dec., 1963): 510–31.

———. "The impact of the American Indian on American culture." *AA* 59 (April, 1957): 212–13.

Hamill, Pete. "Breaking the silence: a letter to a black friend." *Esquire* 109 (March, 1988): 92.

Hamilton, David L., ed. *Cognitive Processes in Stereotyping and Intergroup Behavior.* Hillsdale, NJ: Lawrence Erlbaum Associates, 1981.

Hannerz, Ulf. *Soulside: Inquiries into Ghetto Culture and Community.* NY: Columbia Univ. Press, 1969

Hardin, Garrett. "The tragedy of the commons." *Science* 162 (Oct. 13, 1968): 1243–48.

Harding, Vincent. "Religion and resistance among ante-bellum Negroes, 1800–1860." In *The Making of Black America.* Meier and Rudwick, 1969: 179–97.

Harrington, C. C. "Bilingual education, social stratification, and cultural pluralism." *Equal Opportunity Review,* Summer, 1978: 1–4.

———. "A psychological anthropologist's view of ethnicity and schooling." *IRCD Bulletin* 10 (1975): 1–9.

Harris, Eddy L. *Native Stranger: A Black American's Journey into the Heart of Africa.* NY: Simon and Schuster, 1992.

Hartman, David. *Conflicting Visions: Spiritual Possibilities of Modern Israel.* NY: Schocken Books, 1990.

Haub, Carl and Nancy Yinger. *The UN Long-Range Population Projections: What They Tell Us.* Washington: Population Reference Bureau, Dec., 1992.

Haug, Marie J. and A. Portes. "The structural assimilation of recent Cuban and Mexican immigrants to the United States: the influence of individual and structural characteristics." Manuscript, 1979.

Havel, Václav. *Summer Meditations.* NY: Knopf, 1992.

———. "Words on words." *NYRB*, Jan. 18, 1990: 5–8.

Haveman, Robert H., ed. *A Decade of Federal Antipoverty Programs: Achievements, Failures, Lessons.* NY: Academic Press, 1977.

Hayes-Bautista, Aida Hurtado, R. Burciaga Valdez, and Anthony C. R. Hernandez. *Redefining California: Latino Social Engagement in a Multicultural Center.* Los Angeles: UCLA Chicano Studies Research Center, 1992.

Heard, J. Norman. *White Into Red: A Study of the Assimilation of White Persons Captured by Indians.* Metuchen, NJ: Scarecrow Press, 1973.

Heath, Shirley Brice. "Language Policies: Patterns of retention and maintenance." In Connor, 1985: 257–82.

———. *Ways with Words: Language, Life, and Work in Communities and Classrooms.* London: Cambridge Univ. Press, 1983.

Hechter, Michael. "Nationalism as group solidarity." *ERS* 10 (Oct. 1987): 415–26.

———. "Group formation and cultural division of labor." *AJS* 84 (Sept, 1978): 293–318.

———. *Internal Colonialism: The Celtic Fringe in British National Development, 1536–1966.* Berkeley: Univ. of California Press, 1977.

———. "Ethnicity and Industrialization: On the proliferation of the cultural division of labor." *Ethnicity* 3 (1976): 214–24.

———. "The political economy of ethnic change." *AJS* 79 (March, 1974): 1151–1178.

Heer, David M. "Intermarriage." *Harvard Encyclopedia of American Ethnic Groups.* Cambridge, MA: Belknap Press, 1980: 513–21.

Heiberg, Marianne. *The Making of the Basque Nation.* Cambridge: Cambridge Univ. Press, 1989.

Heilig, Gerhard, Thomas Buttner, and Wolfgang Lutz. "Germany's population, turbulent past, uncertain future." *Population Bulletin* 45 (Dec., 1990).

Heirich, Max. "Change of heart: a test of some widely held theories about religious conversion." *AJS* 83 (Nov., 1977): 653–80.

Heisler, Barbara Schmitter. "From migrant workers to ethnic minorities? The political and organizational aspects of the process of settlement in Western Europe." Manuscript, July, 1985. (See also Schmitter, Barbara.)

Heisler, Martin O., issue ed. "Ethnic conflict in the world today." ANNALS 433 (Sept., 1977): whole issue.

———and Barbara Schmitter Heisler, special eds. "From foreign workers to settlers? Trans-national migration and the emergence of new minorities." *Annals,* 485 (May, 1986): whole issue.

Heiss, Jerold and Susan Owens. "Self-evaluations of blacks and whites. *AJS* 72 (1972): 360–70.

Heller, Mark A. and Sari Nusseibeh. *No Trumpets, No Drums: A Two-State Settlement of the Israeli-Palestinian Conflict.* NY: Hill and Wang, 1991.

Helms, Janet E. *Black and White Racial Identity.* Westport, CN: Greenwood Press, 1990.

Henderson, R. D. and M. Euler. "What research and experience teach us about desegregating large northern cities." *Clearinghouse for Civil Rights Research* 7 (1979): 2–14.

Henry, D. "Love and discipline spawn education in midst of despair." *NYT:* Nov. 16, 1980: 14.

Herman, Edward S. *Beyond Hypocrisy: Decoding the News in an Age of Propaganda.* Monroe, Maine: South End Press, 1992.

Herskovits, M. J. *Acculturation: The Study of Culture Contact.* NY: Augustin, 1938.

Hertzberg, Arthur. "A lost chance for peace." *NYRB,* March 5, 1992: 20–24.

————. "The impasse over Israel." *NYRB,* Oct. 25, 1990: 41–47.

Hertzberg, Hazel W. *The Search for an American Indian Identity: Modern Pan-Indian Movements.* Syracuse, NY: Syracuse Univ. Press, 1971.

Herzen, Alexander I. *My Past and Thoughts: The Memoirs of Alexander Herzen.* (Trans. by Constance Garnett. Revised by Humphrey Higgins.) NY: Knopf, 1968, 4 vols.

Hewitt, Roger. *White Talk Black Talk: Inter-Racial Friendship and Communication amongst Adolescents.* Cambridge: Cambridge Univ. Press, 1986.

Heyns, Barbara. *Summer Learning and the Effects of Schooling.* NY: Academic Press, 1978.

Hickey, John. *Religion and the Northern Ireland Problem.* Dublin: Gill and Macmillan, 1984.

Higginbotham, A. Leon. *In the Matter of Color.* London: Oxford Univ. Press, 1978.

Higham, John. *Send These to Me: Immigrants in Urban America,* rev. ed. Baltimore: Johns Hopkins Univ. Press, 1984.

Hill, Martha S. and Michael Ponza. "Poverty and welfare dependence across generations." *Economic Outlook USA,* 1983 (Summer): 61–64.

Hill, Richard J. "Attitudes and behavior." In Rosenberg and Turner, 1981: 347–77.

Hilterman, Joost R. *Behind the Intifada.*Princeton, NJ: Princeton Univ. Press, 1991.

Himes, Joseph H. *The South Moves into the Future.* Tuscaloosa: Univ. of Alabama Press, 1991.

Hinde, Robert A. and Jo Groebel, eds. *Cooperation and Prosocial Behavior.* Cambridge: Cambridge Univ. Press, 1992.

Hirschman, Charles. "America's melting pot reconsidered." *ARS* 9 (1983): 397–423.

Hitchens, Christopher. "Why Bosnia matters: appointment in Sarajevo." *Nation,* Sept. 14, 1992: 236–41.

Hobsbawm, E. J. *Nations and Nationalism Since 1870.* NY: Cambridge Univ. Press, 1990.

Hochschild, Jennifer L. *The New American Dilemma: Liberal Democracy and School Desegregation.* New Haven, CT: Yale Univ. Press, 1984.

———. *What's Fair? American Beliefs about Distributive Justice.* Cambridge, MA: Harvard Univ. Press, 1981.

Hodgson, Marshall G. S. *The Venture of Islam: Conscience and History in a World Civilization*, 3 vols. Chicago: Univ. of Chicago Press, 1974.

Hoffman, Carl. "Affirmative action programs that work." *New Perspectives* 17 (Summer, 1985): 16–23.

Hoffman, Stanley. "France self-destructs." *NYRB*, May 28, 1992: 25–30.

Hoffman, Stanley. "Goodbye to a United Europe?" *NYRB*, May 27, 1993, 27–31.

Hofstadter, Richard. *Social Darwinism*, rev. ed. NY: George Braziller, 1959.

Hofstetter, Richard R., ed. *U.S. Immigration Policy.* Durham, NC: Duke Univ. Press, 1984.

Hoge, Dean R., with Kenneth McGuire and Bernard F. Stratman. *Converts, Dropouts, Returnees: A Study of Religious Change among Catholics.* Washington: The Pilgrim Press, 1981.

Holloway, Joseph E., ed. *Africanisms in American Culture.* Bloomington, Univ. of Indiana Press, 1990.

Homans, George C. *Social Behavior.* NY: Harcourt, Brace, and World, 1961.

Horkheimer, Max. *Critical Theory.* NY: Herder and Herder, 1972.

Hornberger, Nancy H. "Bilingual education and English-only: a language planning framework." In Cazden and Snow, 1990: 12–26.

Hornby, Peter A. *Bilingualism: Psychological, Social, and Educational Implications.* NY: Academic Press, 1977.

Horowitz, Donald L. *A Democratic South Africa?* Berkeley: Univ. of California Press, 1991.

———. *Ethnic Groups in Conflict.* Berkeley: Univ. of California Press, 1985a.

———. "After apartheid." *New Republic*, November 4, 1985b: 19–23.

———. "Ethnic identity." In Glazer and Moynihan, 1975: 111–40.

Hourani, Albert. *A History of the Arab Peoples.* Cambridge, MA: Harvard Univ. Press, 1991.

Howells, William W. *The Heathens: Primitive Man and His Religions.* Garden City, NY: Doubleday, 1948.

Hughes, Michael and David H. Demo. "Self-perceptions of black Americans: self-esteem and personal efficacy." *AJS* 95 (July, 1989): 132–59.

Hultkrantz, Ake. *The Religions of the American Indians*. Berkeley: Univ. of California Press, 1979.

Hunt, J. G. "Assimilation or marginality? Some school integration effects reconsidered." *SF* 56 (1977): 604–10.

Hunter, Robert F. *The Palestinian Uprising: A War by Other Means*. Berkeley: Univ. of California Press, 1991.

Hurh, Won Moo, Hei Chu Kim, and Kwange Chung Kim. *Assimilation Patterns of Immigrants in the United States: A Case Study of Korean Immigrants in the Chicago Area*. Washington: University Press of America, 1979.

Husband, Charles, ed. *Race in Britain: Continuity and Change*. London: Hutchinson, 1984.

Husbands, Christopher T. "The main stream right and the politics of immigration in France: major developments in the 1980s." *ERS* 14 (April, 1991): 170–98.

Hwang, Sean-Shong and Rogelio Saenz. "The problem posed by immigrants married abroad on immigration research; the case of Asian Americans." *IMR* 24 (Fall, 1990): 563–76.

Iacovetta, Franca. "Ordering in bulk: Canada's postwar immigration policy and the recruitment of contract workers from Italy." *Journal of American Ethnic History* 11/1 (Fall, 1991): 50–80.

Ignatieff, Michael. "The Balkan tragedy." *NYRB*, May 13, 1993: 3–5.

Ikeda, Kiyoshi. "On the shoulders of giants—Romanzo Adams and the study of interracial marriage in Hawaii." Manuscript, Aug., 1991.

Imhoff, Gary. "The position of U.S. English on bilingual education. *Annals* 508 (March, 1990): 48–61.

Isaacs, Harold R. *Idols of the Tribe: Group Identity and Political Change* Cambridge, MA: Harvard Univ. Press, 1989 (1975).

Ivanov, Miroslav. *From the New World*. (Trans. by Stania Slahor, Nan Karel, and Leon Karel.) Prague: Panorama Press, 1984. (English translation in press, Kirksville, MO: Thomas Jefferson Press, 1993).

Jackman, Mary R. and Michael J. Muha. "Education and intergroup attitudes: moral enlightenment, superficial democratic commitment, or ideological refinement." *ASR* 49 (Dec., 1984): 751–69.

Jackson, James S. and Gerald Gurin. *National Survey of Black Americans.* (1979–80) (machine readable codebook) Ann Arbor, Mich.: Inter-University Consortium for Political and Social Research, Institute For Social Research, 1987.

Jackson, Jesse L. "Give the people a vision." *NYT Magazine,* April 18, 1976: 13, 71–73.

Jacobson, Cardell K. "Religiosity in a black community: an examination of secularization and political variables." *RRR* 33/3 (March, 1992): 215–228.

———. "Desegregation rulings and public attitude changes: white resistance or resignation?" *AJS* 84 (1978): 698–705.

Janowski, Martin Sanchez. *City Bound: Urban Life and Political Attitudes among Chicano Youth.* Albuquerque: Univ. of New Mexico, 1986.

Janowsky, Oscar I. *Nationalities and National Minorities.* NY: Macmillan, 1945.

Jaynes, Gerald David and Robin M. Williams, Jr. *A Common Destiny: Blacks and American Society.* Washington: National Academy Press, 1989.

Jencks, Christopher. *Rethinking Social Policy: Race, Poverty, and the Underclass.* Cambridge, MA: Harvard Univ. Press, 1991.

———, and Paul E. Peterson, eds. *The Urban Underclass.* Washington: The Brookings Institution, 1991.

Jenkins, J. Craig. "Resource mobilization theory and the study of social movements." *ARS* 9 (1983): 527–53.

———, and Augustine J. Kposowa. "Explaining military coups d'etat: Black Africa, 1957–84. *ASR* 55 (Dec., 1990): 861–75.

Jiobu, Robert M. *Ethnicity and Assimilation: Blacks, Chinese, Japanese, Koreans, Mexicans, Vietnamese, and Whites.* Albany: State Univ. of New York Press, 1988.

———. "Ethnic hegemony and the Japanese of California." *ASR* 53 (June, 1988a): 353–67.

Johnson, Charles S. *Growing Up in the Black Belt.* Washington: American Council on Education, 1941.

Johnston, B. V. and Yoels, W. C. "On linking cultural and structural models of ethnicity: a synthesis of Schooler and Yancy, Ericksen, and Juliani." *AJS* 83 (1977): 729–36.

Jones, Faustine C. "Internal crosscurrents and internal diversity: an assessment of black progress, 1960–80." *Daedalus* 110 (Spring, 1981): 71–101.

Jones, Gareth Stedman. *Language of Class: Studies in English Working-Class HIstory, 1932–1982.* Cambridge: Cambridge Univ. Press, 1983.

Jones, Jacqueline.*The Dispossessed: America's Underclass from the Civil War to the Present.* NY: Basic Books, 1992.

Jones, Peter R. "Ethnic intermarriage in Britain: a further assessment." *ERS* 7 (July, 1984): 398–405.

Jones, R. Kenneth. "Paradigm shifts and identity theory: alternation as a form of identity management." In *Identity and Religion,* Hans Mol, ed. Beverly Hills, CA: Sage, 1978: 59–82.

Joó, Rudolf. "Slovenes in Hungary and Hungarians in Slovenia: ethnic and state identity." *ERS* 14 (Jan., 1991): 100–106.

Judd, Elliot. "The English Language Amendment: a case study on language and politics." *TESOL Quarterly* 21 (1987): 113–35.

Kahn, Herman, William Brown, and Leon Martel. *The Next 200 Years: A Scenario for America and the World.* NY: William Morrow, 1976.

Kalish, Susan. "Blacks and Hispanics poised for increase in Congress." *Population Today* 20 (May, 1992a): 3–4.

———. "Immigration IRCA Tops Out." *Population Today* 20/11 (Nov., 1992b): 4.

———. "Interracial baby boomlet in progress? *Population Today,* Vol. 20/12 (Dec., 1992c): 1–2, 9.

Kalmijn, Mattijs. "Shifting boundaries: trends in religious and educational homogamy." *ASR* 56 (Dec., 1991): 786–800.

Kanter, Rosabeth Moss. "Some effects of proportions on group life: skewed sex ratios and responses to token women." *AJS* 82 (March, 1977): 965–90.

Karklins, Rasma. "Determinants of ethnic identification in the USSR: the Soviet Jewish case." *ERS* 10 (Jan., 1987): 27–47.

———. *Ethnic Relations in the USSR: The Perspective from Below.* Boston: Allen and Unwin, 1986.

Kasarda, John D. "Urban industrial transition and the underclass." *Annals* 501 (Jan., 1989): 26–47.

Katz, Mark N., ed. *Soviet-American Conflict Resolution in the Third World*. Washington: United States Institute of Peace Press, 1991.

———. "Yemeni unity and Saudi security." MIDDLE EAST POLICY 1/1 (1992): 117–35.

———. "Analyzing the changing foreign and domestic politics of the former USSR." *Studies in Comparative Communism* 25/2 (June, 1992): 139–49.

———. "The legacy of empire on international relations." Manuscript, 1993.

Katz, Michael B., ed. *The Underclass Debate: Views from History*. Princeton, NJ: Princeton Univ. Press, 1993.

Katz, Phyllis A., ed. *Towards the Elimination of Racism*. NY: Pergamon Press, 1976.

———and Dalmas A. Taylor, eds. *Eliminating Racism: Profiles in Controversy*. NY: Plenum Press, 1988.

Katz, Schlomo. *Negro and Jew: An Encounter in America*. NY: Macmillan, 1967.

Katznelson, Ira. *Black Men White Cities: Race Politics and Migration in the United States, 1900–1930, and Britain, 1948–68*. London: Oxford Univ. Press, 1973.

Kauffmann, Sam. "Human rights in South Africa: a continuing struggle." Ford Foundation Letter, Fall, 1991: 6–9.

Kaufman, Robert L. "A structural decomposition of black-white earning differentials." *AJS* 89 (Nov., 1983): 585–611.

Kearney, Hugh. *The British Isles: A History of Four Nations*. Cambridge: Univ. of Cambridge Press, 1989.

Kedourie, Elie and Sylvia G. Haim, eds. *Zionism and Arabism in Palestine and Israel*. London: Frank Cass, 1982.

Keefe, Susan E. and Amado M. Padilla. *Chicano Ethnicity*. Albuquerque: Univ. of New Mexico Press, 1987.

Keith, Verna M. and Cedric Herring. "Skin tone and stratification in the black community." *AJS* 97/3 (Nov., 1991): 760–78.

Kelly, Aileen. "Revealing Bakhtin." *NYRB*, Sept. 24, 1992: 44–48.

Kelman, Herbert C. "Violence without moral restraint: reflections on the dehumanization of victims and victimizers." *JSI* 29 (1973): 25–61.

Kennedy, Paul. *Preparing for the Twenty-First Century.* NY: Random House, 1993.

Kennedy, Ruby Jo Reeves. "Single or triple melting pot? Intermarriage in New Haven, 1870–1950. *AJS* 58 (July, 1952): 56–59.

Kenworthy, Tom and Thomas B. Edsall. "The voices of those who think civil rights have gone too far." *Washington Post National Weekly,* June 10–16, 1991: 14.

Kerckhoff, Alan C. "Effects of ability grouping in British secondary schools." *ASR* 51 (Dec., 1986): 842–58.

Kershaw, David and Jerilyn Fair. *The New Jersey Income-Maintenance Experiment,* Vol. 1 NY: Academic Press, 1976.

Keyes, Charles F., ed. *Ethnic Change.* Seattle: Univ. of Washington Press, 1981.

Kilgore, Sally B. "The organizational context of tracking in schools." *ASR* 56 (April, 1991): 189–203.

Kim Bok-lim C. "Asian wives of U.S. servicemen: women in shadows." *Amerasia* 4 (1977): 91–115.

Kimmerling, Baruch, ed. *The Israeli State and Society: Boundaries and Frontiers.* Albany: State University of New York Press, 1989.

———and Joel S. Migdal. *Palestinians: The Making of a People.* NY: Free Press, 1993.

Kinder, Donald R. and David O. Sears. "Prejudice and politics: symbolic racism versus racial threats to the good life. *Journal of Personality and Social Psychology* 40 (1983): 414–31.

King, Martin Luther, Jr. *The Trumpet of Conscience.* NY: Harper and Row, 1968.

———. *Why We Can't Wait.* NY: Harper and Row, 1963.

———. *Stride toward Freedom.* NY: Harper and Row, 1958.

Kingkade, Ward. "USSR ethnic composition: preliminary 1989 census results." *Population Today* 18 (March, 1990): 6–7.

Kirscht, John P. and Ronald C. Dillehay. *Dimensions of Authoritarianism: A Review of Research and Theory.* Lexington: Univ. of Kentucky Press, 1967.

Kivisto, Peter, ed. *The Ethnic Enigma: The Salience of Ethnicity for European-Origin Groups.* Philadelphia: The Balch Institute Press, 1989.

―――. "The transplanted then and now: the reorientation of immigration studies from the Chicago school to the new social history." *ERS* 13/4 (Oct., 1990): 455–81.

Kluckhohn, Clyde. *Navaho Witchcraft*. Papers of the Peabody Museum of American Archaeology and Ethnology, no. 22. Cambridge, MA: Harvard Univ. Press, 1944.

Kluegel, James R. and Eliot R. Smith. "Affirmative action attitudes: effects of self-interest, racial affect, and stratification beliefs on whites' views." *SF* 61 (March, 1983): 797–824.

Knutson, Jeanne N., ed. *Handbook of Political Psychology*. San Francisco: Jossey-Bass, 1973.

Kochman, Thomas, ed. *Rappin' and Stylin' Out*. Urbana: Univ. of Illinois Press, 1972.

Kozol, Jonathan. *Savage Inequalities: Children in America's Schools*. NY: Crown, 1991.

Krebs, D. L. "Altruism: an examination of the concept and a review of the literature." *Psychological Bulletin* 73 (1970): 258–302.

Kriesberg, Louis, ed. *Research in Social Movements, Conflicts, and Change*. Greenwich, CT: JAI Press, 1979.

Krymkowski, Daniel H. and Raymond L. Hall. "The African development dilemma revisited: theoretical and empirical explorations." *ERS* 13/3 (July, 1990): 315–44.

Kuper, Leo. "The prevention of genocide: cultural and structural indicators of genocidal threat." *ERS* 12 (April, 1989): 157–73.

―――. *Genocide: Its Political Use in the Twentieth Century*. New Haven, CT.: Yale Univ. Press, 1982.

―――. *The Pity of it All*. Minneapolis: Univ. of Minnesota Press, 1977.

―――. *Race, Class, and Power: Ideology and Revolutionary Change in Plural Societies*. Chicago: Aldine, 1974.

―――. *Passive Resistance in South Africa*. New Haven, CT: Yale Univ. Press, 1957.

―――and M. G. Smith, eds. *Pluralism in Africa*. Berkeley: Univ. of California Press, 1971.

Kuttner, Robert. "Notes from underground; clashing theories about the 'underclass.' " *Dissent*, Spring, 1991: 212–17.

LaBarre, Weston. *The Ghost Dance: The Origins of Religion.* NY: Dell, 1972.

Labov, William. "Are black and white vernaculars diverging?" In Fasold, Labov, et al., 1987: 5–12.

————. *Language in the Inner City: Studies in the Black English Vernacular.* Philadelphia: Univ. of Pennsylvania Press, 1972.

LaCoste, Yves, ed. *Géopolitique des Régions Française.* Paris: Fayard, 1986.

Lacy, W. B. and E. Middleton. "Are educators really prejudiced? A cross-occupational comparisons." *Sociological Focus* 14 (1981): 87–95.

Ladd, Helen F. and John Yinger, *America's Ailing Cities: Fiscal Health and the Design of Urban Policy.* Baltimore: Johns Hopkins Univ. Press, 1989.

Lal, Barbara Ballis. "Perspectives on ethnicity; old wine in new bottles." *ERS* 6 (April, 1983): 154–73.

Lane, Robert E. *The Market Experience.* Cambridge: Cambridge Univ. Press, 1991.

Lanternari, Vittorio. "Ethnocentrism and ideology." *ERS* 3 (Jan., 1980): 52–67.

Lapidus, Gail W. "Gorbachev's nationalities problem." *Foreign Affairs* 68 (Fall, 1989): 92–108.

LaPierre, Jean-William. *Le Pouvoir Politique et les Langues: Babel et Leviathan.* Paris: Presses Universitaires de France, 1988.

Laqueur, Walter. "Russian Nationalism." Foreign Affairs 71/8 (Winter, 1992–93): 103–116.

Lasch, Christopher. *The True and Only Heaven: Progress and its Critics.* NY: W. W. Norton, 1991.

Laski, Harold. *The American Democracy.* NY: Viking Press, 1948.

Laumann, Edward O. *Bonds of Pluralism: The Forms and Substance of Urban Social Networks.* NY: Wiley, 1973.

————and Franz U. Pappi. *Networks of Collective Action.* NY: Academic Press, 1976.

Lehman, Edward C., Jr. "Religion and race in the United States." *RRR* 30 (Dec., 1988): whole issue.

Leifer, Eric M. "Competing models of political mobilization: the role of ethnic ties." *AJS* 87 (July, 1981): 23–47.

Lemann, Nicholas. *The Promised Land: The Great Black Migration and How it Changed America.* NY: Knopf, 1991.

Lenski, Gerhard. "Marxist Experiments in destratification: an appraisal." *SF* 57 (Dec., 1978): 364–83.

Léons, M. B. "Race, ethnicity, and political mobilization in the Andes." *AE* 5 (1978): 484–94.

Lernoux, Penny. *Cry of the People: The Struggle for Human Rights in Latin America—The Catholic Church in Conflict With U.S. Policy.* NY: Penguin, 1982.

Lesser, Alexander. "Cultural significance of the ghost dance." *AA* 35 (Jan.-March, 1933): 108–15.

Levine, Daniel H. *Religion and Politics in Latin America.* Princeton, NJ: Princeton Univ. Press, 1981.

Levine, Robert. *Culture, Behavior and Personality.* Boston: Aldine, 1973.

——and Donald T. Campbell. *Ethnocentrism: Theories of Conflict, Ethnic Attitudes, and Group Behavior.* NY: Wiley, 1972.

Levinson, Sanford. "Lingo Fracas." *Nation,* Nov. 9, 1992: 549–51.

Lewin, Kurt. *A Dynamic Theory of Personality.* NY: McGraw-Hill, 1935.

Lewis, Bernard. "Muslims, Christians, and Jews: the dream of coexistence." *NYRB,* March 26, 1992: 48–52.

——. *Race and Slavery in the Middle East: An Historical Enquiry.* Oxford: Oxford Univ. Press, 1990.

Lewis, Michael. *The Culture of Inequality.* Amherst: Univ. of Massachusetts Press, 1978.

Lewis, Oscar. "The culture of poverty." *Scientific American* 215 (October, 1966a): 19–25.

——. *La Vida: A Puerto Rican Family in the Culture of Poverty.* NY: Random House, 1966b.

——. *The Children of Sanchez.* NY: Random House, 1961.

——. *Five Families: Mexican Case Studies in the Culture of Poverty.* NY: Basic Books, 1959.

Lieberson, Stanley. "Unhyphenated whites in the United States." *ERS* 8 (Jan., 1985): 159–80.

————. *Language Diversity and Language Contact*. (Essays selected and introduced by Anwar S. Dil) Stanford, CA: Stanford Univ. Press, 1981.

————. *A Piece of the Pie: Blacks and White Immigrants Since 1880*. Berkeley: Univ. of California Press, 1980.

————. *Ethnic Patterns in American Cities*. NY: Free Press, 1963.

————, Guy Dalto, and Mary Ellen Johnston. "The course of mother-tongue diversity in nations." *AJS* 81 (July, 1975): 34–61.

————and Glenn V. Fuguitt. "Negro-white occupational differences in the absence of discrimination." *AJS* 73 (Sept., 1977): 188–200.

————and Mary Waters. *From Many Strands: Ethnic and Racial Groups in Contemporary America*. NY: Russell Sage Foundation, 1988.

Liebow, Elliot. *Tally's Corner: A Study of Negro Streetcorner Men*. Boston: Little, Brown, 1967.

Lifton, Betty J. "The cruel legacy: the children our GI's left behind in Asia." *Saturday Review*, Nov. 29, 1975: 10–11ff.

Light, Ivan. "Numbers gambling among Blacks: A financial institution." *ASR* 42 (Dec., 1977): 892–904.

Lim, Mah Lui. "Affirmative action, ethnicity and integration: the case of Malaysia." *ERS* 8 (April, 1985): 250–76.

Lincoln, C. Eric, ed. *The Black Experience in Religion*. NY: Anchor Press, 1974.

————. *The Black Muslims in America*. Boston: Beacon Press, 1961.

————and Lawrence H. Mamiya. *The Black Church in the American Experience*. Durham, NC: Duke Univ. Press, 1990.

Lind, Andrew W., ed. *Race Relations in World Perspective*. Honolulu: Univ. of Hawaii Press, 1955.

Linton, Ralph, ed. *The Science of Man in the World Crisis*. NY: Columbia Univ. Press, 1945.

————, ed. *Acculturation in Seven American Indian Tribes*. NY Appleton-Century, 1940.

————. "One hundred percent American." *American Mercury* 40 (April, 1937): 427–29.

Linz, Juan J. "From primordialism to nationalism." In *New Nationalisms of the Developed West*. Edward Tiryakian and Ronald Rogowski, eds. London: Allen and Unwin, 1985.

Lipset, Seymour Martin. *Continental Divide: The Values and Institutions of the United States and Canada.* NY: Routledge, 1990.

Lithman, Yngve George. *The Practice of Underdevelopment and the Theory of Development-The Canadian Indian Case.* Stockholm: Univ. of Stockholm, 1983.

Loewen, James W. "Desegregating schools can help desegregate neighborhoods." *Clearing House for Civil Rights Research* 7 (Spring, 1979): 14–18.

Long, Larry and Dana DeAre. "The suburbanization of Blacks." *American Demographics* 3 (Sept., 1981): 16–21, 44.

Lopez, David E. *Language Maintenance and Shift in the United States Today: The Basic Patterns and Their Social Implications,* 4 vols. Los Alamitos, CA: National Center for Bilingual Research, 1983.

————. "The social-consequences of Chicano home/school bilingualism." *Social Problems* 24 (Dec., 1976): 234–46.

Lorenz, Konrad. *On Aggression.* NY: Harcourt-Brace, and World, 1960.

Louden, Delroy. "A Comparative study of self-concepts among minority and majority group adolescents in English multi-racial schools." *ERS* 4 (April, 1981): 153–74.

Louw-Potgieter, Joha. *African Dissidents: A Social Psychological Study of Identity and Dissent.* Clevedon, Eng.: Multilingual Matters, 1988.

Lucas, J. Anthony. *Common Ground: A Turbulent Decade in the Lives of Three American Families.* NY: Knopf, 1985.

Lukacs, Georg. *History and Class-Consciousness.* London: Merlin, 1971.

Lukes, Steven. *Individualism.* NY: Harper and Row, 1973.

Lustick, Ian. *Arabs in the Jewish State: Israel's Control of a National Minority.* Austin: Univ. of Texas Press, 1980.

Lynch, Owen M. *The Politics of Untouchability: Social Mobility and Social Change in a City of India.* NY: Columbia Univ. Press, 1969.

Lyon, Patricia J., ed. *Native South Americans: Ethnology of the Least Known Continent.* Boston: Little, Brown, 1974.

Macaulay, J. and L. Berkowitz, eds. *Altruism and Helping Behavior.* NY: Academic Press, 1970.

MacGregor, Gordon. *Warriors Without Weapons.* Chicago: Univ. of Chicago Press, 1946.

Mack, John E. "Cultural amplifiers in ethno-nationalistic affiliation and differentiation." Manuscript, 1984.

———. "Nationalism and the self.: *Psychohistory Review* 2 (1983): 47–69.

MacKaye, Suzannah D. H. "California Proposition 63: Language attitudes reflected in the public debate." *Annals* 508 (March, 1990): 135–46.

MacLeod, Scott. "The new PLO?" and "Inside the PLO." *NYRB*, April 13, 1989: 44–49; and Nov. 7, 1991: 15–18.

———. "South Africa on the edge." *NYRB*, Feb. 11, 1993: 24–28.

Macy, Michael W. "Learning to cooperate: stochastic and tacit collusion in social exchange." *AJS* 97/3 (Nov., 1991): 808–43.

Madrid, Arturo. "Official English: A false policy issue." *Annals* 508 (March, 1990): 62–66.

Malcolm X, with Alex Haley. *The Autobiography of Malcolm X.* NY: Grove Press, 1966.

Maldonando, Lionel and Joan Moore, eds. *Urban Ethnicity in the United States.* Beverly Hills, CA: Sage, 1985. (Urban Affairs Annual Review.)

Malhotra, M. K. "The educational problems of foreign children of different nationalities in West Germany." *ERS* 8 (April, 1985): 291–309.

Malik, Yogendra K. and D. K. Vajpeyi. "The rise of Hindu militancy." *Asian Survey* 33/3 (March, 1989): 308–25.

Malinowski, Bronislaw. *Argonauts of the Western Pacific.* London: Routledge and Kegan Paul, 1922.

Mallaby, Sebastian, *After Apartheid: The Future of South Africa.* NY: Times Books, 1992.

Mamiya, Lawrence H. "From Black Muslim to Bilalian." *JSSR* 21 (June, 1982): 138–52.

Maran, Rita. *Torture: The Role of Ideology in the French-Algerian War.* NY: Praeger, 1989.

Margalit, Avishai. "The great white hope." *NYRB* June 27, 1991: 19–25.

Markham, Edwin. *The Book of Poetry,* vol. 1. NY: William H. Wise, 1927.

Marks, Carole. "The urban underclass." *ARS* 17 (1991): 445–66.

Marks, Stephen R. "Multiple roles and role strain: some notes on human energy, time, and commitment." *ASR* 42 (Dec., 1977): 921–36.

Marrus, Michael Robert. *The Unwanted: European Refugees in the Twentieth Century.* NY: Oxford Univ. Press, 1985.

Marshall, Ray. "The economics of racial discrimination: a survey." *Journal of Economic History,* Sept., 1974: 849–71.

Marshall, T. H. *Citizenship and Social Class and Other Essays.* Cambridge: Cambridge Univ. Press, 1960.

Martin, David. *Tongues of Fire: The Explosion of Protestantism in Latin America.* Cambridge, MA.: Basil Blackwell, 1990.

Martin, Philip L. *Guestworker Programs: Lessons from Europe.* United States Department of Labor: Bureau of International Labor Affairs. Washington: Government Printing Office, 1980.

———, Elmar Hönekopp, and Hans Ullman. "Europe 1992: effects of labor migration." *IMR* 24 (Fall, 1990): 591–603.

Marty, Martin E. "Fundamentalism reborn: faith and fanaticism." *Saturday Review* (May, 1980): 37–42.

———and R. Scott Appleby, eds. *Fundamentalism Observed.* Chicago: Univ. of Chicago Press, 1991.

Marx, Anthony W. *Lessons of Struggle: South African Internal Opposition.* NY: Oxford Univ. Press, 1992.

Marx, Karl. "Theses on Feuerbach." In *Friedrich Engels, Ludwig Feuerbach and the Outcome of Classical German Philosophy.* NY: International Publishers, 1935: 73–75.

———. *Selected Writings in Sociology and Social Philosophy.* (Edited and introduced by T. B. Bottomore and Maximillien Rubel.) NY: McGraw-Hill, 1956: 243–258.

Mason, David. "Race relations, group formation and power: a framework for analysis." *ERS* 5 (Oct., 1982): 421–39.

Massey, Douglas D. "American apartheid: Segregation and the making of the underclass." *AJS* 96 (Sept., 1990): 329–57.

———. "Understanding Mexican migration to the United States." *AJS* 92 (May, 1987): 1372–1403.

———, Rafael Alarcon, Jorge Durand, and Humberto González. *Return to Aztlan: The Social Process of International Migration from Western Mexico.* Berkeley: Univ. of California Press, 1986.

———and Nancy A. Denton. "Hypersegregation in U.S. metropolitan areas: Blacks and Hispanic segregation along five dimensions." *Demography* 26 (1989): 373–91.

———and ———. "Suburbanization and segregation in U.S. metropolitan areas." *AJS* 94 (Nov., 1988): 592–626.

———and ———. *American Apartheid: Segregation and the Making of an Underclass.* Cambridge, MA: Harvard Univ. Press, 1993.

Matsueda, Ross L. "Reflected appraisals, parental labeling, and delinquency: specifying a symbolic interactionist theory." *AJS* 97/6 (May, 1992): 1577–1611.

Matthews, William. *Cockney Past and Present.* NY: E. P. Dutton, 1938.

Mauss, Marcel. *The Gift: Forms and Functions of Exchange in Archaic Societies.* NY: Free Press, 1954.

Maybury-Lewis, David, ed. *The Prospects for Plural Societies.* Washington: American Ethnological Society, 1984.

Maynard, Douglas W., with Allen Grimshaw, Deidre Boden, Marilyn Whalen, Timothy Halkowski, and Paul Colomy. "Symposium: Language and Social Life." *Contemporary Sociology* 20 (Nov., 1991): 841–56.

Mazur, Allan and Leon S. Robertson. *Biology and Social Behavior.* NY: Free Press, 1972.

McCarthy, John D. and W. L. Yancey. "Uncle Tom and Mr. Charlie: Metaphysical pathos in the study of racism and personal disorganization." *AJS* 76 (1971): 648–72.

———and Mayer N. Zald. "Resource mobilization and social movements: a partial theory." *AJS* 86 (May, 1977): 1212–41.

McCormack, Wayne, ed. *The Bakke Decision: Implications for Higher Education Admissions.* Washington: American Council on Education and the Association of American Law Schools, 1978.

McCrone, David. "Explaining nationalism: the Scottish experience." *ERS* 7/1 (Jan., 1984): 129–37.

McDermott, R. P. "Social relations as contexts for learning in school." *Harvard Educational Review* 47 (May, 1977): 198–213.

McDowall, David. *Palestine and Israel: The Uprising and Beyond.* Berkeley: Univ. of California Press, 1990.

McGowan, William. *Only Man is Vile: The Tragedy of Sri Lanka.* NY: Farrar, Straus, and Giroux, 1991.

McKay, James. "An exploratory synthesis of primordial and mobilizationist approaches to ethnic phenomena." *ERS* 5 (Oct., 1982): 395–420.

McRae, James A. "Changes in religious communalism desired by Protestants and Catholics." *SF* 61 (March, 1983): 709–30.

McRae, Kenneth D. *Conflict and Compromise in Multilingual Societies:* Vol. 1: Switzerland (1984); Vol. 2: Belgium (1986). Waterloo, Ontario: Wilfrid Laurier Univ. Press.

McWilliams, Wilson Carey. *The Idea of Fraternity in America.* Berkeley: Univ. of California Press, 1973.

Mead, Lawrence M. "The logic of workfare: The underclass and work policy." In Wilson, 1989: 156–69.

Meadwell, Hudson. "Cultural and Instrumental approaches to ethnic nationalism." *ERS* 12 (July, 1989): 309–28.

Meier, August and Elliott Rudwick, eds. *Making of Black America.* NY: Atheneum, 1969.

Melendez, Edwin, Clara Rodriquez, and Janis Barry Figueroa, eds. *Hispanics in the Labor Force: Issues and Policies.* NY: Plenum, 1991.

Melman, Yossi. *The New Israel: An Intimate View of a Changing People.* NY: Carol Publ. Group for the Birch Lane Press, 1992.

Melville, Margarita B. "Ethnicity: an anlysis of its dynamism and variability, focusing on the Mexican/Anglo/Mexican interface." *AE* 10 (May, 1983): 272–89.

Merton, Robert K. "Insiders and outsiders: a chapter in the sociology of knowledge." *AJS* 78 (July, 1972): 9–47.

———. *Social Theory and Social Structure,* 3rd ed. NY: Free Press, 1968.

Metz, M. H. *Classrooms and Corridors: The Crisis of Authority in Desegregated Schools.* Berkeley: Univ. of California Press, 1978.

Michnik, Adam. "The two faces of Europe." *NYRB*, July 19, 1990: 7.

Miles, Robert and Jeanne Singer-Kérel, guest eds. "Migration and migrants in France." *ERS* 14 (July, 1991): whole issue.

Mill, John Stuart. "On Liberty." *Harvard Classics*, vol. 25: 193–312. NY: Collier and Sons, 1937.

Miller, Arthur G., ed. *In the Eye of the Beholder: Contemporary Issues in Stereotyping.* NY: Praeger, 1982.

Miller, Jane. *Many Voices: Bilingualism, Culture and Education.* London: Routledge and Kegan Paul, 1983.

Miller, Judith. "Strangers at the gate." *NYT Magazine,* Sept. 15, 1991: 32–37.

———. "Iraq, a case of genocide." *NYT Magazine,* Jan. 3, 1993; 12–17ff.

Miller, Neal and M. B. Brewer, eds. *Groups in Contact: The Psychology of Desegregation.* NY: Academic Press, 1984.

Miller, Walter B. "Lower class culture as a generating milieu of gang delinquency." *JSI* 14 (1958): 5–19.

Milosz, Czeslaw. *Beginning with My Streets: Essays and Recollections.* NY: Farrar, Straus, and Giroux, 1991.

Mincy, Ronald B., Isabel Sawhill, and Douglas A. Wolf. "The underclass definitions and measurement." *Science,* April 27, 1990: 450–53.

Mirande, Alfredo and Evangelina Enriquez. *La Chicana: The Mexican-American Woman.* Chicago: Univ. of Chicago Press, 1980.

Mittelbach, Frank G. and Joan W. Moore. "Ethnic endogamy—the case of Mexican Americans." *AJS* 74 (July, 1968): 50–62.

Moch, Leslie Page. *Moving Europeans: Migration in Western Europe Since 1650.* Bloomington: Univ. of Indiana Press, 1992.

Montagu, Ashley. *The Nature of Human Aggression.* NY: Oxford Univ. Press, 1975.

Moodie, T. Dunbar. *The Rise of Afrikanerdom: Power, Apartheid, and the Afrikaner Civil Religion.* Berkeley: Univ. of California Press, 1974.

Mooney, James. *The Ghost Dance Religion and the Sioux Outbreak of 1890,* abridged. Chicago: Univ. of Chicago Press, 1965.

Moore, Joan W. "Minorities in the American class system." *Daedalus* 110 (Spring, 1981): 275–99.

———and Harry Pachon. *Hispanics in the United States.* Englewood Cliffs, NJ: Prentice Hall, 1985.

Morgan, Kenneth O. *Rebirth of a Nation: Wales 1880–1980.* London: Oxford Univ. Press, 1981.

Morgan, Lewis Henry. *Ancient Society.* Cambridge, MA: Belknap, 1964 (1877).

Morris, Benny. *The Birth of the Palestinian Refugee Problem: 1947–1949.* NY: Cambridge Univ. Press, 1987.

Morris, Desmond. *The Naked Ape.* NY: McGraw-Hill, 1967.

Mount, C. Eric, Jr. "American individualism reconsidered." *RRR* 22 (June, 1981): 362–76.

Moynihan, Daniel Patrick. *Pandaemonium: Ethnicity in International Politics.* NY: Oxford Univ. Press, 1993.

Muhammad, Wallace Deen. *As the Light Shineth from the East.* Cedarhurst, NY: WMD Publications, 1980.

Munnell, Alicia H., Lynn E. Browne, James McEneaney, and Geoffrey M. B. Tootell. *Mortgage Lending in Boston: Interpreting HMDA Data.* Boston, MA: Federal Reserve Bank of Boston, Working Paper 92–7, Oct., 1992.

Murgúia, Edwards, *Chicano Intermarriage: A Theoretical and Empirical Study.* San Antonio, TX: Trinity Univ. Press, 1982.

————. *Assimilation, Colonialism and The Mexican American People.* Austin: Univ. of Texas Press, 1975.

Murphree, Marshall W. "The salience of ethnicity in African states: a Zimbabwean case study." *ERS* 11 (April, 1988): 119–38.

Murray, Charles A. *Losing Ground: American Social Policy, 1950–1980.* NY: Basic Books, 1984.

Mussen, Paul and Nancy Eisenberg-Berg. *Roots of Caring, Sharing, and Helping.* Freeman, 1977.

Myrdal, Gunnar, with the assistance of Richard Sterner and Arnold Rose. *An American Dilemma: The Negro Problem and Modern Democracy,* 2 vols. NY: Harper and Row, 1944.

————. *Challenge to Affluence.* NY: Pantheon Books, 1962.

Nabokov, Peter, ed. *Native American Testimony: A Chronicle of Indian-White Relations from Prophecy to the Present.* NY: Viking, 1991.

Naipaul, V. S. *India: A Million Mutinies Now.* NY: Viking, 1991.

————. "Our universal civilization." *NYRB,* Jan. 31, 1991a: 22–25.

Nakamura, Masako Sasamoto. *Beyond 'Cultural Deprivation': A View of Democracy of Culture.* Dissertation, Cornell Univ., 1988.

Naroll, R., E. C. Benjamin, F. K. Fohl, M. J. Fried, R. E. Hildreth, and J. M. Schaefer. "Creativity: A cross-historical pilot study." *Journal of Cross-Cultural Psychology* 2 (1971): 191–98.

Nash, Manning. *The Cauldron of Ethnicity in the Modern World.* Chicago: Univ. of Chicago Press, 1989.

Natriello, Gary, Edward L. McDill, and Aaron M. Pallas. *Schooling Disadvantaged Children: Racing against Catastrophe.* NY: Teachers College Press, 1990.

Navarro, Juan Carlos. "Liberation theology: its implications for Latin American politics and American Catholicism." In Roof, 1991: 99–111.

Nayar, Baldev Raj. *National Communication and Language Policy in India.* NY: Praeger, 1969.

Neier, Aryeh. "Watching rights." *Nation,* March 11, 1991: 295.

Neihardt, John G. *Black Elk Speaks: Being the Life Story of a Holy Man of the Oglala Sioux.* Lincoln: Univ. of Nebraska Press, 1979.

Nelson, Candace and Marta Tienda. "The structuring of Hispanic identity: Historical and contemporary perspectives." In Alba, 1985: 49–74.

Newell, R. C. "Giving good weight to black English." *Perspectives,* Spring, 1981: 25–29.

New York State Department of Education. *A Curriculum of Inclusion.* Albany, 1989.

Nisbet, Robert. *Twilight of Authority.* NY: Oxford Univ. Press, 1975.

Novak, Michael. *The Rise of the Unmeltable Ethnics: Politics and Culture in the Seventies.* NY: Macmillan, 1971.

Niebuhr, Reinhold. "Foreward." In Cutler, 1968: x.

Nunis, Doyce B., Jr. "American Identities." *Society,* Nov.-Dec., 1981: 29–30.

Oakes, Jeannie. *Keeping Track: How Schools Structure Inequality.* New Haven, CN: Yale Univ. Press, 1985.

O'Brien, Conor Cruise. "Paradise lost." (A commentary on *The Crooked Timber of Humanity* by Isaiah Berlin.) *NYRB,* April 25, 1991: 52–60.

———. *God Land: Reflections on Religion and Nationalism.* Cambridge, MA: Harvard Univ. Press, 1988.

Ogbu, John. *Minority Education and Caste.* NY: Academic PRESS, 1978.

O'Hare, William P. "Can the underclass concept be applied to rural areas?" Working Papers, Population Reference Bureau, Jan., 1992.

———. "America's minorities—the demographics of diversity." *Population Bulletin* 47/4 (Dec., 1992).

————. *Redistricting in the 1990's: A Guide for Minority Groups.* Washington: Population Reference Bureau, 1989.

————, Melvin M. Pollard, Taynia L. Mann, and Mary M. Kent. "African Americans in the 1990's." *Population Bulletin* 46 (July, 1991).

Okamura, Jonathan Y. "Situational ethnicity." *ERS* 4 (Oct., 1981): 452–65.

Oliner, Samuel P. and Pearl M. Oliner. *The Altruistic Personality: Rescuers of Jews in Nazi Europe.* NY: Free Press, 1988.

Olson, Mancur. *The Logic of Collective Action: Public Goods and the Theory of Groups.* Cambridge, MA: Harvard Univ. Press, 1965.

Olzak, Susan. "Contemporary ethnic mobilization." *ARS* 9 (1983): 355–74.

Omi, Michael and Howard Winant. *Racial Formation in the United States.* NY: Routledge, 1986.

Orfield, Gary. *Must We Bus?* Washington: Brookings Institution, 1978.

————and Carole Ashkinaze. *The Closing Door: Conservative Policy and Black Opportunity.* Chicago: Univ. of Chicago Press, 1991.

Orlans, Harold and June O'Neill, eds. *Affirmative Action Revisited. Annals,* Vol. 523 (Sept., 1992): whole issue.

Orr, Eleanor Wilson. *Twice as Less: Black English and the Performance of Black Students in Mathematics and Science.* NY: W. W. Norton, 1987.

Osgood, Charles. *An Alternative to War or Surrender.* Urbana: Univ. of Illinois Press, 1962.

Ostrom, Elinor. *Governing the Commons: The Evolution of Institutions for Collective Action.* Cambridge: Cambridge Univ. Press, 1990.

Padilla, Amado M., ed. *Acculturation: Theory, Models and Some New Findings.* Boulder, CL: Westview Press, 1980.

Pagdon, Anthony. *European Encounters with the New World.* New Haven, CN: Yale Univ. Press, 1993.

Pagnini, Deanna L. and S. Philip Morgan. "Intermarriage and social distance among U.S. immigrants at the turn of the century." *AJS* 96/2 (Sept., 1990): 405–32.

Pakenham, Thomas. *The Scramble for Africa: The White Man's Conquest of the Dark Continent From 1876–1912.* NY: Random House, 1991.

Parsons, Talcott. *The Structure of Social Action.* NY: McGraw-Hill, 1937.

Parthé, Kathleen F. *Russian Village Prose: The Radiant Past.* Princeton, NJ: Princeton Univ. Press, 1992.

Partner, Peter. "In a fratricidal country." Review of *Tribes with Flags* by Charles Glass. *NYRB,* July 19, 1990: 25–27.

Patterson, Orlando. *Freedom.* Vol. 1: *Freedom in the Making of Western Culture.* NY: Basic Books, 1991.

————. *Slavery and Social Death.* Cambridge, MA: Harvard Univ. Press, 1982.

————. *Ethnic Chauvinism: The Reactionary Impulse.* NY: Stein and Day, 1977.

Peach, Ceri. "The Muslim population of Great Britain." *ERS* 13/3 (July, 1990): 414–19.

————. "Which triple melting pot? A re-examination of ethnic intermarriage in New Haven." *ERS* 3 (Jan., 1980): 1–16.

Peled, Yoav. "Ethnic exclusiveness in the periphery: the case of Oriental Jews in Israel's development towns." *ERS* 13 (July, 1990): 345–67.

Pelto, Pertti and Gretel H. Pelto. "Intra-cultural diversity: some theoretical issues." *AE* 2 (Feb., 1975): 1–18.

Perlmutter, Amos. "Israel's dilemma." *Foreign Affairs* 68 (Winter, 1989–90): 119–132.

Perlmutter, Lawrence C. and Richard A. Monty. "The importance of perceived control: fact or fantasy." *American Scientist* 65 (Nov.-Dec., 1977): 759–65.

Pettigrew, Thomas F. "Race and class in the 1980s: an interactive view." *Daedalus* 110 (Spring, 1981): 233–55.

————. "New black-white patterns: how best to conceptualize them?" *ARS* 11 (1985): 329–46.

————. "Placing Adam's argument in a broader perspective: comment on the Adam paper." *Social Psychology* 41 (1978): 58–61.

————. "Three issues in ethnicity: boundaries, deprivations, and perceptions." In Yinger and Cutler, 1978: 25–49.

————. "Racially separate or together?" *JSI* 25 (Jan., 1969): 43–69.

————and Robert L. Green. "School desegregation in large cities: a critique of the Coleman 'white flight' thesis." *Harvard Educational Review* 46 (Feb., 1976): 1–53.

440   Bibliography

————and Marylee C. Taylor. "Discrimination." *Encyclopedia of Sociology*, Vol. 1 (198): 498–503.

————and Joanne Martin. "Organizational inclusion of minority groups; a social psychological analysis." In van Oudenhoven et al, 1989: 169–200.

————and Joanne Martin. "Shaping the organizational context for Black American inclusion." *JSI* 43 (1987): 41–78.

Phillips, Kevin. *The Politics of Rich and Poor: Wealth and the American Electorate in the Reagan Aftermath*. NY: Random House, 1990.

Piliavin, Jane Allyn and Hong-Wen Charng. "Altruism: A review of recent theory and research." *ARS* 16 (1990): 27–65.

Poggie, John H., Jr. *Between Two Cultures: The Life of an American-Mexican*. Tuscon: Univ. of Arizona Press, 1973.

Pogrund, Benjamin. *Sobukwe and Apartheid*. New Brunswick, NJ: Rutgers Univ. Press, 1991.

Polgar, Steven. "Biculturation of Mesquakie teenage boys." *AA* 62 (April, 1960): 217–35.

Pollitt, Katha. "Canon to the Right of me. . ." *Nation*, Sept. 23, 1991: 328–32.

Porter, Judith R. *Black Child, White Child: The Development of Racial Attitudes*. Cambridge, MA: Harvard Univ. Press, 1971.

————and Robert E. Washington. "Black identity and self-esteem: a review of studies of black self-concept." *ARS* 5 (1979): 53–74.

Porter, Rosalie Pedalino. *Forked Tongue: The Politics of Bilingual Education*. NY: Basic Books, 1990.

Porterfield, Ernest. *Black and White Mixed Marriages*. Chicago: Nelson-Hall, 1978.

Portes, Alejandro. "The rise of ethnicity; determinant of ethnic perceptions among Cuban exiles in Miami." *ASR* 49 (June, 1984): 383–97.

————and Robert L. Bach. *Latin American Journey: Cuban and Mexican Immigrants in the United States*. Berkeley: Univ. of California Press, 1985.

————and Rubén G. Rumbaut. *Immigrant America*. Berkeley: Univ. of California Press, 1990.

———and John Walton. *Labor, Class, and the International System*. NY: Academic Press, 1981.

Powdermaker, Hortense. "The channeling of Negro aggression by the cultural process." *AJS* 48 (May, 1943): 750–58.

Powers, William K. *Oglala Religion*. Lincoln: Univ. of Nebraska Press, 1977.

Prager, Jeffrey. "American political culture and the shifting meaning of race." *ERS* 10 (Jan., 1987): 62–81.

———, Douglas Longshore, and Melvin Seeman, eds. *Advancing the Art of Inquiry in School Desegregation Research*. NY: Plenum, 1986.

Prosser, William R. "The underclass: assessing what we have learned." *Focus* 13 (Summer, 1991): 1–18.

Prozesky, Martin, ed. *Christianity amidst Apartheid: Selected Perspectives on the Church in South Africa*. NY: St. Martin's Press, 1990.

Pryor, Edward T., Gustave J. Goldmann, Michael J. Sheridan, and Pamela M. White. "Measuring ethnicity: is 'Canadian' an evolving indigenous category?" *ERS* 15 (April, 1992): 214–35.

Raboteau, Albert J. *Slave Religion: "The Invisible Religion" in the Antebellum South*. Oxford, Oxford Univ. Press, 1978.

Rainwater, Lee. "The problem of lower class culture." *JSI* 26 (Spring, 1970): 133–48.

Rainwater, Lee et al. "The American Underclass: Red, White, and Black." *Trans-Action* 6/4 (Feb., 1969): 9–53.

Rakowska-Harmstone, Teresa. "Ethnicity in the Soviet Union." *Annals* 433 (Sept., 1977): 73–87.

Ramirez, Manuel III and Alfred Castaneda. *Cultural Democracy, Biocognitive Development, and Education*. NY: Academic Press, 1974.

Rawls, John. *A Theory of Justice*. Cambridge, MA: Harvard Univ. Press, 1971.

Razi, G. Hossein. "Legitimacy, religion, and nationalism in the Middle East." *American Political Science Review* 84/1 (March, 1990): 69–91.

Reed, John Shelton. *Southerners: The Social Psychology of Sectionalism*. Chapel Hill: Univ. of North Carolina Press, 1983.

Reich, Robert B. *The Work of Nations: Preparing Ourselves for 21st Century Capitalism*. NY: Knopf, 1991a.

———. "Secession of the Successful." *NYT Magazine*, Jan. 20, 1991b: 16ff.

Reid, John. "Immigration and the future of the U.S. Black population." *Population Today* 14/2 (Feb., 1986): 6–8.

Resnick, Melvyn C. "Beyond the ethnic community: Spanish language roles and maintenance in Miami." *International Journal of the Sociology of Language* 69 (1988): 89–104.

Rex, John. *The Ghetto and the Underclass: Essays on Race and Social Policy.* Aldershot: Avebury, 1988.

———and David Mason, eds. *Theories of Race and Ethnic Relations.* Cambridge: Cambridge Univ. Press, 1986.

———and Sally Tomlison. *Colonial Immigrants in a British City: A Class Analysis.* London: Routledge and Kegan Paul, 1979.

Richardson, Alan. *British Immigrants and Australia: A Psycho-Social Inquiry.* Canberra: Australian National University Press, 1974.

Richmond, Anthony H., issue ed. "Ethnic Nationalism and Postindustrialism." *ERS* 7 (Jan., 1984): whole issue.

———. *Color Prejudice in Britain.* London: Routledge and Kegan Paul, 1951.

Ricketts, Erol and Isabel Sawhill. "Defining and measuring underclass." *Journal of Policy Analysis and Management* 7 (Winter, 1988): 316–25.

Rieder, Jonathan. *Canarsie: The Jews and Italians of Brooklyn against Liberalism.* Cambridge, MA: Harvard Univ. Press, 1985.

Riehl, Carolyn, Gary Natriello, and Aaron M. Pallas. "Losing Track: The Dynamics of Student Assignment Processes in High School." Manuscript, Aug., 1992.

Rist, Ray E. *Guest Workers in Germany: The Prospects of Pluralism.* NY: Praeger, 1978.

———. "Student social class and teacher expectations; the self-fulfilling prophecy in ghetto education." *Harvard Educational Review* 40 (Aug., 1970): 411–51.

Roach, Jack L. and Orville R. Gursslin. "An evaluation of the concept of 'culture of poverty.' " *SF* 45 (March, 1967): 383–92.

Roberts, J. Deotis. *A Black Political Theology.* Philadelphia: Westminster Press, 1974.

Robinson, J. W., Jr. and J. D. Preston. "Equal-status contact and modification of racial prejudice: a reexamination of the contact hypothesis." *SF* 54 (1976): 911–24.

Robinson, Vaughan. "Roots to mobility: the social mobility of Britain's black population, 1971–87." *ERS* 13 (April, 1990): 274–86.

———. "The new Indian middle class in Britain." *ERS* 11 (Nov., 1988): 456–73.

———. "Patterns of South Asian ethnic exogamy and endogamy in Britain." *ERS* 3 (Oct., 1980): 427–43.

Rodman, Hyman. "Technical note on two rates of mixed marriage." *ASR* 30 (Oct., 1965): 776–78.

———. "The lower-class value stretch." *SF* 42 (Dec., 1963): 205–15.

Rodriquez, Clara E. and Hector Cordero-Guzman. "Placing race in context." *ERS* 15/4 (Oct., 1992): 523–42.

Rodriquez, Richard. *Hunger of Memory: The Education of Richard Rodriquez.* NY: Bantam, 1983.

Roediger, David R. *The Wages of Whiteness: Race and the Making of the American Working Class.* London: Verso, 1991.

Rogers, Rosemarie. "The transnational nexus of migration." *Annals* 485 (May, 1986): 34–50.

Rokeach, Milton. *The Nature of Human Values.* NY: Free Press, 1973.

———. *The Open and Closed Mind.* NY: Basic Books, 1960.

Romaine, Suzanne. *Bilingualism.* Oxford: Blackwell, 1989.

Romann, Michael and Alex Weingrod. *Living Together Separately: Arabs and Jews in Contemporary Jerusalem.* Princeton, NJ: Princeton Univ. Press, 1991.

Roof, Wade Clark, ed. *World Order and Religion.* Albany: State Univ. of New York Press, 1991.

Roosens, Eugene E. *Creating Ethnicity: The Process of Ethnogenesis.* Newbury Park, CA: Sage, 1989.

Root, Maria P. P., ed. *Racially Mixed People in America.* Newbury Park, CA: Sage, 1992.

Rorty, Richard. *Contingency, Irony, and Solidarity.* Cambridge: Cambridge Univ. Press, 1989.

Rosenbaum, James E. *Making Inequality: The Hidden Curriculum of High School Tracking.* NY: Wiley, 1976.

Rosenberg, Morris. "Self-concept research: a historical overview." *SF* 68 (Sept., 1989): 33–44.

——. *Conceiving the Self.* NY: Basic Books, 1979.

——and R. G. Simmons. *Black and White Self-Esteem: The Urban School Child.* Washington: American Sociological Association, 1972.

Rosenfeld, Michel. *Affirmative Action and Justice: A Philosophical and Constitutional Inquiry.* New Haven, CN: Yale Univ. Press, 1991.

Rossell, C. *Assessing the Unintended Impacts of Public Policy.* Washington: National Institute of Education, 1978.

Rossi, Peter H. *Down and Out in America: The Origins of Homelessness.* Chicago: Univ. of Chicago Press, 1989.

Roszak, Theodore. *Person/Planet: The Creative Disintegration of Industrial Society.* Garden City, NY: Doubleday, 1978.

Rotberg, Robert I., ed. *The Mixing of Peoples: Problems of Identity and Ethnicity.* Stamford, CN: Greylock Publishers, 1978.

Rotter, J. B. "Generalized expectancies for internal versus external control of reinforcement." *Psychological Monographs* 80, no. 1 (1966).

Rousseau, Mark O. and Raphael Zariski. *Regionalism and Regional Devolution in Comparative Perspective.* NY: Praeger, 1987.

Roy, Prodipto. "The measurement of assimilation: the Spokane Indians." *AJS* 67 (March, 1962): 541–51.

Royce, Anya Peterson. *Ethnic Identity: Strategies of Diversity.* Bloomington: Indiana Univ. Press, 1982.

Rubin, Joan and Bjorn H. Jernudd, eds. *Can Language Be Planned? Sociolinguistic Theory and Practice for Developing Nations.* Honolulu: Univ. of Hawaii Press, 1971.

Ruether, Rosemary Radford and Herman J. Ruether. *The Wrath of Jonah: The Crisis of Religious Nationalism in the Israeli-Palestinian Conflict.* San Francisco: Harper and Row, 1989.

Rusinow, Dennison, ed. *Yugoslavia: A Fractured Federalism.* Washington: The Wilson Center Press, 1988.

Ryan, Alan. "Professor Hegel goes to Washington." *NYRB*, March 26, 1992: 7–13.

———. "Twenty-first century limited." *NYRB*, Nov. 19, 1992: 20–24.

Ryan, William. *Blaming the Victim*. NY: Vintage Books, 1971.

Rytina, Steven, Peter M. Blau, Terry Blum, and Joseph Schwartz. "Inequality and intermarriage: a paradox of motive and constraint." *SF* 66 (March, 1988): 645–75.

Sabaratnam, Lakshmanan. "The boundries of the state and the state of ethnic boundaries: Sinhala-Tamil relations in Sri Lankan history." *ERS* 10/3 (July, 1987): 291–316.

Safran, William. "Islamization in Western Europe: political consequences and historical parallels." *Annals* 485 (May, 1986): 98–112.

Sahlins, Marshall D. *The Use and Abuse of Biology: An Anthropological Critique of Sociobiology*. Ann Arbor: Univ. of Michigan Press, 1976.

———. *Stone Age Economics*. Chicago: Aldine, 1972.

Sahlins, Peter. *Boundaries: The Making of France and Spain in the Pyrenees*. Berkeley: Univ. of California Press, 1989.

Said, Edward W. "Ignorant armies clash by night." *Nation*, Feb. 11, 1991: 145ff.

———. *Culture and Imperialism*. NY: Knopf, 1993.

Salgado de Snyder, Nelly and Amado Padilla. "Cultural and ethnic maintenance of interethnically married Mexican Americans." *Human Organization* 41 (1982): 359–62.

Sanders, Jimy M. "Public transfers: safety nets or inducements into poverty?" *SF* 68 (March, 1990): 813–34.

Sandomirsky, Sharon and John Wilson. "Processes of disaffiliation." *SF* 68 (June, 1990): 1211–29.

Sanjek, Roger. "Cognitive maps of the ethnic domain in urban Ghana: reflections on variability and change." *AE* 4 (Nov., 1977): 603–22.

Sapir, Edward. "Fashion." *Encyclopedia of the Social Sciences*. NY: Macmillan, 1931, vol. 6: 139–44.

Sayari, Sabri. "Migration policies of sending countries: perspectives on the Turkish experience." *Annals* 485 (May, 1986): 87–97.

Schechtman, Joseph B. *Postwar Population Transfers in Europe, 1945–1955*. Philadelphia: Univ. of Pennsylvania Press, 1962.

Scheepers, Peer, Albert Felling, and Jan Peters. "Ethnocentrism in the Netherlands: a typological analysis." *ERS* 12 (July, 1989): 289–308.

Schelling, Thomas C. *Micromotives and Macrobehavior.* NY: W. W. Norton, 1978.

Schermerhorn, Richard. *Ethnic Plurality in India.* Tuscon: Univ. of Arizona Press, 1978.

———. *Comparative Ethnic Relations: A Framework for Theory and Research.* NY: Random House, 1970.

Schlesinger, Arthur M., Jr. *The Disuniting of America: Reflections on a Multicultural Society.* NY: W. W. Norton, 1992.

———. "Toward a divisive diversity." *Wall Street Journal,* June 25, 1991: A-22.

Schmidt. William E. "Some Chicagoans are moved out of projects into a future." *NYT,* Feb. 3, 1989: 1, 10.

Schmitter, Barbara E. "Immigrant minorities in West Germany: some theortical concerns." *ERS* 6 (July, 1983): 308–19. (See also Barbara Heisler.)

———. "Immigrants and associations: their role in the socio-political process of immigrant worker integration in West Germany and Switzerland." *IMR* 14 (1980): 179–92.

Schofield, J. W. "The impact of positively structured contact on intergroup behavior: does it last under adverse conditions? *Social Psychology Quarterly* 42 (1979): 280–84.

Schooler, C. "Serfdom's legacy: an ethnic continuum." *AJS* 81 (1976): 1265–86.

Schöpflin, George. "National identity in the Soviet Union and East Central Europe." *ERS* 14/1 (Jan., 1991): 3–14.

Schumacher, E. F. *Small is Beautiful.* NY: Harper and Row, 1973.

Schuman, Howard and Lawrence Bobo. "Survey-based experiments on white racial attitudes toward residential integration." *AJS* 94 (Sept., 1988): 273–99.

———and Shirley Hatchett. *Black Racial Attitudes: Trends and Complexities.* Institute for Social Research, Univ. of Michigan, 1974.

———and M. P. Johnson. "Attitudes and behavior." *ARS* 2 (1976): 167–207.

———, Charlotte Steeh, and Lawrence Bobo. *Racial Attitudes in America: Trends and Interpretations.* Cambridge, MA: Harvard Univ. Press, 1985.

Scott, George M., Jr. "A resynthesis of the primordial and circumstantial approaches to ethnic group solidarity: towards an explanatory model." *ERS* 13 (April, 1990): 147–71.

Scott, James C. *Domination and the Arts of Resistance: Hidden Transcripts.* New Haven, CN: Yale Univ. Press, 1990.

See, Katherine O'Sullivan. *First World Nationalisms: Class and Ethnic Politics in Northern Ireland and Quebec.* Chicago: Univ. of Chicago Press, 1986.

Seeman, Melvin. "Intergroup Relations." In Rosenburg and Turner, 1981: 378–410.

———. "Alienation and Engagement." In *The Human Meaning of Social Change.* Angus Campbell and P. E. Converse, eds. NY: Russell Sage, 1972: 467–527.

Segal, Daniel A. " 'The European': Allegories of racial purity." *Anthropology Today* 7 (Oct., 1991): 7–9.

Seligman, Adam B. *The Idea of Civil Society.* NY: Free Press, 1992.

Selznick, Philip. *The Moral Commonwealth: Social Theory and the Promise of Community.* Berkeley: Univ. of California PRESS, 1992.

Semyonov, Moshe and Noah Lewin-Epstein. "Segregation and competition in occupational labor markets." *SF* 68 (Dec., 1989): 379–96.

———& ———. *Hewers of Wood and Drawers of Water: Noncitizen Arabs in the Israeli Labor Market.* Ithaca, NY: ILR Press, 1987.

Sen, Amartya. "The threats to secular India." *NYRB*, April 8, 1993: 26–32.

Senghor, Léopold Sédar. *LIBERTY.* Vol. 1: *Négritude et Humanisme.* Vol. 2: *Nation et Voie Africaine du Socialisme.* Vol. 3: *Négritude et Civilization de L'Universel.* Paris: Editions du Seuil, 1964, 1971, 1977.

Shadid, W. A. "The integration of Muslim minorities in the Netherlands." *IMR* 25 (Summer, 1991): 355–74.

Shaefer, R. T. "Racial endogamy in Great Britain: a cross-national perspective." *ERS* 3 (1980): 224–35.

Shafir, Gershon. "The meeting of Eastern Europe and Yemen: 'idealistic workers' and 'natural workers' in early Zionist settlements in Palestine." *ERS* 13 (April, 1990): 172–97.

Shattuck, Roger and Samba Ka. "Born again African." *NYRB*, Dec. 20, 1990: 11–21.

Shavit, Yossi. "Tracking and ethnicity in Israeli secondary education." *ASR* 49 (April, 1984): 210–20.

Shepard, Paul. *The Subversive Science: Essays Toward an Ecology of Man.* Boston: Houghton Mifflin, 1969.

Sherkat, Darren E. and Christopher G. Ellison. "The politics of black religious change: disaffiliation from black mainline denominations." *SF* 70 (Dec., 1991): 431–54.

Shipler, David. *Arab and Jew: Wounded Spirits in a Promised Land.* NY: Times Books, 1986.

Shorris, Earl. *Latinos: A Biography of the People.* NY: W. W. Norton, 1992.

Sieber, Sam D. *Fatal Remedies: The Ironies of Social Intervention.* NY: Plenum, 1981.

———. "Toward a theory of role accumulation." *ASR* 39 (Aug., 1974): 567–78.

Siegel, Fred, ed. " 'Social Breakdown'. A special section." *Dissent,* Spring, 1991: 163–304.

Sigelman, Lee and Susan Welch. *Black Americans' Views of Racial Inequality: The Dream Deferred.* NY: Cambridge Univ. Press, 1991.

———and ———. "The contact hypothesis revisited: black-white interactions and positive racial attitudes." *SF* 70/3 (March, 1993): 781–95.

Silva, K. M. de, Pensri Duke, Ellen S. Goldberg, and Nathan Katz. *Ethnic Conflict in Buddhist Societies: Sri Lanka, Thailand and Burma.* London: Pinter Publishers, 1988.

Silverman, Irwin and Marvin E. Shaw. "Effects of sudden mass school desegregation on interracial interaction and attitudes in one southern city." *JSI* 29 (1973): 133–42.

Silverman, Maxim. "Citizenship and the nation-state in France." *ERS* 14/3 (July, 1991): 333–349.

Silverman, Maxim. *Deconstructing the Nation: Immigration, Racism, and Citizenship in Modern France.* London: Routledge, 1992.

Simmel, Georg. "A Contribution to the sociology of religion." *AJS* 9 (1905). (Trans. by W. W. Elwang.)

Simon, Rita, special ed. "Immigration and American public policy." *Annals* 487 (Sept., 1986): whole issue.

Simpson, George E. *Black Religions in the New World.* NY: Columbia Univ. Press, 1978.

———. "Assimilation." *International Encyclopedia of the Social Sciences.* NY: Macmillan and the Free Press, 1968: vol. 1: 438–44.

———and J. Milton Yinger. *Racial and Cultural Minorities: An Analysis of Prejudice and Discrimination,* 5th ed. NY: Plenum, 1985.

Singer, Daniel. "The resistable rise of Jean-Marie Le Pen." *ERS* 14 (July, 1991): 368–81.

Sinyavsky, Andrei (Abram Tertz). *Soviet Civilization: A Cultural History.* (Trans. by Joanne Turnbull, with the assistance of Nikolai Formosov.) NY: Arcade (Little, Brown), 1990.

Sleeper, Jim. *The Closest of Strangers.* NY: W. W. Norton, 1990.

Sly, David F. and Louis G. Pol. "The demographic context of school segregation and desegregation." *SF* 56 (June, 1978): 1072–86.

Smelser, Neil, with Andrew Mecca and John Vasconcellos. *The Social Importance of Self-Esteem.* Berkeley: Univ. of California Press, 1989.

———. *Social Paralysis and Social Change: British Working-Class Education in the Nineteenth Century.* Berkeley: Univ. of California Press and NY: Russell Sage Foundation, 1991.

Smith, Anthony D. "The origins of nations." *ERS* 12 (July, 1989): 340–67.

———. "The myth of the 'modern nation' and the myth of nations." *ERS* 11 (Jan., 1988): 1–26.

———. "Ethnic myths and ethnic revivals." *Archives Europeenes de Sociologie* 24 (1984): 283–303.

Smith, A. W. "Tolerance of school desegregation, 1954–1977." *SF* 59 (1981): 1256–74.

Smith, Christian. *The Emergence of Liberation Theology: Radical Religion and Social Movement Theory.* Chicago: Univ. of Chicago Press, 1991.

Smith, Hedrick. *The New Russians.* NY: Random House, 1990.

Smith, Lillian. *Killers of the Dream.* NY: W. W. Norton, 1949.

Smith, M. G. "Some problems with minority concepts and a solution." *ERS* 10 (Oct., 1987): 342–62.

Smith, Tom W. "What do Americans think about Jews." NY: American Jewish Committee, 1991.

―――. "Ethnic images." Chicago: National Opinion Research Center. *GSS Topical Report no. 19*, 1990.

―――. "Problems in ethnic measurement: over-, under-, and misidentification." *GSS Technical Report no. 29*, 1982.

―――. "Ethnic measurement and identification." *Ethnicity* 7 (March, 1980): 78–95.

Smolicz, J. J. "Tradition, core values and intercultural development in plural societies." *ERS* 11 (Nov., 1988): 387–410.

Smooha, Sammy. "Minority status in an ethnic democracy; the status of the Arab minority in Israel." *ERS* 13/3 (July, 1990): 389–413.

―――. "Jewish and Arab ethnocentrism in Israel." *ERS* 10/1 (Jan., 1987): 1–26.

Snipp, C. Matthew. *American Indians: The First of this Land.* NY: Russell Sage Foundation, 1989.

Snow, David A. and Richard Machalek. "The convert as a social type." Manuscript, Aug., 1980.

Snowden, Frank M. *Before Color Prejudice: The Ancient View of Blacks.* Cambridge, MA: Harvard Univ. Press, 1983.

Solaún, Mauricio and Sidney Kronus. *Discrimination Without Violence: Miscegenation and Racial Conflict in Latin America.* NY: Wiley, 1973.

Solé, Robert. "Les immigrants dans l'école." *Le Monde,* Feb. 10–11, 1985.

Solé, Yolanda Russinovich. "Bilingualism: stable or transitional? The case of Spanish in the United States." *International Journal of the Sociology of Language* 84 (1990): 35–80.

Soucy, Robert. *Fascism in France: The Case of Maurice Barrès.* Berkeley: Univ. of California Press, 1972.

Sparks, Allister. *The Mind of South Africa.* NY: Knopf, 1990.

Spicer. Edward H. *The American Indians.* Cambridge, MA: Harvard Univ. Press, 1982.

―――. "Acculturation." *International Encyclopedia of the Social Sciences.* NY: Macmillan and the Free Press, 1968: vol. 1: 21–27.

Spickard, Paul R. *Mixed Blood: Intermarriage and Ethnic Identity in Twentieth-Century America.* Madison: Univ. of Wisconsin Press, 1989.

Spindler, George and Louise S. Spindler. *Dreamers Without Power: The Menomini Indians*. NY: Holt, Rinehart, and Winston, 1971.

Spiro, Melford E. *Culture and Human Nature: Theoretical Papers by Melford E. Spiro*. (Edited by Benjamin Kilborne and L. L. Langness.) Chicago: Univ. of Chicago Press, 1987.

Spitz, Rene A., in collaboration with Godfrey Cobliner. *The First Year of Life*. NY: International Universities Press, 1965.

Sprinzak, Ehud. *The Ascendance of Israel's Radical Right*. NY: Oxford Univ. Press, 1991.

Srinivas, M.N. *Social Change in Modern India*. Berkeley: Univ. of California Press, 1969.

Srinivasan, Nirmala. *Prisoners of Faith: A View from Within*. New Delhi: Sage, 1989.

Stack, Carol B. *All Our Kin: Strategies for Survival in a Black Community*. NY: Harper and Row, 1974.

Stampp, Kenneth. *The Peculiar Institution: Slavery in the Ante-Bellum South*. NY: Knopf, 1965.

Stark, David. "The great transformation? Social change in Eastern Europe." *Contemporary Sociology* 21/3 (May, 1992): 299–304.

Starr, S. Frederick. "The road to reform." In *Chronicle of a Revolution*. Abraham Brumberg, ed. NY: Pantheon Books, 1990: 17–29.

Staub, Ervin. "Instigation to goodness: the role of social norms and interpersonal influence." *JSI* 28 (1972): 131–50.

Stavrianos, L. S. *The Promise of the Coming Dark Age*. San Francisco: W. H. Freeman, 1976.

Stayman, Douglas M. and Rohit Deshpande. "Situational ethnicity and consumer behavior." *Journal of Consumer Research* 16 (Dec., 1989): 361–71.

Steeh, Charlotte and Howard Schuman. "Young white adults: did racial attitudes change in the 1980s?" *AJS* 98/2 (Sept., 1992): 340–67.

Steele, Shelby. *The Content of our Character: a new vision of race in America*. New York: St. Martin's Press, 1990.

Stein, Howard F. and Robert F. Hill. *The Ethnic Imperative: Examining the New White Ethnic Movement*. University Park: Pennsylvania State Univ. Press, 1977.

Steinberg, Stephen. *The Ethnic Myth: Race, Ethnicity, and Class in America.* NY: Atheneum, 1981 (revised, 1989).

Steinfels, Peter. "Debating intermarriage and Jewish survival." *NYT,* Oct. 18, 1992: 1.

Stephen, James Fitzjames. *Liberty, Equality, Fraternity.* (Edited with an Introduction by R. J. White.) Cambridge: Cambridge Univ. Press, 1967 (from the 1874 edition).

Stevens, Gillian. "The social and demographic context of language use in the United States." *ASR* 57 (April, 1992): 171–185.

———and Gray Swicegood. "The linguistic context of ethnic endogamy." *ASR* 52 (Feb., 1987): 733–82.

Stinchcombe, Arthur L. *Constructing Social Theories.* NY: Harcourt, Brace, and World, 1968.

Stoetzel, Jean. *Les Valeurs de Temps Present: Une Enquete Europeene.* Paris: Presses Universitaires de France, 1983.

Stolzenberg, Ross M. "Ethnicity, geography, and occupational achievement of Hispanic men in the United States." *ASR* 55 (Feb., 1990): 143–54.

Stone, John. *Racial Conflict in Contemporary Society.* Cambridge, MA: Harvard Univ. Press, 1985.

———, issue ed. "Internal Colonialism." *ERS* 2 (July, 1979): whole issue.

———, ed. *Race, Ethnicity, and Social Change.* North Scituate, MA: Duxbury Press, 1977.

Stonequist, Everett V. *The Marginal Man: A Study in Personality and Culture Conflict.* NY: Scribners, 1937.

Stuckert, Robert P. " 'Race' mixture: the black ancestry of white Americans." In *Physical Anthropology and Archaeology.* NY: Macmillan, 1976: 135–39.

Studlar, Donley T. and Ian McAllister. "Nationalism in Scotland and Wales: a post-industrial phenomenon." *ERS* 11 (Jan., 1988): 48–62.

Sullivan, Harry Stack. *The Interpersonal Theory of Psychiatry.* NY: W. W. Norton, 1953.

Sullivan, John. *ETA and Basque Nationalism: The Fight for Euskadi, 1890–1986.* London: Routledge, 1988.

Summers, A. A. and B. L. Wolfe. "Do schools make a difference?" *American Economic Review* 67 (1977): 639–52.

Sumner, William Graham. *Folkways*. Lexington, MA: Ginn, 1906.

Suny, Ronald Grigor. "Transcaucasia: cultural cohesion and ethnic revival in a multinational society." In Hajda and Beissinger, 1990: 228–52.

———. "Nationalities and nationalism." In Brumberg, 1990a: 108–28.

———. *The Making of the Georgian Nation*. Bloomington: Indiana Univ. Press, 1988.

Surace, Samuel J. "Achievement, discrimination, and Mexican Americans." *Comparative Studies in Society and History* 24 (April, 1982): 315–339.

Sutherland, Robert L. *Color, Class, and Personality*. Washington: American Council on Education, 1942.

Suttles, Gerald D. *The Social Order of the Slum: Ethnicity and Territory in the Inner City*. Chicago: Univ. of Chicago Press, 1968.

———. *The Man-Made City: The Land Use Confidence Game in Chicago*. Chicago: Univ. of Chicago Press, 1990.

Swanson, Guy E. "Monotheism, materialism, and collective purposes: an analysis of Underhill's correlations." *AJS* 80 (Jan., 1975): 862–69.

Swietochowski, Tadeusz. "The politics of a literary language and the rise of national identity in Russian Azerbaijan before 1920." *ERS* 14 (Jan., 1991): 55–63.

Taeuber, Karl. "Housing, schools, and incremental segregative effects." *Annals* 441 (1979): 157–67.

Tajfel, Henri. "Social psychology of intergroup relations." *Annual Review of Psychology* 33 (1982): 1–39.

———. "Cognitive aspects of prejudice." *JSI* 25 (Autumn, 1969): 79–97.

———and J. C. Turner. "The social identity theory of intergroup behavior." In *Psychology of Intergroup Behavior*. S. Worchel and W. G. Austin, eds. Chicago: Nelson Hall, 1985: 7–24.

———& ———. *An Integrative Theory of Intergroup Conflict: The Social Psychology of Intergroup Relations*. Monterey, CA: Brooks/Cole, 1979.

Takaki, Ronald. *Strangers from a Different Shore: A History of Asian Americans*. Boston: Little, Brown, and Co., 1989.

Tambiah, S. J. *Sri Lanka—Ethnic Fratricide and the Dismantling of Democracy*. Chicago: Univ. of Chicago Press, 1986.

Tambs-Lyche, Harold. *London Patidars: A Case Study in Urban Ethnicity.* London: Routledge and Kegan Paul, 1980.

Tandon, Yash. *Problems of a Displaced Minority: The New Positions of East Africa's Asians.* London: Minority Rights Group, Report no. 16, 1973.

Tarzi, Shah M. "The nation-state, victim groups and refugees." *ERS* 14/4 (Oct., 1991): 441–52.

Tawney, R. H. *Eqality.* NY: Harcourt, Brace, 1931.

Tax, Sol. "The impact of urbanization on American Indians." *Annals* 436 (March, 1978): 121–36.

Taylor, M. C. and E. J. Walsh. "Explanations of black self-esteem: some empirical tests." *Social Psychology Quarterly* 42 (1979): 242–53.

Taylor, Ronald L. "Black ethnicity and the persistence of ethnogenesis." *AJS* 84 (May, 1979): 1401–23.

Taylor, S. E. "A categorization approach to stereotyping." In Hamilton, 1981.

Terkel, Studs. *Race: How Blacks and Whites Think and Feel About the American Obsession.* NY: The New Press, 1992.

Thernstrom, Stephan, ed. *Harvard Encyclopedia of American Ethnic Groups.* Cambridge, MA: Harvard Univ. Press, 1980.

Thomas, Melvin E. and Michael Hughes. "The continuing significance of race: a study of race, class, and quality of life in America, 1972–1985." *ASR* 51 (Dec., 1986): 830–41.

Thomas, W. I. and Florian Znaniecki. *The Polish Peasant in Europe and America.* NY: Knopf, 1918–21 (5 vols.).

Thompson, John L. P. "The plural society approach to class and ethnic political mobilization." *ERS* 6 (April, 1983): 127–53.

Thompson, Leonard. *The Political Mythology of Apartheid.* New Haven, CN. Yale Univ. Press, 1985.

Thornton, Russell. "Demographic antecedents of a revitalization movement: population change, population size, and the 1890 Ghost Dance." *ASR* 46 (Feb., 1981): 88–96.

Tienda, Marta. "Puerto Ricans and the underclass debate." *Annals* 501 (Jan., 1989): 105–119.

Tillich, Paul. *Christianity and the Encounter of the World Religions.* NY: Columbia Univ. Press, 1963.

Tilly, Charles. *From Mobilization to Revolution.* Reading, MA: Addison-Wesley, 1978.

———. *Coercion, Capital, and European States,* A.D. 990–1990. Cambridge, MA: Basil Blackwell, 1990.

Timm, Leonora A. "Bilingualism and bilingual education in the United States." *AA* 87 (June, 1985): 334–42.

Tinbergen, Niko. "On war and peace in animals and man." *Science* 160 (1969): 1411–18.

Tiryakian, Edward A. and Ronald Rogowski, eds. *New Nationalisms of the Developed West: Toward Explanation.* London: Allen and Unwin, 1985.

Triandis, Harry C. "The future of pluralism." *JSI* 32 (1976): 179–208.

———, ed. *Variations in Black and White Perceptions of the Social Environment.* Urbana: Univ. of Illinois Press, 1976b.

Tricaraico, Donald. "In a new light: Italian-American ethnicity in the mainstream." In Kivisto, 1989: 24–46.

Trivers, R. L. "The evolution of reciprocal altruism." *Quarterly Review of Biology* 46 (1971): 35–37.

Troyna, Barry and Bruce Carrington. *Education, Racism and Reform.* London: Routledge, 1990.

Turner, J. H. and Edna Bonacich. "Toward a composite theory of middleman minorities." *Ethnicity* 7 (1980): 144–58.

Turner, Margery Austin, Michael Fix, and Raymond J. Struyk. *Opportunities Denied, Opportunities Diminished in Hiring.* Washington: The Urban Institute, 1991.

———, Raymond J. Struyk, and John Yinger. *Housing Discrimination Study: Synthesis.* Washington and Syracuse: The Urban Institute and Syracuse University, Aug., 1991.

———, ——— & ———. *Access Denied, Access Constrained: Synthesis Report of the Housing Discrimination Study.* Washington: The Urban Institute, 1990.

Turner, Paul R. "Religious conversion and community development." *JSSR* 18/3 (1979): 252–60.

Underhill, Ruth. *Red Man's Religion: Beliefs and Practices of the Indians North of Mexico.* Chicago: Univ. of Chicago Press, 1965.

United Nations. "Human Rights and Refugee Law." *Bulletin of Human Rights 91* (March, 1992): 63–123.

———. Centre for Human Rights. *Second Decade to Combat Racism and Racial Discrimination.* Human Rights Publication 90/8. NY: United Nations, 1991.

———. Population Division. World Population Prospects. NY: United Nations, 1992.

———. Subcommission on Prevention and Protection of Minorities. *Yearbook of Human Rights for 1950.* NY: United Nations, 1952.

United States, Army Defense Western Command and Fourth Army. *Japanese in the United States, Final Report: Japanese Evacuation from the West Coast.* Washington: Government Printing Office, 1943.

———, Bureau of the Census. *Money Income and Poverty Status in the United States: 1989.* Current Population Reports. Series P–60, no. 168, 1990.

———. 1980 *Census of Population. Supplementary Reports.* PC–80, S1–3, 6 July, 1981.

———. Bureau of the Census. "Persons of Spanish origin in the United States, March, 1976." *Current Population Reports,* P-20, no. 310, July, 1977.

———, Department of Justice: Immigration and Naturalization Service. *1989 Statistical Yearbook of the Immigration and Naturalization Service.* Washington: Gov't Printing Office, Sept., 1990.

———. Department of Justice: Immigration and Naturalization Service. *1987 Statistical Yearbook of the Immigration and Naturalization Service.* Washington: Government Printing Office, Oct., 1988.

———. *Advanced Report: Immigration Statistics, Fiscal Year, 1991.* Washington: Gov't. Printing Office, April, 1992.

———. *1987 Statistical Yearbook of the Immigration and Naturalization Service.* Washington: Gov't Printing office, Oct., 1988.

———, Department of Labor, Bureau of International Labor Affairs. *Guestworker Programs: Lessons from Europe.* Washington: Gov't. Printing Office, 1980.

Urofsky, Melvin I. *A Conflict of Rights: The Supreme Court and Affirmative Action.* NY: Scribner's, 1991.

Valdivieso, Rafael and Cary Davis. *U.S. Hispanics: Challenging Issues for the 1990s.* (Population Trends and Public Policy, no. 17 (Dec., 1988). Washington: Population Reference Bureau.

Valentine, BettyLou. *Hustling and Other Hard Work: Life Styles in the Ghetto.* NY: Free Press, 1978.

Valentine, Charles. "Deficit, difference, and bicultural models of Afro-American behavior. *Harvard Educational Review* 41 (May, 1971): 137–57.

———. *Culture and Poverty.* Chicago: Univ. of Chicago Press, 1968.

van den Berghe, Pierre L. "Class, race, and ethnicity in Africa." *ERS* 6 (April, 1983): 221–36.

———. *The Ethnic Phenomenon.* NY: Elsevier Press, 1981.

———. *Race and Racism: A Comparative Perspective,* 2nd ed. NY: Wiley, 1978.

———, ed. *Africa: Social Problems of Change and Conflict.* San Francisco: Chandler, 1965.

van Haitsma, Martha. "A conceptual definition of the underclass." *Focus* 12 (Spring and Summer, 1989): s 27–31, 42.

van Oudenhoven, Jan Pieter and Tineke M. Willimsen, eds. *Ethnic Minorities: Social Psychological Perspectives.* Amsterdam: Swets and Zeitlinger, 1989.

Veltman, Calvin. *The Future of the Spanish Language in the United States.* Washington: Hispanic Policy Development Project, 1990a.

———. "The status of the Spanish language in the United States at the beginning of the 21st century." *IMR* 24 (Spring, 1990b): 108–123.

Volkan, Vamik D. *The Need to Have Enemies and Allies.* Northvale, NJ: Jason Aronson, 1988.

Wagley, Charles and Marvin Harris. *Minorities in the New World.* NY: Columbia Univ. Press, 1958.

Waldron, Ann. "The Demopolis story: a star shines in Alabama." *Nation,* May 15, 1989: 664–66.

Wallace, Anthony F. C. *The Death and the Rebirth of the Seneca.* NY: Knopf, 1970.

———. "Revitalization movements." *American Anthropologist* 58 (April, 1956): 264–81.

Wallach, Janet and John Wallach. *Arafat: in the Eyes of the Beholder.* NY: Lyle Stuart, 1990.

Wallman, Sandra. "Ethnicity and the boundary process in context." In Rex and Mason, 1986: 226–45.

Wardhaugh, Ronald. *Language and Nationhood: The Canadian Experience.* Vancouver: NewStar Press, 1983.

Washington, Joseph R., Jr., ed. *Jews in Black Perspective: A Dialogue.*

Waters, Mary C. *Ethnic Options: Choosing Identities in America.* Berkeley: Univ. of California Press, 1990.

Watkins, Susan Cotts. *From provinces into Nations: Demographic Integration in Western Europe, 1870–1960.* Princeton, NJ: Princeton Univ. Press, 1990.

Watson, James L. *Between Two Cultures: Migrants and Minorities in Britain.* Oxford: Basil Blackwell, 1977.

Watts, Harold W. and Albert Rees, eds. *The New Jersey Income-Maintenance Experiment,* vol. 2, *Labor Supply Responses.* NY: Academic Press, 1977a.

————& ————. *The New Jersey Income-Maintenance Experiment,* vol. 3, *Expenditures, Health, and Social Behavior, and the Quality of the Evidence.* NY: Academic Press, 1977b.

Waxman, Chaim I. *The Stigma of Poverty: A Critique of Poverty Theories and Policies.* NY: Pergamon, 1977.

Weber, David J. *The Spanish Frontier in North America.* New Haven, CN: Yale Univ. Press, 1992.

Weber, Eugen. *My France: Politics, Culture, Myth.* Cambridge, MA: Harvard Univ. Press, 1991.

————. *Peasants into Frenchmen: The Modernization of Rural France, 1870–1914.* Stanford, CA: Stanford Univ. Press, 1976.

Weber, Max. *From Max Weber: Essays in Sociology,* (Trans. and edited, with an Introduction, by H. H. Gerth and C. Wright Mills.). NY: Oxford Univ. Press, 1946.

Weigert, Andrew J, J. Smith Teitge, and Dennis W. Teitge. *Society and Identity: Towards a Sociological Psychology.* Cambridge: Cambridge Univ. Press, 1986.

Weinberg, M. "The relationshp between school desegregation and academic achievement." *Law and Contemporary Problems* 39 (1975): 241–70.

Weiner, Annette B. *Inalienable Possessions: The Paradox of Keeping-while-Giving.* Berkeley: Univ. of California Press, 1992.

Weinreich, Peter. "The operationalisation of identity theory in racial and ethnic relations." In Rex and Mason, 1986: 299–320.

West, Cornel. *Race Matters.* Boston: Beacon Press, 1993.

Westergaard, John. "About and beyond 'underclass': some notes on the influence of social climate on British sociology today." *Sociology* 26/4 (Nov., 1992): 575–87.

Wheeler, Geoffrey. *Racial Problems in Soviet Muslim Asia,* 2nd ed. Oxford: Oxford Univ. Press, 1962.

White, Clovis L. "African American Belief Systems; A Critical Review of Research and Theory on Self-Esteem and Black Identity During the 1980s." Manuscript, Aug., 1991.

White, L. C. and Bruce A. Chadwick. "Urban residence, assimilation, and identity of the Spokane Indians." In *Native Americans Today,* Howard Bahr, Bruce Chadwick, and Robert Day, eds. (NY: Harper and Row, 1972): 239–49.

White, Richard. *The Middle Ground: Indians, Empires, and Republics in the Great Lakes Region, 1650–1815.* NY: Cambridge Univ. Press, 1991.

Whitehurst, James E. "The mainstreaming of Black Muslims: Healing the Hate." *Christian Century,* Feb. 27, 1980: 225–29.

Wiley, Norbert. "The ethnic mobility trap and stratification theory." *Social Problems* 15 (1967): 147–59.

Wilkerson, Isabel. "Separate senior proms reveal an unspanned racial divide." *NYT,* May 5, 1991: 1,17.

Wilkinson, Doris, ed. *Black Male/White Female: Perspectives on Interracial Marriage and Courtship.* Morristown, NJ: Shenkman, 1975.

Williams, J. E. and J. K. Morland. *Race and the Young Child.* Chapel Hill: Univ. of North Carolina Press, 1976.

Williams, Robin M., Jr. "Competing models of multiethnic and multiracial societies; an appraisal of possibilities." In Yinger and Cutler, 1978: 50–65.

———. *Mutual Accommodation: Ethnic Conflict and Cooperation.* Minneapolis: Univ. of Minnesota Press, 1977.

———. "Race and Ethnic Relations." *ARS* 1 (1975): 125–64.

———. *American Society: A Sociological Interpretation*, 3rd ed. NY: Knopf, 1970.

———, John P. Dean, and Edward A. Suchman. *Strangers Next Door.* NY: Prentice-Hall, 1964.

Williamson, Joel. *New People: Miscegenation and Mulattoes in the United States.* NY: Free Press, 1980.

Willie, Charles. "Racial balance of quality education." *School Review* 84 (1976): 313–25.

———. *Oreo: A Perspective on Race and Marginal Men and Women.* Wakefield, MA: Parameter Press, 1975.

Wills, Garry. "A Tale of Three Cities." *NYRB*, March 28, 1991: 11–16.

———. *Under God: Religion and American Politics.* NY: Simon and Schuster, 1990.

Wilmore, Gayraud S., Jr. Black Religion and Black Radicalism. NY: Doubleday, 1973.

Wilson, E. O. *Sociobiology: The New Frontiers.* Cambridge, MA: Harvard Univ. Press, 1975.

Wilson, Franklin D. "Patterns of white avoidance." *Annals* 441 (Jan., 1989): 132–41.

Wilson, William J. "Studying inner-city social dislocations: the challenge of public agenda research." *ASR* 56 (Feb., 1991): 1–14.

———, special ed. "The ghetto underclass: social science perspectives." *Annals* 501 (Jan., 1989): whole issue.

———. *The Truly Disadvantaged: The Inner City, The Underclass, and Public Policy.* Chicago: Univ. of Chicago Press, 1987.

———. *The Declining Significance of Race: Blacks and Changing American Institutions.* Chicago: Univ. of Chicago Press, 1978.

Wirth, Louis. "The problem of minority groups." In Linton, 1945: 347–72.

Wispe, Lauren C. *The Psychology of Sympathy.* NY: Plenum, 1991.

———, issue ed. "Positive forms of social behavior." *JSI* 28 (1972): whole issue.

Wolf, Eric R. *Europe and the People Without History.* Berkeley: Univ. of California Press, 1982.

Wood, Forrest G. *The Arrogance of Faith: Christianity and Race in America from the Colonial Era to the Twentieth Century.* NY: Knopf, 1990.

Woodrum, Eric. "An assessment of Japanese American assimilation, pluralism, and subordination." *AJS* 87 (July, 1981): 157–69.

Woolard, Kathryn A. *Double Talk: Bilingualism and the Politics of Ethnicity in Catalonia.* Stanford, CA: Stanford Univ. Press, 1989.

Wren, Christopher S. "A strident, well-armed minority of South African whites is preparing to foil further dismantling of apartheid." *NYT Magazine,* Oct. 7, 1990: 32–6, 56–9.

Wright, Roy Dean and Susan N. Wright. "A plea for a further refinement of the marginal man theory." *Phylon* 33 (1972): 361–68.

Wuthnow, Robert. *Acts of Compassion: Caring for Others and Helping Ourselves.* Princeton, NJ: Princeton Univ. Press, 1991.

Yancey, W. L., E. P. Ericksen, and R. N. Juliani. "Emergent ethnicity: a review and reformulation." *ASR* 41 (June, 1976): 391–403.

Yiftachel, Oren. "The concept of 'ethnic democracy' and its application to the case of Israel." *ERS* 15/1 (Jan., 1992): 125–36.

Yinger, J. Milton. "The research agenda: new directions for desegregation studies." In Prager, Longshore, and Seeman, 1986a: 229–54.

———. "Intersecting strands in the theorisation of race and ethnic relations." In Rex and Mason, 1986b: 20–41.

———. "Ethnicity." *ARS* 11 (1985a): 151–80.

———. "Assimilation in the United States: with particular reference to Mexican Americans." In Connor (1985b): 30–55.

———. "Ethnicity and social change: the interaction of structural, cultural, and personality factors." *ERS* 6 (Oct., 1983): 395–409.

———. *Countercultures: The Promise and the Peril of a World Turned Upside Down.* NY: Free Press, 1982.

———. "Towards a theory of assimilation and dissimilation. *ERS* 4 (July, 1981): 249–64.

———. "Ethnicity in Complex Societies." In Coser and Larsen, eds., 1976: 197–216.

———. "Anomie, Alienation, and Political Behavior." In Knutson, 1973: 171–202.

———. *The Scientific Study of Religion.* NY: Macmillan, 1970.

———. "A research note on interfaith marriage statistics." *JSSR* 7 (Spring, 1968a): 97–103.

———. "On the definition of interfaith marriage." *JSSR* 7 (Spring, 1968b): 104–07.

———. *A Minority Group in American Society.* NY: McGraw-Hill, 1965a.

———. *Toward a Field Theory of Behavior.* NY: McGraw-Hill, 1965b.

———. "Integration and pluralism viewed from Hawaii." *Antioch Review* 22 (Winter, 1962–63): 397–410.

———. *Religion, Society, and the Individual.* NY: Macmillan, 1957.

———. *Religion in the Struggle for Power.* Durham, NC: Duke Univ. Press, 1946. (Reprinted, Arno Press of the Times, 1981.)

———and Stephen J. Cutler, eds. *Major Social Issues: A Multidisciplinary View.* NY: Free Press, 1978.

———, Kiyoshi Ikeda, Frank Laycock, and Stephen Cutler. *Middle Start: An Experiment in the Educational Enrichment of Young Adolescents.* London: Cambridge Univ. Press, 1977.

———and George E. Simpson, eds. *American Indians Today.* Annals 436 (March, 1978): whole issue.

Yinger, John. *Housing Discrimination Study: Incidence of Discrimination and Variation in Discriminatory Behavior.* Prepared for the Office of Policy Development and Research, United States Department of Housing and Urban Development, May, 1991.

———. "Access denied, access constrained: results and implications for discrimination in America." Manuscript, April, 1993. Forthcoming in *Clear and Convincing Evidence: Testing for Discrimination in America.* Michael Fix and Raymond Struyk, eds. Washington: Urban Institute Press, 1993.

———. "Measuring discrimination with fair housing audits: caught in the act." *AER* 76 (Dec., 1986): 881–93.

———. "On the possibility of achieving racial integration through subsidized housing." Manuscript, 1980.

———. "Prejudice and discrimination in the urban housing market." In *Current Issues in urban Economics.* Peter Mieszkowski and Mahlon Straszheim, eds. Baltimore, MD: Johns Hopkins Univ. Press, 1979: 430–68.

Yishai, Yael. "Responsiveness to ethnic demands: the case of Israel." *ERS* 7 (April, 1984): 283–300.

Yogev, Abraham. "Modernity and ethnic affiliation in Israeli schools: a dependence approach." *ERS* 10 (April, 1987): 203–223.

Young, Crawford. *The Politics of Cultural Pluralism*. Madison: Univ. of Wisconsin Press, 1976.

Zald, Mayer N. and John D. McCarthy, eds. *The Dynamics of Social Movements: Resource Mobilization, Social Control, and Tactics*. Cambridge, MA: Winthrop Publishers, 1979.

Zaslavskaya, Tatyana. *The Second Socialist Revolution: An Alternative Soviet Strategy*. (Foreword by Theodore Shanin; trans. by Susan M. Davies, with Jenny Warren.) Bloomington: Univ. of Indiana Press, 1990.

———. "The Novosibirsk report." *Survey* 28 (Spring, 1984): 83–108.

Zerubavel, Eviatar. *The Fine Line: Making Distinctions in Everyday Life.* NY: The Free Press, 1991.

Zurcher, Louis A. *The Mutable Self: A Self-Concept for Social Change.* Beverly Hills, CA: Sage, 1977.

Name Index

T

SUBJECT INDEX

A

Acculturation, 69–82
  additive vs. substitutive,
    72–75
  individual vs. group meaning
    of, 71–72
  mutuality of, 71
  of European Americans to Na-
    tive American ways, 74–75
Additive acculturation, 72–75
Affirmative action, 213–27
  Bakke decision on, 219, 224
  contrasting views of, 213–14
  dilemma of, 225–27
  effects of, 220
  Griggs vs. Duke Power decision
    on, 214
  in India, 215, 226
  in Malasia, 215
  in the Netherlands, 224
  in the United States, 215–24
  objections to, 217–18, 220–21
  questions related to, 218,
    221, 225
  short view and long view of,
    222–23

Africa, sub-Saharan, 42
  changing ethnic relations in, 2,
    111–16
  forced migration from, 31
  shifts in personal identities
    in 147
  state boundaries in, 14
African Americans, 18–19, 74, 81
  and Black Muslims, 268–70
  black vernacular among,
    307–12
  discrimination against, 63,
    216–17, 242
  effects on, of redistricting,
    195–96
  in predominantly white
    churches, 267–68
  intermarriages of, 161–62
  miscegenation among, 153–54
  mobilization for changes of,
    189–90
  public opinions of, 230
  religion among, 265–70
  self-identifications among,
    265–70
  sources of political activity of,
    177–78